Table of Contents

Lecture Notes in Artificial Intelligence 927

Subseries of Lecture Notes in Computer Science
Edited by J. G. Carbonell and J. Siekmann

Lecture Notes in Computer Science
Edited by G. Goos, J. Hartmanis and J. van Leeuwen

Springer
Berlin
Heidelberg
New York
Barcelona
Budapest
Hong Kong
London
Milan
Paris
Tokyo

Jürgen Dix Louis Moniz Pereira
Teodor C. Przymusinski (Eds.)

Non-Monotonic Extensions of Logic Programming

ICLP '94 Workshop
Santa Margherita Ligure, Italy, June 17, 1994
Selected Papers

Springer

Series Editors

Jaime G. Carbonell
School of Computer Science
Carnegie Mellon University
Pittsburgh, PA 15213-3891, USA

Jörg Siekmann
University of Saarland
German Research Center for Artificial Intelligence (DFKI)
Stuhlsatzenhausweg 3, D-66123 Saarbrücken, Germany

Volume Editors

Jürgen Dix
Institut für Informatik, Universität Koblenz-Landau
Rheinau 1, D-56075 Koblenz, Germany

Louis Moniz Pereira
Departamento de Informàtica, Universidade Nova de Lisboa
P-2825 Monte da Caparica, Portugal

Teodor Przymusinski
Department of Computer Science, University of California
Riverside, CA 92521, USA

CR Subject Classification (1991): I.2.3, F.4.1, D.1.6

ISBN 3-540-59467-1 Springer-Verlag Berlin Heidelberg New York

CIP data applied for

Printed in Germany

Typesetting: Camera ready by author
SPIN: 10486216 06/3142-543210 - Printed on acid-free paper

Preface

This book is the outcome of an original compilation of extended and revised versions of selected papers presented at the workshop on *Non-Monotonic Extensions of Logic Programming*, held in Santa Margherita Ligure, Italy, on June 17, 1994. It also includes additional papers solicited from the participants. As some workshop papers were published elsewhere, they do not appear in this volume.

The workshop on *Non-Monotonic Extensions to Logic Programming* was organized in conjunction with ICLP '94, the Eleventh International Conference on Logic Programming. It was the fourth in a series of workshops held jointly with logic programming conferences (NACLP'90, ILPS'91, and ILPS'93) and received financial support from the *ESPRIT Network of Excellence Compulog-Net* and the *University of Koblenz*.

The motivation for these workshops stems from the fact that during the last decade a significant body of knowledge has been accumulated providing us with a better understanding of the semantic issues in logic programming and the theory of deductive databases. In particular, the class of perfect models for (locally) stratified logic programs and two closely related extensions to normal, non-disjunctive, logic programs were introduced and extensively investigated: the *well-founded* models and the *stable* models.

Semantics of logic programs rely on a non-monotonic operator, often referred to as *negation-by-failure* or *negation-by-default*. The non-monotonicity of this operator allows us to view logic programs as special non-monotonic theories and thus makes it possible to draw from the extensive research in the area of non-monotonic reasoning and use it as a guidance in the search for a suitable semantics for logic programs.

Furthermore, the problem of extending the well-founded and the stable models approaches, by defining a suitable semantics for normal and disjunctive programs extended with a second type of negation, turned out to be a difficult one, as evidenced by a large number of papers devoted to the subject.

As a result, research work aimed at better understanding of the relationships existing between logic programming (LP) and a variety of nonmonotonic formalisms (NMF) has been mutually beneficial to both areas. NMFs help us to determine suitable semantics for logic programs and they help us as well to understand how they can be applied to express and solve various AI problems. Conversely, the NMFs can utilize the wide body of knowledge already gathered about LP and use logic programs as inference engines for query answering.

The 10 papers in this collection address the issues stemming from this outlook. Because new semantics often require new computational procedures, the papers can be naturally divided into two sections: **Semantics** (5 papers) and **Computation** (5 papers). We give more specific comments about the papers and their interrelationship in the Introduction (page 1).

All contributions were refereed by the Program Committee members, who are all to be thanked for their invaluable help and effort. Thanks are due as well to the external reviewers (see next page).

Last but not least, let us congratulate all the authors, whose high quality research and text formatting abilities made this book a reality. We are sure it will spur on further research into this exciting and open field.

March 1995

Jürgen Dix, Koblenz
Luís Moniz Pereira, Lisboa
Teodor C. Przymusinski, Riverside

Previous Workshops

1990	WS at NACLP '90, U.S.A.	1991	WS at ILPS '91, U.S.A.
1993	WS at ILPS '93, U.S.A.	1994	WS at ICLP '94, Italy

Sponsors

Compulog Network of Excellence, University of Koblenz.

Organizing Committee

Jürgen Dix	University of Koblenz
Luís Moniz	Universidade Nova di Lisboa
Teodor Przymusinski	University of California at Riverside

Program Committee

Jürgen Dix	University of Koblenz, Germany
Michael Gelfond	University of Texas at El Paso, U.S.A.
Jorge Lobo	University of Illinois at Chicago, U.S.A.
Wiktor Marek	University of Kentucky at Lexington, U.S.A.
Luís Moniz Pereira	Universidade Nova di Lisboa, Portugal
Teodor Przymusinski	University of California at Riverside, U.S.A.

Additional Referees

J.J. Alferes, C.V. Damasio, L. Degerstedt, A. Provetti, and Carlos Uzcátegui.

Introduction

In order to facilitate reading this book, we now give a brief overview of the contents of the presented papers. We follow our classification of papers into two categories, one devoted to *semantics* and the other to *computation*.

Semantics: While Alferes/Pereira as well as Witteveen deal with extended normal programs, all other papers in this section deal with extended disjunctive programs.

The first paper, *An argumentation theoretic semantics based on non-refutable falsity* by J. J. Alferes and L. M. Pereira, extends previous works of the authors (O-semantics) by presenting a new semantics for extended logic programs. The intuition behind is that the well-founded semantics often is overly careful in deciding about the falsity of some atoms by leaving them undefined. Default literals are viewed as arguments a rational agent can sustain along with the program.

The second paper, *From Disjunctive Programs to Abduction* by V. Lifschitz and H. Turner, deals with the problem of representing incomplete information using different formalisms (classical negation and epistemic disjunction versus two variants of abductive logic programming). Three formalisms are applied to a particular action-domain (the Yale Shooting) and the presented results show that they are very closely related (by simple syntactic transformations).

The third paper, *Semantics of Normal and Disjunctive Logic Programs: A unifying framework* by T. Przymusinski, introduces a uniform semantic framework that isomorphically contains the major semantics for normal, disjunctive and extended logic programs. The framework is based on the *Autoepistemic Logic of Knowledge and beliefs*, AELB, introduced recently by the author.

C. Witteveen's paper, *Every Normal Program has a Nearly-Stable Model*, investigates the inconsistency-problem of the stable semantics: stable models need not always exist. He presents two simple syntactic transformations, *shifting* and *condensation* that allow to transform any program in another one having at least one stable model.

The last paper in the Semantics group, *Logic Programming with Assumption Denial* by J.-H. You and L.-Y. Yuan, deals with arbitrary extended disjunctive programs. The authors define a framework which allows to explicitely represent *defeats* of assumptions, so called *assumption denials*. Their method is related to abduction and reveals interesting relationships between disjunctive and non-disjunctive programs.

Computation: With the exception of the first, all remaining papers deal with *transformations*. Different syntactical transformations are applied to the original program to obtain a certain normal form which is used to compute the semantics more efficiently. While Degerstedt/Nilsson consider the well-founded semantics, the other authors compute (partial) stable models or the static semantics for disjunctive programs.

The first paper of this section, *A Resolution-based Procedure for Default*

Theories with Extensions by M. Barback and J. Lobo, deals with a problem in general non-monotonic reasoning: to determine if a given formula is true in *all* (sceptical entailment) or in *some* (credulous entailment) extensions of a default theory. The authors relate this problem to logic programming, by defining a sound and complete proof-procedure that is closely related to SLDNF and abduction-like procedures for logic programs.

In the second paper, *A General Approach to Bottom-Up Computation of Disjunctive Semantics* by St. Brass and J. Dix, a method for deriving bottom-up query evaluation algorithms from the abstract properties of the underlying negation semantics is described. An important ingredient is to derive first the *residual program* (using partial evaluation and reductions). The authors argue that this approach is applicable to a large class of disjunctive semantics, like the stable, and the static semantics and its variants.

The next paper, *Static Semantics as Program Transformation and Well-founded Computation* by S. Costantini and G. Lanzarone, describes a general framework of computing semantics for disjunctive logic programs that are similar to the static semantics. They distinguish between a *program transformation phase*, which absorbs most of the complexity and a *constructive phase*, which is similar to the well-founded computation for normal programs.

The paper by L. Degerstedt and U. Nilsson, *Magic Computation for Well-founded Semantics*, deals with non-disjunctive semantics under the well-founded semantics. The authors introduce a new magic templates transformation and show a step-by-step correspondence between the naive bottom-up evaluation of the transformed program and a class of top-down search strategies. They show their method to be sound and complete.

Finally, the last paper of this book, *Computing Stable and Partial Stable Models of Extended Disjunctive Logic Programs* by C. Ruiz and J. Minker, again deals with extended disjunctive logic programs. The authors describe a procedure to compute the collection of all partial stable models of a program. This is done by transforming the program into a constrained disjunctive program without any non-monotonic negation such that the classical minimal models of the transformed program correspond to the set of partial stable models of the original program.

An argumentation theoretic semantics based on non–refutable falsity*

José Júlio Alferes[1] and Luís Moniz Pereira[2]

[1] DMAT, Universidade de Évora and CRIA, Uninova
2825 Monte da Caparica, Portugal
jja@fct.unl.pt

[2] DCS, U. Nova de Lisboa and CRIA, Uninova
2825 Monte da Caparica, Portugal
lmp@fct.unl.pt

Abstract. We contend that the well-founded semantics (WFS), for normal program, and similarly the well-founded semantics with explicit negation (*WFSX*), for extended ones are, by design, overly careful in deciding about the falsity of some atoms, by leaving them undefined.
We've dealt with this issue in normal programs and have previously defined the O-semantics, one that extends WFS by addjoining to it more negative assumptions, at the expense of undefined literals. The goal of this paper is to generalize that work to extended programs, and define a semantics for such programs that enlarges *WFSX* with more negative assumptions.
To achieve this we view default literals as arguments a rational agent can sustain along with the program. As our goal is to enlarge *WFSX*, we consider the latter as the common reasoning ground and argumentation tool of agents.
With this basis, and in order to define the semantics, we first formalize the concepts of consistent and non-refutable sets of arguments (or of hypotheses). In general several such sets may exist. So, and in order to define a unique semantics, given by a single set of additional assumptions, we introduce an additional non-refutability of arguments criterium – tenability – for always and finally preferring just one set of arguments over another.

1 Introduction

The Well Founded Semantics (WFS) [GRS91] has been proposed as a suitable semantics for normal logic programs. Unlike other semantics, WFS gives meaning to every normal program, is cumulative [Dix91], and can be obtained by a bottom-up fixpoint construction. Because it is a relevant semantics [Dix92] it is susceptible of top-down existencial query procedures. However, as argued in [KM91, PAA92a, PAA93], the WFS is by design overly careful in deciding about the falsity of some atoms, leaving them undefined.

* We thank Esprit BR project Compulog 2 (no. 6810) for its support.

In [PAA92a, PAA93] we introduce a suitable form of closed world assumption (CWA), and use it to safely and undisputably assume false some of the atoms absent from the well founded model of a program. There we contend that a set S of negative literals (assumptions) *added* to a program model $MOD(P)$ by CWA must obey four precepts:

- $MOD(P) \cup S \not\models L$ for any *not* $L \in S$. I.e. the program model added with the set of assumptions identified by our CWA rule must be **consistent**.
- There is no other set of assumptions A such that $MOD(P) \cup A \models L$ for some *not* $L \in S$.
- S must be **unique**.
- S must, additionally, be **maximal**.

Based on these we've then defined the so-called O-semantics for normal logic programs, one more credulous than WFS in the sense that it accepts more negative assumptions.

A number of authors have underscored the advantages of extending logic programming with a second kind of negation $\neg$, for use in deductive databases, knowledge representation, and nonmonotonic reasoning [GL90, KS90, PAA91, Wag91]. Different semantics for extended logic programs with $\neg$-negation (ELP) have appeared [DR91, GL90, KS90, PA92, Prz90, Prz91, Wag91]. [AP92] contrasts some of these, where distinct meanings of $\neg$-negation are identified: classical, strong and explicit. It is argued there that explicit negation is preferable. The well-founded semantics with explicit negation (*WFSX*) [PA92] incorporates this preferred $\neg$-negation, and also inherits the above mentioned desirable properties of WFS (e.g. cumulativity, relevance, bottom-up fixpoint construction, cf. [Alf93]).

However, as for the WFS of normal programs, the *WFSX* of extended programs too is by design overly careful in deciding about the falsity of some atoms, leaving them also undefined.

Example 1.
The extended program:

$$\begin{aligned} win(X) &\leftarrow move(X,Y), not\ win(Y) \\ worthBetting(X) &\leftarrow win(X) \\ bet(X) &\leftarrow worthBetting(X) \\ \neg bet(X) &\leftarrow not\ worthBetting(X) \\ move(a,a)& \\ move(b,c)& \end{aligned}$$

expresses that:

- "X is a winning position if there is a move from X to Y and Y is not a winning position";
- "winning position bets are worth betting";

- "bet if a position is worth betting";
- "do not bet if it can be assumed that it is not worth betting" or, in other words, "if there is the possibility of it not being worth betting";
- "moves from position a to position a, and from b to c are legal".

c is not a winning position since it is impossible to move from c. b is a winning position because it is possible to move from b to c and c is not a winning position. a is a position of draw.

Neither $win(a)$ nor $not\ win(a)$ should hold. This is correctly handled by *WFSX*, which assigns the truth-value *undefined* to $win(a)$.

The semantics of this program should also capture the intended meaning that one should not bet in a position of draw. This is not captured by *WFSX*, which leaves $\neg bet(a)$ undefined.

Moreover note that, despite the fact that $win(a)$ is undefined, and the only rule for $worthBetting(a)$ has that atom in the body, $not\ worthBetting(a)$ could be safely assumed, thus giving $\neg bet(a)$.

Example 2.
Consider the program:

$$\begin{array}{lcl} go\_to\_movie & \leftarrow & not\ go\_to\_beach \\ go\_to\_beach & \leftarrow & not\ go\_to\_movie \\ stay\_home & \leftarrow & not\ go\_to\_beach, not\ go\_to\_movie \\ \neg stay\_home & \leftarrow & not\ stay\_home \end{array}$$

By *WFSX* all of go_to_movie, go_to_beach, $stay\_home$, and $\neg stay\_home$ are undefined.
However $not\ stay\_home$ can safely be assumed because the two premises of the only rule for $stay\_home$ are incompatible. Moreover, assuming $not\ stay\_home$ does not cause any inconsistency. Thus $\neg stay\_home$ follows unproblematically.

The main result of this paper is an argumentation semantics for ELPs that:

- enlarges the *WFSX* of noncontradictory programs by adding more default assumptions, thus reducing undefinedness.
- generalizes the O-semantics of normal programs to extended ones.

To achieve this we view, as usual, default literals as assumptions that might be added to (or imposed on) a program. In other words, default literals correspond to arguments a rational agent can sustain along with the program. As one of our goals is to enlarge *WFSX*, we consider this semantics the common reasoning and argumentation tool of agents. Whereas our approach is based on a pre-defined semantics, and uses argumentation to enlarge that semantics, others (e.g. [BTK93, Dun93]) use argumentation to defined the semantics from scratch. On this basis, and in order to define the semantics, in this paper we formalize the following informally expressed concepts:

First, as we'll see, a set of assumptions A is consistent with a program P if neither of them is contradicted by the *WFSX* of P when A is imposed on it. Inconsistent sets of assumptions correspond to self-refuting sets of arguments.

Then we introduce the notion of sustainable sets of assumptions (or arguments). Intuitively, a set of assumptions A is sustainable if it is consistent and there is no other set of consistent assumptions that can be adopted together with P whose joint *WFSX* contradicts A. An unsustainable set of assumptions A can be seen as refutable sets of arguments, in the sense that there exists another consistent set of assumptions B which if imposed on P produces a model that contradicts A, even if A plus P contradicts B. In the latter case both are unsustainable.

Example 3.
In program P :

$$c \leftarrow not\ b \qquad a \leftarrow not\ a$$
$$b \leftarrow not\ a$$

the assumption *not a* is inconsistent because when imposed on P the resulting *WFSX* would entail a. In other words, no agent can sustain the argument *not a* because using *WFSX* makes this argument together with the program self-refuting.

The assumption *not c* is consistent but not sustainable: by imposing *not b*, c follows, and so the argument *not c* is refuted by *not b*. In other words, on the basis of P and *WFSX* rationality, an agent upholding argument *not c* can be refuted (or counterargued) by any other agent sustaining the argument *not b*.

The assumption *not b* is consistent and sustainable. An agent sustaining argument *not b* cannot be refuted by any consistent set of arguments.

To maximally reduce undefinedness we need to identify maximal sustainable sets of assumptions. In the example above $\{not\ b\}$ is the single maximal one. Naturally, in this case the semantics is defined as the result of imposing *not b* on the program.

In general several maximal sustainable sets of assumptions may exist (cf. examples 8 and 9). So, and in order to define a unique semantics given by a single set of additional assumptions, a first approach would be to add only those assumptions common to all maximal sets, i.e. those arguments that are nonrefutable and consensual. However this is too extreme a measure. In fact, and in order to further enlarge the *WFSX* with nonrefutable assumptions, one can introduce an additional criterium – tenability – for always and finally preferring one set of assumptions over another. Or, if you will, we introduce a new form of argument refutation: the tenability of a maximal set of sustainable assumptions requires that it be not refuted when conjoined with another such competing set.

The structure of this paper is as follows: we begin with a brief review of *WFSX*. Then, in section 3, we show how to consistently add nonrefutable negative assumptions to the *WFSX* of an extended program P. In section 4 we introduce tenability, define the O-semantics for extended programs, and show that it accomplishes the goals we've proposed. Finally we draw some comparisons with related work.

2 Preliminary definitions

In this section we define the language of extended logic programs and briefly review the *WFSX* semantics [PA92]. Proof of the results in this section can be found in [Alf93].

An extended program is a set of rules of the form:

$$L_0 \leftarrow L_1, \ldots, L_m, not\ L_{m+1}, \ldots, not\ L_n \quad (0 \leq m \leq n)$$

where each L_i is an objective literal. An objective literal is either an atom A or its explicit negation $\neg A$. The set of all objective literals of a program P is called the extended Herbrand base of P and denoted by $\mathcal{H}(P)$. The symbol *not* stands for negation by default[1]. *not* L is called a default literal. Literals are either objective or default literals. By *not* $\{a_1, \ldots, a_n, \ldots\}$ we mean $\{not\ a_1, \ldots, not\ a_n, \ldots\}$.

An interpretation of an extended program P is denoted by $T \cup not\ F$, where T and F are disjoint subsets of $\mathcal{H}(P)$. Objective literals in T are said to be *true* in I, objective literals in F *false by default* in I, and in $\mathcal{H}(P) - (T \cup F)$ *undefined* in I.

WFSX follows from WFS for normal programs plus the coherence requirement relating the two forms of negation:

> *"for any objective literal L, if ¬L is entailed by the semantics then not L must also be entailed".*

This requirement states that whenever some literal is explicitly false then it must be assumed false by default.

Here we present *WFSX* differently from its original definition, based on the application of the Gelfond-Lifschitz Γ operator and on a notion of semi-normal programs. The equivalence between both definitions is proven in [Alf93].

Definition 1 GL-transformation([GL90]).
Let P be an extended program and S a set of objective literals. The GL-transformation of P modulo S is the program $\frac{P}{S}$ obtained from P by first substituting every explicitly negated literal $\neg A$ by a new atom $\neg\_A$ and then performing the following operations:

- remove from P all rules containing a default literal *not* A such that $A \in S$;
- remove from the remaining rules all default literals.

Since $\frac{P}{S}$ is a definite program, it has a unique least model J. Let I be the set of objective literals obtained by substituting every atom $\neg\_A$ in J by $\neg A$. We define $\Gamma_P(S) = I$.

In order to impose coherence[2] we introduce:

---

[1] This designation has been used in the literature instead of the more operational *"negation as failure (to prove)"*.

[2] See [PAA92b] for how the use of semi-normal programs present below imposes coherence in partial stable models.

Definition 2 Semi-normal Version of a Program.
The semi-normal version of a program P is the program P_s obtained from P by adding to the (possibly empty) *Body* of each rule $L \leftarrow$ *Body* the default literal *not* $\neg L$, where $\neg L$ is the complement of L wrt explicit negation.

Whenever P is understood from the context, we use $\Gamma(S)$ to denote $\Gamma_P(S)$, and $\Gamma_s(S)$ to denote $\Gamma_{P_s}(S)$.

Definition 3 Partial Stable Model.
An interpretation $T \cup$ *not* F is called a partial stable model of P iff:

- $T = \Gamma\Gamma_s T$ and
- $F = \mathcal{H}(P) - \Gamma_s T$.

Not every extended program has partial stable models.

Example 4.
The program $P = \{a; \quad \neg a\}$ has no partial stable models.

Definition 4 Contradictory Programs.
A program P is *WFSX*-contradictory iff it has no partial stable model.

Theorem 5 Well-founded Model.
Every noncontradictory program P has a least (wrt $\subseteq$) partial stable model, the well-founded model of P.

3 Adding nonrefutable negative assumptions

In this section we show how to consistently add nonrefutable negative assumptions to the *WFSX* of an extended program P. Informally, it is consistent to add a negative assumption to *WFSX*(P) if no contradiction follows from that addition, and if the assumption atom is not among *WFSX*(P) after adding the assumption to P. A set of assumptions A is refuted (or defeated) by another set, B, if by adding B the complement of some element in A follows.

More formally, to add a negative assumption to the *WFSX* of a program means to first "compile" that assumption into the program. This is achieved simply by substituting, in all body rule occurences, *true* for any of the assumptions to be added, and *false* for their atoms.

Definition 6 Program plus assumptions ($P + A$).
The program $P + A$ obtained by adding to an extended program P a set of negative assumptions $A \subseteq$ *not* $\mathcal{H}(P)$ is the result of:

- Deleting from P all rules

  $$H \leftarrow B_1, \ldots, B_n, not\ C_1, \ldots, not\ C_m,$$

  such that some *not* $B_i \in A$;

– Deleting from the remaining rules all literals *not* $L \in A$.

Then, since we are interested in adding negative assumptions to the *WFSX* of a program, after adding the assumptions to P we compute the *WFSX* of the resulting program. Moreover, there is no reason not to consider the addition of negative assumptions belonging to the *WFSX* of the original program. Note here the difference, mentioned in the introduction, between this approach and other approaches of using argumentation systems to define the semantics of programs. Whereas our approach is based on a pre-defined semantics, and uses argumentation to enlarge that semantics, others (e.g. [BTK93, Dun93]) use argumentation to defined the semantics from scratch.

Unlike the case of WFS for normal programs, by using *WFSX* of extended programs not every program has a semantics. Thus, care must be taken in considering only the addition of assumptions guaranteeing the existence of *WFSX*:

Example 5.
The assumption *not* b cannot be added to program P :

$$\begin{aligned} \neg a &\leftarrow not\ b \\ b &\leftarrow not\ b \\ a &\leftarrow not\ b \end{aligned}$$

because

$$P + \{not\ b\} = \begin{aligned} \neg a &\leftarrow \\ a &\leftarrow \\ b &\leftarrow \end{aligned}$$

is contradictory.

Definition 7 Assumption Model.
An assumption model, or A-model for short, of an extended program P with $WFSX(P) = T \cup not\ F$ is a pair $\langle A; M \rangle$, where $not\ F \subseteq A \subseteq not\ \mathcal{H}(P)$, $P + A$ is a noncontradictory program, and

$$M = WFSX(P + A)$$

The meaning of an A-model $\langle A; WFSX(P + A) \rangle$ is

$$A \cup WFSX(P + A)$$

i.e. the result of adding assumptions A to the *WFSX* of P.

As argued above, sets of negative assumptions that lead to an inconsistency are not to be considered. An inconsistency can be obtained either by having both some L and $\neg L$ in the meaning of the A-model, or some A and *not* A. By not considering sets of assumptions that when added to a program lead to a contradiction the first condition for consistency of A-models is guaranteed by definition.

Definition 8 Consistent A-model.
An A-model $\langle A; M\rangle$ is consistent iff its meaning is consistent i.e., since by definition M is always consistent, iff there exists no assumption $not\ L \in A$ such that $L \in M$.

Note that for consistency we do not impose that $not\ L \in M$. In other words our notion of consistency is not one that guarantees that arguments are stable. Instead, we just impose consistent A-models to be the result of adding to the *WFSX* of a program a set of assumptions that *cannot be contradicted by the program itself.* However one such A-model can be contradicted by another consistent A-model:

Example 6.
Recall the program of example 3,

$$P = \{c \leftarrow not\ b;\quad b \leftarrow not\ a;\quad a \leftarrow not\ a\}$$

whose *WFSX* is $\{not\ \neg a, not\ \neg b, not\ \neg c\}$
P has three consistent A-models:

$$\begin{array}{rcl} M_1 &=& \langle\ \{not\ \neg a, not\ \neg b, not\ \neg c\}\ ;\ \{not\ \neg a, not\ \neg b, not\ \neg c\}\ \rangle \\ M_2 &=& \langle\ \{not\ \neg a, not\ \neg b, not\ \neg c, not\ b\}\ ;\ \{c, not\ \neg a, not\ \neg b, not\ \neg c\}\ \rangle \\ M_3 &=& \langle\ \{not\ \neg a, not\ \neg b, not\ \neg c, not\ c\}\ ;\ \{not\ \neg a, not\ \neg b, not\ \neg c\}\ \rangle \end{array}$$

An agent which argues in favour of any of these sets of assumptions cannot be contradicted by an agent armed with the same program. However $\{not\ c\}$ can be counterargued (or defeated) by $\{not\ b\}$. Accordingly we say that $\{not\ c\}$ is refutable, since there is an alternative consistent additions of assumptions that defeats it, i.e. proves its complement c.

As argued in the introduction, we are interested only in sets of assumptions that cannot be refuted. Note that, like for normal programs, also in extended programs the only way of defeating assumption $not\ L$ is by proving L. To capture the notion of non-refutability (or sustainability) we now formally define how an A-model can defeat another, and define sustainable A-model as a non-defeated consistent one.

Definition 9 Defeating.
A consistent A-model $\langle A; M\rangle$ is defeated by consistent A-model $\langle A'; M'\rangle$ iff $\exists not\ a \in A |\ a \in M'$.

Definition 10 Sustainable A-model.
An A-model $\langle A; M\rangle$ is sustainable iff it is consistent and not defeated by any consistent A-model.

Note that every noncontradictory program has at least one sustainable A-model. Indeed, it follows from lemma 12 below that the A-model whose negative assumptions are all the negative literals of $WFSX(P)$ is sustainable.

Because we wish to maximally enlarge the *WFSX* of a program, we are especially interested in sustainable A-models that have a maximal number of added assumption, i.e. are maximal according to the partial order $\leq_a$ where:

$$\langle A_1; M_1\rangle \leq_a \langle A_2; M_2\rangle \quad \text{iff} \quad A_1 \subseteq A_2$$

Example 7.
The $\leq_a$-maximal sustainable A-model of the program of example 6 is M_2. Thus, the meaning of P is $\{c, not\ b\} \cup WFSX(P)$.

However several noncompatible maximal sustainable A-models may exist:

Example 8.
Let P be:

$$\begin{aligned} c &\leftarrow not\ c, not\ \neg b \\ a &\leftarrow not\ a \\ \neg b &\leftarrow a \end{aligned}$$

whose *WFSX* is $\{not\ \neg a, not\ b, not\ \neg c\}$.

Its sustainable A-models are (where $not\ \neg a, not\ b, not\ \neg c$ are omitted for simplicity):

$$\begin{array}{l} \langle\ \{\}\ ; \{\}\ \rangle \\ \langle\ \{not\ \neg b\}\ ; \{\}\ \rangle \\ \langle\ \{not\ c\}\ ; \{\}\ \rangle \end{array}$$

the last two being maximal. Note that we cannot both add $not\ \neg b$ and $not\ c$ to P to obtain a sustainable A-model since

$$\langle\{not\ \neg b, not\ c\}; \{c\}\rangle$$

is inconsistent.

Example 9.
Consider program P :

$$\begin{aligned} \neg a &\leftarrow not\ b \\ b &\leftarrow not\ d \\ d &\leftarrow not\ d \\ a &\leftarrow not\ c \\ c &\leftarrow not\ d \end{aligned}$$

Its sustainable A-models are:

$$\begin{aligned} M_1 &= \langle\ \{\}\ ; \{not\ \neg b, not\ \neg c, not\ \neg d\}\ \rangle \\ M_2 &= \langle\ \{not\ b\}\ ; \{\neg a, not\ a, not\ \neg b, not\ \neg c, not\ \neg d\}\ \rangle \\ M_3 &= \langle\ \{not\ c\}\ ; \{a, not\ \neg a, not\ \neg b, not\ \neg c, not\ \neg d\}\ \rangle \end{aligned}$$

The last two are maximal. We cannot add both $not\ b$ and $not\ c$ to the program because $P + \{not\ b, not\ c\}$ is contradictory.

So, in general, sustainable A-models are not organized into a complete lattice. However:

Theorem 11.
The set of all sustainable A-models of a program is nonempty iff the program is noncontradictory. On the basis of set union and set intersection among their assumption sets, the A-models ordered by $\leq_a$ form a lower semilattice.

Proof. If a program P is noncontradictory then, given the definitions of A-model and sustainability, $\langle\{\}; WFSX(P)\rangle$ is a sustainable A-model.

If there is a sustainable A-model $\langle A; WFSX(P+A)\rangle$ then, by definition of A-model, $P+A$ is noncontradictory. By lemma 12 below, it follows that P is also noncontradictory.

We have now to prove that for any two consistent A-models $\langle A; M\rangle$ and $\langle A'; M'\rangle$, their meet $\langle A\cap A'; M''\rangle$ exists, is unique, and is a consistent A-model. The uniqueness is guaranteed by definition of A-model, given the uniqueness of *WFSX* of any program.

We begin by proving (by contradiction) that $P+(A\cap A')$ is noncontradictory, i.e. $\langle A\cap A'; M''\rangle$ is an A-model.

Assume that $P+(A\cap A')$ is contradictory. Then there are in $P+(A\cap A')$ at least two rules with complementary heads whose bodies are true in the paraconsistent *WFSX* [Alf93]. If none of these rules is deleted in one of $P+A$ or $P+A'$ then either $P+A$ or $P+A'$ is contradictory. If one of the rules is deleted, say in $P+A$, then there exists in the body of that rule one B_i such that *not* $B_i \in A$. Since B_i is true in $P+(A\cap A')$, similarly to the proof of lemma 12 one can prove that $B_i \in WFSX(P+A)$, i.e. $\langle A; M\rangle$ is inconsistent, thus contradicting one of our hypotheses. □

In order to define a semantics based on a unique set of additional assumptions that are sustainable and consensual, a first approach would be to consider the meet of all maximal sustainable A-models. This would already strictly enlarge the *WFSX* of some programs (cf. example 6). Moreover, it would be a generalization of *WFSX* in the sense that every literal in the *WFSX* of a program is in the meaning of that meet. Also, for every noncontradictory program that meet exist, i.e. a semantics based on that meet is defined for the same programs as *WFSX*:

Lemma 12.
Let $\langle A; \text{WFSX}(P+A)\rangle$ *be a consistent A-model of the extended logic program* P*. Then for every literal* L *:*

$$L \in \text{WFSX}(P) \quad\Rightarrow\quad L \in \text{WFSX}(P+A)$$

Proof. First let us assume that L is an objective literal.

If $L \in WFSX(P)$ then there exists a rule in P

$$L \leftarrow B_1, \ldots, B_n, not\ C_1, \ldots, not\ C_m$$

such that

$$\{B_1, \ldots, B_n, not\ C_1, \ldots, not\ C_m\} \subseteq WFSX(P)$$

If this rule is not deleted in $P + A$, i.e.

$$\{not\ B_1, \ldots, not\ B_n\} \cap A = \{\}$$

then this theorem applies recursively, ending up in a rule with empty body, an atom with no rules or a loop without an interposing *not l*. The truth value of literals in these conditions can never be changed: since the $P + A$ operation only involves deleting rules with literals at the body and literals from the body of rules, the truth value of atoms without rules is always false no matter which A is being considered, and the truth value of atoms with a fact is always true. Literals in a loop without interposing *not l* are false in P, and remain false if rules of the loop are deleted. So:

$$\{B_1, \ldots, B_n, not\ C_1, \ldots, not\ C_m\} \subseteq WFSX(P + A)$$

Given that the rule is not deleted:

$$L \leftarrow B_1, \ldots, B_n, not\ D_1, \ldots, not\ D_k \in P + A$$

where

$$\{not\ D_1, \ldots, not\ D_k\} \subseteq \{not\ C_1, \ldots, not\ C_m\}$$

Thus $L \in WFSX(P + A)$.

If the rule is deleted then there exists in A one *not* B_i where B_i is one elements of the rule body. Applying this theorem recursively for B_i it follows that $B_i \in WFSX(P+A)$, i.e. $\langle A; WFSX(P+A)\rangle$ is not consistent, contradicting this way one of our hypotheses.

The proof for a literal *not L* goes along the same lines, and is omitted. □

Theorem 13.
An extended logic program P has at least one consistent A-model iff P is noncontradictory. The meaning of any consistent A-model of a noncontradictory program P is a superset of WFSX(P).

Proof. Follows directly from theorem 11 and lemma 12 □

4 O-semantics for extended programs

To further enlarge the *WFSX* of a program, additional criteria for preferring among competing sets of sustainable assumptions must be introduced. This is achieved in the O-semantics of normal programs by means of tenability. Whereas sustainability of a consistent set of negative assumptions insists that there must be no other consistent set that defeats it (i.e. no hypothetical evidence whose consequences contradict the sustained assumptions), tenability requires additionally that a maximal sustainable set of assumptions be not contradicted by the consequences of adding to it another competing (nondefeating and nondefeated) maximal sustainable set.

In this section we introduce tenability for extended programs, and use this criterium to define a recursive peeling process that takes a lower semilattice of sustainable A-models and obtains a subsemilattice of it, by deleting maximal untenable A-models[3]. This peeling process is repeated and ends up with a complete lattice of sustainable A-models which, for every program P, is by definition its O-semantics. The meaning of P is then specified by the greatest A-model of the semantics, its O-Model.

To illustrate the problem of preference among maximal A-models recall examples 8 and 9 above.

Example 10.
Because we wish to maximize the number of negative assumptions, we consider the maximal A-models, which in the case of example 8 are:

$$\langle\ \{not\ \neg b\}\ ;\ \{\}\ \rangle$$
$$\langle\ \{not\ c\}\ ;\ \{\}\ \rangle$$

The join of these maximal A-models:

$$\langle \{not\ \neg b, not\ c\}; \{c\}\rangle$$

is inconsistent wrt c. This signifies that when assuming *not* c there is an additional set of assumptions entailing c, making this A-model *untenable*. But the same does not apply to *not* $\neg b$. So we can say that *not* $\neg b$ is more primal than *not* c, in the sense that when added jointly with *not* c it causes an inconsistency in c but not one in $\neg b$. In the program that is indeed intuitively the case: *not* c depends on *not* b but not vice-versa, and so *not* b is more primal and unaffeted by *not* c. Thus the preferred A-model is

$$\langle \{not\ \neg b\}, \{\}\rangle$$

and the A-model $\langle \{not\ c\}; \{\}\rangle$ is said untenable. The rationale for the preference is grounded in that the inconsistency of the join arises wrt c but not wrt $\neg b$.

Example 11.
The maximal sustainable A-models of example 9 are both untenable because by adding the assumptions of them both to P the resulting program is contradictory. In fact:

$$P + \{not\ b, not\ c, not\ \neg b, not\ \neg c, not\ \neg d\} = \quad \begin{array}{l} \neg a \\ a \\ b \leftarrow not\ d \\ c \leftarrow not\ d \\ d \leftarrow not\ d \end{array}$$

[3] Note that by deleting maximal A-models, a greater meet is obtained.

The rationale for saying that both maximal sustainable A-models are untenable is grounded in that there is no reason to prefer one over the other, and they cannot be both assumed jointly. Thus in the end none of them is tenable.

Definition 14 Candidate Structure.
A candidate structure CS of a program P is any subsemilattice of the lower semilattice of all sustainable A-models of P.

Definition 15 Untenable A-model.
Let $\{\langle A_k; M_k\rangle \mid k \in K\}$ be the set of all maximal A-models in candidate structure CS, and let:

$$P_J = P + \bigcup_{k\in K} A_j$$

An A-model $\langle A_i; M_i\rangle$ is untenable wrt CS iff it is maximal in CS and either:

- P_J is contradictory, or
- there exists $not\ a \in A_i$ such that $a \in WFSX(P_J)$.

The candidate structure left after removing all untenable A-models of a CS may itself have several untenable elements, some of which might not be untenable A-models in the initial CS. If the removal of untenable A-models is performed repeatedly on the retained Candidate Structure, a structure with no untenable models is eventually obtained, albeit the bottom element of the candidate structure. If this structure has a single maximal element then it denotes the O-semantics. Otherwise the lemma below guarantees that the join of maximal tenable A-models can be safely added to the structure.

Lemma 16.
Let $\{\langle A_k; M_k\rangle \mid k \in K\}$ be the set of all maximal A-models in Candidate Structure CS. If none of those A-models is untenable then

$$\langle \bigcup_{k\in K} A_k; \mathrm{WFSX}(P + \bigcup_{k\in K} A_k)\rangle$$

is a sustainable A-model.

Proof. Let:

$$A_J = \bigcup_{k\in K} A_k$$

We have to prove that:

1. $P + A_J$ is noncontradictory.
   - By contradiction, assume that $P+A_J$ is contradictory. Then by definition all maximal A–models are untenable (contradiction).
2. There exists no $not\ L \in A_J$ such that $L \in WFSX(P + A_J)$.
   - Again by contradiction, assume that there exists one $not\ L \in A_J$ such that $L \in WFSX(P + A_J)$. If $not\ L \in A_J$ then there exist one A–model $\langle A_i; M_i\rangle$, maximal in CS, such that $not\ L \in A_i$. Since $L \in WFSX(P + A_J)$, $\langle A_i; M_i\rangle$ is untenable (contradiction).

3. There exists no consistent A–model $\langle A; M\rangle$ such that $L \in M$ and *not* $L \in A_J$.
   - By definition of candidate structure, every A–models $\langle A_i; M_i\rangle$ in CS is sustainable. Thus there is no A–model $\langle A; M\rangle$ such that $L \in M$ and *not* $L \in A_i$ and so, given that this holds for all A_i in CS, there is no A–model $\langle A; M\rangle$ such that $L \in M$ and

$$not\ L \in \bigcup_{k\in K} A_i$$

   i.e. the join is sustainable. □

Definition 17 Retained Candidate Structure.
Let CS be a candidate structure, and let A be the union of all assumptions in all A-models of CS. The retained candidate structure $R(CS)$ of CS is defined recursively in the following way:

- $\langle A; WFSX(P + A)\rangle \cup CS$ if there are no untenable A-models in CS;
- Otherwise, let Unt be the set of all untenable A-models wrt CS. Then

$$R(CS) = R(CS - Unt).$$

Definition 18 O-semantics for Extended Programs.
The O-semantics of an extended logic program P is the retained candidate structure of the semilattice of all sustainable A-models of P.

Let $AM = \langle A; M\rangle$ be its maximal element. The O-model of P is the meaning of AM, i.e. $A \cup M$.

The theorems below go to show that in fact the O-semantics defined herein for extended programs is a generalization of that for normal programs, and that it enlarges the *WFSX*, by leaving less literals undefined.

Theorem 19 Relation to O-semantics of Normal Programs.
Let P be a normal logic program. The "O-semantics" of P (as in [PAA92a, PAA93]) coincides with the "O-semantics for extended programs" of P.

Proof. Given that for normal programs WFS and *WFSX* coincide (cf. [PA92]), and that no normal program can be contradictory, it is easy to check that each of the definition modified in order to obtain the "O-semantics of extended programs" coincide with the original ones for normal programs. □

Theorem 20 Existence of the O-semantics.
An extended logic program P is WFSX-*noncontradictory iff it has O-semantics.*

Proof. From theorem 11, P is *WFSX*-noncontradictory iff P has sustainable A-models. From lemma 16 and the definition of retained candidate structure it follows directly that P has sustainable A-models iff P has O-semantics. □

Theorem 21 Extension of *WFSX*.
Let P be a WFSX-*noncontradictory program, whose* WFSX *well-founded model is M, and whose O-model is O. Then* $M \subseteq O$.

Proof. By lemma 12, for every consistent A-model $\langle A, WFSX(P+A)\rangle$:

$$WFSX(P) \subseteq WFSX(P+A) \qquad (*)$$

Since the O–model is by definition the meaning of one A-model, let

$$\langle A_O; WFSX(P+A_O)\rangle$$

be that A-model. Then, and using the result of $(*)$:

$$M = WFSX(P) \subseteq WFSX(P+A_O) \subseteq A_O \cup WFSX(P+A_O) = O$$

□

Example 12.
The *WFSX* of program P of example 1 is (with obvious abbreviations):

$$WF = \left\{ \begin{array}{llll} m(a,a), & m(b,c), & & \\ win(b), & wB(b), & b(b), & not\ \neg b(b), \\ not\ win(c), & not\ wB(c), & not\ b(c), & \neg b(c), \\ not\ \neg m(X,Y), & not\ \neg w(Z), & not\ \neg wB(W)^4 & \end{array} \right\}$$

Its consistent A-models, where N is the set of default literals in WF, are:

$$\begin{array}{lll} M_1 = & \langle\ N \cup \{not\ wB(a)\} & ;\ WF \cup \{\neg b(a), not\ b(a)\}\ \rangle \\ M_2 = & \langle\ N \cup \{not\ b(a)\} & ;\ WF \cup \{\}\ \rangle \\ M_3 = & \langle\ N \cup \{not\ \neg b(a)\} & ;\ WF \cup \{\}\ \rangle \\ M_4 = & \langle\ N \cup \{not\ wB(a), not\ b(a)\} & ;\ WF \cup \{\neg b(a), not\ b(a)\}\ \rangle \end{array}$$

M_3 is defeated by M_1 (and also by M_4). All other A-models are sustainable. Thus, the maximal sustainable A-model is M_4, and the O-model is:

$$WF \cup \{not\ worthBetting(a), \neg bet(a), not\ bet(a)\}$$

Example 13.
The *WFSX* of the program P of example 2 is (with obvious abbreviations):

$$WF = \{not\ \neg g\_m, not\ \neg g\_b\}$$

Its consistent A-models are:

$$\begin{array}{lll} M_1 = & \langle\ WF \cup \{not\ g\_m\} & ;\ WF \cup \{g\_b, \neg s\_h, not\ s\_h\}\ \rangle \\ M_2 = & \langle\ WF \cup \{not\ g\_b\} & ;\ WF \cup \{g\_m, \neg s\_h, not\ s\_h\}\ \rangle \\ M_3 = & \langle\ WF \cup \{not\ s\_h\} & ;\ WF \cup \{\neg s\_h\}\ \rangle \\ M_4 = & \langle\ WF \cup \{not\ \neg s\_h\} & ;\ WF \cup \{\}\ \rangle \\ M_5 = & \langle\ WF \cup \{not\ g\_m, not\ s\_h\} & ;\ WF \cup \{g\_b, \neg s\_h, not\ s\_m\}\ \rangle \\ M_6 = & \langle\ WF \cup \{not\ g\_b, not\ s\_h\} & ;\ WF \cup \{g\_m, \neg s\_h, not\ s\_m\}\ \rangle \end{array}$$

[4] Where $not\ \neg m(X,Y)$, $not\ \neg w(Z)$, and $not\ \neg wB(W)$ stand for all ground literals resulting from these by replacing any variables by all possible constants of the program.

A-model M_1 defeats both M_2 and M_6. Intuitively, an agent hypothesizing that one not go to the beach is defeated by an agent hypothesizing one go to the movie.

A-model M_2 defeats both M_1 and M_5. Intuitively, an agent that hypothesizes that one not go to the movie is defeated by an agent hypothesizing that one go to the beach.

A-model M_3 defeats M_4. Intuitively, an agent that hypothesizes to stay at home is defeated by an agent that hypothesizes not to stay at home.

M_3 is not defeated by any other A-model, i.e. an agent sustaining that one does not stay home cannot be counterargued.

Thus M_3 is the (unique) maximal sustainable A-models, and so the O-model is:

$$WF \cup \{\neg stay\_home, not\ stay\_home\}$$

Example 14.
Recall P of example 8, whose sustainable A-models are:

$$\begin{array}{l} \langle \quad \{\} \quad ; \{\} \rangle \\ \langle \{not\ \neg b\} ; \{\} \rangle \\ \langle \ \{not\ c\} \ ; \{\} \rangle \end{array}$$

As several maxima exist, we start removing untenable ones. The join of maximal A-models is $\langle\{not\ \neg b, not\ c\}; \{c\}\rangle$. So the third A-model is untenable, and removed.

After this step a single maximal element obtains, and so the process stops, returning the O-model $WF(P) \cup \{not\ \neg b\}$.

5 Comparisons

Although several semantics that extend WFS of normal programs by producing less undefinedness exist, to the best of our knowledge, apart from the "improved semantics for extended programs" of [BTK93], no other attempt has been made to combine these extension of WFS with explicit negation. So, in this section we not only compare our approach with the approach of [BTK93], but also compare the application of O-semantics for normal programs with other approaches that extend WFS for those programs.

Semantics for normal programs extending WFS are the extended well-founded semantics (EWFS) [Dix91], and the similar WFS$^+$ ([Dix92]) resp. WFS$_C$ ([Sch92]). WFS$^+$ and WFS$_C$ have been recently shown to be equivalent in [Dix95]. For simplicity, the following discussion only compares the O-Model with EWFS. But our comments literally apply to WFS$^+$ (resp. WFS$_C$).

Roughly, EWFM moves closer than the WFM (in the sense of being less undefined) to being the intersection of all minimal Herbrand models of P. With a different notation from that of [Dix91]:

$$EWFM(P) =_{def} WFM(P) \cup T(WFM(P)) \cup not\ F(WFM(P))$$

where:

$$T(\mathcal{I}) =_{def} True(MIN\_MOD(\mathcal{I}, P)),$$
$$F(\mathcal{I}) =_{def} False(MIN\_MOD(\mathcal{I}, P))$$

$\mathcal{I}$ is a three-valued interpretation, and $MIN\_MOD(\mathcal{I}, P)$ is the collection of all minimal two-valued Herbrand models of P consistent with $\mathcal{I}$. For a set $\mathcal{S}$ of interpretations, $True(\mathcal{S})$ (resp. $False(\mathcal{S})$) denotes the set of all atoms which are true (resp. false) in all interpretations of $\mathcal{S}$.

For the program $P = \{a \leftarrow not\ a\}$ we have:

$$WFM(P) = \{\}, MIN\_MOD(\{\}, P) = \{\{a\}\} \quad EWFM(P) = \{a\}$$

The O-Model of P is empty.

The main differences between ours and Schlipf/Dix's approach are:

- Like WFS and unlike EWFM (WFS^+), we insist on the supportedness of positive literals, i.e.:

  An atom $A \in M_P$ iff $\exists\ A \leftarrow Body \mid Body \subseteq M_P$

- Unlike WFS and unlike EWFM (WFS^+), we relax, by allowing undefined bodies with false heads under certain conditions, the requirement of supportedness of negative literals, i.e. we relax:

  $not\ A \in M_P$ iff $\forall\ A \leftarrow Body \mid Body$ is false in M_P

In other words, unlike the approach of Dix and Schlipf, we impose that positive literals be *derived* from program rules plus the assumption of some negative literals.
Negative literals are assumed if that can be safely done (according to the argumentation principles we've stated).

Example 15.
Consider program P:

$$c \leftarrow not\ b$$
$$b \leftarrow not\ a$$
$$a \leftarrow not\ a$$

The O-Model of P is $\{c, not\ b\}$. Note that c has a rule whose body is true in the O-Model and it is not the case that all rules for b are false in it. However $not\ b$ can be safely assumed.

The $EWFM$ is $\{a, c, not\ b\}$. The atom a is true in the $EWFM$ and has no rule with a body true in it. All rules for b have a false body in the $EWFM$.

Another semantics also extending the WFS of normal programs is the "stable theories semantics" [KM91]. Like O-semantics, stable theories also enlarge the WFS by adding more negative assumptions. In order to avoid some unintuitive results of stable theories, Kakas and Mancarella (personal communication) modified their definition, and presented the "acceptability semantics" . In this recent work, instead of our notion of "sustainable" they present:

> A is **KM-coherent**[5] if all assumptions B that defeat A are defeated by A.

i.e., if one insists on the set of assumptions A, no consistent nondefeatable evidence to the contrary can be found. No preferred unique model is identified in their approach, the semantics being defined as the set of consequences common to all KM-coherent sets of assumptions.

However, their approach is still conservative (as noted in [BTK93]). For example consider the program:

$$\begin{array}{l} a \leftarrow not\ b \\ b \leftarrow not\ a, not\ b \end{array}$$

Its consistent A-models are:

$$\begin{array}{lcll} \langle & \{\} & ; & \{\} & \rangle \\ \langle & \{not\ a\} & ; & \{\} & \rangle \\ \langle & \{not\ b\} & ; & \{a, not\ b\} & \rangle \end{array}$$

Given that the second A-model is defeated by the third one, the O-model is $\{a, not\ b\}$, i.e. $not\ b$ is added.

Using the acceptability semantics approach, both $\{not\ a\}$ and $\{not\ b\}$ are KM-coherent, and so the semantics is $\{\}$.

More recently, in [BTK93], a flexible framework for defining logic programming semantics is presented, based on an argumentation framework similar to the one in [Dun91] but where different notions of evidence to the contrary, and of how a scenario defeats contrary evidence, are used.

Within this framework the authors can define the well-founded, stable models, preferred extensions, and acceptability semantics. Then, motivated by the very same example presented here that shows the acceptability semantics is too conservative, they define what they call an "improved semantics".

This "improved semantics" views program rules as inference rules, and default literals as new atoms that are abducible. The semantics is defined as the result of adding to the program some sets of abducible atoms, called preferred extensions. A preferred extension must be consistent with the program (i.e. for no A can A and $not\ A$ hold), and must *counterattack* every *attack* made on it. A set of abducibles A *attacks* another B iff $P \cup A$ derives some L such that $not\ L \in B$, and B *counterattacks* A iff it attacks A or A itself is inconsistent.

As shown by the example below, the "improved semantics" exhibits some "strange" behaviour:

Example 16.
Consider a program with the single rule:

$$a \leftarrow not\ a, not\ b$$

[5] The authors just call it coherent. Here we use KM-coherent to avoid confusion with our coherence principle, which is completely unrelated.

whose WFS and O-model is $\{not\ b\}$. Note that this is indeed the expected result: since b has no rules, *not* b must belong to the semantics independently of the truth value of a. Thus, from the standpoint of *not* a this program should be equivalent to the one containing the single rule $a \leftarrow not\ a$, and so *not* a cannot be safely added.

However, according to the "improved semantics" $\{not\ a\}$ is a preferred extension of this program since $\{not\ a, not\ b\}$ is the only attack on $\{not\ a\}$, but $P \cup \{not\ a, not\ b\}$, is inconsistent. Accordingly, there are two preferred extensions $P \cup \{not\ a\}$ and $P \cup \{not\ b\}$, so that neither *not* a nor *not* b follow.

This example shows that the "improved semantics" does not always enlarge WFS. In this case the former sustains more undefinedness than the latter.

In [BTK93] the authors also generalize their "improved semantics" for extended programs, by renaming every explicitly negated literal $\neg A$ to a new atom, say $\neg\_A$, and by introducing inference rules stating that A and $\neg\_A$ derive an inconsistency. In our opinion this approach not only suffers from the problems inherited from the "improved sermantics" of normal programs, but also some new ones due to the way explicit negation is introduced. In particular, their semantics does not comply with the coherence requirement of section 2:

Example 17.
The program P :

$$\neg a$$
$$a \leftarrow not\ a$$

has one preferred extension $P \cup \{\}$. Thus according to this semantics the consequences of P are $\{\neg a\}$, so that a is explicitly false and cannot be assumed false by default.

In our opinion this program should be contradictory: a is explicitly declared as false; thus a must be assumed false by default, i.e. *not* a should hold; *not* a derives a so contradiction ensues. This is what O-semantics proclaims.

References

[Alf93] José Júlio Alferes. *Semantics of Logic Programs with Explicit Negation.* PhD thesis, Universidade Nova de Lisboa, October 1993.

[AP92] J. J. Alferes and L. M. Pereira. On logic program semantics with two kinds of negation. In K. Apt, editor, *Int. Joint Conf. and Symp. on LP*, pages 574–588. MIT Press, 1992.

[BTK93] A. Bondarenko, F. Toni, and R. Kowalski. An assumption-based framework for nonmonotonic reasoning. In L. M. Pereira and A. Nerode, editors, *2nd Int. Ws. on LP & NMR*, pages 171–189. MIT Press, 1993.

[Dix91] J. Dix. Classifying semantics of logic programs. In A. Nerode, W. Marek, and V. S. Subrahmanian, editors, *LP & NMR*, pages 166–180. MIT Press, 1991.

[Dix92] J. Dix. A framework for representing and characterizing semantics of logic programs. In B. Nebel, C. Rich, and W. Swartout, editors, *3rd Int. Conf. on Principles of Knowledge Representation and Reasoning.* Morgan Kaufmann, 1992.

[Dix95] Jürgen Dix. A Classification-Theory of Semantics of Normal Logic Programs: I. Strong Properties. *Fundamenta Informaticae*, XXII(3):227-255 , 1995.

[DR91] P. M. Dung and P. Ruamviboonsuk. Well founded reasoning with classical negation. In A. Nerode, W. Marek, and V. S. Subrahmanian, editors, *LP & NMR*, pages 120–132. MIT Press, 1991.

[Dun91] P. M. Dung. Negation as hypotheses: An abductive framework for logic programming. In K. Furukawa, editor, *8th ICLP*, pages 3–17. MIT Press, 1991.

[Dun93] P. M. Dung. An argumentation semantics for logic programming with explicit negation. In D. S. Warren, editor, *10th ICLP*, pages 616–630. MIT Press, 1993.

[GL90] M. Gelfond and V. Lifschitz. Logic programs with classical negation. In Warren and Szeredi, editors, *7th ICLP*, pages 579–597. MIT Press, 1990.

[GRS91] A. Van Gelder, K. A. Ross, and J. S. Schlipf. The well-founded semantics for general logic programs. *Journal of the ACM*, 38(3):620–650, 1991.

[KM91] A. C. Kakas and P. Mancarella. Stable theories for logic programs. In Ueda and Saraswat, editors, *Int. LP Symp.*, pages 85–100. MIT Press, 1991.

[KS90] R. Kowalski and F. Sadri. Logic programs with exceptions. In Warren and Szeredi, editors, *7th ICLP*. MIT Press, 1990.

[PA92] L. M. Pereira and J. J. Alferes. Well founded semantics for logic programs with explicit negation. In B. Neumann, editor, *European Conf. on AI*, pages 102–106. John Wiley & Sons, 1992.

[PAA91] L. M. Pereira, J. N. Aparício, and J. J. Alferes. Nonmonotonic reasoning with well founded semantics. In Koichi Furukawa, editor, *8th ICLP*, pages 475–489. MIT Press, 1991.

[PAA92a] L. M. Pereira, J. J. Alferes, and J. N. Aparício. Adding closed world assumptions to well founded semantics. In *Fifth Generation Computer Systems*, pages 562–569. ICOT, 1992.

[PAA92b] L. M. Pereira, J. J. Alferes, and J. N. Aparício. Default theory for well founded semantics with explicit negation. In D. Pearce and G. Wagner, editors, *Logics in AI. Proceedings of the European Ws. JELIA'92*, pages 339–356. LNAI 633, Springer-Verlag, 1992.

[PAA93] L. M. Pereira, J. J. Alferes, and J. N. Aparício. Adding closed world assumptions to well founded semantics (extended improved version). *Theoretical Computer Science. Special issue on selected papers from FGCS'92*, 1993.

[Prz90] T. Przymusinski. Extended stable semantics for normal and disjunctive programs. In Warren and Szeredi, editors, *7th ICLP*, pages 459–477. MIT Press, 1990.

[Prz91] T. Przymusinski. A semantics for disjunctive logic programs. In Loveland, Lobo, and Rajasekar, editors, *ILPS'91 Ws. in Disjunctive Logic Programs*, 1991.

[Sch92] John S. Schlipf. Formalizing a Logic for Logic Programming. *Annals of Mathematics and Artificial Intelligence*, 5:279–302, 1992.

[Wag91] G. Wagner. A database needs two kinds of negation. In B. Thalheim, J. Demetrovics, and H-D. Gerhardt, editors, *Mathematical Foundations of Database Systems*, pages 357–371. LNCS 495, Springer-Verlag, 1991.

From Disjunctive Programs to Abduction*

Vladimir Lifschitz[1] and Hudson Turner[2]

[1] Department of Computer Sciences and Department of Philosophy
University of Texas at Austin
vl@cs.utexas.edu
[2] Department of Computer Sciences
University of Texas at Austin
hudson@cs.utexas.edu

Abstract. The purpose of this work is to clarify the relationship between three approaches to representing incomplete information in logic programming. Classical negation and epistemic disjunction are used in the first of these approaches, abductive logic programs with classical negation in the second, and a simpler form of abductive logic programming — without classical negation — in the third. In the literature, these ideas have been illustrated with examples related to properties of actions, and in this paper we consider an action domain also. We formalize this domain as a disjunctive program with classical negation, and then show how two abductive formalizations can be obtained from that program by a series of simple syntactic transformations. The three approaches under consideration turn out to be parts of a whole spectrum of different, but equivalent, ways of representing incomplete information.

1 Introduction

The purpose of this work is to clarify the relationship between three approaches to representing incomplete information in logic programming. Classical negation and epistemic disjunction are used in the first of these approaches ([GL91], [Tur94]), abductive logic programs with classical negation in the second [Gel91], and a simpler form of abductive logic programming — without classical negation — in the third [DDS93], [Dun93].

All these ideas have been illustrated with examples related to properties of actions, and in this paper we consider an action domain also. The theorems stated in this paper show, however, that the observations made here are of a general nature, and they may be applicable to other knowledge representation problems. Our example domain is the enhancement of Yale Shooting [HM87] in which two guns are available and it is assumed that at least one of them is loaded. This is a case of temporal projection with incomplete information about the initial situation.

After a brief review of the syntax and semantics of the relevant logic programming languages (Section 2), we formalize the two gun domain as a disjunctive

* This work was partially supported by the National Science Foundation under grant IRI-9306751. The second author is also supported by an IBM Graduate Fellowship.

program with classical negation, along the lines of [Tur94] (Section 3). Then, in Sections 4–9, we apply a series of six simple syntactic transformations to that program, so that a formulation in the spirit of [Gel91] is generated at one point along the way, and then a formulation in the spirit of [DDS93] is obtained. All programs formed in the process are equivalent to each other. Thus, the three approaches under consideration turn out to be parts of a whole spectrum of different, but equivalent, ways of representing incomplete information.

Each of Sections 4–9 concludes with a subsection called "Generalization," in which we present the underlying theorems, based for the most part on syntactic criteria, that are used to establish the correctness of the transformations. Thus, this sequence of theorems itself further illustrates the close relationships between the different approaches to representing incomplete information. Readers uninterested in the details of the underlying theorems can safely skip the "Generalization" subsections.

2 Rules, Constraints and Abduction

The answer set semantics [GL91] is defined for programs that consist of rules of the form

$$L_1 \mid \ldots \mid L_k \leftarrow L_{k+1}, \ldots, L_m, not\ L_{m+1}, \ldots, not\ L_n, \tag{1}$$

where $n \geq m \geq k \geq 0$, and each L_i is a literal (an atom possibly preceded by the classical negation sign $\neg$). If the "epistemic disjunction" $L_1 \mid \ldots \mid L_k$ in the head consists of a single literal ($k = 1$) then the rule is called *nondisjunctive*. If the head is empty ($k = 0$) then the rule is called a *constraint*. Given a rule r of the form (1), we define: $head(r) = \{L_1, \ldots, L_k\}$, $pos(r) = \{L_{k+1}, \ldots, L_m\}$, $neg(r) = \{L_{m+1}, \ldots, L_n\}$, and $lit(r) = head(r) \cup pos(r) \cup neg(r)$.

A program Π is *positive* if, for every rule $r \in \Pi$, $neg(r) = \emptyset$. The notion of an answer set is first defined for positive programs, as follows. A set X of literals is *closed under* a positive program Π if, for every rule $r \in \Pi$ such that $pos(r) \subset X$, $head(r) \cap X \neq \emptyset$.[1] A set of literals is *logically closed* if it is consistent or contains all literals. An *answer set* for a positive program Π is a minimal set of literals that is both closed under Π and logically closed.

Now let Π be an arbitrary program. Take a set X of literals. For each rule $r \in \Pi$ such that $neg(r) \cap X = \emptyset$, consider the rule r' defined by

$$head(r') = head(r),\ pos(r') = pos(r),\ neg(r') = \emptyset.$$

The positive program consisting of all rules r' obtained in this way is the *reduct* of Π relative to X, denoted by Π^X. We say that X is an *answer set* for Π if X is an answer set for Π^X.

It is clear from the definition of an answer set that adding a constraint to a program affects its meaning in a simple, "monotonic" way: this can only eliminate some of its answer sets. For instance, adding the constraint $\leftarrow not\ L$ to a program eliminates the answer sets that do not contain L.

[1] We write $X \subset Y$ when X is a subset of Y, not necessarily proper.

The definition of abduction accepted here follows Inoue and Sakama ([IS93], [IS94]), whose work is based on [KM90] and [Gel91]. An *abductive program* is a pair $\langle \Pi, \Gamma \rangle$, where Π is a program and Γ is a set of ground literals, called *abducibles*. A set X of ground literals is a *belief set* for an abductive program $\langle \Pi, \Gamma \rangle$ if it is a consistent answer set for the program $\Pi \cup (X \cap \Gamma)$.[2] The intersection $X \cap \Gamma$ is the *explanation* of X. When the set Γ of abducibles is clear from context, we will sometimes refer to an abductive program $\langle \Pi, \Gamma \rangle$ as Π.

3 A Disjunctive Program

There is a pilgrim and a turkey. The pilgrim has two guns, and at least one of them is initially loaded. The turkey is initially alive. The available actions are loading and shooting.

We are interested in representing this action domain using the situation calculus and negation as failure. Early work of this kind is described in [EK89], [Eva89], [AB90] and [Gel91]. The subject is treated more systematically in several recent papers, including [GL93], [DDS93] and [Dun93]. We assume that the reader is familiar with the main ideas of this work.

The following formulation of the two gun example is close to the one proposed in [Tur94]. It uses variables for situations (s), actions (a), propositional fluents (f) and guns (x).

We will call this program Π_0.

1. *Initial conditions:*

$$Holds(Alive, S0) \leftarrow$$
$$Holds(Loaded(Gun1), S0) \mid Holds(Loaded(Gun2), S0) \leftarrow$$

2. *Effects of actions:*

$$Holds(Loaded(x), Result(Load(x), s)) \leftarrow$$
$$Noninertial(Loaded(x), Load(x), s) \leftarrow$$
$$\neg Holds(Alive, Result(Shoot(x), s)) \leftarrow Holds(Loaded(x), s)$$
$$Noninertial(Alive, Shoot(x), s) \leftarrow not\ \neg Holds(Loaded(x), s)$$

3. *Commonsense law of inertia:*

$$Holds(f, Result(a, s)) \leftarrow Holds(f, s), not\ Noninertial(f, a, s)$$
$$\neg Holds(f, Result(a, s)) \leftarrow \neg Holds(f, s), not\ Noninertial(f, a, s)$$

4. *Completeness rule:*

$$Holds(f, S0) \mid \neg Holds(f, S0) \leftarrow$$

The last rule guarantees that each answer set X for Π_0 includes a complete description of the initial state of affairs: for every ground instance A of

[2] For notational convenience we sometimes identify a set Y of literals with the corresponding program $\{L \leftarrow\ : L \in Y\}$.

Holds$(f, S0)$, either A or $\neg A$ belongs to X. The answer sets for Π_0 are in a 1–1 correspondence with the possible initial states of the system.

Here is a somewhat more detailed description of the answer sets for Π_0. There are exactly 3 such sets: X_1, which includes the literals

$$Holds(Loaded(Gun1), S0) \text{ and } \neg Holds(Loaded(Gun2), S0),$$

X_2, which includes the literals

$$\neg Holds(Loaded(Gun1), S0) \text{ and } Holds(Loaded(Gun2), S0),$$

and X_3, which includes the literals

$$Holds(Loaded(Gun1), S0) \text{ and } Holds(Loaded(Gun2), S0).$$

Each answer set is complete, in the sense that, for every ground atom A that begins with *Holds*, either $A \in X_i$ or $\neg A \in X_i$.

4 Expressing Initial Conditions by Constraints

The first step in the sequence of syntactic transformations to be described here is the replacement of the first two rules of Π_0 — those that express the initial conditions — by the corresponding constraints:

$$\begin{array}{l} \leftarrow not\ Holds(Alive, S0), \\ \leftarrow not\ Holds(Loaded(Gun1), S0), not\ Holds(Loaded(Gun2), S0). \end{array}$$

We will denote the new program by Π_1.

Generally, the effect of a rule $A \leftarrow$ is quite different from the effect of the corresponding constraint $\leftarrow not\ A$. For instance, the only answer set for the program

$$\begin{array}{l} A \leftarrow \\ B \leftarrow A \end{array}$$

(where A and B are ground atoms) is $\{A, B\}$; whereas the program

$$\begin{array}{l} \leftarrow not\ A \\ B \leftarrow A \end{array}$$

has no answer sets. In the case of the transition from Π_0 to Π_1, however, the meaning of the program does not change:

Proposition 1. *Program Π_1 has the same answer sets as Π_0.*

This is not surprising. We have observed that the last rule of Π_0 forces each answer set to include a complete description of the initial state of the system. For this reason, the only effect of the initial conditions of Π_0 is to eliminate the answer sets corresponding to some of the initial states; these rules function as constraints.

Generalization

Given a rule r of form (1), let *constraint*(r) denote the constraint

$$\leftarrow not\ L_1, \ldots, not\ L_k, L_{k+1}, \ldots, L_m, not\ L_{m+1}, \ldots, not\ L_n\ . \qquad (2)$$

Given a program Π, let

$$constraint(\Pi) = \{constraint(r) : r \in \Pi\}\ .$$

We'll consider a condition under which we can guarantee that a program $\Pi \cup \Pi'$ has the same consistent answer sets as the program $\Pi \cup constraint(\Pi')$.

For instance, take Π to be the program Π_0 minus the rules representing initial conditions, and take Π' to be $\Pi_0 \setminus \Pi$. So we have $\Pi_0 = \Pi \cup \Pi'$. Notice that we also have $\Pi_1 = \Pi \cup constraint(\Pi')$. What we wish to ensure is that the initial condition rules in Π_0 function exactly as the initial condition constraints in Π_1. We do this by showing that Π' and $constraint(\Pi')$ are interchangeable, in the sense that programs $\Pi \cup \Pi'$ and $\Pi \cup constraint(\Pi')$ have the same consistent answer sets.

We'll say that a set X of literals is *saturated* if every literal in X has its complement in X.

Given a set X of literals, we'll say that a set Y of literals is *complete in* X if for every literal $L \in X$ at least one of the complementary literals $L, \overline{L}$ belongs to Y.

Following is the definition from [Tur94] of a "signing" of a program.

Let Π be a constraint-free program, and let *Lit* denote the set of ground literals in the language of Π. Let S be a subset of *Lit* such that no literal in S that appears in the head of a rule in Π has its complement in the head of a rule in Π. We say that S is a *signing* for Π if each rule $r \in \Pi$ satisfies the following two conditions:

- $head(r) \cup pos(r) \subset S$ and $neg(r) \subset Lit \setminus S$, or
  $head(r) \cup pos(r) \subset Lit \setminus S$ and $neg(r) \subset S$,
- if $head(r) \subset S$, then $head(r)$ is a singleton.

Theorem 1. *Let Π and Π' be programs, and let Γ be a saturated set of literals such that $Lit \setminus \Gamma$ is a signing for the program $\Pi \cup \Pi'$. If every answer set for Π is complete in Γ and if the head of every rule in Π' is a subset of Γ, then programs $\Pi \cup \Pi'$ and $\Pi \cup constraint(\Pi')$ have the same consistent answer sets.*

We can use Theorem 1 to prove Proposition 1 as follows. Take Π and Π' as described above, so that $\Pi_0 = \Pi \cup \Pi'$ and $\Pi_1 = \Pi \cup constraint(\Pi')$. Let Γ be the set of all *Holds* literals. Clearly Γ is saturated. Furthermore, $Lit \setminus \Gamma$ is the set of all *Noninertial* literals, which is a signing for program Π_0. Every answer set for Π is complete in Γ, and for both rules $r \in \Pi'$ we have $head(r) \subset \Gamma$. So Theorem 1 guarantees that programs $\Pi \cup \Pi'$ and $\Pi \cup constraint(\Pi')$ have the same consistent answer sets.

Theorem 1 is proved using the following additional definitions, and theorem, from [Tur94].

Given rules r and r', we say that r *is subsumed by* r', and we write $r \preceq r'$, if the following three conditions hold:

- $neg(r') \subset neg(r)$,
- $pos(r') \subset pos(r)$,
- every literal in $head(r') \setminus head(r)$ appears complemented in $pos(r)$.

Given programs Π and Π', we say that Π *is subsumed by* Π', and we write $\Pi \preceq \Pi'$, if for each rule $r \in \Pi$ there is a rule $r' \in \Pi'$ such that $r \preceq r'$.

Given a program Π with signing S,

$$h_S(\Pi) = \{r \in \Pi : head(r) \subset S\} ,$$
$$h_{\overline{S}}(\Pi) = \{r \in \Pi : head(r) \subset Lit \setminus S\} .$$

Restricted Monotonicity Theorem. *Let Π, Π' be programs in the same language, both with signing S. If $h_{\overline{S}}(\Pi) \preceq h_{\overline{S}}(\Pi')$ and $h_S(\Pi') \preceq h_S(\Pi)$, then for every consistent answer set X' for program Π', there is a consistent answer set X for program Π such that $X \setminus S \subset X' \setminus S$.*

We'll also use the following lemma in the proof of Theorem 1.

Lemma 1. *Let Π be a program with signing S. A consistent set X of literals is an answer set for Π if and only if $X \setminus S$ is an answer set for program $h_{\overline{S}}(\Pi)^{X \cap S}$ and $X \cap S$ is the unique answer set for program $h_S(\Pi)^{X \setminus S}$.*

Proof. Let X be a consistent set of literals. Of course X is an answer set for Π if and only if X is an answer set for Π^X. Since S is a signing for Π, we have the following.

$$\begin{aligned} \Pi^X &= h_S(\Pi)^X \cup h_{\overline{S}}(\Pi)^X \\ &= h_S(\Pi)^{X \setminus S} \cup h_{\overline{S}}(\Pi)^{X \cap S} \end{aligned}$$

Observe that only literals from S appear in program $h_S(\Pi)^{X \setminus S}$, and similarly only literals not from S appear in program $h_{\overline{S}}(\Pi)^{X \cap S}$. It follows that X is an answer set for Π^X if and only if $X \setminus S$ is an answer set for program $h_{\overline{S}}(\Pi)^{X \cap S}$ and $X \cap S$ is an answer set for program $h_S(\Pi)^{X \setminus S}$. Finally, since program $h_S(\Pi)^{X \setminus S}$ is a nondisjunctive program without negation as failure, it has a unique answer set. □

Proof of Theorem 1. Assume that X is an answer set for $\Pi \cup constraint(\Pi')$. Thus, X is an answer set for Π that is closed under $constraint(\Pi')^X$. Since X is closed under $constraint(\Pi')^X$, it is also closed under $(\Pi')^X$. So X is closed under $\Pi^X \cup (\Pi')^X$. It follows that some subset X' of X is an answer set for $\Pi^X \cup (\Pi')^X$. So X' is a subset of X that is closed under Π^X. But X is an answer set for Π^X, so we can conclude that $X' = X$. Thus X is an answer set for $\Pi^X \cup (\Pi')^X = (\Pi \cup \Pi')^X$. That is, X is an answer set for program $\Pi \cup \Pi'$.

Assume that X' is a consistent answer set for program $\Pi \cup \Pi'$. Since X' is closed under $(\Pi')^X$, it is also closed under $constraint(\Pi')^X$. Notice that if

X' is also an answer set for Π, it will follow that X' is an answer set for $\Pi \cup$ *constraint*(Π'). So we'll complete the proof by showing that X' is an answer set for Π. Let $S = Lit \setminus \Gamma$. Observe that $h_{\overline{S}}(\Pi) \preceq h_{\overline{S}}(\Pi \cup \Pi')$ and $h_S(\Pi \cup \Pi') \preceq h_S(\Pi)$. By the Restricted Monotonicity Theorem, there is a consistent answer set X for program Π such that $X \setminus S \subset X' \setminus S$. Thus, $X \cap \Gamma \subset X' \cap \Gamma$. But we know that X is complete in Γ and Γ is saturated, from which we can conclude that $X \cap \Gamma = X' \cap \Gamma$. It remains to show that $X \setminus \Gamma = X' \setminus \Gamma$. We can conclude by Lemma 1 that $X \setminus \Gamma$ is the unique answer set for program $h_S(\Pi)^{X \cap \Gamma}$. Similarly, $X' \setminus \Gamma$ is the unique answer set for program $h_S(\Pi \cup \Pi')^{X' \cap \Gamma}$. But $h_S(\Pi) = h_S(\Pi \cup \Pi')$, and $X \cap \Gamma = X' \cap \Gamma$; so we've shown that $X \setminus \Gamma = X' \setminus \Gamma$. □

5 Introducing Abduction

The next step is to turn Π_1 into an abductive program. The literals occurring in the ground instances of the completeness rule

$$Holds(f, S0) \mid \neg Holds(f, S0) \leftarrow \tag{3}$$

are declared abducibles, and the rule is replaced with the constraint

$$\leftarrow not\ Holds(f, S0), not\ \neg Holds(f, S0). \tag{4}$$

This constraint forces every explanation to contain one member of each complementary pair of abducibles.

The result is the following abductive program Π_2.

1. *Initial conditions:* (same as Π_1)

$\leftarrow not\ Holds(Alive, S0)$
$\leftarrow not\ Holds(Loaded(Gun1), S0), not\ Holds(Loaded(Gun2), S0)$

2. *Effects of actions:* (same as Π_0 and Π_1)

$Holds(Loaded(x), Result(Load(x), s)) \leftarrow$
$Noninertial(Loaded(x), Load(x), s) \leftarrow$
$\neg Holds(Alive, Result(Shoot(x), s)) \leftarrow Holds(Loaded(x), s)$
$Noninertial(Alive, Shoot(x), s) \leftarrow not\ \neg Holds(Loaded(x), s)$

3. *Commonsense law of inertia:* (same as Π_0 and Π_1)

$Holds(f, Result(a, s)) \leftarrow Holds(f, s), not\ Noninertial(f, a, s)$
$\neg Holds(f, Result(a, s)) \leftarrow \neg Holds(f, s), not\ Noninertial(f, a, s)$

4. *Completeness rule:*

$$\leftarrow not\ Holds(f, S0), not\ \neg Holds(f, S0)$$

Abducibles: The ground instances of $Holds(f, S0)$ and $\neg Holds(f, S0)$.

At this stage, epistemic disjunctions have been completely eliminated in favor of abduction: every rule of Π_2 is a nondisjunctive rule or a constraint.

The transition from Π_1 to Π_2 does not change the meaning of the program:

Proposition 2. *The belief sets for Π_2 are the same as the answer sets for Π_1.*

It is interesting to relate the process used in constructing Π_2 to the view of abduction developed by Inoue and Sakama [IS94]. They show that declaring a literal L abducible has the same effect as adding the rule

$$L \mid not\ L \leftarrow .$$

Such rules are syntactically different than the rules introduced in Section 2, because they contain the negation as failure operator in the head. However, the answer set semantics can be easily extended to rules like these [LW92]. In the case of Π_2, this approach to characterizing the abducibles leads to the rule

$$Holds(f, S0) \mid not\ Holds(f, S0) \leftarrow .$$

This rule differs from the completeness rule (3) only in that it uses negation as failure *not* instead of classical negation $\neg$. Proposition 2 shows that this difference can be offset by constraint (4).

The use of abduction in Π_2 is similar to the style of formalization proposed by Gelfond [Gel91]. One difference is that he does not introduce constraints like (4). (Without this constraint, Π_2 would have two additional belief sets, and the correspondence with the answer sets of Π_0 and Π_1 would be lost.)

Formulations of this kind are symmetric, in the sense that the rules expressing "positive facts" (such as the effect of *Load* on *Loaded*) look similar to the rules expressing "negative facts" (such as the effect of *Shoot* on *Alive*). This attractive feature will be lost in further transformations, but the final version will be in some ways more economical than the one presented in this section.

Generalization

In the presence of completeness of belief sets in a saturated set of abducibles, the interchangeability of abduction and disjunction is a general fact. Below we make this assertion precise.

Given a set X of literals, let

$$CC(X) = \{ \leftarrow not\ L, not\ \overline{L} : L \in X\} .$$

Notice that if we take X to be the set of abducibles for program Π_2 above, then the rules in $CC(X)$ are precisely the "completeness rules" (or completeness constraints) of Π_2.

If Π is an abductive program with set Γ of abducibles, adding $CC(\Gamma)$ to Π simply eliminates the beliefs sets that are not complete in Γ. That is, a set X of literals is a belief set for $\langle \Pi \cup CC(\Gamma), \Gamma\rangle$ if and only if X is a belief set for $\langle \Pi, \Gamma\rangle$ that is complete in Γ.

Given a set X of literals, let

$$DCR(X) = \{L \mid \overline{L} \leftarrow : L \in X\} .$$

Notice that if we take X to be the set of abducibles for program Π_2 above, then the rules in $DCR(X)$ are precisely the disjunctive "completeness rules" of program Π_1.

Theorem 2. *Let Π be a program, and Γ a saturated set of abducibles. The belief sets for the abductive program $\langle \Pi \cup CC(\Gamma), \Gamma \rangle$ are the same as the consistent answer sets for the program $\Pi \cup DCR(\Gamma)$.*

Proposition 2 is a special case of Theorem 2, in which we take Π to be the program Π_1 without the completeness rule.

Proof of Theorem 2 follows.

Lemma 2. *Let Π be a program, and Γ a saturated set of abducibles. A set X of literals is a belief set for $\langle \Pi \cup CC(\Gamma), \Gamma \rangle$ if and only if X is a consistent answer set for program $\Pi \cup (X \cap \Gamma)$ and $X \cap \Gamma$ is complete in Γ.*

Proof. We've already observed that X is a belief set for $\langle \Pi \cup CC(\Gamma), \Gamma \rangle$ if and only if X is a belief set for $\langle \Pi, \Gamma \rangle$ that is complete in Γ. Furthermore, by definition, X is a belief set for $\langle \Pi, \Gamma \rangle$ if and only if X is a consistent answer set for program $\Pi \cup (X \cap \Gamma)$. Finally, because Γ is saturated, we know that X is complete in Γ if and only if $X \cap \Gamma$ is complete in Γ. □

Lemma 3. *Let Π be a program, and Γ a saturated set of literals. A set X of literals is a consistent answer set for program $\Pi \cup DCR(\Gamma)$ if and only if X is a consistent answer set for program $\Pi \cup (X \cap \Gamma)$, with $X \cap \Gamma$ complete in Γ.*

Proof. Assume that X is a consistent answer set for program $\Pi \cup DCR(\Gamma)$. Thus X is an answer set for $\Pi^X \cup DCR(\Gamma)$. So X is closed under Π^X, and of course it's also closed under $X \cap \Gamma$. That is, X is closed under $\Pi^X \cup (X \cap \Gamma)$; and since X is consistent, some subset X' of X must be an answer set for $\Pi^X \cup (X \cap \Gamma)$. We know that X is closed under $DCR(\Gamma)$, from which it follows that X is complete in Γ. In fact, since Γ is saturated, we can conclude that $X \cap \Gamma$ is complete in Γ. It follows that any set closed under $\Pi^X \cup (X \cap \Gamma)$ must be complete in Γ. So X' is complete in Γ. But from this we can conclude that X' is also closed under $DCR(\Gamma)$. We already know that X' is closed under Π^X. Thus we see that X' is closed under $\Pi^X \cup DCR(\Gamma)$. It follows that $X' = X$, since X is an answer set for $\Pi^X \cup DCR(\Gamma)$. So X is an answer set for $\Pi^X \cup (X \cap \Gamma)$; and thus X is an answer set for $\Pi \cup (X \cap \Gamma)$.

Assume that X is a consistent answer set for program $\Pi \cup (X \cap \Gamma)$, with $X \cap \Gamma$ complete in Γ. So X is an answer set for $\Pi^X \cup (X \cap \Gamma)$, and thus X is closed under $\Pi^X \cup (X \cap \Gamma)$. It's clear that since X is complete in Γ, X is also closed under $DCR(\Gamma)$. We already know that X is closed under Π^X. Thus we see that X is closed under $\Pi^X \cup DCR(\Gamma)$. And since X is consistent, some subset X' of X is an answer set for $\Pi^X \cup DCR(\Gamma)$. But any set that is closed under $DCR(\Gamma)$ must be complete in Γ. Since X is consistent and complete in Γ, we can conclude that $X' \cap \Gamma = X \cap \Gamma$; so X' is closed under $X \cap \Gamma$. We know that X' is also closed under Π^X. Thus we see that X' is closed under $\Pi^X \cup (X \cap \Gamma)$. It follows that $X' = X$, since X is an answer set for $\Pi^X \cup (X \cap \Gamma)$. So X is an answer set for $\Pi^X \cup DCR(\Gamma)$; and thus X is an answer set for $\Pi \cup DCR(\Gamma)$. □

The theorem follows directly from the lemmas.

6 Eliminating Negative Abducibles

The explanation of every belief set for Π_2 contains exactly one element of each complementary pair of abducibles. In the next modification of the program, the instances of $\neg Holds(f, S0)$ are dropped from the set of abducibles, and constraint (4) is replaced with the "closed world assumption" (CWA) rule that generates these negative literals:

$$\neg Holds(f, S0) \leftarrow not\ Holds(f, S0).$$

Here is the resulting program Π_3.

1. *Initial conditions:* (same as Π_1 and Π_2)

$$\leftarrow not\ Holds(Alive, S0)$$
$$\leftarrow not\ Holds(Loaded(Gun1), S0), not\ Holds(Loaded(Gun2), S0)$$

2. *Effects of actions:* (same as Π_0 - Π_2)

$$Holds(Loaded(x), Result(Load(x), s)) \leftarrow$$
$$Noninertial(Loaded(x), Load(x), s) \leftarrow$$
$$\neg Holds(Alive, Result(Shoot(x), s)) \leftarrow Holds(Loaded(x), s)$$
$$Noninertial(Alive, Shoot(x), s) \leftarrow not\ \neg Holds(Loaded(x), s)$$

3. *Commonsense law of inertia:* (same as Π_0 - Π_2)

$$Holds(f, Result(a, s)) \leftarrow Holds(f, s), not\ Noninertial(f, a, s)$$
$$\neg Holds(f, Result(a, s)) \leftarrow \neg Holds(f, s), not\ Noninertial(f, a, s)$$

4. *Closed world assumption:*

$$\neg Holds(f, S0) \leftarrow not\ Holds(f, S0)$$

Abducibles: The ground instances of $Holds(f, S0)$.

Proposition 3. *Program Π_3 has the same belief sets as Π_2.*

Generalization

A saturated set Γ of abducibles along with the associated completeness constraints can always be replaced by a complete subset of Γ along with the appropriate closed world assumption rules. We make this precise below.

Given a set X of literals, let

$$CWA(X) = \{\overline{L} \leftarrow not\ L : L \in X\}$$

and let

$$\overline{X} = \{\overline{L} : L \in X\}\ .$$

Theorem 3. *Let Π be a program, and Γ a saturated set of abducibles. Let Γ' be a subset of Γ that is complete in Γ. The abductive program $\langle \Pi \cup CC(\Gamma), \Gamma \rangle$ has the same belief sets as the abductive program $\langle \Pi \cup CWA(\Gamma'), \Gamma' \rangle$.*

Proposition 3 is the special case of Theorem 3 in which we take Π to be the program Π_2 without the completeness rule, Γ to be the set of ground instances of $Holds(f, S0)$ and $\neg Holds(f, S0)$, and Γ' to be the set of ground instances of $Holds(f, S0)$.

Proof of Theorem 3 follows.

Lemma 4. *Let Π be a program, and Γ a saturated set of abducibles. Let Γ' be a complete subset of Γ. A set X of literals is a consistent answer set for $\Pi \cup CWA(\Gamma') \cup (X \cap \Gamma')$ if and only if X is a consistent answer set for program $\Pi \cup (X \cap \Gamma)$ and $X \cap \Gamma$ is complete in Γ.*

Proof. Assume that X is a consistent answer set for $\Pi \cup CWA(\Gamma') \cup (X \cap \Gamma')$. So X is closed under $\Pi^X \cup CWA(\Gamma')^X \cup (X \cap \Gamma')$. We need to show that X is an answer set for $\Pi \cup (X \cap \Gamma)$ and that $X \cap \Gamma$ is complete in Γ. Notice that $CWA(\Gamma')^X$ is $\overline{\Gamma' \setminus X}$; so $X \cap \overline{\Gamma'}$ is closed under $\overline{\Gamma' \setminus X}$. That is, $\overline{\Gamma' \setminus X} \subset X \cap \overline{\Gamma'}$. Since Γ' is complete in Γ, we have $\Gamma = \Gamma' \cup \overline{\Gamma'}$. So we see that $(X \cap \Gamma') \cup (\overline{\Gamma' \setminus X}) \subset X \cap \Gamma$. Furthermore it is easy to show, again using the completeness of Γ' in Γ, that $(X \cap \Gamma') \cup \overline{\Gamma' \setminus X}$ must be complete in Γ. It follows that $X \cap \Gamma$ is also complete in Γ. It remains to show that X is an answer set for $\Pi \cup (X \cap \Gamma)$. We already know that X is closed under Π^X. Thus X is closed under $\Pi^X \cup (X \cap \Gamma)$. Since X is consistent, some subset X' of X is an answer set for $\Pi^X \cup (X \cap \Gamma)$. Since X is consistent and $X \cap \Gamma$ is complete in Γ, and since X' is closed under $X \cap \Gamma$, we can can conclude that $X' \cap \Gamma = X \cap \Gamma$. It follows that X' is closed under $CWA(\Gamma')^X \cup (X \cap \Gamma')$. We already know that X' is closed under Π^X. Thus X' is closed under $\Pi^X \cup CWA(\Gamma')^X \cup (X \cap \Gamma')$. It follows that $X' = X$, since X is an answer set for $\Pi^X \cup CWA(\Gamma')^X \cup (X \cap \Gamma')$. So X is an answer set for $\Pi^X \cup (X \cap \Gamma)$; and thus X is an answer set for $\Pi \cup (X \cap \Gamma)$.

Assume that X is a consistent answer set for program $\Pi \cup (X \cap \Gamma)$, with $X \cap \Gamma$ complete in Γ. So X is closed under $\Pi^X \cup (X \cap \Gamma)$. Clearly X is closed under $X \cap \Gamma'$. As before, $CWA(\Gamma')^X$ is $\overline{\Gamma' \setminus X}$. Let L be a literal in $\overline{\Gamma' \setminus X}$. So $\overline{L} \in \Gamma' \setminus X$, and thus $\overline{L} \notin X$. Since $\Gamma' \subset \Gamma$, we have $\overline{L} \in \Gamma$. Since X is complete in Γ, we can conclude that L belongs to X. So we've shown that $\overline{\Gamma' \setminus X} \subset X$. That is, X is closed under $CWA(\Gamma')^X$. Since X is also closed under Π^X, we have shown that X is closed under $\Pi^X \cup CWA(\Gamma')^X \cup (X \cap \Gamma')$. Since X is consistent, some subset X' of X is an answer set for $\Pi^X \cup CWA(\Gamma')^X \cup (X \cap \Gamma')$. We can see that X' must contain $X \cap \Gamma'$. Since $CWA(\Gamma')^X$ is $\overline{\Gamma' \setminus X}$, we also see that X' must contain $\overline{\Gamma' \setminus X}$. Let L be a literal in $X \cap (\Gamma \setminus \Gamma')$. So $L \notin \Gamma'$, and since Γ' is complete in Γ, we see that $L \in \overline{\Gamma'}$. Thus $L \in \overline{\Gamma'} \cap X$. And since X is consistent, we can conclude that $L \in \overline{\Gamma' \setminus X}$. So X' also contains $X \cap (\Gamma \setminus \Gamma')$. Thus $X \cap \Gamma \subset X'$; so X' is closed under $X \cap \Gamma$. We already know that X' is closed under Π^X, so X' is closed under $\Pi \cup (X \cap \Gamma)$. It follows that $X' = X$, since X is an answer set for $\Pi \cup (X \cap \Gamma)$. So X is an answer set for $\Pi \cup CWA(\Gamma') \cup (X \cap \Gamma')$.

□

Proof of Theorem 3. By Lemma 2 from the previous section, we know that X is a belief set for $\langle \Pi \cup CC(\Gamma), \Gamma \rangle$ if and only if X is a consistent answer set for program $\Pi \cup (X \cap \Gamma)$, with $X \cap \Gamma$ complete in Γ. By the definition of belief set, we know that X is a belief set for $\langle \Pi \cup CWA(\Gamma'), \Gamma' \rangle$ if and only if X is a consistent answer set for $\Pi \cup CWA(\Gamma') \cup (X \cap \Gamma')$. Now the theorem follows immediately from the lemma. □

7 Using the CWA to Generate Negative Facts

Every belief set for Π_3 contains exactly one element of each complementary pair of *Holds* literals. This "semantic" fact, along with several "syntactic" ones, allows us to replace two rules of Π_3 whose heads are negative with the closed world assumption rule

$$\neg Holds(f,s) \leftarrow not\ Holds(f,s).$$

This rule is more general than the closed world assumption of Π_3, so the latter can be dropped. Using the CWA, instead of specialized rules with negative heads, for generating negative conclusions seems to be the main distinctive feature of the use of abduction by Denecker and De Schreye [DDS93] and Dung [Dun93], in comparison with Gelfond's approach [Gel91].

The result of this transformation is the following program Π_4.

1. *Initial conditions:* (same as Π_1 - Π_3)

$$\leftarrow not\ Holds(Alive, S0)$$
$$\leftarrow not\ Holds(Loaded(Gun1), S0), not\ Holds(Loaded(Gun2), S0)$$

2. *Effects of actions:*

$$Holds(Loaded(x), Result(Load(x), s)) \leftarrow$$
$$Noninertial(Loaded(x), Load(x), s) \leftarrow$$
$$Noninertial(Alive, Shoot(x), s) \leftarrow not\ \neg Holds(Loaded(x), s)$$

3. *Commonsense law of inertia:*

$$Holds(f, Result(a,s)) \leftarrow Holds(f,s), not\ Noninertial(f,a,s)$$

4. *Closed world assumption:*

$$\neg Holds(f,s) \leftarrow not\ Holds(f,s)$$

Abducibles: The ground instances of $Holds(f, S0)$. (same as Π_3)

Proposition 4. *Program Π_4 has the same belief sets as Π_3.*

Generalization

A *level mapping* is a function from literals to ordinals. A program Π is *stratified* if it includes no constraints and if there is a level mapping f such that, for all rules $r \in \Pi$ and all literals L, L', the following three conditions are satisfied:

- if $L, L' \in head(r)$ then $f(L) = f(L')$,
- if $L \in head(r)$ and $L' \in pos(r)$ then $f(L) \geq f(L')$,
- if $L \in head(r)$ and $L' \in neg(r)$ then $f(L) > f(L')$.

We'll say that such a level mapping *stratifies* Π.[3]

Let Π be a nondisjunctive program. For ground literals L, L', we say that L *refers to* L' in Π if there is a rule in Π with L in the head and L' in the body. If the pair $\langle L, L' \rangle$ belongs to the reflexive transitive closure of the "refers to" relation, we say that L *depends on* L' in Π.[4]

We observe that if Π is a stratified nondisjunctive program, then a literal L depends on a literal L' in Π if and only if for every level mapping f that stratifies Π we have $f(L) \geq f(L')$.

Take Π to be the program Π_3 minus the rules for initial conditions. Let $R(L)$ denote the number of occurences of *Result* in a literal L. We define a level mapping f as follows:

$$f(L) = \begin{cases} 3R(L) & , \textit{if } L \textit{ is a ground instance of } Holds(f,s), \\ 3R(L)+1 & , \textit{if } L \textit{ is a ground instance of } \neg Holds(f,s), \\ 3R(L)+2 & , \textit{otherwise.} \end{cases}$$

It's easy to verify that f stratifies Π. Furthermore, we see that no *Holds* atom depends on its complement.

Theorem 4. *Let Π be a stratified nondisjunctive program, and let Γ be a set of abducibles such that for each consistent subset X of Γ, program $\Pi \cup X$ is consistent. Let C be a consistent set of literals such that every belief set for $\langle \Pi, \Gamma \rangle$ is complete in C. Let $\Pi' = \{r \in \Pi : head(r) \not\subset C\}$. If no literal in $\overline{C}$ depends on its complement, then the abductive programs $\langle \Pi, \Gamma \rangle$ and $\langle \Pi' \cup CWA(\overline{C}), \Gamma \rangle$ have the same belief sets.*

Proposition 4 can be shown to follow from Theorem 4.

We omit the proof of Theorem 4, which relies on the fact that a stratified nondisjunctive program has at most one consistent answer set.

[3] The definition given here is equivalent to the usual definition of a "locally stratified" program [Prz88] when the set of atoms is defined as the set of ground atoms of a first-order language, and there is no classical negation.

[4] This definition extends in a natural way the standard notion of "depends on" for non-disjunctive programs without classical negation [ABW88]. In the following section, we further extend this notion to disjunctive programs (also with classical negation).

8 Eliminating Classical Negation in the Bodies of Rules

In the presence of the general closed world assumption included in Π_4, $\neg$*Holds* and *not Holds* are interchangeable in the bodies of rules, and *not* $\neg$ in front of *Holds* can be dropped in the bodies of rules.

Let Π_5 be the program obtained from Π_4 by dropping *not* $\neg$ from the last rule of Group 2.

Proposition 5. *Program Π_5 has the same belief sets as Π_4.*

We have eliminated classical negation from all rules other than the closed world assumption.

Generalization

Let C be a consistent set of literals. Given a rule r, let $r|C$ denote the rule obtained from r by replacing, for each literal $L \in C$, all occurences of *not* L in the body by $\overline{L}$ and all occurences of L in the body by *not* $\overline{L}$. Notice that no literal from C appears in the body of a rule $r|C$. More formally, $r|C$ is defined as follows:

- $head(r|C) = head(r)$,
- $pos(r|C) = (pos(r) \setminus C) \cup \overline{(neg(r) \cap C)}$,
- $neg(r|C) = (neg(r) \setminus C) \cup \overline{(pos(r) \cap C)}$.

We'll be interested in conditions guaranteeing that a program Π has the same consistent answer sets as the program $\{r|C : r \in \Pi\}$, for a consistent set C of literals. In order to state our theorem, we further extend the notion of "depends on" to programs with disjunction as well as classical negation, as follows.

A *splitting set* for a program Π is any set U of literals such that, for every rule $r \in \Pi$, if $head(r) \cap U \neq \emptyset$ then $lit(r) \subset U$.[5] For any program Π and literals L, L', we'll say that L *depends on* L' *in* Π if there is no splitting set U for Π with $L \in U$ and $L' \notin U$.

Theorem 5. *Let Π be a program with set Γ of abducibles. Let C be a consistent set of literals satisfying the following three conditions: no literal in C appears in Γ; no literal in $\overline{C}$ depends on its complement; and*

$$\{r \in \Pi : head(r) \cap C \neq \emptyset\} = CWA(\overline{C}) .$$

The abductive programs $\langle \Pi, \Gamma \rangle$ and $\langle \{r|C : r \in \Pi\}, \Gamma \rangle$ have the same belief sets.

Proposition 5 is a special case of Theorem 5. To see this, take Π to be Π_4, with Γ as in Π_4, and take C to be the set of ground instances of $\neg Holds(f, s)$.

The proof of Theorem 5 is based on a series of lemmas. The first of them allows us to replace literals $L \in C$ that occur in the body of a rule with *not* $\overline{L}$. Notice that in this lemma we needn't require that no literal in $\overline{C}$ depend upon its complement.

[5] This definition comes from [LT94].

Lemma 5. *Let Π be a program, and L a literal such that the only rule in Π with L in its head is the rule $L \leftarrow not\ \overline{L}$. For every rule $r \in \Pi$, let r_L be the rule such that $head(r_L) = head(r)$ and $pos(r_L) = pos(r) \setminus \{L\}$ and $neg(r_L) = neg(r) \cup \overline{(pos(r) \cap \{L\})}$. Let $\Pi_L = \{r_L : r \in \Pi\}$. Programs Π and Π_L have the same consistent answer sets.*

Proof. The proof proceeds in four parts.

(i) Assume that X is a consistent answer set for Π^Y. We'll show that X is closed under Π_L^Y. Notice that for all rules $r_L \in \Pi_L$, $r_L \neq r$ if and only if $L \in pos(r)$; so we need only consider rules $r_L \in \Pi_L$ such that $L \in pos(r)$. Let r_L be such a rule. Consider two cases. Case 1: $\overline{L} \in Y$. We know that $\overline{L}$ belongs to $neg(r_L)$, so $neg(r_L) \cap Y$ is nonempty and we're done. Case 2: $\overline{L} \notin Y$. Notice that L must belong to X, since Π includes the rule $L \leftarrow not\ \overline{L}$. If $neg(r_L) \cap Y$ is nonempty or $pos(r_L) \not\subset X$, we're done; so assume that $neg(r_L) \cap Y$ is empty and $pos(r_L) \subset X$. We must show that $head(r_L) \cap X$ is nonempty. To do this, we show that $neg(r) \cap Y$ is empty and $pos(r) \subset X$. Since $neg(r) \subset neg(r_L)$ and $neg(r_L) \cap Y$ is empty, we know that $neg(r) \cap Y$ is empty. We know that $pos(r) = pos(r_L) \cup \{L\}$, and that $pos(r_L) \subset X$. Since $L \in X$, we're done.

(ii) Assume that X is a consistent answer set for Π_L^Y. We'll show that X is closed under Π^Y. As before, for all rules $r \in \Pi$, $r \neq r_L$ if and only if $L \in pos(r)$; so we need only consider rules $r \in \Pi$ such that $L \in pos(r)$. Let r be such a rule. Consider two cases. Case 1: $\overline{L} \in Y$. Since the rule $L \leftarrow not\ \overline{L}$ is the only rule in Π_L with L in its head, we can conclude that L doesn't belong to X. Since $L \in pos(r)$, we have $pos(r) \not\subset X$; and we're done. Case 2: $\overline{L} \notin Y$. If $neg(r) \cap Y$ is nonempty or $pos(r) \not\subset X$, we're done; so assume that $neg(r) \cap Y$ is empty and $pos(r) \subset X$. We must show that $head(r) \cap X$ is nonempty. To do this, we show that $neg(r_L) \cap Y$ is empty and $pos(r_L) \subset X$. We know that $pos(r_L) \subset pos(r)$, so we conclude that $pos(r_L) \subset X$. We also know that $neg(r_L) = neg(r) \cup \{\overline{L}\}$. Since $\overline{L} \notin Y$ and $neg(r) \cap Y$ is empty, so is $neg(r_L) \cap Y$.

(iii) Assume that X is a consistent answer set for Π. By part (i), X is closed under Π_L^X; so some subset X' of X is an answer set for Π_L^X. By part (ii), X' is closed under Π^X. It follows that $X' = X$; so X is an answer set for Π_L.

(vi) Assume that X is a consistent answer set for Π_L. By part (ii), X is closed under Π^X; so some subset X of X is an answer set for Π^X. By part (i), X' is closed under Π_L^X. It follows that $X' = X$; so X is an answer set for Π. □

The next lemma uses the following additional definitions, and theorem, from [LT94].

Let U be a splitting set for a program Π. The set of rules $r \in \Pi$ such that $lit(r) \subset U$ is denoted by $b_U(\Pi)$. Let X be a set of literals. For each rule $r \in \Pi$ such that $pos(r) \cap U$ is a subset of X and $neg(r) \cap U$ is disjoint from X, take the rule r' defined by

$$head(r') = head(r),\ pos(r') = pos(r) \setminus U,\ neg(r') = neg(r) \setminus U.$$

The program consisting of all rules r' obtained in this way will be denoted by $e_U(\Pi, X)$. A *solution* to Π (with respect to U) is a pair $\langle X, Y \rangle$ of sets of literals such that

- X is an answer set for $b_U(\Pi)$,
- Y is an answer set for $e_U(\Pi \setminus b_U(\Pi), X)$,
- $X \cup Y$ is consistent.

Splitting Set Theorem. *Let U be a splitting set for a program Π. A set A of literals is a consistent answer set for Π if and only if $A = X \cup Y$ for some solution $\langle X, Y \rangle$ to Π with respect to U.*

Lemma 6. *Let Π be a program, and L a literal such that the only rule in Π with L in its head is the rule $L \leftarrow not\ \overline{L}$. Furthermore, assume that $\overline{L}$ does not depend on L in Π. For every rule $r \in \Pi$, let $r_{\overline{L}}$ be the rule such that $head(r_{\overline{L}}) = head(r)$ and $pos(r_{\overline{L}}) = pos(r) \cup \overline{(neg(r) \cap \{L\})}$, and $neg(r_{\overline{L}}) = neg(r) \setminus \{L\}$. Let $\Pi_{\overline{L}} = \{r_{\overline{L}} : r \in \Pi\}$. Programs Π and $\Pi_{\overline{L}}$ have the same consistent answer sets.*

Proof. Since $\overline{L}$ doesn't depend on L in Π, there is a splitting set U for Π such that $\overline{L}$ belongs to U while L does not. Notice that U is also a splitting set for program $\Pi_{\overline{L}}$, and that no rule in $b_U(\Pi)$ has L in its body. Thus we have $b_U(\Pi) = b_U(\Pi_{\overline{L}})$. What we will show is that for any consistent answer set X for program $b_U(\Pi)$, programs $e_U(\Pi \setminus b_U(\Pi), X)$ and $e_U(\Pi_{\overline{L}} \setminus b_U(\Pi_{\overline{L}}), X)$ have the same consistent answer sets. Since $b_U(\Pi) = b_U(\Pi_{\overline{L}})$, it follows by the Splitting Set Theorem that programs Π and $\Pi_{\overline{L}}$ have the same consistent answer sets.

Assume that X is a consistent answer set for program $b_U(\Pi)$. The proof will proceed in four parts.

(*i*) Assume that Y is a consistent answer set for $e_U(\Pi \setminus b_U(\Pi), X)^Z$, with $Z \cap U$ empty, and with $L \in Z$ if and only if $L \in Y$. We'll show that Y is closed under $e_U(\Pi_{\overline{L}} \setminus b_U(\Pi_{\overline{L}}), X)^Z$. What we must show is that for every rule $r_{\overline{L}} \in \Pi_{\overline{L}} \setminus b_U(\Pi_{\overline{L}})$, if $pos(r_{\overline{L}}) \subset X \cup Y$ and $neg(r_{\overline{L}}) \cap (X \cup Z)$ is empty, then $head(r_{\overline{L}}) \cap Y$ is nonempty. Notice that for all rules $r_{\overline{L}} \in \Pi_{\overline{L}}$, $r_{\overline{L}} \neq r$ if and only if $L \in neg(r)$; so we need only consider rules $r_{\overline{L}} \in \Pi_{\overline{L}} \setminus b_U(\Pi_{\overline{L}})$ such that $L \in neg(r)$. Let $r_{\overline{L}}$ be such a rule in $\Pi_{\overline{L}} \setminus b_U(\Pi_{\overline{L}})$. Consider two cases. Case 1: $L \in Y$. Notice that since L belongs to Y, we know that $\overline{L} \notin X$, because the rule $L \leftarrow not\ \overline{L}$ is the only rule in Π with L in its head. Since $L \in neg(r)$, we have $\overline{L} \in pos(r_{\overline{L}})$. Since $\overline{L} \notin X$ (and of course $\overline{L} \notin Y$), we have $pos(r_{\overline{L}}) \not\subset X \cup Y$ and we're done. Case 2: $L \notin Y$. Notice that since L doesn't belong to Y, we know that $\overline{L} \in X$, since the rule $L \leftarrow not\ \overline{L}$ occurs in Π. If $pos(r_{\overline{L}}) \not\subset X \cup Y$ or $neg(r_{\overline{L}}) \cap (X \cup Z)$ is nonempty, then we're done; so assume that $pos(r_{\overline{L}}) \subset X \cup Y$ and $neg(r_{\overline{L}}) \cap (X \cup Z)$ is empty. We need to show that $head(r_{\overline{L}}) \cap Y$ is nonempty. We do this by showing that $pos(r) \subset X \cup Y$ and $neg(r) \cap (X \cup Z)$ is empty. To begin, $pos(r) \subset pos(r_{\overline{L}})$, so we have $pos(r) \subset X \cup Y$. We also know that $neg(r) = neg(r_{\overline{L}}) \cup \{L\}$, so all that remains is to verify that L doesn't belong to $X \cup Z$. Since $L \notin Y$, we know that $L \notin Z$. And since $\overline{L} \in X$ and X is consistent, $L \notin X$. So $L \notin X \cup Z$.

(*ii*) Assume that Y is a consistent answer set for $e_U(\Pi_{\overline{L}} \setminus b_U(\Pi_{\overline{L}}), X)^Z$, with $Z \cap U$ empty, and with $L \in Z$ if and only if $L \in Y$. We'll show that Y is closed under $e_U(\Pi \setminus b_U(\Pi), X)^Y$. What we must show is that for every rule $r \in \Pi \setminus b_U(\Pi)$, if $pos(r) \subset X \cup Y$ and $neg(r) \cap (X \cup Z)$ is empty, then $head(r) \cap Y$

is nonempty. Notice that for all rules $r \in \Pi$, $r \neq r_{\overline{L}}$ if and only if $L \in \mathit{neg}(r)$; so we need only consider rules $r \in \Pi \setminus b_U(\Pi)$ such that $L \in \mathit{neg}(r)$. Let r be such a rule. Consider two cases. Case 1: $L \in Y$. Since $L \in Y$, we know $L \in Z$. And since $L \in \mathit{neg}(r)$, we see that $\mathit{neg}(r) \cap (X \cup Z)$ is nonempty; so we're done. Case 2: $L \notin Y$. Notice that since $L \notin Y$, we know that $\overline{L} \in X$, since the rule $L \leftarrow \mathit{not}\ \overline{L}$ occurs in $\Pi_{\overline{L}}$. If $\mathit{pos}(r) \not\subset X \cup Y$ or $\mathit{neg}(r) \cap (X \cup Z)$ is nonempty, then we're done; so assume that $\mathit{pos}(r) \subset X \cup Y$ and $\mathit{neg}(r) \cap (X \cup Z)$ is empty. We need to show that $\mathit{head}(r) \cap Y$ is nonempty. To do this, we show that $\mathit{pos}(r_{\overline{L}}) \subset X \cup Y$ and $\mathit{neg}(r_{\overline{L}}) \cap (X \cup Z)$ is empty. To begin, $\mathit{neg}(r_{\overline{L}}) \subset \mathit{neg}(r)$, so we see that $\mathit{neg}(r_{\overline{L}}) \cap (X \cup Z)$ is empty. We know that $\mathit{pos}(r_{\overline{L}}) = \mathit{pos}(r) \cup \overline{(\mathit{neg}(r) \cap \{L\})}$, so all that remains is to verify that $\overline{L}$ belongs to $X \cup Y$, which is true since $\overline{L} \in X$.

(*iii*) Assume Y is a consistent answer set for program $e_U(\Pi \setminus b_U(\Pi), X)$. That is, Y is a consistent answer set for program $e_U(\Pi \setminus b_U(\Pi), X)^Y$. By part (*i*), Y is closed under program $e_U(\Pi_{\overline{L}} \setminus b_U(\Pi_{\overline{L}}), X)^Y$, so some subset Y' of Y is an answer set for $e_U(\Pi_{\overline{L}} \setminus b_U(\Pi_{\overline{L}}), X)^Y$. Notice that $L \in Y'$ if and only if $L \in Y$. So by part (*ii*), Y' is closed under program $e_U(\Pi \setminus b_U(\Pi), X)^Y$. It follows that $Y' = Y$; so Y is an answer set for $e_U(\Pi_{\overline{L}} \setminus b_U(\Pi_{\overline{L}}), X)^Y$, which is to say that Y is an answer set for $e_U(\Pi_{\overline{L}} \setminus b_U(\Pi_{\overline{L}}), X)$.

(*iv*) Assume Y is a consistent answer set for program $e_U(\Pi_{\overline{L}} \setminus b_U(\Pi_{\overline{L}}), X)$. That is, Y is a consistent answer set for program $e_U(\Pi_{\overline{L}} \setminus b_U(\Pi_{\overline{L}}), X)^Y$. By part (*ii*), Y is closed under program $e_U(\Pi \setminus b_U(\Pi), X)^Y$, so some subset Y' of Y is an answer set for $e_U(\Pi \setminus b_U(\Pi), X)^Y$. Notice that $L \in Y'$ if and only if $L \in Y$. So by part (*i*), Y' is closed under program $e_U(\Pi_{\overline{L}} \setminus b_U(\Pi_{\overline{L}}), X)^Y$. It follows that $Y' = Y$; so Y is an answer set for $e_U(\Pi \setminus b_U(\Pi), X)^Y$, which is to say that Y is an answer set for $e_U(\Pi \setminus b_U(\Pi), X)$. □

Lemma 7. *Let Π be a program, with C a consistent set of literals such that no literal in $\overline{C}$ depends on its complement and*

$$\{r \in \Pi : \mathit{head}(r) \cap C \neq \emptyset\} = \mathit{CWA}(\overline{C}) .$$

If L belongs to C, then programs Π and $\{r|\{L\} : r \in \Pi\}$ have the same consistent answer sets.

Proof. Follows by one application each of Lemmas 6 and 7. □

The following lemma is a consequence of Lemma 7.

Lemma 8. *Let Π be a program, with C a consistent set of literals such that no literal in $\overline{C}$ depends on its complement and*

$$\{r \in \Pi : \mathit{head}(r) \cap C \neq \emptyset\} = \mathit{CWA}(\overline{C}) .$$

Programs Π and $\{r|C : r \in \Pi\}$ have the same consistent answer sets.

Theorem 5 is an easy consequence of Lemma 8.

9 Dropping the CWA

Now we can eliminate classical negation altogether.

Let Π_6 be Π_5 without the closed world assumption rule:

1. *Initial conditions:* (same as $\Pi_1 - \Pi_5$)

$$\leftarrow not\ Holds(Alive, S0)$$
$$\leftarrow not\ Holds(Loaded(Gun1), S0), not\ Holds(Loaded(Gun2), S0)$$

2. *Effects of actions:* (same as Π_5)

$$Holds(Loaded(x), Result(Load(x), s)) \leftarrow$$
$$Noninertial(Loaded(x), Load(x), s) \leftarrow$$
$$Noninertial(Alive, Shoot(x), s) \leftarrow Holds(Loaded(x), s)$$

3. *Commonsense law of inertia:* (same as Π_4 and Π_5)

$$Holds(f, Result(a, s)) \leftarrow Holds(f, s), not\ Noninertial(f, a, s)$$

Abducibles: The ground instances of $Holds(f, S0)$. (same as $\Pi_3 - \Pi_5$)

This representation follows the method advocated in [DDS93].

The last transformation, unlike the ones performed earlier, does change the meaning of the program, of course. But the way the belief sets change when we drop the CWA is easy to describe.

In the following proposition, GA stands for the set of all ground atoms.

Proposition 6. *The map $X \mapsto X \cap GA$ establishes a 1–1 correspondence between the belief sets for Π_5 and the belief sets for Π_6. Moreover, each belief set X for Π_5 can be obtained from $X \cap GA$ by adding the negations of all ground atoms that begin with Holds and do not belong to $X \cap GA$.*

Generalization

The following theorem is an easy consequence of Proposition 2 from [LT94].

Theorem 6. *Let Π be a program and Γ a set of abducibles. Let C be a consistent set of literals such that no literal in C appears in Π or in Γ. If a set X of literals is a belief set for $\langle \Pi \cup CWA(\overline{C}), \Gamma \rangle$, then $X \setminus C$ is a belief set for $\langle \Pi, \Gamma \rangle$. Moreover, if X is a belief set for $\langle \Pi, \Gamma \rangle$, then $X \cup (C \setminus \overline{X})$ is a belief set for $\langle \Pi \cup CWA(\overline{C}), \Gamma \rangle$.*

Proposition 6 follows from Theorem 6. To see this, take Π to be Π_6, with Γ as in Π_6, and take C to be the set of ground instances of $\neg Holds(f, s)$.

10 Conclusion

We have presented a sequence of simple, syntactic, equivalence-preserving transformations of a program for reasoning about action. These transformations illustrate some of the close relationships between three approaches to representing incomplete information in logic programming: namely, disjunctive logic programs with classical negation; abductive logic programs with classical negation; and abductive logic programs without classical negation. The correctness of these transformations is proved by means of more general underlying theorems, which rely on various, mostly syntactic criteria that are not unique to programs for reasoning about action.

Among the seven programs in this paper formalizing the two gun domain, we prefer the program Π_2 presented in Section 5. Firstly, program Π_2 is symmetric, in the sense that the rules expressing "positive facts" (such as the effect of *Load* on *Loaded*) look similar to the rules expressing "negative facts" (such as the effect of *Shoot* on *Alive*). Secondly, on the basis of Lemma 2 (from Section 5), we can understand the abductive program Π_2 in terms of the family of simpler non-abductive programs $\Pi_2 \cup X$, where X is a set of literals representing a complete, consistent description of the initial situation.

Acknowledgments

The authors would like to thank Marc Denecker, Michael Gelfond and Norman McCain for useful discussions on the subject of this paper.

References

[AB90] Krzysztof Apt and Marc Bezem. Acyclic programs. In David Warren and Peter Szeredi, editors, *Logic Programming: Proc. of the Seventh Int'l Conf.*, pages 617–633, 1990.

[ABW88] Krzysztof Apt, Howard Blair, and Adrian Walker. Towards a theory of declarative knowledge. In Jack Minker, editor, *Foundations of Deductive Databases and Logic Programming*, pages 89–148. Morgan Kaufmann, San Mateo, CA, 1988.

[DDS93] Mark Denecker and Danny De Schreye. Representing incomplete knowledge in abductive logic programming. In Dale Miller, editor, *Logic Programming: Proceedings of the 1993 Int'l Symposium*, pages 147–163, 1993.

[Dun93] Phan Minh Dung. Representing actions in logic programming and its applications in database updates. In *Logic Programming: Proceedings of the Tenth Int'l Conf. on Logic Programming*, pages 222–238, 1993.

[EK89] Kave Eshghi and Robert Kowalski. Abduction compared with negation as failure. In Giorgio Levi and Maurizio Martelli, editors, *Logic Programming: Proc. of the Sixth Int'l Conf.*, pages 234–255, 1989.

[Eva89] Chris Evans. Negation-as-failure as an approach to the Hanks and McDermott problem. In *Proc. of the Second Int'l Symp. on Artificial Intelligence*, 1989.

[Gel91] Michael Gelfond. Epistemic approach to formalization of commonsense reasoning. Technical Report TR-91-2, University of Texas at El Paso, Department of Computer Science, 1991.

[GL91] Michael Gelfond and Vladimir Lifschitz. Classical negation in logic programs and disjunctive databases. *New Generation Computing*, 9:365–385, 1991.

[GL93] Michael Gelfond and Vladimir Lifschitz. Representing action and change by logic programs. *The Journal of Logic Programming*, 17:301–322, 1993.

[HM87] Steve Hanks and Drew McDermott. Nonmonotonic logic and temporal projection. *Artificial Intelligence*, 33(3):379–412, 1987.

[IS93] Katsumi Inoue and Chiaki Sakama. Transforming abductive logic programs to disjunctive programs. In *Logic Programming: Proceedings of the Tenth Int'l Conf. on Logic Programming*, pages 335–353, 1993.

[IS94] Katsumi Inoue and Chiaki Sakama. On positive occurrences of negation as failure. In *Proc. of the Fourth Int'l Conf. on Principles of Knowledge Representation and Reasoning*, pages 293–304, 1994.

[KM90] Antonis Kakas and Paolo Mancarella. Generalized stable models: a semantics for abduction. In *Proc. of ECAI-90*, pages 385–391, 1990.

[LT94] Vladimir Lifschitz and Hudson Turner. Splitting a logic program. In *Logic Programming: Proceedings of the Eleventh Int'l Conf. on Logic Programming*, pages 23–37, 1994.

[LW92] Vladimir Lifschitz and Thomas Woo. Answer sets in general nonmonotonic reasoning (preliminary report). In Bernhard Nebel, Charles Rich, and William Swartout, editors, *Proc. of the Third Int'l Conf. on Principles of Knowledge Representation and Reasoning*, pages 603–614, 1992.

[Prz88] Teodor Przymusinski. On the declarative semantics of deductive databases and logic programs. In Jack Minker, editor, *Foundations of Deductive Databases and Logic Programming*, pages 193–216. Morgan Kaufmann, San Mateo, CA, 1988.

[Tur94] Hudson Turner. Signed logic programs. In *Logic Programming: Proceedings of the 1994 Int'l Symposium*, pages 61–75, 1994.

Semantics of Normal and Disjunctive Logic Programs A Unifying Framework*

Teodor C. Przymusinski[1]

Department of Computer Science,
University of California,
Riverside, CA 92521, USA,
(teodor@cs.ucr.edu)

Abstract. We introduce a simple uniform semantic framework that isomorphically contains major semantics proposed recently for normal, disjunctive and extended logic programs, including the perfect model, stable, well-founded, disjunctive stable, stationary and static semantics and many others. The existence of such a natural framework allows us to compare major proposed semantics, analyze their properties, provide simpler definitions and generate new semantics satisfying a specific set of conditions.

1 Introduction

Various semantics have been recently proposed for normal, disjunctive and extended logic programs, including[1] the following:

- Perfect model semantics [ABW88, VG89, Prz88] and disjunctive perfect model semantics [Prz88].
- Stable [GL88, BF91] and disjunctive stable semantics [GL90, Prz91b].
- Well-founded semantics [VGRS90].
- Partial stable semantics [Prz90] and disjunctive partial stable semantics [Prz91b].
- Stationary semantics [Prz91c].
- Static semantics [Prz94b].
- Extended semantics with "classical", or, more precisely, "strong" negation [GL90, AP92, Prz90, Prz91c].

Different approaches are typically based on very different premises and involve different terminology and notation. Their features and mutual relationships are not always clear and sometimes confusing. Moreover, their exact relationship to major non-monotonic formalisms is often difficult to assess. In short, there is no common framework available to study such semantic approaches, investigate their properties and possible extensions

* Partially supported by the National Science Foundation grant #IRI-9313061.

[1] See e.g. [Dix92, LMR92, Prz94c] for more information.

We introduce a uniform semantic framework that isomorphically includes, among others, all of the above listed semantics and thus allows us to:

- Compare major proposed semantics.
- Analyze their properties.
- Provide simpler, more natural definitions.
- Introduce more general logic programs.
- Generate semantics satisfying a specific set of axioms.

We first recall the definition of the Autoepistemic Logic of Knowledge and Beliefs, *AELB*, originally introduced in [Prz94a]. *AELB* was obtained by augmenting Moore's Autoepistemic Logic, *AEL*, with the new belief operator, $\mathcal{B}$ and was proved to be a powerful non-monotonic formalism which, in particular, isomorphically contains AutoEpistemic Logic, AEL [Moo85], Circumscription, CIRC [McC80, Lif85], AutoEpistemic logic of Beliefs, AEB, [Prz94a], Epistemic Specifications [Gel92] and yet is more expressive than each one of these non-monotonic formalisms considered individually. We then show that all the semantics of logic programs discussed above can be obtained by means of a suitable translation of logic programs into *AELB* . The resulting semantic framework is quite simple, flexible and modular and thus allows easy modifications and extensions. The results presented in this paper extend those obtained in [Prz94b].

2 Autoepistemic Logic of Knowledge and Beliefs

Moore's autoepistemic logic, *AEL* [Moo85], is obtained by augmenting classical propositional logic with a modal operator $\mathcal{L}$. The intended meaning of the modal atom $\mathcal{L}F$ is "F is provable" or "F is logically derivable" (in the stable autoepistemic expansion). Thus Moore's modal operator $\mathcal{L}$ can be viewed as a "knowledge operator" which allows us to reason about formulae *known* to be true in the expansion. However, often times we need to reason about formulae that are only *believed*, rather than known, to be true, where what is believed or not believed is determined by some specific *non-monotonic formalism*. In particular, we may want to express beliefs based on *minimal entailment*, or, more generally, on some form of *circumscription* and thus we may need a modal "belief operator" $\mathcal{B}$ with the intended meaning of $\mathcal{B}F$ given by "F is true in all minimal models" or "F is minimally entailed" (in the expansion).

In order to be able to explicitly reason about beliefs, in [Prz94a] the author introduced a new non-monotonic formalism, called the *Autoepistemic Logic of Knowledge and Beliefs*, *AELB*, obtained by augmenting Moore's Autoepistemic Logic, *AEL*, with a new *belief operator*, $\mathcal{B}$. Below we briefly recall the definition and basic properties of the *AELB*.

The language of *AELB*, is a propositional modal language, $\mathcal{K}_{\mathcal{B},\mathcal{L}}$, with standard connectives ($\vee$, $\wedge$, $\supset$, $\neg$), the propositional letter $\perp$ (denoting *false*) and two modal operators $\mathcal{B}$ and $\mathcal{L}$, called, respectively, the *belief* and the *knowledge* operator. The atomic formulae of the form $\mathcal{B}F$ (respectively, $\mathcal{L}F$) where F is an arbitrary formula of $\mathcal{K}_{\mathcal{B},\mathcal{L}}$, are called *belief atoms* (respectively, knowledge atoms). The formulae of $\mathcal{K}_{\mathcal{B},\mathcal{L}}$ in which $\mathcal{B}$ and $\mathcal{L}$ do not occur are called *objective* and the set of all such formulae is denoted by $\mathcal{K}$. Similarly, the set of all formulae of $\mathcal{K}_{\mathcal{L},\mathcal{B}}$ in which only $\mathcal{L}$ (respectively, only $\mathcal{B}$) occurs is denoted by $\mathcal{K}_{\mathcal{L}}$ (respectively, $\mathcal{K}_{\mathcal{B}}$). Any theory T in the language $\mathcal{K}_{\mathcal{B},\mathcal{L}}$ is called an *autoepistemic theory of knowledge and beliefs*, or, briefly, a *belief theory*.

Definition 1 Belief Theories.
By an *autoepistemic theory of knowledge and beliefs* or just a *belief theory* we mean an arbitrary theory in the language $\mathcal{K}_{\mathcal{L},\mathcal{B}}$, i.e., a (possibly infinite) set of arbitrary clauses of the form:

$$B_1 \wedge \ldots \wedge B_m \wedge \mathcal{B}G_1 \wedge \ldots \wedge \mathcal{B}G_k \wedge \mathcal{L}H_1 \wedge \ldots \wedge \mathcal{L}H_s \supset$$
$$\supset A_1 \vee \ldots \vee A_l \vee \mathcal{B}F_1 \vee \ldots \vee \mathcal{B}F_n \vee \mathcal{L}K_1 \vee \ldots \vee \mathcal{L}K_t$$

where $m, n, k, l, s, t \geq 0$, A_i's and B_i's are objective atoms and F_i's, G_i's, H_i's and K_i's are arbitrary formulae of $\mathcal{K}_{\mathcal{L},\mathcal{B}}$.

Equivalently, a belief theory consists of a set of arbitrary clauses of the form:

$$B_1 \wedge \ldots \wedge B_m \wedge \mathcal{B}G_1 \wedge \ldots \wedge \mathcal{B}G_k \wedge \mathcal{L}H_1 \wedge \ldots \wedge \mathcal{L}H_s \wedge$$
$$\wedge \neg\mathcal{B}F_1 \wedge \ldots \wedge \neg\mathcal{B}F_n \wedge \neg\mathcal{L}K_1 \wedge \ldots \wedge \neg\mathcal{L}K_t \supset A_1 \vee \ldots \vee A_l$$

which say that if the B_i's are true, the G_i's are believed, the H_i's are known, the F_i's are not believed and the K_i's are not known then one of the A_i's is true.

By an *affirmative belief theory* we mean any belief theory all of whose clauses satisfy the condition that $l > 0$. In other words, affirmative belief theories are precisely those belief theories that satisfy the condition that all of their clauses contain at least one *objective* atom in their heads[2]. □

We assume the following two simple axiom schemata and one inference rule describing the arguably obvious properties of belief and knowledge atoms, which we jointly call *introspective atoms*:

(D) Consistency Axiom:

$$\neg\mathcal{B}\bot \quad \text{and} \quad \neg\mathcal{L}\bot \tag{1}$$

(K) Normality Axiom: For any formulae F and G:

$$\begin{array}{c} \mathcal{B}(F \supset G) \supset (\mathcal{B}F \supset \mathcal{B}G) \\ \mathcal{L}(F \supset G) \supset (\mathcal{L}F \supset \mathcal{L}G) \end{array} \tag{2}$$

(N) Necessitation Rule: For any formula F:

$$\frac{F}{\mathcal{B}F} \quad \text{and} \quad \frac{F}{\mathcal{L}F} \tag{3}$$

[2] More precisely, we require that all clauses contain at least one *positive objective* atom in their heads. Later, we introduce *negative objective atoms*, namely, the so called "strong negation" atoms.

The first axiom states that tautologically false formulae are neither known nor believed. The second axiom states that if we know (respectively, believe) that a formula F implies a formula G and if we know (respectively, believe) that F is true then we also know (respectively, believe) that G is true as well. The necessitation inference rule states that if a formula F has been proven to be true then F is both known and believed to be true.

Remark. It is worth mentioning that for our purposes it would be sufficient to restrict the axioms (D) and (K) to belief atoms $\mathcal{B}F$ only and to remove the necessitation rule (N) entirely because the corresponding axioms (D) and (K) for $\mathcal{L}F$ and the necessitation rule (N) are in fact *automatically* satisfied in all static autoepistemic expansions introduced later in this section. Moreover, if $\mathcal{L}F$ belongs to any static autoepistemic expansion then so does $\mathcal{B}F$.

It is easy to see that, in the presence of the axioms (K), the axioms (D) are equivalent to the axioms:

$$\begin{aligned} &\mathcal{B}F \supset \neg\mathcal{B}\neg F \\ &\mathcal{L}F \supset \neg\mathcal{L}\neg F. \end{aligned} \tag{4}$$

stating that if we know (respectively, believe) that a formula F is true then we do not know (respectively, believe) that its negation $\neg F$ is also true.

One can also easily verify (see [MT94]) that the axioms (D) and (K) imply the distributivity of the operators $\mathcal{B}$ and $\mathcal{L}$ with respect to conjunctions. More precisely, for any formulae F and G:

$$\begin{aligned} \mathcal{B}(F \wedge G) &\equiv \mathcal{B}F \wedge \mathcal{B}G \\ \mathcal{L}(F \wedge G) &\equiv \mathcal{L}F \wedge \mathcal{L}G. \end{aligned} \tag{5}$$

For readers familiar with modal logics it should be clear by now that we are, in effect, considering here a *normal* modal logic with two modalities $\mathcal{B}$ and $\mathcal{L}$ which both satisfy the consistency axiom (D) [MT94]. The axioms (K) are called "normal" because all normal modal logics satisfy them [MT94].

Definition 2 Formulae Derivable from a Belief Theory.
We say that a formula F is *derivable* from a given belief theory T in the logic $AELB$ if it belongs to the smallest set, $Cn_*(T)$, of formulae of the language $\mathcal{K}_{\mathcal{B},\mathcal{L}}$ which contains the theory T and all the (substitution instances of) the axioms (K) and (D), and is closed under standard propositional consequence and under the necessitation rule (N). We denote this by $T \vdash_* F$. Consequently, $Cn_*(T) = \{F : T \vdash_* F\}$. We call a belief theory T *consistent* if the theory $Cn_*(T)$ is consistent. Thus T is consistent if $T \not\vdash_* \bot$.

Definition 3 Formulae Derivable from a Belief Theory.
For any belief theory T, we denote by $Cn_*(T)$ the smallest set of formulae of the language $\mathcal{K}_{\mathcal{B},\mathcal{L}}$ which contains the theory T, all the (substitution instances of) the axioms (K) and (D) and is closed under standard propositional consequence and under the necessitation rule (N).

We say that a formula F is *derivable* from theory T in the logic $AELB$ if F belongs to $Cn_*(T)$. We denote this fact by $T \vdash_* F$. We call a belief theory T *consistent* if the theory $Cn_*(T)$ is consistent.

Consequently, $Cn_*(T) = \{F : T \vdash_* F\}$ and clearly T is consistent if and only if $T \not\vdash_* \bot$.

2.1 Intended Meaning of Belief Atoms

The intended meaning of $\mathcal{L}F$ is "*F is known*", or, more precisely, "*F can be logically inferred*", i.e., $T \models F$. On the other hand, the intended meaning of $\mathcal{B}F$ is "*F is believed*", or, more precisely, "*F can be non-monotonically inferred*", i.e., $T \models_{nm} F$, where $\models_{nm}$ denotes a specific non-monotonic inference relation.

In general, different non-monotonic inference relations, $\models_{nm}$, can be used, including various forms of predicate and formula *circumscription* [McC80, Lif85]. In this paper, the intended meaning of belief atoms $\mathcal{B}F$ is based on Minker's *GCWA* (see [Min82, GPP89]) or McCarthy's *Predicate Circumscription* [McC80], and is described by the principle of *predicate minimization*:

$$\mathcal{B}F \;\equiv\; F \text{ is minimally entailed } \;\equiv\; F \quad \text{is true in all minimal models.}$$

Accordingly, beliefs considered in this paper can be called *minimal beliefs*.

We now give a precise definition of minimal models and minimal entailment. Throughout the paper we represent *models* as (consistent) *sets of literals*. An atom A is *true* in a model M if A belongs to M and an atom A is *false* in a model M if $\neg A$ belongs to M. We denote by M^+ (respectively, by M^-) the set of all positive (respectively, negative) literals in a model M. A model M is *total* if for every atom A either A or $\neg A$ belongs to M. Otherwise, the model is called *partial*. Unless stated otherwise, all models are assumed to be total models. A total model M is *smaller* than a total model N if it contains fewer positive literals (atoms), i.e., if M^+ is a proper subset of N^+. When describing models we usually list *only* those of their members that are *relevant* to our considerations, typically those whose predicate symbols appear in the theory that we are currently discussing.

Definition 4 Minimal Models. [Prz94a]
By a *minimal model* of a belief theory T we mean a model M of T with the property that there is *no* smaller model N of T which coincides with M on introspective atoms $\mathcal{B}F$ and $\mathcal{L}F$. If a formula F is true in all minimal models of T then we write:

$$T \models_{\min} F$$

and say that F is *minimally entailed* by T.

For readers familiar with *circumscription*, this means that we are considering predicate circumscription $CIRC(T;\mathcal{K})$ of the theory T in which atoms from the objective language $\mathcal{K}$ are minimized while the introspective atoms $\mathcal{B}F$ and $\mathcal{L}F$ are fixed:

$$T \models_{\min} F \equiv CIRC(T;\mathcal{K}) \models F.$$

In other words, minimal models are obtained by first assigning *arbitrary* truth values to the introspective atoms and then *minimizing* objective atoms.

2.2 Static Autoepistemic Expansions

Like in Moore's Autoepistemic Logic, also in the Autoepistemic Logic of Knowledge and Beliefs we introduce sets of beliefs that an ideally rational and introspective agent may hold, given a set of premises T. We do so by defining *static autoepistemic expansions* $T^\diamond$ of T, which constitute plausible sets of such rational beliefs.

Definition 5 Static Autoepistemic Expansion. [Prz94a]
A belief theory $T^\diamond$ is called a *static autoepistemic expansion* of a belief theory T if it satisfies the following fixed-point equation:

$$T^\diamond = Cn_*(T \cup \{\mathcal{L}F : T^\diamond \models F\} \cup \{\neg\mathcal{L}F : T^\diamond \not\models F\} \cup \{\mathcal{B}F : T^\diamond \models_{\min} F\}),$$

where F ranges over all formulae of $\mathcal{K}_{\mathcal{B},\mathcal{L}}$.

The definition of static autoepistemic expansions is based on the idea of building an expansion $T^\diamond$ of a belief theory T by closing it with respect to: (i) the derivability in the logic $AELB$, (ii) the addition of knowledge atoms $\mathcal{L}F$ for which the formula F is logically implied by $T^\diamond$ and negations $\neg\mathcal{L}F$ of the remaining knowledge atoms, and, (iii) the addition of those belief atoms $\mathcal{B}F$ for which the formula F is minimally entailed by $T^\diamond$. Consequently, the definition of static expansions *enforces* the intended meaning of knowledge and belief atoms as discussed before. Note, however, that negations $\neg\mathcal{B}F$ of the remaining belief atoms are not *explicitly* added to the expansion although some of them will be forced in by the Normality and Consistency Axioms (2) and (1).

Definition 6 Static Semantics.
By the *(skeptical) static semantics* of a belief theory T we mean the set of all formulae that belong to all static autoepistemic expansions $T^\diamond$ of T.

Example 1.
Suppose that you plan to rent a movie if you believe that you will neither go to a baseball game nor to a football game. Moreover, you do not plan to buy tickets to any game if you don't know that you will actually go to see it. We could describe this scenario as follows:

$$\mathcal{B}\neg baseball \wedge \mathcal{B}\neg football \supset rent\_movie$$
$$\neg\mathcal{L}baseball \wedge \neg\mathcal{L}football \supset dont\_buy\_tickets.$$

This theory has a unique static autoepistemic expansion (we use obvious abbreviations):

$$T_1^\diamond = Cn_*(T\cup\{\mathcal{B}\neg b\_ball, \mathcal{B}\neg f\_ball, \neg\mathcal{L}b\_ball, \neg\mathcal{L}f\_ball, \mathcal{L}r\_movie, \mathcal{L}d\_b\_tickets\})$$

in which you rent a movie, because you believe that you will not go to see any games (i.e., $\neg baseball \wedge \neg football$ holds in all minimal models) and you do not buy any tickets because you don't know that you will go to see any of the games (i.e., neither *baseball* nor *football* are provable). Here and in the rest of the paper we list only the "relevant" introspective atoms belonging to the expansion $T^\diamond$, skipping, e.g., $\mathcal{B}$*dont_buy_tickets*, $\mathcal{LB}\neg$*baseball*, etc.

Suppose now that you learn that you either go to a baseball game or to a football game, i.e., suppose that we add the clause:

$$baseball \vee football$$

to T obtaining the theory T_2. Now T_2 has a unique static autoepistemic expansion:

$$T_2^\diamond = Cn_*(T \cup \{\mathcal{B}(b\_ball \vee f\_ball), \neg\mathcal{L}b\_ball, \neg\mathcal{L}f\_ball, \mathcal{B}\neg r\_movie, \mathcal{L}d\_b\_tickets\})$$

in which you believe you should *not* rent a movie. Indeed, we know that $T_2^\diamond \models baseball \vee football$ and thus $T_2^\diamond \models \mathcal{B}(baseball \vee football)$. By the Consistency Axiom (1), we get $T_2^\diamond \models \neg\mathcal{B}(\neg baseball \wedge \neg football)$ and thus, by distributivity of conjunctions (5), $T_2^\diamond \models \neg\mathcal{B}\neg baseball \vee \neg\mathcal{B}\neg football$. As a result *rent_movie* is false in all minimal models of $T_2^\diamond$ and consequently $T_2^\diamond \models \mathcal{B}\neg rent\_movie$.

However, you still do not buy any tickets, because you don't know yet which game you are going to see, i.e., neither *baseball* nor *football* are provable in $T_2^\diamond$.

Finally, suppose that you learn that you actually go to see a baseball game. After adding the clause:

$$baseball$$

to T_2, the new theory T_3 has a unique static autoepistemic expansion consisting of:

$$T_3^\diamond = Cn_*(T \cup \{\mathcal{B}b\_ball, \mathcal{B}\neg f\_ball, \mathcal{L}b\_ball, \neg\mathcal{L}f\_ball, \mathcal{B}\neg r\_movie, \mathcal{B}\neg d\_b\_tickets\})$$

in which you still believe you should *not* rent any movies but you no longer believe in not buying tickets because you now know that you are going to see a specific game. Indeed, $T_3^\diamond \models baseball$ and thus $T_3^\diamond \models \mathcal{B}baseball$. By the Consistency Axiom (4), we get $T_3^\diamond \models \neg\mathcal{B}\neg baseball$ and thus *rent_movie* is false in all minimal models of $T_3^\diamond$. Consequently $T_3^\diamond \models \mathcal{B}\neg rent\_movie$. Similarly, since $T_3^\diamond \models \mathcal{L}baseball$ we deduce that $T_3^\diamond \models_{min} \neg dont\_buy\_tickets$ and therefore $T_3^\diamond \models \mathcal{B}\neg dont\_buy\_tickets$.

As we can see, the semantics assigned to the discussed belief theories by their static autoepistemic expansions seem to agree with their intended meaning. Observe, that we cannot replace the premise $\mathcal{B}\neg baseball \wedge \mathcal{B}\neg football$ in the first clause by $\mathcal{L}\neg baseball \wedge \mathcal{L}\neg football$ because that would result in *rent_movie* not being true in $T^\diamond$. Similarly, we cannot replace it by $\neg\mathcal{L}baseball \wedge \neg\mathcal{L}football$ because that would result in *rent_movie* becoming true in $T_2^\diamond$. We also cannot replace the premise $\neg\mathcal{L}baseball \wedge \neg\mathcal{L}football$ in the second implication by $\neg\mathcal{B}baseball \wedge \neg\mathcal{B}football$ or by $\mathcal{B}\neg baseball \wedge \mathcal{B}\neg football$, because it would no longer imply that we should not buy tickets in $T_2^\diamond$. Thus the roles of the two operators are quite different and one cannot be substituted by the other.

2.3 Moore's Autoepistemic Logic

The first part of the definition of static expansions is identical to the definition of *stable autoepistemic expansions* in Moore's autoepistemic logic, *AEL*. As a result, it is not difficult to prove that *AEL* is properly *embeddable* into the autoepistemic logic of knowledge and beliefs, *AELB*.

Theorem 7 Embeddability of Autoepistemic Logic. *[Prz94a]*
Moore's autoepistemic logic, AEL, is properly embeddable into the autoepistemic logic of knowledge and beliefs, AELB. More precisely, for any autoepistemic theory T in the language $\mathcal{K}_{\mathcal{L}}$, i.e., for any theory that does not use belief atoms $\mathcal{B}F$, there is a natural one-to-one correspondence between stable *autoepistemic expansions of T in AEL and static autoepistemic expansions of T in AELB.*

However, the addition of belief atoms $\mathcal{B}F$ to *AELB* results in a *much more powerful non-monotonic logic* which contains, as special cases, several well-known non-monotonic formalisms and semantics of logic programs.

2.4 Autoepistemic Logic of Beliefs

From the preceding Theorem it follows that the restriction $AELB|\mathcal{K}_{\mathcal{L}}$ of *AELB* to the language $\mathcal{K}_{\mathcal{L}}$ is isomorphic to Moore's autoepistemic logic, *AEL*. On the other hand, the restriction $AELB|\mathcal{K}_{\mathcal{B}}$ of *AELB* to the language $\mathcal{K}_{\mathcal{B}}$, i.e., its restriction to theories using only the belief operator $\mathcal{B}$, constitutes an entirely new logic, which will be called the *Autoepistemic Logic of Beliefs* and will be denoted by *AEB*.

The following table illustrates the relationships between the three autoepistemic logics discussed in the paper:

Acronym	Logic	Language
AELB	Autoepistemic Logic of Knowledge and Beliefs	$\mathcal{K}_{\mathcal{L},\mathcal{B}}$
AEL	Autoepistemic Logic (of Knowledge)	$\mathcal{K}_{\mathcal{L}}$
AEB	Autoepistemic Logic of Beliefs	$\mathcal{K}_{\mathcal{B}}$

It turns out that *AEB* has some quite natural and interesting properties. In particular, *every* belief theory T in *AEB* has the *least* (in the sense of inclusion) static expansion $T^{\diamond}$ which has an *iterative* definition as the *least fixed point* of a monotonic belief closure operator Ψ_T defined below. Although least static expansions may, in general, be inconsistent theories, they are in fact consistent for all *affirmative* belief theories. These properties of static expansions in the Autoepistemic Logic of Beliefs, *AEB*, sharply contrast with the properties of stable autoepistemic expansions in *AEL* which do not admit natural least fixed point definitions and, in general, do not have least elements.

Definition 8 Belief Closure Operator. [Prz94a]
For any belief theory T define the *belief closure* operator Ψ_T by the formula:

$$\Psi_T(S) = Cn_*(T \cup \{\mathcal{B}F : S \models_{\min} F\}),$$

where S is an arbitrary belief theory and the F's range over all formulae of $\mathcal{K}_{\mathcal{B}}$.

Thus $\Psi_T(S)$ augments the theory T with all those belief atoms $\mathcal{B}F$ with the property that F is minimally entailed by S. It is easy to see that a theory $T^\diamond$ is a static autoepistemic expansion of the belief theory T in AEB if and only if $T^\diamond$ is a fixed point of the operator Ψ_T, i.e. if $T^\diamond = \Psi_T(T^\diamond)$.

Theorem 9 Least Static Expansion. *[Prz94a]*
Every belief theory T in AEB has the least *static expansion, namely, the least fixed point $T^\diamond$ of the monotonic belief closure operator Ψ_T. Moreover, the least static expansion $T^\diamond$ of a belief theory T can be constructed as follows. Let $T^0 = Cn_*(T)$ and suppose that T^α has already been defined for any ordinal number $\alpha < \beta$. If $\beta = \alpha + 1$ is a successor ordinal then define[3]:*

$$T^{\alpha+1} = \Psi_T(T^\alpha) = Cn_*(\ T \cup \{\mathcal{B}F : T^\alpha \models_{\min} F\}\ ),$$

where F ranges over all formulae in $\mathcal{K}_{\mathcal{B}}$. Else, if β is a limit ordinal then define:

$$T^\beta = \bigcup_{\alpha<\beta} T^\alpha.$$

The sequence $\{T^\alpha\}$ is monotonically increasing and has a unique fixed point $T^\diamond = T^\lambda = \Psi_T(T^\lambda)$, for some ordinal λ.

Observe that the *least* static autoepistemic expansion $T^\diamond$ of T contains those and only those formulae which are true in *all* static autoepistemic expansions of T, and thus it always coincides with the static semantics of T. It is easy to verify that a belief theory T in AEB either has a *consistent* least static expansion $T^\diamond$ or it does *not* have any consistent static expansions at all. However, it turns out that least static expansions are always consistent for *affirmative* belief theories.

Theorem 10 Consistency of Least Static Expansions. *[Prz94a]*
The least static expansion $T^\diamond$ of any affirmative belief theory T in AEB is always consistent.

As shown by the following result, which is analogous to Theorem 7, the restriction to the language of $\mathcal{K}_{\mathcal{B}}$ does not constitute any limitation because any static autoepistemic expansion T^* of a belief theory T in AEB can be uniquely extended to a static autoepistemic expansion $T^\diamond$ of T in $AELB$:

[3] Since the sequence $\{T^\alpha\}$ is monotonically increasing we can equivalently define $T^\beta = Cn_*(\ T^\alpha \cup \{\mathcal{B}F : T^\alpha \models_{\min} F\}\ )$.

Theorem 11 Embeddability of Autoepistemic Logic of Beliefs. *[Prz94a]*

Autoepistemic logic of Beliefs, AEB, is properly embeddable into the autoepistemic logic of knowledge and beliefs, AELB. More precisely, for any autoepistemic theory T in the language $\mathcal{K}_{\mathcal{B}}$, i.e., for any theory that does not use knowledge atoms $\mathcal{L}F$, there is a natural one-to-one correspondence between static *autoepistemic expansions of T in AEB and static autoepistemic expansions of T in AELB.*

Let us now discuss a simple example. As we mentioned before, unless explicitly needed, when describing static expansions we ignore nested beliefs and we list only those elements of the expansion that are "relevant" to our discussion.

Example 2.
Consider the following belief theory T:

$$\begin{array}{l} Car \\ Car \wedge \mathcal{B}\neg Broken \supset Runs \end{array}$$

In order to iteratively compute its least static expansion $T^{\diamond}$ we let $T^0 = Cn_*(T)$. Clearly, $T^0 \models Car$ and one easily checks that $T^0 \models_{min} \neg Broken$. Indeed, in order to find minimal models of T^0 we need to assign an *arbitrary* truth value to the only belief atom $\mathcal{B}\neg Broken$, and then *minimize* the objective atoms *Broken*, *Car* and *Runs*. We easily see that T^0 has the following two minimal models (truth values of the remaining belief atoms are irrelevant and are therefore omitted):

$$\begin{array}{l} M_1 = \{\mathcal{B}\neg Broken, Car, \ Runs, \ \neg Broken\}; \\ M_2 = \{\neg\mathcal{B}\neg Broken, Car, \ \neg Runs, \ \neg Broken\}. \end{array}$$

Since in both of them *Car* is true, and *Broken* is false, we deduce that $T^0 \models_{min} Car$ and $T^0 \models_{min} \neg Broken$. Consequently, since $T^1 = \Psi_T(T^0) = Cn_*(T \cup \{\mathcal{B}F : T^0 \models_{\min} F\})$, we obtain:

$$T^1 = Cn_*(T \cup \{\mathcal{B}Car, \mathcal{B}\neg Broken\}).$$

Since $T^1 \models Runs$ and $T^2 = \Psi_T(T^1) = Cn_*(T \cup \{\mathcal{B}F : T^1 \models_{\min} F\})$, we obtain:

$$T^2 = Cn_*(T \cup \{\mathcal{B}Car, \mathcal{B}\neg Broken, \mathcal{B}Runs\}).$$

It is easy to check that $T^2 = \Psi_T(T^2)$ is a fixed point of Ψ_T (we recall that, for simplicity, we ignore nested beliefs). Consequently, $T^{\diamond} = T^2 = Cn_*(T \cup \{\mathcal{B}Car, \mathcal{B}\neg Broken, \mathcal{B}Runs\})$ is the least static expansion of T. The static semantics of T asserts therefore our belief that the car is not broken and thus runs fine. One easily verifies that T does not have any other (consistent) static expansions.

3 Logic Programs as Belief Theories

We now show that major semantics defined for normal and disjunctive *logic programs* can be obtained by translating logic programs into belief theories in *AELB*. We argue therefore that the Autoepistemic Logic of Knowledge and Beliefs, *AELB*, constitutes a broad and flexible *semantic framework* for logic programming which not only enables us to reproduce many of the semantics recently introduced for logic programs but also allows us to introduce new semantics, analyze their properties and study their mutual relationships.

Let us first recall that by a *disjunctive logic program* (or a disjunctive deductive database) P we mean a set of *informal* clauses of the form

$$A_1 \vee \ldots \vee A_l \leftarrow B_1 \wedge \ldots \wedge B_m \wedge not\ C_1 \wedge \ldots \wedge not\ C_n \tag{6}$$

where $l \geq 1$; m, $n \geq 0$ and A_i, B_i and C_i's are atomic formulae. If $l = 1$, for all clauses, then the program is called *normal* or *non-disjunctive*. As usual, we assume (see [PP90]) that the program P has been already *instantiated* and thus all of its clauses (possibly infinitely many) are propositional. This assumption allows us to restrict our considerations to a fixed *objective propositional language* $\mathcal{K}$. In particular, if the original (uninstantiated) program is finite and function-free then the resulting objective language $\mathcal{K}$ is also finite.

Clauses (6) are informal because the negation symbol *not* C does not denote the *classical negation* $\neg C$ of C but rather a *non-monotonic (default) negation*. Moreover, the implication symbol $\rightarrow$ may not necessarily be interpreted as the standard *material implication* $\supset$. By translating the informal logic programs into formal belief theories in *AELB* various meanings can be associated with "*not* C" and $\rightarrow$ leading to different semantics for logic programs.

In this paper, we will always interpret the implication symbol $\rightarrow$ as standard *material implication* $\supset$. We will consider the following four natural ways in which default negation "*not* C" can be interpreted:

Translation	Intended meaning
$not\ C \equiv \neg\mathcal{L}C$	C is not known
$not\ C \equiv \mathcal{B}\neg C$	$\neg C$ is believed
$not\ C \equiv \mathcal{L}\neg C$	$\neg C$ is known
$not\ C \equiv \neg\mathcal{B}C$	C is not believed

It is easy to see that the third translation $not\ C \equiv \mathcal{L}\neg C$ is not very useful for default reasoning because it requires us to actually prove falsity of C in order to conclude *not* C. As we will see later, the fourth interpretation $not\ C \equiv \neg\mathcal{B}C$ is also not very interesting. In particular, for normal programs it coincides with the second translation. Accordingly, we will concentrate on the first two interpretations.

The expressive power of *AELB* allows us to ensure additional semantic properties by assuming additional, optional axioms. We will consider the effects of adding the following axioms, or, more precisely, axiom schemas:

Acronym	Name	Definition	Restrictions
DBA	Disjunctive Belief Axiom	$\mathcal{B}(F \vee G) \equiv \mathcal{B}F \vee \mathcal{B}G$	
DKA	Disjunctive Knowledge Axiom	$\mathcal{L}(F \vee G) \equiv \mathcal{L}F \vee \mathcal{L}G$	
GCWA	Generalized Closed World	$\mathcal{LB}F \supset F$	
BCA	Belief Completeness Axiom	$\mathcal{LB}A \vee \mathcal{LB}\neg A$	A is an atom
PIA	Positive Introspection Axiom	$A \supset \mathcal{L}A$	A is an atom

The Disjunctive Belief Axiom (DBA): states that our beliefs are distributive with respect to disjunctions. Note that, by virtue of (5), our beliefs are always distributive with respect to conjunctions (5).

The Disjunctive Knowledge Axiom (DKA): states that our knowledge is distributive with respect to disjunctions. Note again that, by virtue of (5), our knowledge is always distributive with respect to conjunctions. Due to the fact that for every formula F either $\mathcal{L}F$ or $\neg\mathcal{L}F$ must hold in any static expansion, this axiom is equivalent to the assumption that if a disjunction $F \vee G$ is true in a static expansion then either F is true or G is true (in the expansion). Thus, it is a strong axiom which, in essence, eliminates truly disjunctive information from static expansions.

The Generalized Closed World Assumption (GCWA): states that if $\mathcal{B}F$ is true in a theory T, i.e., if a formula F holds in all minimal models of T, then F itself holds in T. Again, this is a powerful axiom which, in essence, erases the distinction between facts *believed* to be true and those which are actually *true* (in the expansion).

The Belief Completeness Axiom (BCA): says that we can always either prove $\mathcal{B}A$ or $\mathcal{B}\neg A$, i.e., that either A holds in all minimal models of a theory T or $\neg A$ holds in all minimal models of a theory T.

The Positive Introspection Axiom (PIA): states that if $\mathcal{L}A$ holds in some model of the theory then so does A itself. In other words, if A is false in some model then it cannot be known in that model.

3.1 Translating *notC* as $\neg\mathcal{L}C$

We first consider the translation $T_{\neg\mathcal{L}}(P)$ of a logic program P obtained by replacing the non-monotonic negation *not* C by the negated knowledge atom $\neg\mathcal{L}C$ which gives it the intended meaning of *"C is not known to be true"* and is patterned after the translation of logic programs into autoepistemic theories originally proposed by Gelfond [Gel87].

Definition 12 Translation $T_{\neg\mathcal{L}}(P)$.
For any disjunctive logic program P consisting of clauses:

$$A_1 \vee \ldots \vee A_n \leftarrow B_1 \wedge \ldots \wedge B_m \wedge not\ C_1 \wedge \ldots \wedge not\ C_n$$

define $T_{\neg\mathcal{L}}(P)$ to be its translation into the (affirmative) belief theory consisting of formulae:

$$B_1 \wedge \ldots \wedge B_m \wedge \neg\mathcal{L}C_1 \wedge \ldots \wedge \neg\mathcal{L}C_n \supset A_1 \vee \ldots \vee A_n.$$

3.1.1 Embeddability of Stable Semantics

Since Moore's autoepistemic logic, AEL, is isomorphic to the subset $AELB|\mathcal{K}_{\mathcal{L}}$ of $AELB$, it follows from the results of Gelfond and Lifschitz [GL88] that stable semantics of normal logic programs can be obtained by means of translating logic programs into belief theories.

Theorem 13 Embeddability of Stable Semantics.
There is a one-to-one correspondence between stable models $\mathcal{M}$ of the normal program P and consistent static autoepistemic expansions $T^\diamond$ of its translation $T_{\neg\mathcal{L}}(P)$ into belief theory. Moreover, for any objective atom A we have:

$$A \in \mathcal{M} \quad \text{iff} \quad \mathcal{L}A \in T^\diamond$$
$$\neg A \in \mathcal{M} \quad \text{iff} \quad \neg\mathcal{L}A \in T^\diamond.$$

Proof. By Theorem 7 there is a one-to-one correspondence between stable autoepistemic expansions and consistent static expansions of $T_{\neg\mathcal{L}}(P)$. The claim now follows from the results obtained in [GL88]. □

3.1.2 Embeddability of Disjunctive Stable Semantics

For disjunctive logic programs the straight translation $T_{\neg\mathcal{L}}(P)$ often leads to an unintuitive meaning.

Example 3.
Consider the following program P reflecting the anxieties of a guy living in Southern California who was informed by a friend that apparently yet another disaster stroked California. The friend was not quite sure, however, whether it was another earthquake or extensive fires this time.

$$Earthquake \vee Fires \leftarrow \tag{7}$$
$$Calm \leftarrow not\, Earthquake, not\, Fires \tag{8}$$

Its translation $T = T_{\neg\mathcal{L}}(P)$ into belief theory:

$$Earthquake \vee Fires \tag{9}$$
$$\neg\mathcal{L}Earthquake \wedge \neg\mathcal{L}Fires \supset Calm. \tag{10}$$

has a unique static expansion

$$T^\diamond = Cn_*(T \cup \{\neg\mathcal{L}Earthquake, \neg\mathcal{L}Fires, \mathcal{L}Calm\}),$$

which produces a rather unintuitive conclusion that our poor Californian should not worry at all.

The reason for this phenomenon lies in the fact that given only the disjunction $F \vee G$ the (autoepistemic) knowledge operator $\mathcal{L}$ concludes that neither F nor G is known and thus our translation leads us to assume negation of both F and G. In order to eliminate this problem we augment the translated program $T_{\neg\mathcal{L}}(P)$ with the Positive Introspection Axiom, *(PIA)*. The resulting translation $T_{\neg\mathcal{L}}(P)$ turns out to be equivalent to the disjunctive stable semantics originally defined in [GL90, Prz91b]:

Theorem 14 Embeddability of Disjunctive Stable Semantics.
There is a natural one-to-one correspondence between disjunctive stable models of a disjunctive program P and consistent static expansions $T^\diamond$ of its translation $T_{\neg\mathcal{L}}(P)$ into belief theory augmented with the axiom (PIA).

Proof. By Theorem 7 there is a one-to-one correspondence between stable autoepistemic expansions and consistent static expansions of $T_{\neg\mathcal{L}}(P)$. The claim now follows from the results obtained in [Prz91d]. □

3.2 Translating *not* C as $\mathcal{B}\neg C$

We now consider the translation $T_{\mathcal{B}\neg}(P)$ of a logic program P obtained by replacing the non-monotonic negation *not* C by the belief atom $\mathcal{B}\neg C$ which gives it the intended meaning of *"$\neg C$ is believed to be true"* or *"$\neg C$ is minimally entailed"* and is patterned after the translation of logic programs into circumscriptive autoepistemic theories originally proposed by Przymusinski in [Prz91a] and subsequently further investigated in [Prz94b].

Definition 15 Translation $T_{\mathcal{B}\neg}(P)$.
For any disjunctive logic program P consisting of clauses:

$$A_1 \vee \ldots \vee A_n \leftarrow B_1 \wedge \ldots \wedge B_m \wedge not\ C_1 \wedge \ldots \wedge not\ C_n$$

define $T_{\mathcal{B}\neg}(P)$ to be its translation into the (affirmative) belief theory consisting of formulae:

$$B_1 \wedge \ldots \wedge B_m \wedge \mathcal{B}\neg C_1 \wedge \ldots \wedge \mathcal{B}\neg C_n \supset A_1 \vee \ldots \vee A_n.$$

3.2.1 Embeddability of Stationary and Well-Founded Semantics

It follows from the results obtained in [Prz94b] that the stationary (or, equivalently, partial stable) semantics, and, in particular, the well-founded semantics, of normal logic programs can be obtained by means of translating logic programs P into belief theories $T_{\mathcal{B}\neg}(P)$.

Theorem 16 Embeddability of Stationary and Well-Founded Sem.
There is a natural one-to-one correspondence between stationary (or, equivalently, partial stable) models $\mathcal{M}$ of the program P and consistent static autoepistemic expansions $T^\diamond$ of its translation $T_{\mathcal{B}\neg}(P)$ into a belief theory. Moreover, for any objective atom A we have:

$$A \in \mathcal{M} \quad \text{iff} \quad \mathcal{B}A \in T^\diamond$$

$$\neg A \in \mathcal{M} \quad \text{iff} \quad \mathcal{B}\neg A \in T^\diamond.$$

Since the well-founded model $\mathcal{M}_0$ of the program P coincides with the least *stationary model of P [Prz91b], it corresponds to the least static expansion of $T_{\mathcal{B}\neg}(P)$, whose existence is guaranteed by Theorem 9.*

Proof. By Theorem 11 there is a one-to-one correspondence between static autoepistemic expansions of $T_{\mathcal{B}\neg}(P)$ in AEB and static expansions of $T_{\mathcal{B}\neg}(P)$ in $AELB$. The claim now follows from the results obtained in [Prz94b]. □

Since (total) stable models form a subclass of the class of all partial stable models, as a corollary we obtain:

Corollary 17 Embeddability of Stable Semantics.
For any normal program P there is a natural one-to-one correspondence between (total) stable models (or answer sets) $\mathcal{M}$ of P and consistent static autoepistemic expansions $T^\diamond$ of the theory $T_{\mathcal{B}\neg}(P)$ augmented with the axiom (BCA).

Proof. By Theorem 11 there is a one-to-one correspondence between static autoepistemic expansions of $T_{\mathcal{B}\neg}(P)$ in AEB and static expansions of $T_{\mathcal{B}\neg}(P)$ in $AELB$. The claim now follows from the results obtained in [Prz94b]. □

Remark. It is worth mentioning that for normal programs an analogous result applies also to the translation $T_{\neg\mathcal{B}}(P)$ defined by:

$$B_1 \wedge \ldots \wedge B_m \wedge \neg\mathcal{B}C_1 \wedge \ldots \wedge \neg\mathcal{B}C_n \supset A$$

and thus giving *not* C the intended meaning " C is not believed". However, as we will see later, for disjunctive programs the two translations $T_{\mathcal{B}\neg}(P)$ and $T_{\neg\mathcal{B}}(P)$ lead, in general, to different results.

Example 4.
It is easy to see that the belief theory T:

$$\begin{array}{l} Car \wedge \mathcal{B}\neg Broken \supset Runs \\ Car \end{array}$$

considered in Example 2 can be viewed as a translation $T_{\mathcal{B}\neg}(P)$ of the logic program P given by:

$$\begin{array}{l} Runs \leftarrow Car, notBroken \\ Car \end{array}$$

Its unique static expansion :

$$T^\diamond = Cn_*(T \cup \{\mathcal{B}Car, \mathcal{B}\neg Broken, \mathcal{B}Runs\}).$$

corresponds therefore to the unique stationary (or stable) model:

$$M = \{Car, \neg Broken, Runs\}$$

of P which is also its unique well-founded model.

3.2.2 Embeddability of Static Semantics

As we have shown, major semantics proposed for *normal* logic programs can be naturally captured by using the translation $T_{\mathcal{B}\neg}(P)$ of logic programs into belief theories in *AELB*. This translation also works very nicely in the class of *disjunctive logic programs.*

Theorem 18 Embeddability of Static Semantics.
There is a one-to-one correspondence between static expansions $P^\diamond$ of the disjunctive logic program P, as defined in [Prz94b], and consistent static autoepistemic expansions $T^\diamond$ of its translation $T = T_{\mathcal{B}\neg}(P)$ into belief theory. Namely, a formula F belongs to $P^\diamond$ if and only if $\mathcal{B}F$ belongs to $T^\diamond$.

Proof. By Theorem 11 there is a one-to-one correspondence between static autoepistemic expansions of $T_{\mathcal{B}\neg}(P)$ in *AEB* and static expansions of $T_{\mathcal{B}\neg}(P)$ in *AELB*. The claim now follows from the results obtained in [Prz94b]. □

Example 5.
Consider the following disjunctive logic program P describing the state of mind of a person planning a trip to either Australia or Europe:

$$\begin{array}{ll} Goto\_Australia \vee Goto\_Europe & \\ Goto\_Both & \leftarrow Goto\_Australia \wedge Goto\_Europe \\ Save\_Money & \leftarrow not\ Goto\_Both \\ Cancel\_Reservation & \leftarrow not\ Goto\_Australia \\ Cancel\_Reservation & \leftarrow not\ Goto\_Europe \end{array}$$

and its translation into the (affirmative) belief theory $T = T_{\mathcal{B}\neg}(P)$:

$$\begin{array}{ll} Goto\_Australia \vee Goto\_Europe & \\ Goto\_Australia \wedge Goto\_Europe & \supset Goto\_Both \\ \mathcal{B}\neg Goto\_Both & \supset Save\_Money \\ \mathcal{B}\neg Goto\_Australia & \supset Cancel\_Reservation \\ \mathcal{B}\neg Goto\_Europe & \supset Cancel\_Reservation. \end{array}$$

Let $T^0 = Cn_*(T)$ and assume obvious abbreviations. Clearly, in all minimal models of T^0 the disjunctions $GA \vee GE$ and $\neg GA \vee \neg GE$ hold true. Therefore:

$$T^0 \models_{\min} GA \vee GE,\ T^0 \models_{\min} \neg GA \vee \neg GE \ \ and\ \ T^0 \models_{\min} \neg GB$$

and, consequently:

$$T^1 = \Psi_T(T^0) = Cn_*(T \cup \{\mathcal{B}(GA \vee GE),\ \mathcal{B}(\neg GA \vee \neg GE),\ \mathcal{B}\neg GB, \ldots\}).$$

Now $T^1 \models_{\min} SM$ and thus

$$T^2 = \Psi_T(T^1) = Cn_*(T \cup \{\mathcal{B}(GA \vee GE),\ \mathcal{B}(\neg GA \vee \neg GE),\ \mathcal{B}\neg GB,\ \mathcal{B}SM, \ldots\}).$$

It is easy to see that there is a minimal model of T^2 in which $\mathcal{B}\neg Goto\_Australia$ is true and thus also *Cancel_Reservation* is true. But there is also is a minimal model of T^2 in which both $\mathcal{B}\neg$*Goto_Australia* and $\mathcal{B}\neg$*Goto_Europe* are false and thus also *Cancel_Reservation* is false. Consequently:

$$T^2 \not\models_{\min} CR \text{ and } T^2 \not\models_{\min} \neg CR .$$

This leads to the conclusion that $T^3 = \Psi_T(T^2) = T^2$ is a fixed point and therefore the least static expansion $T^\diamond$ of T is given by:

$$T^\diamond = Cn_*(T \cup \{\mathcal{B}(GA \vee GE),\ \mathcal{B}(\neg GA \vee \neg GE),\ \mathcal{B}\neg GB,\ \mathcal{B}SM, \ldots\}).$$

It establishes that the individual is expected to travel either to Australia or to Europe but is not expected to do both trips and thus will save money. One easily verifies that T does not have any other (consistent) static expansions.

It is important to stress that *Cancel_Reservation* is *not* a logical consequence of the static semantics $T^\diamond$ of the previously considered (translated) program $T = T_{\mathcal{B}\neg}(P)$. This follows from the fact that the least static expansion $T^\diamond$ does *not* infer $\mathcal{B}\neg$*Goto_Australia* $\vee$ $\mathcal{B}\neg$*Goto_Europe* even though it derives $\mathcal{B}(\neg$*Goto_Australia* $\vee \neg$*Goto_Europe*$)$. This reflects the notion that from the fact that a disjunction $F \vee G$ is believed to be true, one does *not* necessarily want to conclude that either F is believed or G is believed. In this particular case, we do not want to cancel our reservations to either Australia or to Europe until we find out precisely *which* one of them we will actually *not* visit. In other words, we usually do *not* want to assume that the belief operator $\mathcal{B}$ is *distributive* with respect to disjunctions.

Remark. Observe that, by the Consistency Axiom (4), $T^\diamond$ implies the weaker formula:

$$\neg\mathcal{B}(Goto\_Australia \wedge Goto\_Europe) \equiv \neg\mathcal{B}Goto\_Australia \vee \neg\mathcal{B}Goto\_Europe.$$

Consequently, if instead of the translation $T_{\mathcal{B}\neg}(P)$ we used the translation $T_{\neg\mathcal{B}}(P)$, i.e., if we translated *not* C into $\neg\mathcal{B}C$, then *Cancel_Reservation* would be a logical consequence of the static semantics $T^\diamond$ of the translated program $T_{\neg\mathcal{B}}(P)$. This implies that for disjunctive programs the translations $T_{\neg\mathcal{B}}(P)$ and $T_{\mathcal{B}\neg}(P)$ no longer coincide.

However, one could easily ensure distributivity of beliefs w.r.t. disjunctions by assuming the *Disjunctive Belief Axiom*, *DBA*, introduced earlier. As the next theorem demonstrates such a translation leads to the *disjunctive stationary semantics*, introduced in [Prz91c].

Theorem 19 Embeddability of Disjunctive Stationary Semantics. *There is a one-to-one correspondence between stationary expansions*[4] *of a disjunctive program P and consistent static autoepistemic expansions of its translation $T_{\mathcal{B}\neg}(P)$ into belief theory augmented with the Disjunctive Belief Axiom, DBA.*

[4] We mean here stationary expansions without the *Disjunctive Inference Rule*, *DIR*, defined in [Prz91c].

Proof. According to [Prz91c], a *stationary expansion* of a disjunctive program (or database) P is any consistent theory P^* which satisfies the following fixed point condition:

$$P^* = P \cup \{not\_F : P^* \models_{\min} \neg F\}$$

where F is an arbitrary formula. Moreover, the operator not_F was assumed to satisfy the following two *distributive axioms*:

$$not\_(F \vee G) \equiv not\_F \wedge not\_G \tag{11}$$
$$not\_(F \wedge G) \equiv not\_F \vee not\_G \tag{12}$$

which state that negation by default is distributive with respect to disjunction and conjunction. The operator not_F was also assumed to satisfy the following *inference rule*:

$$\frac{F}{\neg not\_F} \tag{13}$$

which says that if a formula F is known to be true then its negation by default not_F must be false.

In order to show that static expansions can be translated into stationary expansions, let us define the following translation between the operators not_F and $\mathcal{B}F$:

$$not\_F \equiv \mathcal{B}\neg F.$$

Clearly, not_F satisfies the above distributivity axioms if and only if $\mathcal{B}F$ is distributive with respect to both conjunctions and disjunctions. Moreover, the definition of stationary expansions translates into:

$$P^\diamond = P \cup \{\mathcal{B}\neg F : P^\diamond \models_{\min} \neg F\} = P \cup \{\mathcal{B}F : P^\diamond \models_{\min} F\}$$

and thus is equivalent to the definition of static expansions in the logic AEB.

Finally, the inference rule:

$$\frac{F}{\neg not\_F} \tag{14}$$

gets translated into:

$$\frac{F}{\neg\mathcal{B}\neg F} \tag{15}$$

and becomes an immediate consequence of the necessitation rule (N) and the consistency axiom (D).

In an analogous way one can prove the that stationary expansions can be translated into static expansions. We recall again that we consider here stationary expansions without the *Disjunctive Inference Rule*, *DIR*, as defined in [Prz91c]. In order to achieve equivalence with the rule *DIR* added, one only has to add the corresponding axiom: $\mathcal{L}(F \vee G) \supset \mathcal{L}(\mathcal{B}\neg F \supset G)$. □

Example 6.
When augmented with the Disjunctive Belief Axiom, DBA, the static semantics of the (translated) program $T = T_{\mathcal{B}\neg}(P)$ from Example 5:

$$\begin{array}{ll} Goto\_Australia \vee Goto\_Europe & \\ Goto\_Australia \wedge Goto\_Europe & \supset Goto\_Both \\ \mathcal{B}\neg Goto\_Both & \supset Save\_Money \\ \mathcal{B}\neg Goto\_Australia & \supset Cancel\_Reservation \\ \mathcal{B}\neg Goto\_Europe & \supset Cancel\_Reservation. \end{array}$$

implies *Cancel_Reservation*. Indeed, belief theory T has a unique static expansion $T^{\diamond}$ of T given by:

$$T^{\diamond} = Cn_{*}(T \cup \{\mathcal{B}(GA \vee GE),\ \mathcal{B}(\neg GA \vee \neg GE),\ \mathcal{B}\neg GB,\ \mathcal{B}SM,\ \mathcal{B}CR, \ldots\}),$$

because now the axiom (DBA) implies $\mathcal{B}\neg Goto\_Australia \vee \mathcal{B}\neg Goto\_Europe$.

Observe also that the definition of static as well as stationary expansions carefully distinguishes between these formulae F which are *known to be true* in the expansion $T^{\diamond}$ (i.e., those for which $T^{\diamond} \models F$), and those formulae F which are only *believed* (i.e., those for which $T^{\diamond} \models \mathcal{B}F$). This important distinction not only increases the *expressiveness* of the language but is in fact quite crucial for many forms of reasoning. However, if we wanted to ensure that a formula F is always true whenever it is believed to be true we could use the *Generalized Closed World Axiom*, $GCWA$, which we also introduced before. In fact, it is not difficult to prove that the *disjunctive stable semantics*, introduced in [Prz91b, GL90] and already discussed in Theorem 14, can be expressed by means of translating logic programs into belief theories augmented with the Disjunctive Knowledge Axiom, DKA, and the Generalized Closed World Assumption, $GCWA$. This observation further clarifies the nature of this semantics and its relationship to other semantics proposed for disjunctive programs

Several other semantics proposed for disjunctive programs can be obtained in a similar way thus demonstrating the expressive power and modularity of $AELB$.

3.3 Combining Knowledge and Belief: Mixing Stable and Well-Founded Negation

As we have seen in Theorems 13 and 16, both stable and well-founded (partial stable) negation in logic programs can be obtained by translating the non-monotonic negation *not* C into introspective literals $\neg\mathcal{L}C$ and $\mathcal{B}\neg C$, respectively. However, the existence of both types of introspective literals in $AELB$ allows us to *combine both types of negation* in one belief theory consisting of formulae of the form:

$$B_1 \wedge \ldots \wedge B_m \wedge \neg\mathcal{L}C_1 \wedge \ldots \wedge \neg\mathcal{L}C_k \wedge \mathcal{B}\neg C_{k+1} \wedge \ldots \wedge \mathcal{B}\neg C_n \supset A_1 \vee \ldots \vee A_l.$$

Such an belief theory may be viewed as representing a more general disjunctive logic program which permits the simultaneous use of both types of negation. In such logic programs, the first k negative premises represent ***stable negation*** and the remaining ones represent the ***well-founded negation***. The ability to use both types of negation significantly increases the expressibility of logic programs. For instance, the example:

$$\mathcal{B}\neg baseball \wedge \mathcal{B}\neg football \supset rent\_movie$$
$$\neg\mathcal{L}baseball \wedge \neg\mathcal{L}football \supset dont\_buy\_tickets.$$

discussed in Example 1 is a special case of such a generalized logic program.

3.4 Strong Negation

Classical negation, $\neg A$, which is part of the propositional language $\mathcal{K}_{\mathcal{B},\mathcal{L}}$ of the Autoepistemic Logic of Knowledge and Beliefs, $AELB$, satisfies the so called *law of the excluded middle*, $A \vee \neg A$, which requires that any given property A be known to be either true or false in every model. However, in many commonsense reasoning domains, including logic programming, such a requirement appears undesirable. Consequently, we need a new notion of negation, which does not necessarily satisfy the law of the excluded middle.

One such notion of non-standard negation[5] for logic programs with stable semantics was introduced by Gelfond and Lifschitz in [GL90] and called, somewhat unfortunately, "classical negation". It was later generalized to other semantics and extended to disjunctive logic programs [AP92, Prz90, Prz91c] and given the name of *"strong negation"* [AP92]. In [Prz94a], we showed that strong negation, can be easily added to the autoepistemic logic of beliefs, AEB, by:

- augmenting the original objective language $\mathcal{K}$ with new *objective* propositional symbols $\sim A$, called *strong negation atoms*, resulting in a new objective language $\mathcal{K}'$ and the new language of beliefs $\mathcal{K}'_{\mathcal{B},\mathcal{L}}$.
- ensuring that the intended meaning of $\sim A$ is "$\sim A$ *is the opposite of* A" by assuming the following *strong negation* axiom:

$$\text{(S)} \qquad A \wedge \sim A \supset \bot \quad \text{or, equivalently,} \quad \sim A \supset \neg A,$$

which says that A and its opposite $\sim A$ cannot be both true. Formally, the addition of the axiom schema (S) means that the set $Cn_*(T)$ of formulae derivable from a given belief theory T, used in the definition of the static expansion, is now replaced by the smallest set, $Cn_*^s(T)$, which contains the theory T and all the (substitution instances of) the axioms (K), (D) and (S) and is closed under the necessitation rule (N).

[5] For other, closely related notions of non-standard negation in logic programming see [PW90, PA92, APP95].

For example, a proposition A may describe the property of being *"good"* while the proposition $\sim A$ describes the property of being *"bad"*. The strong negation axiom states that things cannot be *both* good and bad. We do not assume, however, that things must always be either good or bad.

Example 7.
Consider the belief theory T with strong negation:

$$\sim Football$$

$$\mathcal{B}\neg Baseball \supset Football$$

$$\mathcal{B}\neg Football \supset Baseball$$

It is easy to verify that T has precisely one consistent static expansion:

$$T^{\diamond} = Cn_{*}(T \cup \{\mathcal{B}\neg Football,\ \mathcal{B}Baseball.\})$$

Indeed, axiom (S) implies that $T^0 \models \neg Football$ and thus $T^1 \models \mathcal{B}\neg Football$, and, consequently, $T^1 \models Baseball$ and $T^{\diamond} = T^2 \models \mathcal{B}Baseball$.

As the following result shows, we can use strong negation to translate extended logic programs with "classical negation", originally introduced in [GL90], into belief theories.

Theorem 20 Embeddability of Extended Stationary and Stable Sem.

There is a one-to-one correspondence between stationary (or partial stable) models $\mathcal{M}$ of an extended logic program P with "classical negation", as defined in [Prz94b], and consistent static autoepistemic expansions $T^{\diamond}$ of its translation $T_{\mathcal{B}\neg}(P)$ into belief theory, in which "classical negation" of an atom A is translated into $\sim A$.

In particular, (total) stable models (or answer sets) $\mathcal{M}$ of a normal extended logic program P, as defined in [GL90], correspond to consistent static autoepistemic expansions $T^{\diamond}$ of the belief theory $T_{\mathcal{B}\neg}(P)$ augmented with the axiom (BCA).

Proof. By Theorem 11 there is a one-to-one correspondence between static autoepistemic expansions of $T_{\mathcal{B}\neg}(P)$ in AEB and static expansions of $T_{\mathcal{B}\neg}(P)$ in $AELB$. The claim now follows from the results obtained in [Prz94b]. □

4 Concluding Remarks

We introduced an extension, $AELB$, of Moore's autoepistemic logic, AEL, obtained by adding a new belief operator, B. We showed that $AELB$ constitutes a powerful knowledge representation framework unifying several well-known nonmonotonic formalisms and major semantics for normal and disjunctive logic programs.

The following table briefly summarizes the results presented in the paper involving embeddability of semantics of *normal* logic programs into belief theories in the logic $AELB$.

Semantics	Translation of *not* C	Axioms
Well-founded	$\mathcal{B}\neg C$	
Stationary	$\mathcal{B}\neg C$	
Stable	$\mathcal{B}\neg C$	(BCA)
Stable	$\neg\mathcal{L}C$	
Extended Stationary	$\mathcal{B}\neg C$	(S)
Extended Stable	$\neg\mathcal{L}C$	(S)

The next table summarizes the results presented in the paper involving embeddability of semantics of *disjunctive* logic programs into belief theories in the logic $AELB$.

Semantics	Translation of *not* C	Axioms
Static	$\mathcal{B}\neg C$	
Disjunctive Stationary	$\mathcal{B}\neg C$	(DBA)
Disjunctive Stable	$\neg\mathcal{L}C$	(PIA)
Extended Static	$\mathcal{B}\neg C$	(S)
Extended Stationary	$\mathcal{B}\neg C$	(S) + (DBA)

Moreover, Brass, Dix and Przymusinski have recently established the embeddability of the *D-WFS*-semantics for disjunctive programs, introduced in [BD95, BD94], into the logic $AELB$ by showing that the *D-WFS*-semantics and the static semantics are equivalent (when restricted to suitable formulae).

As we can see, the proposed formalism allows us to compare different formalisms, better understand their mutual relationships and introduce simpler and more natural definitions. It is also quite flexible and modular by allowing various extensions and modifications, including the use of different formalisms defining the meaning of beliefs and introduction of additional axioms.

Acknowledgments

The author is grateful to Jose Alferes, Jürgen Dix, Michael Gelfond, Vladimir Lifschitz, Luis Pereira and Halina Przymusinska for their helpful comments and discussions. The author is especially grateful to Grigorij Schwartz for his extensive remarks.

References

[ABW88] K. Apt, H. Blair, and A. Walker. Towards a theory of declarative knowledge. In J. Minker, editor, *Foundations of Deductive Databases and Logic Programming*, pages 89–142. Morgan Kaufmann, Los Altos, CA., 1988.

[AP92] J. J. Alferes and L. M. Pereira. On logic program semantics with two kinds of negation. In K. Apt, editor, *International Joint Conference and Symposium on Logic Programming*, pages 574–588. MIT Press, 1992.

[APP95] J. Alferes, L. Pereira, and T. C. Przymusinski. Strong and explicit negation in non-monotonic reasoning and logic programming. (In preparation.), University of Lisbon and University of California at Riverside, 1995.

[BD94] Stefan Brass and Jürgen Dix. A disjunctive semantics based on unfolding and bottom-up evaluation. In Bernd Wolfinger, editor, *Innovationen bei Rechen- und Kommunikationssystemen, (IFIP-Congress, Workshop FG2: Disjunctive Logic Programming and Disjunctive Databases)*, pages 83–91. Springer-Verlag, 1994.

[BD95] Stefan Brass and Jürgen Dix. Disjunctive Semantics based upon Partial and Bottom-Up Evaluation. In Leon Sterling, editor, *Proceedings of the 12th Int. Conf. on Logic Programming, Tokyo*. MIT, June 1995.

[BF91] N. Bidoit and C. Froidevaux. General logical databases and programs: Default logic semantics and stratification. *Journal of Information and Computation*, pages 15–54, 1991.

[Dix92] Jürgen Dix. Classifying Semantics of Disjunctive Logic Programs. In K. Apt, editor, *LOGIC PROGRAMMING: Proceedings of the 1992 Joint International Conference and Symposium*, pages 798–812. MIT Press, November 1992.

[Gel87] M. Gelfond. On stratified autoepistemic theories. In *Proceedings AAAI-87*, pages 207–211, Los Altos, CA, 1987. American Association for Artificial Intelligence, Morgan Kaufmann.

[Gel92] M. Gelfond. Logic programming and reasoning with incomplete information. Technical report, University of Texas at El Paso, 1992.

[GL88] M. Gelfond and V. Lifschitz. The stable model semantics for logic programming. In R. Kowalski and K. Bowen, editors, *Proceedings of the Fifth Logic Programming Symposium*, pages 1070–1080, Cambridge, Mass., 1988. Association for Logic Programming, MIT Press.

[GL90] M. Gelfond and V. Lifschitz. Logic programs with classical negation. In *Proceedings of the Seventh International Logic Programming Conference, Jerusalem, Israel*, pages 579–597, Cambridge, Mass., 1990. Association for Logic Programming, MIT Press.

[GPP89] Michael Gelfond, Halina Przymusinski, and Teodor C. Przymusinski. On the relationship between circumscription and negation as failure. *Journal of Artificial Intelligence*, 38(1):75–94, February 1989.

[Lif85] V. Lifschitz. Computing circumscription. In *Proceedings IJCAI-85*, pages 121–127, Los Altos, CA, 1985. American Association for Artificial Intelligence, Morgan Kaufmann.

[LMR92] J. Lobo, J. Minker, and A. Rajasekar. *Foundations of Disjunctive Logic Programming*. MIT Press, Cambridge, Massachusetts, 1992.

[McC80] J. McCarthy. Circumscription – a form of non-monotonic reasoning. *Journal of Artificial Intelligence*, 13:27–39, 1980.

[Min82] J. Minker. On indefinite data bases and the closed world assumption. In *Proc. 6-th Conference on Automated Deduction*, pages 292–308, New York, 1982. Springer Verlag.

[Moo85] R.C. Moore. Semantic considerations on non-monotonic logic. *Journal of Artificial Intelligence*, 25:75–94, 1985.

[MT94] W. Marek and M. Truszczynski. *Non-Monotonic Logic*. Springer Verlag, 1994.

[PA92] L. M. Pereira and J. J. Alferes. Well founded semantics for logic programs with explicit negation. In B. Neumann, editor, *European Conference on Artificial Intelligence*, pages 102–106. John Wiley & Sons, 1992.

[PP90] H. Przymusinska and T. C. Przymusinski. Semantic issues in deductive databases and logic programs. In R. Banerji, editor, *Formal Techniques in Artificial Intelligence*, pages 321–367. North-Holland, Amsterdam, 1990.

[Prz88] T. C. Przymusinski. On the declarative semantics of deductive databases and logic programs. In J. Minker, editor, *Foundations of Deductive Databases and Logic Programming*, pages 193–216. Morgan Kaufmann, Los Altos, CA., 1988.

[Prz90] T. C. Przymusinski. The well-founded semantics coincides with the three-valued stable semantics. *Fundamenta Informaticae*, 13(4):445–464, 1990.

[Prz91a] T. C. Przymusinski. Autoepistemic logics of closed beliefs and logic programming. In A. Nerode, W. Marek, and V.S. Subrahmanian, editors, *Proceedings of the First International Workshop on Logic Programming and Non-monotonic Reasoning, Washington, D.C., July 1991*, pages 3–20, Cambridge, Mass., 1991. MIT Press.

[Prz91b] T. C. Przymusinski. Stable semantics for disjunctive programs. *New Generation Computing Journal*, 9:401–424, 1991. (Extended abstract appeared in: Extended stable semantics for normal and disjunctive logic programs. *Proceedings of the 7-th International Logic Programming Conference, Jerusalem*, pages 459–477, 1990. MIT Press.).

[Prz91c] T. C. Przymusinski. Stationary semantics for normal and disjunctive logic programs. In C. Delobel, M. Kifer, and Y. Masunaga, editors, *Proceedings of the Second International Conference on Deductive and Object-Oriented Databases DOOD'91*, pages 85–107, Munich, Germany, December 1991. Springer Verlag.

[Prz91d] T. C. Przymusinski. Three-valued non-monotonic formalisms and semantics of logic programs. *Journal of Artificial Intelligence*, 49(1-3):309–343, January 1991. (Extended abstract appeared in: Three-valued non-monotonic formalisms and logic programming. *Proceedings of the First International Conference on Principles of Knowledge Representation and Reasoning (KR'89), Toronto, Canada*, pages 341–348, Morgan Kaufmann, 1989.).

[Prz94a] T. C. Przymusinski. Autoepistemic logic of knowledge and beliefs. (In preparation), University of California at Riverside, 1994. (Extended abstract appeared in 'A knowledge representation framework based on autoepistemic logic of minimal beliefs' In *Proceedings of the Twelfth National Conference on Artificial Intelligence, AAAI-94, Seattle, Washington, August 1994*, pages 952-959, Los Altos, CA, 1994. American Association for Artificial Intelligence, Morgan Kaufmann.).

[Prz94b] T. C. Przymusinski. Static semantics for normal and disjunctive logic programs. *Annals of Mathematics and Artificial Intelligence*, Special Issue on Disjunctive Programs, 1994. (in print).

[Prz94c] T. C. Przymusinski. Well-founded and stationary models of logic programs. *Annals of Mathematics and Artificial Intelligence*, 12:141–187, 1994.

[PW90] D. Pearce and G. Wagner. Reasoning with negative information I: Strong negation in logic programs. In L. Haaparanta, M. Kusch, and

I. Niiniluoto, editors, *Language, Knowledge and Intentionality*, pages 430–453. Acta Philosophica Fennica 49, 1990.

[VG89] A. Van Gelder. Negation as failure using tight derivations for general logic programs. *Journal of Logic Programming*, 6(1):109–133, 1989. Preliminary versions appeared in *Third IEEE Symposium Logic Programming* (1986), and *Foundations of Deductive Databases and Logic Programming*, J. Minker, ed., Morgan Kaufmann, 1988.

[VGRS90] A. Van Gelder, K. A. Ross, and J. S. Schlipf. The well-founded semantics for general logic programs. *Journal of the ACM*, 1990. (to appear). Preliminary abstract appeared in Seventh ACM Symposium on Principles of Database Systems, March 1988, pp. 221–230.

Every Normal Program has a Nearly-Stable Model

Cees Witteveen[1]

Delft University of Technology,
Dept of Mathematics and Computer Science,
P.O.Box 356, 2600 AJ Delft, The Netherlands,
e-mail: witt@cs.tudelft.nl

Abstract. We discuss a revision method for normal logic programs that do not have a stable model. The method we propose is a revision-by-transformation method: we apply some rule transformations which do not affect the meaning of such a program as a first-order theory, but ensure that the transformed program has at least one stable model.
The stable models of such a transformation are called the *nearly-stable models* of the original program.
The transformation method we propose is a generalization of program transformation approaches as shift operations and dependency-directed backtracking which can be shown to be too weak to provide a suitable model for every normal logic program.
Furthermore, our results can be used to extend the weakly-stable model semantics as recently proposed by Schaerf ([Sch93]).

1 Introduction

It is well-known that some (normal) logic programs are not well-behaved with respect to the stable model semantics. This means that, viewed as a first-order theory, such a program has classical models, but does not have a stable model. In this paper we want to to find a suitable meaning for such a program by (i) transforming it to classically equivalent programs and (ii) using the stable models of these transformations as the (nearly)-stable models of the original program.

What is the motivation for this approach? Like Schaerf in [Sch93], we would like to make a distinction between a *model-theoretical* view of a program and a *proof-theoretical* view. In the first view, a program is just a first order theory and its interpretation is independent from the special syntactical form the theory is framed in. According to the latter view, the rule-based syntax does matter, in fact the rules making up the program are considered to be a kind of inference rules.

Now, in our view, the stable model semantics of [GL88] can be viewed as an attempt to use a proof-theoretical semantics as a refinement of a model-theoretical semantics: Based on the program as a first order theory, the minimal models of the program are selected in order to maximize its informational content. Then, taking into account the syntactical form of the program, we make a further selection among these minimal models, thereby keeping the stable models and rejecting the non-stable ones. According to this view we should distinguish semantically between e.g. $P_1 : a \leftarrow \neg b$ and $P_2 : b \leftarrow \neg a$ although, classically, these programs are equivalent and have the same minimal models $M_1 = \{a, \neg b\}$ and $M_2 = \{b, \neg a\}$ respectively. Viewing these rules as inference rules, however, only M_1 is adequate for the first rule and M_2 for the second rule. The stable semantics then comes down to preferring those minimal models that respect the view of a program as a specification of a set of arguments or inference rules.

This sketch, however, of the stable semantics as establishing a complementary relationship between two different views on semantics of programs is an idealized one. In practice, we have to face the following problem of incongruity: although normal programs may have minimal models, sometimes we are not able to select a stable one from them. In this case, the program is said to be not well-behaved. Of course, one might leave it at that, but there are some clear cases in which such an attitude of resignation is unjustified.

Let us give some examples. Consider the following simple program:

$$P : \; c \leftarrow \neg a$$
$$\bot \leftarrow c$$

where the last rule is a *constraint* having the effect that c should be considered as false in every model of the program[1]. This program has no stable model, since a has no support, so $\neg a$ should be considered true, making c true and then we run into a contradiction. Note that P has a minimal model $M = \{a, \neg c\}$ which expresses the intuitively right interpretation of P:

> *If the only reason for c to be true is by assuming that a does not hold and you are told that c cannot be true then you are not entitled to assume that a is false.*

So, as a two-valued reasoner, your only option is to consider a to be true.

It is clear that the stable semantics is too weak to adapt to this kind of *reductio ad absurdum* reasoning.

Now we might ask: Is there another well-behaved[2] program P', closely resembling P, such that P' has the same model-theoretical meaning as P? The answer, of course, is *yes*: just by taking a logical contrapositive of the first rule, we have such a program:

$$P' : \; a \leftarrow \neg c$$
$$\bot \leftarrow c$$

having $M = \{a, \neg c\}$ as its stable model.

So, at least in normal programs with constraints, such transformations might be useful to recover a suitable meaning for the original program.

---

[1] We will allow such constraints to occur in normal programs as long as they do not make the program inconsistent

[2] A program P is called well-behaved if it has at least one stable model.

Also for programs without a constraint such modifications can be justified: Take, for example, the following well-known, but not well-behaved, program:

$$\begin{aligned} P:\ & a \leftarrow \neg b \\ & b \leftarrow \neg c \\ & c \leftarrow \neg a \end{aligned}$$

Note, that again in this example, we need to incorporate reductio ad absurdum to find a nearly-stable model: If we assume b to be false, then, according to the first rule, a is true. Now, according to the second rule, if c would be considered false, b would be true: contradiction; hence, taking the contrapositive $c \leftarrow \neg b$, we have a reason to consider c as true and $M = \{a, c, \neg b\}$ is a stable model of a (minimal) transformation:

$$\begin{aligned} P':\ & a \leftarrow \neg b \\ & c \leftarrow \neg b \\ & c \leftarrow \neg a \end{aligned}$$

Looking back at these examples, we notice that if the original program P does not have a stable model, we tried to find some transformation P' of P such that

1. P' is classically equivalent to P,
2. P' has at least one stable model
3. P' may differ from P in the syntactical form of some rules.

If there exists such small "perturbations" of P having a stable model M, we call such a model a *nearly-stable* model of P.

The important questions with respect to these transformations, of course, are:

> *Which (first-order preserving) transformations or perturbations of programs are allowed?*

and

> *Does every normal program have at least one nearly-stable model under these transformations?*

With respect to the examples given, the reader might become suspicious: in both examples it was sufficient to take contrapositives of existing rules, i.e. shifting literals between heads and bodies to transform it into an equivalent well-behaved program. But does this shifting method work for every normal program?

The answer, (un)fortunately, is *no*: there are some clear cases in which shifting of literals is of no help and cannot be used in combination with the stable model semantics to model reductio-ad-absurdum-like reasoning patterns.

In order to guarantee that for every program a nearly-stable model can be found, we have to supplement shifting operations with another rule-transformation technique, called *condensation*. This technique, although not a local transformation like shifting, removes some literals from rules, but preserves the classical meaning of the program. If we combine condensation with shifting, we can prove that for every normal logic program a nearly-stable model can be found. This transformation can also be used to extend the weakly-stable semantics, as introduced by [Sch93].

Remark. The idea of taking contrapositives for strengthening non-monotonic reasoning patterns in rule-based systems like logic programs is not new and can be traced back to the application of dependency-directed backtracking (ddb) in truth-maintenance, as introduced in [Doy79]. Giordano and Martelli ([GM90]) showed that, logically, ddb can be reconstructed as taking logical contrapositives of rules.

Shifting is a closely related technique introduced in [Sch93] and [JDM94] to transform disjunctive programs into normal ones and using the stable models of the latter ones to give the original disjunctive a so-called *weakly* stable meaning. As they already have shown, not for every disjunctive program a weakly stable model could be found[3].

In this paper we will use a generalization of their shifting technique to extend the stable model semantics *within* the class of normal logic programs. Our idea of nearly-stable models should be conceived as a generalization of transformation techniques like dependency-directed backtracking as well as an extension of the stable model semantics, like the weakly-stable model semantics. In fact, taking nearly-stable models as the weakly stable models of a consistent program, we can easily show that every consistent (disjunctive) logic program has at least one nearly-stable model.

1.1 Preliminaries

We assume the reader to be familiar with some basic terminology used in logic programming, as for example in Lloyd [Llo87]. A *normal program rule* r is a directed propositional clause of the form $A \leftarrow B_1, \ldots, B_m, \neg D_1, \ldots, \neg D_n$, where $A, B_1, \ldots, D_1, \ldots, D_n$ are all atomic propositions. The head of such a rule r is denoted by $hd(r)$ and its body by $body(r) = \alpha(r) \wedge \beta(r)$, where $\alpha(r)$ denotes the conjunction of the B_i atoms and $\beta(r)$ denotes the conjunction of the negative atoms $\neg D_j$. The head of a rule r is denoted by $hd(r)$. A program is called *positive* if for every rule r, $\beta(r) = \top$ (the empty conjunction).

Constraints are special rules r with $hd(r) = \bot$, expressing that the conjunction of the literals occurring in $body(r)$ cannot be true. We do not allow $\bot$ (*falsum*) to occur in the body of any rule r.

[3] Elsewhere (see [Wit94]), we have shown that taking contrapositives is adequate for the supported semantics, but is too weak as a transformation technique for the stable semantics.

As usual, interpretations and models of a program are denoted by maximal consistent subsets I of literals over the Herbrand base B_P of P, i.e., for every atom $a \in B_P$, either a or $\neg a$ occurs in I. If L is a set of literals over B_P, $atoms(L)$ denotes the set of atoms $a \in B_P$ occurring positively or negatively in L and L^+ (L^-) denotes the subset of atoms occurring positively (negatively) in L. If l is a literal, $\bar{l}$ equals $\neg l$ if l is a positive atom and equals s if $l = \neg s$ for some $s \in B_P$. If L is a set of literals, $\neg L = \{\bar{l} \mid l \in L\}$.

A *model* of a program P is an interpretation I satisfying all the rules and constraints of P. Here, a rule r is said to be satisfied by an interpretation I iff $I \models body(r)$ implies $I \models hd(r)$ and a constraint $\bot \leftarrow \alpha \wedge \beta$ is satisfied by I iff $I \not\models \alpha \wedge \beta$ or, equivalently, I is a model of the constraint as a rule and I^+ does not contain the special atom $\bot$.

T_P denotes the immediate consequence operator associated with the program P and $lfp(T_P) = T_P \uparrow \omega$ denotes the least fixpoint of this operator.

The intended meaning of a normal logic program is given by the two-valued *stable model* semantics ([GL88]):

Definition 1. A model M of a logic program P is called stable iff M^+ equals the least fixpoint of the Gelfond-Lifschitz reduction $G(P, M)$ of P, where

$$G(P, M) = \{c \leftarrow \alpha \mid c \leftarrow \alpha \wedge \beta \in P,\ M \models \beta\}$$

Note that $G(P, M)$ is a positive program, i.e., does not contain any rule with a negative antecedent.

The set of stable models of a program P is denoted by $Stable(P)$. P is called *consistent*, if it has a non-empty set $Mod(P)$ of classical models.

In the subsequent sections, we will also need *clause-representations* of rules. If r is the rule

$$c \leftarrow a_1, \ldots, a_m, \neg b_1, \ldots, \neg b_n,$$

then the clause $C(r)$ *associated with* r is

$$C(r) = \{c, \neg a_1, \ldots, \neg a_m, b_1, \ldots, b_n\}.$$

If P is a logic program, $C(P) = \{C(r) \mid r \in P\}$ is the set of clauses associated with P. Conversely, if $\mathcal{C}$ is a set of clauses, $Normal(\mathcal{C})$ refers to the set of *normal* logic programs P such that $\mathcal{C} = C(P)$.

Since we are allowed to include constraints, it is not difficult to see that, for every set of clauses $\mathcal{C}$, there exists at least one normal program P, such that $C(P) = \mathcal{C}$.

A clause C is called *positive* if it contains only positive atoms. A clause C is said to be a *prime implicate* of a set of clauses Σ iff $\Sigma \models C$ and there is no proper subset $C' \subset C$ such that $\Sigma \models C'$.

We will need the following lemma's pertaining to properties of stable models:

Lemma 2 Marek & Truszczyński [MT93].
Let M be a model of a program P. Then $T_{G(P,M)} \uparrow \omega \subseteq M^+$.

Lemma 3. *Let P be a program and $M_{neg} = \{\neg a \mid a \in B_P\}$ an interpretation of P. Then the following statements are equivalent:*

1. *M_{neg} is a model of P.*
2. *M_{neg} is a stable model of P.*
3. *The body of every rule r of P contains at least one positive literal.*

Proof. $(1 \Rightarrow 2)$ Let M_{neg} be a model of P. By Lemma 2,

$$\emptyset \subseteq \mathit{lfp}(T_{G(P,M_{neg})}) \subseteq M^+_{neg} = \emptyset,$$

hence, $\mathit{lfp}(T_{G(P,M_{neg})}) = M^+_{neg}$ and therefore, M_{neg} is stable.

$(2 \Rightarrow 3)$ Since $\mathit{lfp}(T_{G(P,M_{neg})}) = M^+_{neg} = \emptyset$, every rule r of P must contain at least one positive literal, for else the rule $hd(r) \leftarrow$ would occur in $G(P, M_{neg})$ and then $\mathit{lfp}(T_{G(P,M_{neg})}) \neq \emptyset = M^+$, contradicting the assumption that M_{neg} is stable.

$(3 \Rightarrow 1)$ If the body of every rule r of P contains at least one positive literal, $M_{neg} \not\models body(r)$. Hence, for every r, $M_{neg} \models r$, so M_{neg} is a model of P. □

The following lemma is useful in finding stable models of a program by looking only at a subset of rules of the program.

Lemma 4 Expansion Lemma.
Let P be a program, $P' \subset P$ and M a model of P. Then, if M is a stable model of P', M also is a stable model of P.

Proof. Assume that M is a stable model of P' and a model of P. Since $G(P', M)$ and $G(P, M)$ are positive programs and $G(P', M) \subseteq G(P, M)$, it immediately follows that $\mathit{lfp}(T_{G(P',M)}) \subseteq \mathit{lfp}(T_{G(P,M)})$.

Hence, since $M^+ = \mathit{lfp}(T_{G(P',M)})$,

$$M^+ \subseteq \mathit{lfp}(T_{G(P,M)}).$$

Since M is a model of P, by Lemma 2, it follows that

$$\mathit{lfp}(T_{G(P,M)}) \subseteq M^+.$$

So $M^+ = \mathit{lfp}(T_{G(P,M)})$, and, by definition of stability, M is a stable model of P. □

2 Revision by transformation

If a logic program does not have a stable model, there is an incongruity between its model-theoretical and its proof-theoretical interpretation, making it impossible to use syntactical information to select between the minimal models of the program. We will, however, try to make use of such syntactical information *as much as possible* by trying to find well-behaved syntactical *adaptations* of the program. This approach we will call a revision-by-transformation approach.

2.1 Shifting as program transformation

The transformations we are primarily interested in are the so-called *shift operations* as proposed by [Sch93] and [JDM94] and transformations by taking (logical) contrapositives of rules, like introduced by [GM90] and [WB93].

In [Sch93] and [JDM94] a *shift operation* simply moves a positive literal c from the head of a disjunctive rule to its body, where it is added as $\neg c$.

While shift operations have been used to transform positive disjunctive data/-bases into normal programs, *contrapositives*, as introduced in [GM90] and further studied in [WB93], have been used to extend the stable model semantics within the class of normal logic programs. Clearly, taking a contrapositive of a rule is a bi-directional generalization of the afore-mentioned shift operation.

In this section we will study the transformational power of such (generalized) shift operations. So we will ask if it is true that for every normal program we can find a shifted variant having a stable model? And if not, which extensions of this shift operation can be found that indeed are successful?

First of all, we will introduce (*bi-directional*) shift operations, slightly generalizing the notion of shift operations introduced in [JDM94] and [Sch93], but applying them to normal rules. This generalization identifies shift-operations and taking contrapositives:

Definition 5 Shifting.
Let r be a rule of some normal program P. Then every *normal rule* r' is said to be the result of *shifting* r, denoted as $r' \in \mathit{Shift}(r)$, if r' is the result of

- moving a positive literal from $hd(r)$ to the body of r and negating it

and/or

- moving a negative literal from $body(r)$ to the head of r and negating it

and subsequently simplifying the resulting rule.

For example, given the rule

$$r:\; a \leftarrow \neg a, \neg b, c$$

the following rules occur in $\mathit{Shift}(r)$:

$a \leftarrow \neg b, c$ (shifting $\neg a$ and simplifying)
$b \leftarrow \neg a, c$ (shifting a and $\neg b$ and simplifying)
$\bot \leftarrow \neg a, \neg b, c$ (shifting a and simplifying)

Note that we do not restrict shifting operations to take place in the head-body direction (uni-directional shifts), like in [JDM94] and [Sch93] but that we also allow for moving literals the other way around.

Let $\mathit{Shift}(P)$ denote the set of normal programs that can be obtained from P by applying zero or more shift operations to the rules of P. It is immediate that for every $P' \in \mathit{Shift}(P)$ we have $Mod(P') = Mod(P)$, i.e. shifted versions of a program are classically equivalent. And, as an immediate consequence, we also have that their *minimal models* are identical:

Proposition 6. *For every logic program P and every $P' \in Shift(P)$, $MinMod(P) = MinMod(P')$.*

It is easy to show that the set of stable models of P is not preserved in shifting P:

Example 1. Consider the following program

$$\begin{aligned} P:\ & b \leftarrow \neg a \\ & c \leftarrow \neg b \\ & a \leftarrow \neg c \end{aligned}$$

Note that $Stable(P) = \emptyset$.
But take the following program $P' \in Shift(P)$:

$$\begin{aligned} P:\ & b \leftarrow \neg a \\ & c \leftarrow \neg b \\ & c \leftarrow \neg a \end{aligned}$$

Then $Stable(P') = \{\neg a, b, c\}$.

Remark. This result shows that, in principle, with our generalized shifting operation we can extend the stable semantics for more programs than Schaerf was able to do, since we also allow for extensions of this semantics ***within*** the class of normal programs.

The big problem, however, is whether such extensions ***always*** can be found, i.e., given a programs P such that $Stable(P) = \emptyset$, -does there ***always*** exist a successful shifting of P to P', i.e. does there alway exist some $P' \in Shift(P)$ such that $Stable(P') \neq \emptyset$?

2.2 The limitations of shifting

In this section we investigate the power of shifting in extending the stable model semantics. In this context, we will define the notion of a successful transformation method:

Definition 7 Successful Transformation.
We say that a transformation method T is ***successful*** for the class of normal programs $\mathcal{P}_{normal}$ iff for every classically consistent program $P \in \mathcal{P}_{normal}$ there exists a normal program $P' \in T(P)$ such that $Stable(P') \neq \emptyset$.

It is not difficult to come up with a principal limitation of our generalized form of (bi-directional) shifting:

Proposition 8. *Shifting is not successful for $\mathcal{P}_{normal}$.*

Proof. Take the following program:

$$P: \quad b \leftarrow \neg a$$
$$a \leftarrow b$$
$$b \leftarrow a$$

The unique (classical) model of P is $M = \{a, b\}$. Since $Mod(P) = Mod(P')$ for every $P' \in Shift(P)$, if there is a stable model of some $P' \in Shift(P)$, it should be equal to M.

Note, however, that for each normal $P' \in Shift(P)$, we have

$$G(P', M) \subseteq \{a \leftarrow b, b \leftarrow a\}$$

Hence, $lfp(T_{G(P',M)}) = \emptyset \neq M^+$ and M cannot be stable. □

Therefore, shifting is not sufficient to provide a nearly-stable model for every normal program.

This should not come as a surprise: intuitively, the program P specified above states by combining the first and third rule that b should be considered as true. Hence, by the second rule, a should be true as well. This conclusion cannot be drawn by taking contrapositives alone and requires another form of (limited) propositional deduction.

3 Condensing programs

In this section we will discuss another operation on a logic program that can be used to modify the proof-theoretical information without affecting the model-theoretical meaning. We will call this operation ***condensing a program*** since it has the effect of removing literals from the rules making up the program. These literals may be removed from some clauses as long as they do not affect the classical meaning of the program. A condensation[4] then of a program P, denoted by $Condens(P)$, is a program in which every rule of P occurs, except for the removal of some literals in the head or body of the rule.

We will show that the combination of shift and condensation operations is a successful transformation for normal logic programs with respect to the stable model semantics. But first we need to introduce some preliminaries.

Definition 9 Condensation.
A set of clauses $\mathcal{C}'$ is said to be a *condensation* of a set of clauses $\mathcal{C}$ iff $\mathcal{C}'$ is an inclusion minimal set of clauses such that

1. for every clause $C \in \mathcal{C}$ there exists a clause $C' \in \mathcal{C}'$ such that $C' \subseteq C$ and
2. $Mod(\mathcal{C}) = Mod(\mathcal{C}')$.

[4] This notion is related to the notion of a condensation of a clause as discussed in [GG93], but not identical. In this latter article, a condensation relation is a relation between two clauses instead of sets of clauses.

Remember that, if a program P' is related to P by shift operations, then $C(P) = C(P')$.

Definition 10 Shiftcondens Operations.
We say that a program P' can be obtained from a program P by *shiftcondens operations*, abbreviated as $P' \in \mathit{ShiftCondens}(P)$, if $C(P')$ is a condensation of $C(P)$.

It is often useful to consider *extreme* condensations of clauses and programs:

Definition 11 Maximal Condensation.
A set of clauses $\mathcal{C}'$ is a *maximal condensation* of a set of clauses $\mathcal{C}$ iff

1. $\mathcal{C}'$ is a condensation of $\mathcal{C}$ and
2. $\mathcal{C}'$ is *maximally condensed*, i.e. for every condensation $\mathcal{C}''$ of $\mathcal{C}'$, $\mathcal{C}'' = \mathcal{C}'$.

Analogously, a program P is called *maximally condensed* iff $C(P)$ is a maximally condensed set of clauses and $C'(P)$ is a *maximal condensation* of P if $C'(P)$ is a maximal condensation of $C(P)$.

The following result shows that maximal condensations of P can be obtained by using prime implicates of $C(P)$:

Proposition 12. *Let $\Pi(P)$ denote a smallest set of prime-implicates*[5] *of $C(P)$ such that for every $C \in C(P)$ there is a prime implicate C' of $C(P)$ with*

- *$C' \subseteq C$ and*
- *$C' \in \Pi(P)$.*

Then $\Pi(P)$ is a maximal condensation of $C(P)$.

Proof. We first prove that $Mod(C(P)) = Mod(\Pi(P))$. Then, from the definition of $\Pi(P)$, it is clear that $\Pi(P)$ is a condensation of $C(P)$.

Since $\Pi(P)$ is a set of prime implicates, it is immediate that $Mod(P) \subseteq Mod(\Pi(P))$. Since for every $C \in C(P)$ there is a prime implicate C' such that $C' \subseteq C$, it follows that $C' \models C$. Hence, $Mod(\Pi(P)) \subseteq Mod(C(P))$. So, $Mod(C(P)) = Mod(\Pi(P))$.

Finally, we have to show that $\Pi(P)$ is a maximal condensation.

But that is immediate, since any condensation $\Pi'(P)$ of $\Pi(P)$ different from $\Pi(P)$, would contain a clause C'' that is a strict subset of a prime implicate C' occurring in $\Pi(P)$. Then, since $Mod(C(P)) = Mod(\Pi(P)) = Mod(\Pi'(P))$, $C(P) \models C''$, contradicting the minimality of the prime implicate C. □

A nice property of maximal condensations we will need in the next section is that in every positive clause C of $\Pi(P)$ every atom $c \in C$ occurs in at least one minimal model M of P that also minimally satisfies C:

[5] Remember that C is a prime implicate of a set of clauses $\mathcal{C}$ iff C is a minimal clause such that $\mathcal{C} \models C$

Observation 13. *For every positive clause C in $\Pi(P)$ and for every atom c in C there exists at least one minimal model M of P such that M minimally satisfies C and M makes c true.*

Proof. Let C be an arbitrary positive clause in $\Pi(P)$ and c an arbitrary positive literal $c \in C$.

If c would be false in every minimal model M of P, c would be false in every model of P, hence c would not occur in any prime implicate of $C(P)$, and therefore, c would not occur in $\Pi(P)$; contradiction.

So there exists at least one minimal model M of P, such that $M \models c$.

Suppose that for every M satisfying $c \in C$, M would also satisfy at least one other literal in C. Then $C - \{c\}$ would be an implicate of $C(P)$, contradicting the fact that C is a prime implicate of $C(P)$. □

This property will be used in the next section to show that given an arbitrary (consistent) normal program P, we can construct a normal program P' from $\Pi(P)$ such that (i) $P' \in \mathit{ShiftCondens}(P)$ and (ii) $\mathit{Stable}(P') \neq \emptyset$.

3.1 Constructing stable models for maximally condensed logic programs

In this section we will show that condensing + shifting is successful for every class of programs with respect to the stable semantics.

The construction idea we will use can be summarized as follows:

1. We assume to be given a maximal condensation $\Pi = \Pi(P)$ of an arbitrary consistent normal program P.
2. From $\Pi(P)$ we construct a normal program P' and a stable model M'.
3. We show that $C(P') = \Pi(P)$, i.e. the model-theoretical interpretations of P' and P are identical.

Since for every logic program P there exists a maximal condensation $\Pi(P)$ of P, this shows that for every program P there exists a program $P' \in \mathit{Shift}(P)$ such that P' has a stable model.

As an important corollary, we note that shift operations are successful for the class of maximally condensed logic programs.

The method we will present constructs P' and M' in a finite number of stages $i = 0, 1, \ldots, n$. At every stage i, $i \geq 0$, the currently partial realization of P' is denoted as P^i and the (partial) model associated with P^i as M^i.

We will show that:

Claim 1 At every stage i, M^i will be a stable model of P^i and a partial model of Π, i.e. there exists at least one complete extension M of M^i which is a model of Π.

Claim 2 After a finite number of stages, P^i will be a member of $\mathit{Shift}(\Pi)$ and M' will be a stable model of P'.

The stages themselves are defined as follows:

At Stage 0, let $P^0 = \emptyset$ and $M^0 = \emptyset$. Since M^0 is a stable model of P^0 and M^0 is extendible to a model M of Π, Claim 1 holds for Stage 0.

At Stage $i+1$, proceeding inductively, we have at our disposal a partial model M^i of Π, which is also a stable model of P^i, where $P^i \in \mathit{Shift}(\Pi')$, for some subset Π' of Π.

Then we consider a set of clauses $\Pi^{i+1} = R(\Pi, M^i)$, derived from Π and M^i as follows:

1. remove every *clause* C' from Π containing a literal c such that $M^i \models c$,
2. remove in the remaining clauses C', every *literal* c such that $M^i \models \neg c$;
3. let the resulting set of clauses be Σ^{i+1} and construct a set Π^{i+1} of maximally condensed clauses from Σ^{i+1}.

Note that, since M^i has an extension M satisfying Π, Σ^{i+1} and Π^{i+1} must be satisfiable.

We distinguish two cases:

Case 1. Π^{i+1} does not contain any positive clause.

By Lemma 3, $M_{neg} = \neg(\mathit{Atoms}(\Pi) - \mathit{Atoms}(P^i))$, is a stable model of Π^{i+1}. Note that $C(P^i) \subseteq \Pi$. Let $P'' \in \mathit{Normal}(\Pi - C(P^i))$ be an arbitrary normal program, $P^{i+1} = P^i \cup P''$ and $M^{i+1} = M^i \cup M_{neg}$.

We will show that

(a) M^{i+1} is a stable model P^{i+1}

(b) $P^{i+1} \in \mathit{Shift}(\Pi)$

This implies that Stage i is a final stage, $M' = M^{i+1}$ and $P' = P^{i+1}$, proving Claim 1+2.

Ad (a)

By assumption, M^i is a stable model of P^i, and since, for every atom $a \in (\mathit{Atoms}(\Pi) - \mathit{Atoms}(P^i)$, $M^{i+1} \models \neg a$, it follows that M^{i+1} is a stable model of P^i.

By Lemma 4, it suffices to show that $M^{i+1} \models P^{i+1} - P^i$. Let $r \in P^{i+1} - P^i$ and let $C(r) = \{c_1, c_2, \ldots, c_m\}$. If there exists some subset C' of $C(r)$ in Σ^{i+1}, then, clearly, $M_{neg} \models C'$ and therefore $M_{neg} \models C(r)$, so, clearly, $M^{i+1} \models r$.

So suppose, there exists no subset $C' \subseteq C(r)$ in Σ^{i+1}. Then, since $C(r) \in \Pi$, by construction of Σ^{i+1}, $C(r)$ contains a literal l such that $M^i \models l$. Hence, $M^i \models r$ and therefore, $M^{i+1} \models r$.

We conclude that $M^{i+1} \models P^{i+1} - P^i$.

Ad (b)

trivial, by construction of P^{i+1}.

Case 2. Π^{i+1} contains at least one positive clause $C'' = \{c_1, \ldots, c_k\}$.

Since Π^{i+1} is a maximally condensed set, by Observation 13, there is a minimal model M_m of Π^{i+1}, making c_1 true and every c_j, $j \geq 2$ false.

Let $C' \supseteq C''$ be a clause in Σ^{i+1} from which C'' has been derived and

$$C = \{c_1, \ldots, c_k, c_{k+1}, \ldots, c_m\}$$

be the clause in Π from which C' has been derived.
Consider the following rule $r(C)$ to be added to P^i to form the program P^{i+1}:

$$r(C) = c_1 \leftarrow \bar{c_2}, \ldots, \bar{c_k}, \bar{c}_{k+1}, \ldots, \bar{c}_m$$

Let $M^{i+1} = M^i \cup \{c_1, \bar{c_2}, \ldots, \bar{c}_m\}$. Now we have to prove that:
(a) M^{i+1} is a stable model of P^{i+1}.
(b) there is at least one extension M of M^{i+1} such that M is a model of Π.
These claims are easy to prove:
Ad (a)
By assumption, M^i is a stable model of P^i. Note that C cannot contain literals c_i such that $M^i \models c_i$. For then, C would have been removed from Π and C'' would not occur in Π^i.
Hence, M^{i+1} is a consistent set of literals. Also note that $c_1 \notin Atoms(P^i)$, hence,

$$G(P^{i+1}, M^{i+1}) = G(P^i, M^i) \cup \{c_1 \leftarrow\}$$

implying that

$$lfp(T_{G(P^{i+1},M^{i+1})}) = lfp(T_{G(P^i,M^i)}) \cup \{c_1\} = (M^{i+1})^+$$

and therefore, M^{i+1} is a stable model of P^{i+1}.
Ad (b)
By definition of M_m, $M_m \cup M^i$ is a model of Π and by construction of M^{i+1}, $M_m \cup M^i$ extends M^{i+1}.

Finally, note that at the end of Stage $i+1$, either

$$C(P^{i+1}) = \Pi(P)$$

or

$$C(P^i) \subset C(P^{i+1}) \subset \Pi(P) \text{ and } C(P^{i+1}) - C(P^i) \neq \emptyset.$$

This means that after a finite number of stages, the construction of P' is completed.

From the properties of this construction, the following result can be easily derived:

Lemma 14. *For every consistent maximally condensed set of clauses Π, there is a normal program $P' \in Shift(\Pi)$, such that $Stable(P') \neq \emptyset$.*

The procedure given in Figure 3.1 is a succinct description of our method to find a nearly-stable model of a normal program P: We present a number of examples to illustrate the application of the method described above.

---

input: the set $\Pi = \Pi(P)$.
output: a transformation $P' \in \mathit{ShiftCondens}(P)$ and a stable model M of P'.
begin

Let $j := 0$
Let $P^j := \emptyset$; let $M^j := \emptyset$; Let $\Pi^j := \Pi$
while Π^j contains a positive clause C containing c_1 derived from
some $C^0 = \{c_1, c_2, \ldots, c_m\} \in \Pi$
$r := c_1 \leftarrow \bar{c}_2, \ldots, \bar{c}_m$;
$P^{j+1} := P^j + r$;
$M^{j+1} := M^j \cup \{c_1, \bar{c}_2, \ldots, \bar{c}_m\}$;
$\Pi^{j+1} := R(\Pi, M^j)$
$j := j + 1$
wend
Let $P'' \in \mathit{Normal}(\Pi - C(P^j))$;
$M' := M^j$;
$P' := P^j \cup P''$
return (P', M');

end;

Fig. 1. Finding a suitable transformation of a normal program P

Example 2. Consider the following program:

$$P: \quad b \leftarrow \neg a$$
$$c \leftarrow \neg b$$
$$a \leftarrow \neg c$$

Since $\mathit{Stable}(P) = \emptyset$, we transform P into a set of clauses

$$C(P) = \{\{a, b\}, \{b, c\}, \{c, a\}\}.$$

Now $\Pi = \Pi(P) = C(P)$.

Note that Π^0 contains a positive clause $\{c, a\}$; so we let P^1 contain the rule

$$r = c \leftarrow \neg a$$

and then

$$M^1 = \{c, \neg a\}$$

Now the clauses $\{a, c\}$ and $\{b, c\}$ can be removed from Π^0 and a can be removed from the remaining clause $\{a, b\}$. Therefore,

$$\Pi^1 = \Sigma^1 = \{b\}$$

Since $\{b\}$ has been derived from $\{a, b\}$, P^2 will include the rule $b \leftarrow \neg a$ and $M^2 = \{b, c, \neg a\}$.

Note that now $\Sigma^3 = \emptyset$ *and therefore, does not contain a positive clause. Now* $\Pi - C(P^2) = \{b, c\}$. *So, let* $P'' = \{c \leftarrow \neg b\}$. *Then*

$$\begin{aligned} P' &= P^2 \cup \{c \leftarrow \neg b\} \\ &= \{c \leftarrow \neg a,\ b \leftarrow \neg a,\ c \leftarrow \neg b\} \end{aligned}$$

and $M' = \{b, c, \neg a\}$ *is a stable model of* P'.

Example 3. Consider the following normal program P, *containing a constraint:*

$$\begin{aligned} \bot &\leftarrow c, \neg a \\ c &\leftarrow \neg b, d \\ d &\leftarrow \\ b &\leftarrow a \end{aligned}$$

Note that P *does not have a stable model. We transform* P *into an equivalent set of clauses*

$$C(P) = \{\{\neg c, a\}, \{c, b, \neg d\}, \{d\}, \{b, \neg a\}\}.$$

Now

$$\Pi = \Pi^0 = \Pi(P) = \{\{\neg c, a\}, \{b\}, \{d\}\}.$$

Let us take the rule $r : b \leftarrow$ *to form* P^1. *Then* $M^1 = \{b\}$. *In the construction of* $R(\Pi, M^1)$, *we can remove the clause* $\{b\}$. *Hence,*

$$Pi^1 = \Sigma^1 = \{\{\neg c, a\}, \{d\}\}.$$

Next, we select $\{d\}$, *since it is positive and so*

$$P^2 = \{b \leftarrow,\ d \leftarrow\}.$$

Then $M^2 = \{b, d\}$ *and* $\Pi^2 = \Sigma^2 = \{\neg c, a\}$. *Note that this set of clauses does not contain a positive clause. Now* $\Pi - C(P^2) = \{\neg c, a\}$. *Choose* $P'' = \{\bot \leftarrow c, \neg a\}$. *Then*

$$\begin{aligned} P' &= P^2 \cup \{\bot \leftarrow c, \neg a\} \\ &= \{b \leftarrow,\ d \leftarrow,\ \bot \leftarrow c, \neg a\} \end{aligned}$$

and $M' = \{b, d, \neg a, \neg c, \}$. *It is easy to see that indeed* M' *is a stable model of* $P' \in CondensShift(P)$.

As an easy consequence we have the following theorem:

Theorem 15 Existence of nearly-stable models.
Every normal program has a nearly-stable model.

Here, we do allow constraints to occur normal programs, but require, of course, the program to be consistent.

4 Discussion

We have discussed some methods to adapt the proof-theoretical semantics of normal logic programs in such a way that in every such a program syntax-dependent information can be used to select a model or a subset of models from a set of models already provided by the model-theoretical interpretation of the program. Basically, these methods extend existing proof-theoretical semantics by allowing for small changes in the syntactical form of the rules involved, without affecting the meaning of the program as a first-order theory.

We have shown that with this goal in mind, ***shift operations*** as a transformation technique are too weak and have to be extended by ***condensations***, i.e. the removal of literals from some rules. These removals also are the result of limited propositional reasoning applied to the program as a first-order theory and they result in a simplification of the rules as inference rules. Together with shifting, this latter operation can be used to provide every consistent normal program with a so-called nearly-stable model.

Since the so-called ShiftCondens operations, when applied to a consistent program P, result in a classically equivalent program P', both programs have the same set of *minimal* models. Since every stable model is a minimal model, this implies that the nearly-stable models of P are also minimal models of P.

Clearly, if we require transformations of P to be minimal transformations, not every minimal model can occur as a nearly-stable model of P. For example, consider the program $P : a \leftarrow \neg b \ , \ \bot \leftarrow \neg c$. Its minimal models are $M_1 = \{a, \neg b, c\}$ and $M_2 = \{\neg a, b, c\}$. If we only allow minimal transformations, M_2 is the unique nearly-stable model of P.

The analysis of minimal transformations and the characterization of nearly-stable models associated with them will be subject of subsequent research.

5 Acknowledgement

I am indebted to Wiktor Marek to pointing out to me the relationship between an earlier idea about revision by transformation and the approach of Marco Schaerf. I am grateful to Marco Schaerf for sending me a recent version of his paper.

References

[Doy79] J. Doyle. A truth maintenance system. *Artificial Intelligence*, 12, 1979.

[GG93] C. G. Fermüller G. Gottlob. Removing redundancy from a clause. *Artificial Intelligence*, 61:263–289, 1993.

[GL88] M. Gelfond and V. Lifschitz. The stable model semantics for logic programming. In *Fifth International Conference Symposium on Logic Programming*, pages 1070–1080, 1988.

[GM90] L. Giordano and A. Martelli. Generalized stable models, truth maintenance and conflict resolution. In D. Warren and P. Szeredi, editors, *Proceedings of the 7th International Conference on Logic Programming*, pages 427–441, 1990.

[JDM94] G. Gottlob J. Dix and V. Marek. Causal models of disjunctive logic programs. In *Proceedings of the Tenth International Conference on Logic Programming ICLP'94*, 1994.

[Llo87] J. W. Lloyd. *Foundations of Logic Programming*. Springer Verlag, Heidelberg, 1987.

[MT93] V. W. Marek and M. Truszczyński. *Nonmonotonic Logic*. Springer Verlag, Heidelberg, 1993.

[Sch93] M. Schaerf. Negation and minimality in non-horn databases. In C. Beeri, editor, *Proceedings of the Twelfth Conference on Principles of Database Systems (PODS-93)*, pages 147–157. ACM-Press, 1993.

[WB93] C. Witteveen and G. Brewka. Skeptical reason maintenance and belief revision. *Artificial Intelligence*, 61:1–36, 1993.

[Wit94] C. Witteveen. Shifting and condensing normal logic programs and disjunctive databases. Technical Report TWI 94-100, Delft University, 1994.

Logic Programming with Assumption Denial*

Jia-Huai You and Li Yan Yuan

Department of Computing Science, University of Alberta
Edmonton, Alberta, Canada T6G 2H1
{you, yuan}@cs.ualberta.ca

Abstract. We present a framework of logic programming using an explicit representation of defeats of assumptions, called *assumption denials*. We study semantics for extended, disjunctive, and extended disjunctive programs, all in the same framework. The framework is based on a fixpoint operator over "uninterpreted programs", and semantics for various kinds of programs are then defined simply by adding appropriate constraint clauses. For extended programs, we present a skeptical semantics that is tractable, and a credulous semantics which is a natural extension of a number of equivalent semantics proposed for normal programs. The generality of this framework is further evidenced by its ability to define semantics for disjunctive programs in terms of non-disjunctive programs. This reveals a relationship between disjunctive programs and non-disjunctive programs, which is known previously to be false in some other formalisms.

1 Introduction

Human reasoning often involves an explicit process of defeating assumptions. For example, suppose we use the clause

$$on \leftarrow \mathbf{not}\, broken$$

to express our knowledge about lights on. If, matter-of-factly, we find out that its opposite is true, expressed by $on^{\sim}$, then we will not assume **not** *broken*, since it will cause a contradiction in our reasoning. In this case we say that the assumption **not** *broken* is *defeated*. The defeat of the assumption is not because we believe *broken* (we really do not know if it is indeed broken). This is different from the typical process of making assumptions in nonmonotonic reasoning, which is characterized by "if there is no evidence to the contrary," where *evidence to the contrary* is usually realized by deriving the contrary.

One finds out the reasons (assumptions) that caused a contradiction by looking into one's own knowledge (program clauses). In our example this can be viewed as employing a *contrapositive*:

$$(\mathbf{not}\, broken)^{\sim} \leftarrow on^{\sim}$$

* This paper is based on the technical report, "Abductive logic programming with assumption denials," ISIS-RR-93-19E, Fujitsu Laboratories, 1993. The work of the first author was performed while visiting ISIS, Fujitsu Laboratories Ltd.

which expresses under what conditions an assumption is defeated. We call an object like (**not** *broken*)$^\sim$ *an assumption denial*, and a clause of the above form *an assumption denial clause*. They are *induced* (or, *compiled*, if one desires) from a given program. Thus our reasoning with two kinds of negation is in fact based on, syntactically, a normal program where all explicitly negated atoms and assumptions are treated as distinct propositions.

This explicit representation of assumption defeat leads to a very general framework in which a variety of semantics can be investigated using different formulations of *acceptability*. The most general formulation of acceptability has been the acceptability relation as given in [KMD94]. Here we employ a particular mechanism of acceptability. A reasoning agent accepts a set A of assumptions if it is *undefeated* under a weak notion of stability. Briefly, given a program P, with B being the set of the assumptions whose atomic counterparts are not derivable from $P \cup A$, if A turns out to be exactly the set of assumptions whose atomic counterparts are not derivable by $P \cup B$, then A should indeed be considered undefeated and hence acceptable. Such a set has been called an *alternating fixpoint* [BS91, Gel89].

Not all alternating fixpoints are intuitive. A subclass, called *normal alternating fixpoints*, is identified [Yua94], and subsequently shown to coincide with a number of promising semantic frameworks for normal programs [YY95]. These include 3-valued stable models [Prz90a, Prz90b], complete scenarios [Dun91], P-stable models [SZ91], three-valued grounded models [WB93], and a subclass of stable classes [BS92]. *Stationary default extensions* defined in [PP91] are also normal alternating fixpoints in a broader context.

In this paper we propose a framework and study its semantics, as well as the properties under these semantics, to accommodate this type of reasoning. We summarize our findings below.

1. The normal alternating fixpoints of an extended program, a normal program in syntax, along with its assumption denial clauses, yield an elegant semantic structure whose least element serves as a skeptical semantics, which we call the *skeptical denial semantics*, and whose maximal elements define a credulous semantics, called the *credulous denial semantics*.
2. The skeptical denial semantics is tractable (bounded by $O(n^3)$). Although tractability is a major advantage for the well-founded semantics, this advantage is lost in some extensions to accommodate explicit negation, e.g., computing the *contradiction removal semantics* [PAA91a] is NP-hard [WB93, WJ93]. This dramatic change in complexity has made tractability an interesting question for extended programs.
3. The credulous denial semantics is a natural extension of the five equivalent extensions to the stable model semantics, i.e., the regular semantics [YY94], the partial stable model semantics [SZ90], the preferential semantics [Dun91], a restricted version of the stable class semantics [BS92], and the semantics based on $\leq_k$-maximal 3-valued stable models [Prz90a]. Recent studies by Dix [Dix94a, Dix94b] show that these semantics possess a number of desirable properties, categorically termed as *well-behaved*.

4. A number of semantical properties for extended logic programs have been argued desirable, such as the *coherence principle*, [PA93, PAA91b] and *logic programming with exceptions* [KD90]. In the proposed framework, these properties can all be enforced for the proposed semantics by simply adding constraint clauses to a program.
5. In this framework, a disjunctive program can be transformed to a normal program and the credulous semantics of the former can be defined in terms of the existing credulous semantics of the latter. To us, this is a rather interesting and deep fact relating the semantics of disjunctive and non-disjunctive programs. This relationship is known previously not to hold in some other semantic formulations. A similar relationship has been shown to hold for a subclass of locally stratified disjunctive programs, known as *acyclic* disjunctive programs [Dun92]. This result enables query answering procedures for normal programs (cf. [EK88]) to be adapted with relative ease for disjunctive programs.

Our work was inspired by the work on *reason maintenance* [GM90, WB93], where the defeat of an assumption **not** ϕ was represented by a contrapositive with the head ϕ. For the lighs on example, for instance, they would have

$$broken \leftarrow on^{\sim}$$

where the defeat of an assumption **not** *broken* is represented by believing *broken*. This appears to the key problem associated with some of the difficulties encountered in these approaches.

In addition, we should mention that, due to the use of contrapositives to reason backward, the second negation introduced in this paper is different from the notion of *explicit negation* as introduced in [PA92]. This second negation lies somewhere in between explicit negation and classic negation. For lack of an appropriate name, we use the terminology explicit negation to mean that it is not classic negation. As we will show in Subsection 4.1, this difference illustrates an advantage of our approach, since, with the introduction of explicit negation, some obvious queries cannot be answered properly without contrapositives.

From the next section we start describing notation conventions, followed by the technical exploration of the results sketched above.

2 Notation Conventions

We assume a language L that contains three classes of objects: H_L is a collection of *individuals* $\phi, \varphi^{\sim}, \ldots$; $L_{\mathbf{not}}$ is a collection of *assumptions* of the form $\mathbf{not}\,\phi$, $\phi \in H_L$; and $L_{\mathbf{not}^{\sim}}$ is a collection of *assumption denials* taking the form $(\mathbf{not}\,\phi)^{\sim}$, $\phi \in H_L$. These are only *syntactic* elements in the language. Only for the purpose of references, elements in H_L are called (objective) *literals*. We use L to denote the collection of all these syntactic objects.

Any subset of $L_{\mathbf{not}}$ is called *an assumption set*.

Normal, extended, disjunctive, extended disjunctive programs are defined as usual. Clauses in these programs are called *program clauses.* We sometimes denote a program clause by $\alpha \leftarrow \beta, \gamma$ where α is the set of literals in the head of the clause, β is the set of literals in the body, and γ the set of assumptions in the body.

In addition, we allow non-program clauses, called *arbitrary clauses* (also called *constraint clauses*), which are of the form $\phi \leftarrow \varphi_1, ..., \varphi_n$, where $n \geq 0$ and ϕ and φ_j's are arbitrary elements from L.

We define a derivation relation $\vdash_d$ as follows. Let Π be a set of arbitrary clauses and Φ be a set of assumptions. $\Pi \cup \Phi \vdash_d \zeta$, for any $\zeta \in L$, iff (i) $\zeta \in \Phi$, or (ii) there is a clause $(\zeta \leftarrow) \in \Pi$, or inductively, there is a clause $\zeta \leftarrow B \in \Pi$ such that $\Pi \cup \Phi \vdash_d \xi$, for each $\xi \in B$.

3 The Framework: Uninterpreted

The fundamental idea in the proposed framework is that semantics for various kinds of logic programs may be expressed syntactically: specify an acceptability operator and then obtain a semantics by adding constraint clauses. In this section, we specify a particular acceptability operator.

Let Π be a set of arbitrary clauses and S an assumption set. We define an operator $\mathcal{F}_\Pi$ over assumption sets as:

$$\mathcal{F}_\Pi(S) = \{\textbf{not}\,\phi \in L_{\textbf{not}} \mid \Pi \cup S \not\vdash_d (\textbf{not}\,\phi)^\sim\}.$$

It is said to be *restricted to* P *for* $P \subseteq \Pi$ when $\mathcal{F}_\Pi(S) = \{\textbf{not}\,\phi \mid \Pi \cup S \not\vdash_d (\textbf{not}\,\phi)^\sim, \phi$ occurs in $P\}$. This restrictive clause can be applied to any set of assumptions. This corresponds to the usual abductive framework (e.g. [BTK93, KM90]) where a set of assumptions is given as a parameter to an abductive system. In this paper whenever there is a need, we specify such a set to avoid confusion (and to avoid listing irrelevant assumptions in examples, too).

Definition 1. An operator $\mathcal{A}$ is called *anti-monotonic* if for S_1 and S_2, $S_1 \subseteq S_2$ implies $\mathcal{A}(S_2) \subseteq \mathcal{A}(S_1)$.

Baral and Subrahmanian [BS91] show that this property holds for an operator, similar to $\mathcal{F}_\Pi$, over normal logic programs. Here we extend this result to arbitrary clauses where the head of a clauses may be an assumption. This extension is the basis for the assumption denial framework.

Proposition 2.
$\mathcal{F}_\Pi$ is anti-monotonic and $\mathcal{F}_\Pi^2$ is monotonic.

Proof. Let S_1 and S_2 be two assumption sets such that $S_1 \subseteq S_2$. Let also $W_1 = \{\phi \mid \Pi \cup S_1 \vdash_d \phi\}$ and $W_2 = \{\phi \mid \Pi \cup S_2 \vdash_d \phi\}$. Since $\vdash_d$ is monotonic, we have $W_1 \subseteq W_2$. It follows that for any $(\textbf{not}\,\phi)^\sim \notin W_2$, we have $(\textbf{not}\,\phi)^\sim \notin W_1$. Therefore, for any $(\textbf{not}\,\phi) \in \mathcal{F}_\Pi(S_2)$, we have $(\textbf{not}\,\phi) \in \mathcal{F}_\Pi(S_1)$. That is, $\mathcal{F}_\Pi(S_2) \subseteq \mathcal{F}_\Pi(S_1)$. Hence, $\mathcal{F}_\Pi^2(S_1) \subseteq \mathcal{F}_\Pi^2(S_2)$. □

The set of all subsets of assumptions with set inclusion forms a complete lattice. From the fact that $\mathcal{F}_{\Pi}^2$ is monotonic we know that $\mathcal{F}_{\Pi}^2$ possesses a unique least fixpoint, possibly among others. It is also known that the set of maximal fixpoints is nonempty.

Definition 3. Let Π be a set of arbitrary clauses and S be an assumption set. S is said to be a *fixpoint* of Π iff $\mathcal{F}_{\Pi}(S) = S$. S is an *alternating fixpoint* of Π iff $\mathcal{F}_{\Pi}^2(S) = S$. S is a *normal alternating fixpoint* of Π iff it is an alternating fixpoint of Π that also satisfies the condition $S \subseteq \mathcal{F}_{\Pi}(S)$.

Now one can write a program of arbitrary clauses and compute its least normal alternating fixpoint or maximal normal alternating fixpoints as its "semantics". However, so far *no* construct of the language has been interpreted semantically. In the next few sections we will see that the intended semantics of default and explicit negation can be interpreted by adding assumption denial clauses and other constraint clauses of the language.

4 Extended Logic Programming

We show here that a set of basic *(assumption) denial clauses* (*d-constraints*) is sufficient to define the well-known semantic structure for normal programs. For extended programs, an additional set of constraints is sufficient to resolve contradictions.

Definition 4. The *set of the basic d-constraints* of language L, denoted $\mathcal{D}_L$, is defined as $\mathcal{D}_L = \{(\mathbf{not}\,\phi)^\sim \leftarrow \phi \mid \phi \in H_L\}$.

In the sequel, for the purpose of including the symmetric case automatically, any occurrence of $(\varphi^\sim)^\sim$ means φ.

Definition 5. Let $r = \varphi \leftarrow \Phi$ be an arbitrary clause. The set $\mathcal{C}(r)$ of *d-constraints* of r is defined as:

$$\mathcal{C}(r) = \{\xi^\sim \leftarrow \Phi' \mid \Phi' = (\Phi - \{\xi\}) \cup \{\varphi^\sim\},\ \xi \in \Phi\}$$

We denote by $\mathcal{C}_P$ the set of d-constraints for all the clauses in P.

Example 1. Assume $r = c \leftarrow b, \mathbf{not}\,d$. Then $\mathcal{C}(r)$ contains two assumption denial constraints:

$$b^\sim \leftarrow c^\sim, \mathbf{not}\,d; \quad (\mathbf{not}\,d)^\sim \leftarrow c^\sim, b$$

These clauses specify under what conditions an assumption is considered defeated.

Definition 6. Let P be an extended program, S be an assumption set, and $\Pi = P \cup \mathcal{D}_L \cup \mathcal{C}_P$. S is said to be an *undefeated assumption set (UAS)* of P iff it is a normal alternating fixpoint of Π, restricted to P.

The *credulous (assumption) denial semantics* is defined by all maximal (set inclusion) UASs of P, and the *skeptical (assumption) denial semantics* is determined by the least UAS of P.

Example 2. Let P be

$$a \leftarrow \textbf{not}\, b$$
$$a^{\sim} \leftarrow \textbf{not}\, c$$
$$p \leftarrow \textbf{not}\, q$$

There are exactly three UASs (restricted to the assumptions that occur in P): $S_1 = \{\textbf{not}\, q\}$, $S_2 = \{\textbf{not}\, q, \textbf{not}\, b\}$, and $S_3 = \{\textbf{not}\, q, \textbf{not}\, c\}$.

Usually, a credulous semantics is intended to capture as much information as possible. The credulous denial semantics proposed here falls into this category.

Example 3. Consider the following program:

$$have\_car \leftarrow$$
$$drive \leftarrow have\_car, \textbf{not}\, broken$$
$$drive^{\sim} \leftarrow \textbf{not}\, good\_weather$$
$$take\_bus \leftarrow drive^{\sim}$$
$$sightseeing \leftarrow drive, \textbf{not}\, rush$$
$$need\_money \leftarrow drive$$
$$need\_money \leftarrow take\_bus$$

There are exactly two maximal UASs:

$$S_1 = \{\textbf{not}\, broken,\ \textbf{not}\, rush\} \text{ and } S_2 = \{\textbf{not}\, good\_weather,\ \textbf{not}\, rush\}$$

Although there is uncertainty about whether to drive or not, in both cases we need money to buy gas or bus ticket. In the case of driving, we would do sightseeing if time permits.

Definition 7. Let Π be a set of clauses and S be an assumption set. $\Pi \cup S$ is said to be *non-contradictory* iff $\Pi \cup S \not\vdash_d \phi, \phi^{\sim}$ for any $\phi \in L$.

Thus a program P is non-contradictory iff $\Pi \not\vdash_d \phi, \phi^{\sim}$ for any $\phi \in L$.

Proposition 8.
There always exists an undefeated assumption set for any extended program P. $P \cup S$ is non-contradictory whenever P is.

Proof. Since $\mathcal{F}^2_{\Pi}$ is monotonic, the least alternating fixpoint W always exists, independent of whether a program is contradictory or not. Let $\mathcal{F}_{\Pi}(W) = W'$. Since W is an alternating fixpoint, we have $\mathcal{F}_{\Pi}(W') = W$. Hence, W' is also an alternating fixpoint of $\mathcal{F}^2_{\Pi}$. Since W is the least such that $\mathcal{F}^2_{\Pi}(W) = W$, we know $W \subseteq W'$, i.e., $W \subseteq \mathcal{F}_{\Pi}(W)$. Thus W is a UAS.

Now let P be non-contradictory and S be a UAS of P. For the sake of contradiction, suppose $P \cup S \vdash_d \phi, \phi^{\sim}$ for some ϕ. Since P is non-contradictory, we know that $S \neq \emptyset$. It is then easy to see that there exists at least one assumption $(\textbf{not}\, \phi) \in S$, $(\textbf{not}\, \phi)^{\sim}$ can be derived from $P \cup \mathcal{D}_L \cup \mathcal{C}_P \cup S$ and hence $(\textbf{not}\, \phi) \notin \mathcal{F}_{\Pi}(S)$. Thus, $S \not\subseteq \mathcal{F}_{\Pi}(S)$. This contradicts the assumption that S is a UAS of P. Therefore, $P \cup S$ must be non-contradictory. □

Since a normal program is always non-contradictory, d-constraints in $\mathcal{C}_P$ have no effect on defeats of assumptions. That is, for normal programs, the inclusion of only $\mathcal{D}_L$ is sufficient. Hence

Proposition 9.
Let P be a normal program. Then an assumption set S is a normal alternating fixpoint of $P \cup \mathcal{D}_L \cup \mathcal{C}_P$ iff it is a normal alternating fixpoint of $P \cup \mathcal{D}_L$.

The following are based on the results given earlier by the authors in [YY95].

Theorem 10.
The semantics of normal programs, that are based on regular models [YY94], partial stable models [SZ90], or preferred extensions [Dun91], are all equivalent to the one based on maximal UASs.

Theorem 11.
Let P be a normal program and S an assumption set. S is a UAS of P iff $P \cup S$ is a complete scenario iff $M = \langle E_{P \cup S}, S_{lit} \rangle$ is a 3-valued stable model of P, where $S_{lit} = \{\phi \mid \mathbf{not}\, \phi \in S\}$ and $E_{P \cup S} = \{\phi \in H_L \mid P \cup S \vdash_d \phi\}$. Furthermore, S is the least UAS of P iff M is the well-founded model of P.

Example 4. Consider P

$$a \leftarrow \mathbf{not}\, b$$
$$b \leftarrow \mathbf{not}\, a, \mathbf{not}\, b$$

P has exactly two UASs: $S_1 = \{\mathbf{not}\, b\}$ and $S_2 = \emptyset$. S_1 is just a fixpoint and S_2 is not a fixpoint but a normal alternating fixpoint. S_1 corresponds to the 3-valued stable model $\langle \{a\}, \{b\} \rangle$, which is in fact a stable model, and S_2 corresponds to $\langle \emptyset, \emptyset \rangle$.

Let n_1 be the size of H_L and n_2 be the number of their occurrences in P. Observe that (1) the least alternating fixpoint is always equivalent to the least normal alternating fixpoint, (2) the program size, plus $\mathcal{D}_L$ and $\mathcal{C}_P$, is bounded by $O(n_1 \times n_2)$, (3) computing the least UAS requires at most $O(n_1)$ steps, and (4) computing the relation $\vdash_d$ is bounded by the size of the expanded program $O(n_1 \times n_2)$ and it is computed twice in every step. This means computing the least UAS of an extended program is bounded by $O(n_1^2 \times n_2)$. Let input size be $n = n_1 + n_2$. Hence,

Theorem 12.
The least UAS of an extended program can be computed in $O(n^3)$ time.

This analysis also tells us that computing the well-founded model is bounded by $O(n^2)$, a previously known result.

4.1 Contrapositives in positive extended logic programming

A key difference between our explicit negation and the ones in the literature (e.g. [ADP93, BTK93, Dun93, PA93, PAA91a]) lies in the use of contrapositives in our approach. The difference becomes especially clear when dealing with extended programs without assumptions. Let us call these programs *positive extended programs*. In this section, we demonstrate that the use of contrapositives can be considered as an economic though incomplete mechanism to approximate the classic connective of negation.

In logic programming with default negation, it is often said that a program clause is oriented and this orientation is important in reflecting the intuition of the programmer that a program clause is a rule rather than a formula of (material) implication in classic logic. In particular, a program clause does not mean that its contrapositive holds. This has been proven essential in discovering a number of important semantics. For example, the *answer set semantics* [GL90] relies on a transformation, the GL-transformation, to fix the orientation of the clauses, the *static semantics* and its variants [Prz95, Prz91] employ a metalevel operator and a special form of circumscription to enforce the orientation, and the *regular semantics* [YY94] uses explicit justification to reason, within a clause, from the body to the head.

With the introduction of the "classic negation" [GL90], since one is allowed to express negative information, one should be allowed to reason about it. Viewing a clause as completely oriented seems too rigid, and in some cases, it may render a logic programming system inadequate, since it cannot give a correct answer to some obvious queries. Consider, for example

$$\begin{array}{l} parent(x,y) \leftarrow father(x,y) \\ parent(x,y) \leftarrow mother(x,y) \\ \neg parent(mary,john) \leftarrow \end{array}$$

It is just too obvious to conclude that *mary* is not father of *john*, nor mother of *john*. That is, the query $\neg mother(mary, john)$ should be answered *true*. But the answer by the answer set semantics and many other semantics is *unknown*.

What is revealed in this example is that sometimes reasoning in the sense of classical logic is so natural and obvious that if a system fails to do so, there is something that seems strange. Of course, one can use the standard model theoretic semantics for these type of programs, as was done in the static semantics [Prz95]. But it needs a general theorem prover to handle disjunction.

An alternative solution is to approximate the classical connective of negation by adding contrapositives:

$$\begin{array}{l} \neg father(x,y) \leftarrow \neg parent(x,y) \\ \neg mother(x,y) \leftarrow \neg parent(x,y) \end{array}$$

These contrapositives can be stated explicitly by the programmer for individual clauses, or added by a compilation process to enforce it uniformly. Operationally, SLD-resolution can be used with each clause being viewed as a definite clause by renaming each $\neg\phi$ to a new predicate, for example, $\phi^{\sim}$, as we have done in this paper.

This is a straightforward, almost trivial extension of positive logic programming. SLD-resolution is always sound, but not complete.

Note that the explicit negation introduced in this paper is not the same as classic negation: it does not accommodate the induced disjunction, e.g., with $P = \{a \leftarrow b;\ a \leftarrow b^{\sim}\}$, we do not have a. In addition, when a positive extended program is contradictory, the derivation relation $\vdash_d$ is also different from the classic derivation relation.

4.2 Semantic properties enforced by constraints

The generality of the proposed framework lies in its accommodation of arbitrary clauses. Thus any semantic property that can be expressed by arbitrary clauses can be enforced syntactically for the semantics defined within the framework.

• **Contradictory Assumptions:**
To disallow conflicting assumptions $\mathbf{not}\,\varphi$ and $\mathbf{not}\,\varphi^{\sim}$, we add the constraints:

$$\mathcal{N}_P = \{(\mathbf{not}\,\varphi^{\sim})^{\sim} \leftarrow \mathbf{not}\,\varphi \mid (\mathbf{not}\,\varphi) \text{ occurs in } P\}$$

This means whenever $\mathbf{not}\,\varphi$ is assumed $\mathbf{not}\,\phi^{\sim}$ is defeated. Clearly, this guarantees that no $\mathbf{not}\,\phi$ and $\mathbf{not}\,\phi^{\sim}$ may co-exist in any undefeated assumption set.

Example 5. Let P be

$$a \leftarrow \mathbf{not}\, b$$
$$c \leftarrow \mathbf{not}\, b^{\sim}$$

There are three UASs (restricted to the assumptions in P): $S_1 = \emptyset$, $S_2 = \{\mathbf{not}\, b\}$, and $S_3 = \{\mathbf{not}\, b^{\sim}\}$.

• **Coherence Property for Explicit Negation:**
The *coherence principle* as given in [PA93] states that whenever ϕ is believed, $\mathbf{not}\,\phi^{\sim}$ should be assumed. In the current framework, this can be expressed by constraint clauses:

$$\mathcal{H}_P = \{\mathbf{not}\,\phi^{\sim} \leftarrow \phi \mid \phi \text{ occurs in the head of a clause in } P\}$$

Note that $\mathcal{H}_P$ need also be used along with P when answering queries.

• **Witteveen and Brewka's Strong Property for Explicit Negation:**
In [WB93] Witteveen and Brewka argue that for the reason maintenance purposes, a stronger explicit negation[1] is more desirable: it satisfies, whenever $\mathbf{not}\,\phi$ is assumed we have $\phi^{\sim}$, and vice versa. To enforce this property for the

[1] The authors call it the *strong negation*, which confuses with the standard use of this terminology where strong negation implies classic negation [AP92].

semantics defined in this paper, we only need to add, in addition to $\mathcal{N}_P$ and $\mathcal{H}_P$ above, the constraints

$$\mathcal{S}_P = \{\phi^{\sim} \leftarrow \mathbf{not}\,\phi \mid \mathbf{not}\,\phi \text{ occurs in } P\}.$$

- **Logic Programs with Exceptions:**
  In [KD90] the clauses with a negative head are treated as *exceptional rules* which have higher priority to be applied when a contradiction arises. For this, one only need include contrapositives of the clauses with a *positive* head.

5 A Credulous Semantics for Disjunctive Programs

In this section we present a credulous semantics for extended disjunctive programs. We first use an illustrative example.

Example 6. Let $P = \{a \vee b \leftarrow \mathbf{not}\, c;\ a \leftarrow b;\ b \leftarrow a\}$. We may transform P to a non-disjunctive program P^T

$$\begin{aligned} &a \leftarrow \mathbf{not}\, b, \mathbf{not}\, c \\ &b \leftarrow \mathbf{not}\, a, \mathbf{not}\, c \\ &a \leftarrow b \\ &b \leftarrow a \end{aligned}$$

That is, each disjunctive clause is transformed into a number of non-disjunctive clauses by retaining exactly one disjunct in the head and moving all the rest, after negated by **not** , to the body.

It is known that this type of transformation in general yields different semantics. For example, P has one answer set $\{a, b\}$, but P^T's answer set semantics is not defined. It is also known that this transformation preserves semantics for *acyclic* disjunctive programs [Dun92], which is a subclass of locally stratified disjunctive programs.

A careful study reveals an interesting relation between these two programs; the undefeated assumption set $S = \{\mathbf{not}\, c\}$ of P^T may serve as a semantic basis for P in the following sense: using S we obtain, from P, a positive program $P_S = \{a \vee b \leftarrow;\ a \leftarrow b;\ b \leftarrow a\}$, whose standard minimal model semantics is sufficient to determine the beliefs held along with S.

We thus obtain a semantics of a disjunctive program in terms of the maximal UASs of its transformed normal program. To extend the semantics to disjunctive programs with explicit negation, we only need to add appropriate constraint clauses to prevent contradictory beliefs. We use an illustrative example below.

Example 7. Let $P = \{a \vee b \leftarrow \mathbf{not}\, c;\ a^{\sim} \leftarrow\}$. Then P^T consists of

$$\begin{aligned} &a \leftarrow \mathbf{not}\, b, \mathbf{not}\, c \\ &b \leftarrow \mathbf{not}\, a, \mathbf{not}\, c \\ &a^{\sim} \leftarrow \end{aligned}$$

Obviously the d-constraints for the disjunctive program P should include the d-constraints of P^T and $(\mathbf{not}\ c)^{\sim} \leftarrow a^{\sim}, b^{\sim}$ as well, which states if both $a^{\sim}$ and $b^{\sim}$ are believed, **not** c should be defeated.

Let us denote this set by $\mathcal{C}_P^d$ and let $\Pi = P^T \cup \mathcal{D}_L \cup \mathcal{C}_P^d$. Suppose we are interested in the assumptions that occur in P^T. There is only one (maximal) UAS $S = \{\mathbf{not}\ c, \mathbf{not}\ a\}$. The corresponding positive program is $P_S = \{b \leftarrow;\ a^{\sim} \leftarrow\}$.

We now give a more formal treatment.

Definition 13. Let P be an extended disjunctive program. The *disjunction elimination transformation* of P results in an extended program, denoted P^T and is defined as

$$P^T = \{\phi \leftarrow \beta, \gamma' \mid \alpha \leftarrow \beta, \gamma \in P,\ \gamma' = \gamma \cup \mathbf{not}\,(\alpha - \{\phi\}),\ \phi \in \alpha\}.$$

We first define a semantics for disjunctive programs.

Definition 14. Let P be a disjunctive program and $\Pi = P^T \cup \mathcal{D}_L$. An assumption set S is said to be an *undefeated assumption set (UAS)* of P iff S is a normal alternating fixpoint of Π, restricted to P.

Let S be an assumption set and α a literal set. Denote $S(\alpha) = \{\phi \in \alpha \mid \mathbf{not}\,\phi \notin S\}$.

Definition 15. Let P be a disjunctive program and S be a maximal UAS of P. The positive program, denoted P_S and obtained from P using S, is defined as:

$$P_S = \{\alpha' \leftarrow \beta \mid \alpha \leftarrow \beta, \gamma \in P,\ \gamma \subseteq S,\ \alpha' = S(\alpha) \neq \emptyset\}.$$

Example 8. Let P be

$$a \vee b \leftarrow$$
$$a \leftarrow \mathbf{not}\ c$$

Then P^T is

$$a \leftarrow \mathbf{not}\ b$$
$$b \leftarrow \mathbf{not}\ a$$
$$a \leftarrow \mathbf{not}\ c$$

There is only one UAS $S = \{\mathbf{not}\ c, \mathbf{not}\ b\}$. $P_S = \{a \leftarrow\}$.

Obviously, for normal programs the semantics outlined above reduces to the *regular semantics* and its equivalents.

Given an extended disjunctive clause $\alpha \leftarrow \beta, \gamma$, an assumption in γ need be defeated when the opposite of each of the literal in the head is believed. This leads to the next definition.

Definition 16. Let $r = \phi_1 \vee ... \vee \phi_m \leftarrow \Phi$ be an extended disjunctive clause and r^T be the set of clauses resulted from r by the disjunction elimination transformation. The set $\mathcal{C}^d(r)$ of *abductive clauses* of r is defined as $\mathcal{C}^d(r) = \mathcal{C}_{r^T} \cup \mathcal{C}(r)$ where

$$\mathcal{C}(r) = \{\xi^{\sim} \leftarrow \Phi' \mid \Phi' = (\Phi - \{\xi\}) \cup \{\phi_1^{\sim}, ..., \phi_m^{\sim}\},\ \xi \in \Phi\}$$

We denote by $\mathcal{C}_P^d$ the set of constraint clauses for all the clauses in P.

Definition 17. Let P be an extended disjunctive program and $\Pi = P^T \cup \mathcal{D}_L \cup \mathcal{C}_P^d$. An assumption set S is said to be an *undefeated assumption set (UAS)* of P iff S is a normal alternating fixpoint of Π, restricted to P.

The minimal model semantics of P_S determines the beliefs held along with S. Thus, the *credulous denial semantics* of P is defined by all maximal UASs of P.

Example 9. Let P be

$$a \vee b \leftarrow$$
$$c \leftarrow \textbf{not}\ a$$

with P^T consisting of

$$a \leftarrow \textbf{not}\ b$$
$$b \leftarrow \textbf{not}\ a$$
$$c \leftarrow \textbf{not}\ a$$

There are exactly two maximal UASs of P, $S_1 = \{\textbf{not}\ a\}$ and $S_2 = \{\textbf{not}\ b\}$. Hence the semantics of P is determined by the two minimal models for $P_{S_1} = \{b \leftarrow;\ c \leftarrow\}$ and $P_{S_2} = \{a \leftarrow\}$.

We now show that the above semantics reduces to the standard minimal model semantics for positive disjunctive programs. This is proved in two separate theorems following the lemma below.

Lemma 18.
Let P be a positive disjunctive program. Let $\Pi = P^T \cup \mathcal{D}_L$. If M is a minimal model of P then $S = \{\textbf{not}\ \phi \mid \phi$ is false in $M\}$ satisfies $S = \mathcal{F}_\Pi^2(S)$.

Proof. Let M be a minimal model of P and $S = \{\textbf{not}\ \phi \mid \phi \text{ is false in } M\}$.

We first show that $S \subseteq \mathcal{F}_\Pi(S)$. Assume $\textbf{not}\ \phi \in S$, i.e. ϕ is false in M. Then, for each clause $r = \alpha \leftarrow \beta \in P$, where $\phi \in \alpha$, we have either (i) $M \models \varphi$ for some $\varphi \in \alpha$, or (ii) $M \models \neg\xi$, for some $\xi \in \beta$. In case (i), for the corresponding transformed clause $r' = \phi \leftarrow \beta'$ in P^T where $\{\textbf{not}\ \varphi\} \cup \beta \subseteq \beta'$, we have $\textbf{not}\ \varphi \notin S$ (note that $\varphi \neq \phi$). Hence, r' cannot be used to derive ϕ (and therefore it cannot be used to derive $(\textbf{not}\ \phi)^\sim$). In case (ii), applying the same reasoning to ξ, we again have either of the two cases. The same argument above applies to case (i). If case (ii) continues, we then have clauses in P^T (where $\xi_0 = \xi$):

$$\phi \leftarrow \ldots, \xi_0, \ldots;\quad \xi_0 \leftarrow \ldots, \xi_1, \ldots;\quad \ldots\ldots;\quad \xi_k \leftarrow \ldots, \xi_{k+1}, \ldots$$

In this case, we have an *unfounded set* $U = \{\phi, \xi_0, \ldots, \xi_{k+1}, \ldots\}$ [GRS88]. Thus $\Pi \cup S \not\vdash_d \phi, \xi_i$ for each i. Therefore, $\textbf{not}\ \phi \in \mathcal{F}_\Pi(S)$, i.e. $S \subseteq \mathcal{F}_\Pi(S)$.

We now show that $\mathcal{F}_\Pi^2(S) = S$. For each $\textbf{not}\ \zeta \notin S$, we know ζ is true in M. Then there exists a clause $\alpha \leftarrow \beta \in P$, $\zeta \in \alpha$ and $M \models \beta$. Without loss of generality, assume α is of the form $\zeta \vee \eta$. If $M \models \neg\eta$ we then have $\Pi \cup S \vdash_d \zeta$ (hence $\Pi \cup S \vdash_d (\textbf{not}\ \zeta)^\sim$), and thus $\textbf{not}\ \zeta \notin \mathcal{F}_\Pi(S)$. If $M \models \eta$ then $M \models \zeta$ iff $M \models \eta$. This implies either both $\textbf{not}\ \zeta, \textbf{not}\ \eta \notin \mathcal{F}_\Pi(S)$, or both $\textbf{not}\ \zeta, \textbf{not}\ \eta \in \mathcal{F}_\Pi(S)$. In the first case, since $\mathcal{F}_\Pi$ is anti-monotonic, from $S \subseteq \mathcal{F}_\Pi(S)$, we have

$\mathcal{F}_\Pi(S) \supseteq \mathcal{F}_\Pi^2(S)$, and therefore both $\mathbf{not}\,\zeta, \mathbf{not}\,\eta \notin \mathcal{F}_\Pi^2(S)$. For the second case, clearly $\Pi \cup \mathcal{F}_\Pi(S) \vdash_d \zeta, \eta$, and thus both $\mathbf{not}\,\zeta, \mathbf{not}\,\eta \notin \mathcal{F}_\Pi^2(S)$. Thus, we have shown that for each $\mathbf{not}\,\zeta \notin S$, $\mathbf{not}\,\zeta \notin \mathcal{F}_\Pi^2(S)$, i.e., $\mathcal{F}_\Pi^2(S) \subseteq S$.

In addition, we observe from the above proof that for any ζ true in M, $\Pi \cup \mathcal{F}_\Pi(S) \vdash_d \zeta$. Also due to the fact that $S \subseteq \mathcal{F}_\Pi(S)$, the cases (i) and (ii) above still apply to the derivations from $\Pi \cup \mathcal{F}_\Pi(S)$. Thus, for any $\mathbf{not}\,\phi \in S$, we have $\mathbf{not}\,\phi \in \mathcal{F}_\Pi^2(S)$, i.e., $S \subseteq \mathcal{F}_\Pi^2(S)$. Therefore $S = \mathcal{F}_\Pi^2(S)$. □

Theorem 19.
Let P be a positive disjunctive program. Let $\Pi = P^T \cup \mathcal{D}_L$ and S be maximal such that $S = \mathcal{F}_\Pi^2(S)$. Then $M = \{\phi \mid \mathbf{not}\,\phi \notin S\}$ is a minimal model of P.

Proof. Assume S is maximal such that $S = \mathcal{F}_\Pi^2(S)$. To satisfy every clause $\alpha \leftarrow \beta \in P$, we only need to show that whenever $M \models \beta$, we have $M \models \alpha$. For the sake of contradiction, we assume $M \not\models \alpha$, i.e., $\mathbf{not}\,(\alpha) \subseteq S$. Then there exists $\xi_i \in \beta$ such that $\Pi \cup \mathcal{F}_\Pi(S) \not\vdash_d \xi_i$. Since $S \subseteq \mathcal{F}_\Pi(S)$, we have $\Pi \cup S \not\vdash_d \xi_i$. Either $\mathbf{not}\,\xi_i \in S$ or $\mathbf{not}\,\xi_i \notin S$. For the former, we have $M \models \neg\xi_i$ which contradicts $M \models \beta$. For the latter case, since $S = \mathcal{F}_\Pi^2(S)$, $\mathbf{not}\,\xi_i \notin \mathcal{F}_\Pi^2(S)$. This implies $\Pi \cup \mathcal{F}_\Pi(S) \vdash_d \xi_i$, again resulting in a contradiction. Thus M is a model of P.

We now show that M is minimal. Again, assume it is not. Then there exists a minimal model $M' \subset M$ of P. Let $S' = \{\mathbf{not}\,\phi \mid \phi \text{ is false in } M'\}$. Note $S' \supset S$. Since M' is a minimal model of P, from Lemma 18, we have $\mathcal{F}_\Pi^2(S') = S'$. This contradicts the fact that S is a maximal normal alternating fixpoint of Π.

We therefore conclude that M is a minimal model of P. □

Theorem 20.
Let P be a positive disjunctive program. Let $\Pi = P^T \cup \mathcal{D}_L$. If M is a minimal model of P then $S = \{\mathbf{not}\,\phi \mid \phi \text{ is false in } M\}$ is maximal satisfying $S = \mathcal{F}_\Pi^2(S)$.

Proof. Let M be a minimal model of P and $S = \{\mathbf{not}\,\phi \mid \phi \text{ is false in } M\}$. From Lemma 18, we know $\mathcal{F}_\Pi^2(S) = S$. We only need to show that S is maximal. Suppose not. Then there exists $S' \supset S$ such that $S' = \mathcal{F}_\Pi^2(S')$. From Theorem 19, S' corresponds to a minimal model M' of P such that $M' \subset M$. This contradicts the assumption that M is a minimal model of P. □

The transformation approach cannot be adopted directly for defining the skeptical semantics for (extended) disjunctive programs. The following example shows the reason.

Example 10. Consider P

$$\begin{aligned} &a \vee b \leftarrow \\ &c \leftarrow a \\ &c \leftarrow b \\ &d \leftarrow \mathbf{not}\,c \end{aligned}$$

Then we have P^T consisting of

$$\begin{aligned} a &\leftarrow \mathbf{not}\, b \\ b &\leftarrow \mathbf{not}\, a \\ c &\leftarrow a \\ c &\leftarrow b \\ d &\leftarrow \mathbf{not}\, c \end{aligned}$$

There are three UASs, $S_1 = \emptyset$, $S_2 = \{\mathbf{not}\, a, \mathbf{not}\, d\}$, and $S_3 = \{\mathbf{not}\, b, \mathbf{not}\, d\}$. While S_2 and S_3 constitute a natural credulous semantics, S_1 misses the fact that c is false in both cases of $a \vee b$, and therefore the assumption **not** d can always be assumed.

Sakama and Inoue [IS93, SI93] also used a transformational approach for disjunctive programs. In general, their approach can provide both exclusive and inclusive readings of disjunction. But their semantics is different; in particular, it is not an extension of the preferential semantics and its equivalents.

6 Concluding Remarks

In almost all of the previously proposed semantics for extended programs, the concept of defeating or retracting assumptions is implicit and is usually captured by semantic definitions. This paper proposes a framework of logic programming using an explicit representation of defeat of assumptions. This yields a semantic structure whose least element serves as a tractable skeptical denial semantics and whose maximal elements define a natural credulous denial semantics. We have also presented a credulous semantics for normal as well as extended disjunctive programs using a transformation approach.

For extended programs, the definition of the skeptical denial semantics automatically provides a bottom-up query answering mechanism. It would be interesting to investigate a top-down query answering procedure. In such a procedure, to prove **not** ϕ amounts to a proof that not only ϕ fails to be derived but also **not** ϕ cannot be defeated. The former is a proof based on negation as failure and the latter requires the use of assumption denial clauses.

Since in our framework an extended program is just a normal program plus constraint clauses, the proof procedure proposed in [EK88] may be adapted to our credulous semantics with relative ease. The credulous semantics for disjunctive programs is based on the semantics of normal programs using a transformation approach. Thus a proof procedure for the latter can be extended for the former, with a subprocedure to compute minimal models. These topics require further study.

Acknowledgement: We would like to thank the two anonymous referees for their constructive comments that helped improve the presentation of this work.

References

[ADP93] J. Alferes, P. Dung, and L. Pereira. Scenario semantics of extended logic programs. In *Proc. Second Workshop on Logic Programming and Nonmonotonic Reasoning*, 1993.

[AP92] J. Alferes and L. Pereira. On logic programs with two kinds of negation. In *Proc. Joint International Conference and Symposium on Logic Programming*, pages 574–588. MIT Press, 1992.

[BS91] C. Baral and V.S. Subrahmanian. Dualities between alternative semantics for logic programming and nonmonotonic reasoning. In *Proc. First Workshop on Logic Programming and Nonmonotonic Reasoning*, pages 69–86, 1991.

[BS92] C. Baral and V.S. Subrahmanian. Stable and extension class theory for logic programs and default logic. *J. Automated Reasoning*, pages 345–366, 1992.

[BTK93] A. Bondarenko, F. Toni, and R.A. Kowalski. An assumption-based framework for nonmonotonic reasoning. In *Proc. Second Workshop on Logic Programming and Nonmonotonic Reasoning*, July, 1993. Invited talk.

[Dix94a] J. Dix. A classification theory of semantics of normal logic programs: I. strong properties. *Foundamenta Informaticae (to appear)*, 1994.

[Dix94b] J. Dix. A classification theory of semantics of normal logic programs: Ii. weak properties. *Foundamenta Informaticae (to appear)*, 1994.

[Dun91] P. Dung. Negations as hypotheses: An abductive foundation for logic programming. In *Proc. 8th ICLP*, pages 3–17, 1991.

[Dun92] P. Dung. Acyclic disjunctive logic programs with abductive procedures as proof procedure. In *Proc. International Conference on Fifth Generation Computer System*, pages 555–561, 1992.

[Dun93] P. Dung. An argumentation semantics for logic programming with explicit negation. In *Proc. 10th ICLP*, pages 615–630, 1993.

[EK88] K. Eshghi and R.A. Kowalski. Abduction compared with negation by failure. In *Proc. 6th ICLP*, pages 234–254, 1988.

[Gel89] A. Van Gelder. The alternating fixpoint of logic programs with negation. In *Proc. 8th ACM PODS*, 1989.

[GL90] M. Gelfond and V. Lifschitz. Logical programs with classical negation. In *Proc. 7th International Conference and Symposium on Logic Programming*, pages 579–597, 1990.

[GM90] L. Giordano and A. Martelli. Generalized stable models, truth maintenance and conflict resolution. In *Proc. 7th ICLP*, pages 427–441, 1990.

[GRS88] A. Van Gelder, K. Ross, and J.S. Schlipf. Unfounded sets and well-founded semantics for general logic programs. In *Proc. 7th ACM PODS*, 1988.

[IS93] K. Inoue and C. Sakama. Transforming abductive logic programs to disjunctive programs. In *Proc. 10th ICLP*, 1993.

[KD90] R.A. Kowalski and F. Dadri. Logic programs with exceptions. In *Proc. 7th ICLP*, pages 490–504, 1990.

[KM90] A. Kakas and P. Mancarella. Generalized stable models: a semantics for abduction. In *Proc. 9th European Conf. for AI*, 1990.

[KMD94] A. Kakas, P. Mancarella, and P.M. Dung. The acceptability semantics for logic programs. In *Proc. 11th ICLP*, pages 504–519, 1994.

[PA92] L. Pereira and J. Alferes. Well-founded semantics with explicit negation. In *Proc. 10th ECAI*, pages 102–106, 1992.

[PA93] L. Pereira and J. Alferes. Optative reasoning with scenario semantics. In *Proc. 10th ICLP*, pages 601–615, 1993.

[PAA91a] L. Pereira, J. Alferes, and J. Aparício. Contradiction removal within well-founded semantics. In *Proc. First Workshop on Logic Programming and Non-monotonic Reasoning*, pages 105–119, 1991.

[PAA91b] L. Pereira, J. Alferes, and J. Aparício. Counterfactual reasoning based on revising assumptions. In *Proc. International Symposium on Logic Programming*, pages 566–580, 1991.

[PP91] H. Przymusinska and T.C. Przymusinski. Stationary default extensions. Technical report, California State Polytechnic and University of California at Riverside, 1991.

[Prz90a] T.C. Przymusinski. Extended stable semantics for normal and disjunctive logic programs. In *Proc. 7th International Conference and Symposium on Logic Programming*, pages 459–477, 1990.

[Prz90b] T.C. Przymusinski. Well-founded semantics coincides with three-valued stable semantics. *Foundamenta Informaticae*, 13:445–463, 1990.

[Prz91] T.C. Przymusinski. Semantics of disjunctive logic programs and deductive databases. In *Proc. 2nd International Conference on Object Oriented and Deductive Databases*, pages 87–107, 1991.

[Prz95] T. C. Przymusinski. Static semantics of logic programs. *Annals of Mathematics and Artificial Intelligence*, 1995. (A short version in this volume).

[SI93] C. Sakama and K. Inoue. Negation in disjunctive logic programs. In *Proc. 10th ICLP*, 1993.

[SZ90] D. Saccà and C. Zaniolo. Stable models and non-determinism in logic programs with negation. In *Proc. 9th ACM PODS*, pages 205–217, 1990.

[SZ91] D. Saccà and C. Zaniolo. Partial models and three-valued stable models in logic programs with negation. In *Proc. First Workshop on Logic Programming and Nonmonotonic Reasoning*, pages 87–101, 1991.

[WB93] C. Witteveen and G. Brewka. Skeptical reason maintenance and belief revision. *Artificial Intelligence*, 61:1–36, 1993.

[WJ93] C. Witteveen and C. M. Jonker. Revision by expansion in logic programs. Technical Report Report 93-02, Faculty of Mathematics and Computer Science, Delft University of Technology, 1993.

[Yua94] L. Yuan. Autoepistemic logic of first order and its expressive power. *J. Automated Reasoning*, 13(1):88–116, 1994.

[YY94] J. You and L. Yuan. A three-valued semantics for deductive databases and logic programs. *J. Computer and System Sciences*, 49(2):334–361, 1994. An extended abstract appeared in *Proc. ACM PODS '90.*

[YY95] J. You and L. Yuan. On the equivalence of semantics for normal logic programs. *Journal of Logic Programming*, 22(3):209–219, 1995.

A Resolution-based Procedure for Default Theories with Extensions*

Monica D. Barback[1] and Jorge Lobo[2]

[1] Department of EECS
Northwestern University
Evanston, Illinois 60208-3118
barback@eecs.nwu.edu
[2] EECS Department M/C 154
University of Illinois at Chicago
851 S. Morgan Street #1120 SEO
Chicago, Illinois 60607-7053
jorge@eecs.uic.edu

Abstract. Default logic, introduced by Reiter, is an effective nonmonotonic reasoning system. In addition to being a stand alone paradigm for nonmonotonic reasoning, default logic has also been used to represent other nonmonotonic reasoning systems such as the stable model semantics and the well-founded semantics of logic programs. This paper complements these results by describing a sound and complete resolution based proof procedure for a large class of default theories.
The procedure can be used to determine if an arbitrary formula is in an extension. It also has the advantage of generating a partial extension, which is contained in the final extension, thus helping to describe the meaning of a given default theory. Further, the procedure does not necessarily have to compute every extension in order for a single query to be answered. The procedure has been implemented in C-Prolog.

1 Introduction

Default logic, introduced by Reiter [Rei80], is an effective nonmonotonic reasoning system (cf.[Eth87, Eth88]). In addition to being a stand alone paradigm for nonmonotonic reasoning, default logic has also been used to represent other nonmonotonic reasoning systems such as the stable model semantics ([MT89], [LS92], [BF91]) and the well-founded semantics [Bar94] of logic programs. We complement this integral relationship between default logic and logic programming by developing a sound and complete proof procedure for certain default theories. Readers familiar with proof procedures for logic programs will notice the similarities with our procedure.

A given default theory may have zero, one, or many extensions. The purpose of a proof procedure is to be able to query the default theory with a formula

* Partial support was provided by the National Science Foundation, under grant Nr. IRI-92-10220.

and determine if it is in one extension (the extension membership problem) or determine if it is in every extension (the entailment problem). Without a way to answer these questions, a default theory becomes meaningless.

In Reiter's original work, a sound and complete resolution based proof procedure was introduced for the class of *normal default theories*, which answered the extension membership problem. The implementation involved successive applications of resolution to the consequents of the defaults in the default theory. At the conclusion of the proof all defaults involved in the proof are subject to a consistency check. However, little work has been done to expand this refutation procedure for general default theories.

There have been several bottom-up approaches to generate extensions. Etherington [Eth87], developed a bottom up algorithm to generate all of the extensions of the class of default theories called *finite ordered default theories*. Finite ordered default theories are more general than normal default theories, thus extending the work of Reiter. Although this algorithm is guaranteed to generate all of the extensions of a finite ordered default theory, the procedure is not guaranteed to halt, even if an extension exists. More general bottom-up procedures are descried by Marek and Truszczynski in [MT93]. There have also been procedures for computing answers to modified versions of default logic. An example of such procedures can be found in [Bes89].

Our goal when we started this investigation was to find a top-down proof procedure based on resolution for the standard definition of default logic.

The proof procedure that we developed is sound and complete for finite semi-normal default theories with the property that each subset of the default theory has an extension. Normal default theories have this property. The set of *even default theories* also has this property. Even default theories are a larger class of default theories than the finite ordered default theories of Etherington. We also show how we could relax the assumption that each subset of the default theory has an extension if we work with alternative definitions of default logic.

The advantages of our procedure can be stated as follows:

- The algorithm can be used to determine if a formula is in any extension of a default theory Π.
- We can determine if a formula is in every extension from a query that must fail.
- The algorithm generates a partial extension that is contained in some extension of the default theory, thus giving us some more information about the structure of the default theory.
- Neither complete extensions nor every extension needs to be generated in order for a query to be answered. Thus, it is possible that generating a proof could be much less expensive than deriving all extensions as in the bottom up approaches.
- The algorithm is implemented in C-Prolog, so the actual cost of the algorithm can be tested with real-world examples.

The organization of the paper is as follows. Section 2 gives some preliminaries, Sections 3 and 4, detail the development of the proof procedure. Many of the propositions in these section have appeared somewhere else. We include most of the proofs since in many cases the proofs reflect the structure of our procedure. Section 5 gives the proof procedure along with the soundness and completeness proofs. Section 6 restates the soundness and completeness results and draws some useful conclusions. Section 7 shows how to relax the assumption that every subset of the default theory has an extension. Section 8 presents some examples. Finally, Section 9 discusses the implications of the work, specifically addressing the question of what the proof procedure does compute when the default theory is not even.

2 Preliminaries

2.1 Defaults

A *default* δ as defined in [Rei80] is an expression of the form,

$$w \leftarrow a_1, \ldots, a_n, Mb_1, \ldots, Mb_m \tag{1}$$

where a_i, b_i, and w are formulas. Informally, the default may be read as; if $a_1 \& \ldots \& a_n$ are true and it is consistent to believe each of $b_1, \ldots, b_m$, then w must be true.

A *default theory* is defined in [Rei80] as a pair (Δ, W), where Δ is a set of defaults and W is a set of closed well-formed formulas (wffs).

However, a default theory (Δ, W) has been shown (cf.[GLPT91, MT93]) to be equivalent to a default theory Π of the form

$$(\Delta \cup \overbrace{\{w \leftarrow \quad \mid w \in W\}}^{\Omega}, \emptyset]$$

Thus the default theory (Δ, W) will always be equivalent to the default theory $(\Delta \cup \Omega, \emptyset)$.

Any default theory $\Pi = (\Delta \cup \Omega, \emptyset)$ will be equivalently represented using the notation (Δ, Ω). Further, when we refer to the defaults in the default theory Π we are referring to the defaults in $\Delta \cup \Omega$.

In Equation 1, above, the set $\{a_1, \ldots, a_n\}$ is referred to as the *prerequisite* of the default, denoted *prereqs*(δ). The set $\{b_1, \ldots, b_m\}$ is called the *justification* of the default, denoted *justs*(δ). The set $\{w\}$ is known as the *consequent* of the default, denoted *cons*(δ).

Similar definitions to those above can be made for a set of defaults Δ. We define, $Prereqs(\Delta) = \bigcup_{\delta \in \Delta} prereqs(\delta)$, $Justs(\Delta) = \bigcup_{\delta \in \Delta} justs(\delta)$, and $Cons(\Delta) = \bigcup_{\delta \in \Delta} cons(\delta)$.

2.2 Extensions

The meaning of a default theory is associated with a set of ground formulas called an *extension*. The following definitions are useful for testing whether or not a set of wffs is indeed an extension.

Definition 1 [Rei80]. Let Π be a default theory and E be a set of sentences, then E is an *extension* if the following holds: It is the smallest deductively closed set of sentences E' such that for every default in Π of the form of Equation 1 if each formula a_i is in E' and $\neg b_i$ is not in E, then w is in E'.

For a set of wffs W, $th(W)$ refers to the deductive closure of W. In an extension E, it is always the case that $E = th(E)$.

The following is an alternate, but equivalent, definition of an extension.

Definition 2 [Rei80]. Let Π be a default theory and E be a set of sentences, where:

$$E_0 = \emptyset$$
$$E_{i+1} = th(E_i) \cup \{w | w \leftarrow a_1, \ldots, a_n, Mb_1, \ldots, Mb_m \in \Pi, \; \textit{each } a_j \in E_i \textit{ and no } \neg b_j \in E\}$$

Then, E is an *extension* for Π iff $E = \cup_{i=0}^{\infty} E_i$.

Although the definition is iterative, it is important to note that E must be known before Definition 2 can be applied.

The following definition of a default is based on the operator Π^E.

Definition 3 [GLPT91]. For any default theory Π and set of sentences E, the operator Π^E is defined. The default

$$w \leftarrow a_1, \ldots, a_n \tag{2}$$

is in Π^E iff for some $b_1, \ldots, b_m$ such that each $\neg b_i \notin E$, a default of the form

$$w \leftarrow a_1, \ldots a_n, Mb_1, \ldots, Mb_m \tag{3}$$

is in Π.

We say that Equation 2 is the *simple form* of Equation 3, because it is the same as Equation 3 except that it does not have any justifications. We write $simple(3) = 2$. For a set of defaults Γ, $Simple(\Gamma)$ refers to the simple form of each default in Γ.

There is a similar definition of the operator Π_E.

Definition 4. For any default theory Π and set of sentences E, the operator Π_E, where $\Pi_E \subseteq \Pi$, is defined. A default of the form of Equation 3 is in Π_E iff each $\neg b_i \notin E$ and a default of the form of Equation 3 is in Π.

Definition 5 [GLPT91]. A set of sentences E is an *extension* for a default theory Π iff E is the minimal set E' closed under provability in propositional calculus and under the defaults of Π^E.

Proposition 6 [GLPT91]. *Definition 2 and Definition 5 are equivalent.*

Proof: Definition 1 is shown to be equivalent to Definition 2 in [Rei80], Theorem 2.1. Definition 5 is shown to be equivalent to Definition 1 in [GLPT91], Theorem 2.3.

Neither of Definitions 2 or 5 can be efficiently used to compute all (or even one) of the extensions of an arbitrary default theory. The computationally expensive aspect of all of the above definitions is that it is necessary to guess at a final extension before the definition can be applied.

Our aim is to find a more rigorous procedure for determining what is in an extension. Defaults have certain properties that limit the types of things that go into extensions.

Definition 7. Let ρ be a default rule and W be a set of ground formulas. The default rule ρ is said to be *activated* in W iff for all $p \in prereqs(\rho)$, $W \models p$, and for no $j \in justs(\rho)$ does $W \models \neg j$.

Proposition 8. *Let Π be a default theory with extension E. Then E is equal to $th(Cons(\Pi'))$, where $\Pi' \subseteq \Pi$ and each $\delta \in \Pi'$ is activated in E.*

Definition 9. Let Π be a default theory with $\Pi' \subseteq \Pi$. We define $E^* = th(Cons(\Pi'))$ to be *the theory set* of Π'. Suppose that E^* has the following properties:

(1) E^* is an extension for Π'.

(2) Each $\delta \in \Pi'$ is activated in E^*.

Then we say that Π' is a *defining set.*[1] If E^* is contained in an extension E of Π, then we say that Π' is a *Π-defining set through E.*

Although a default theory has only one theory set it may have many defining and Π-defining sets.

Example 1. Let Π be the following default theory:

1. $p \leftarrow a, M(\neg q)$
2. $q \leftarrow a, M(\neg p)$
3. $a \leftarrow$

There are two extensions of Π, $E_1 = th(\{a, p\})$, and $E_2 = th(\{a, q\})$. The set of defaults $\{1., 3.\}$ is a defining set, since the extension of $\{1., 3.\}$ is the theory set of $\{1., 3.\}$ or $E^* = th(\{a, p\})$. It is also a Π-defining set through E_1, since $E^* \subseteq E_1$. Similar arguments can be made for $\{2., 3.\}$, and $\{3.\}$. There are no other Π-defining sets.

Proposition 10. *Suppose Π is a default theory with extension E. Then E is the theory set of some Π-defining set $\Pi' \subseteq \Pi$.*

[1] In [MT93] there is a similar notion called generating set. Given a default theory Π and an extension E of Π, a generating set for E is the subset of defaults ¿from Π that are activated in E.

2.3 Classes of default theories

By restricting default theories to different classes, the problem of finding extensions becomes easier.

Simple default theories A default theory $\Pi = (\Delta, \Omega)$ is said to be *simple* if every default $\delta \in \Delta$ has the form,

$$w \leftarrow a_1, \ldots, a_n.$$

Simple default theories have the nice property that their extensions can be generated iteratively.[2] In other words it is not necessary to guess at the final extension to generate the extension of a simple default theory. Definition 2 shows how this can be done.

They also have the unusual property that they have one and only one extension.

Proposition 11 [MT93]. *Suppose Π is a simple default theory. Then Π has one and only one extension.*

Proof: Consider an extension generated by Definition 2. It is clear that no matter what set of wffs are in E, E_i is always the same. Thus, there can be only one extension. □

Normal default theories The default theory $\Pi = (\Delta, \Omega)$ is said to be *normal* if every default $\delta \in \Delta$ has the form,

$$w \leftarrow a_1, \ldots, a_n, M(w).$$

The following theorem is useful.

Proposition 12 [Rei80]. *Every normal default theory has an extension.*

Normal default theories are studied here, because Reiter's original proof procedure was valid only for normal default theories. We can see that there is a strong relationship between simple default theories and normal default theories.

Definition 13. Let $\Pi = (\Delta, \Omega)$ be a simple default theory. Define,

$$norm(\Pi) = (\{w \leftarrow a_1, ..., a_p, Mw \mid w \leftarrow a_1, ..., a_p \in \Delta\}, \Omega)$$

Proposition 14 cf. [MT93]. *Let Π be a simple default theory with extension E. Then $norm(\Pi)$ has the single extension E.*

---

[2] Simple default theories are called justification-free default theories in [MT93].

Proof: Suppose Π has an extension E, but $norm(\Pi)$ does not. By Proposition 12, $norm(\Pi)$ has an extension F. We assume that $F \neq E$.

Consider the extension generated by Definition 2. We prove that $F_i \subseteq E_i$. Clearly $F_0 = \emptyset \subseteq E_0 = \emptyset$.

Consider the iteration in E_i and F_i in Definition 2 and assume that $F_i \subseteq E_i$. Suppose $F_{i+1} \not\subseteq E_{i+1}$. Then there is a default δ

$$w \leftarrow a_1, ..., a_n, M(w)$$

such that $\{a_1, ..., a_n\} \subseteq F_i$ and $\neg w \notin F$. But $simple(\delta)$ is not activated in E_{i+1}. This is a contradiction, since $\{a_1, ..., a_n\} \subseteq E_i \supseteq F_i$.

Consider a Π-defining set through E, Π'. Clearly, $\Pi' \subseteq norm(\Pi)^E$. Since $F \subseteq E$, we know that $\Pi' \subseteq norm(\Pi)^F$. Hence, $F = E$. □

Semi-normal default theories The default theory Π is said to be *semi-normal* if every default $\delta \in \Delta$ is simple or it has the form

$$w \leftarrow a_1, \ldots, a_n, M(w \,\&\, b),$$

where b is a formula.

Semi-normal default theories are not as well behaved as simple default theories or normal default theories. Semi-normal default theories may have zero, one or many extensions and their is no easy way to tell how many extensions a given default theory has.

2.4 Assumptions

For this work, some simplifying assumptions are made. First, we do not address default theories that are more general than semi-normal default theories. It is shown in [MT93] that every default theory can be represented using a semi-normal default theory,[3] therefore this assumption does not seem to be restrictive. Second, we assume that the set of consequences of all simple defaults in the theory are consistent. This condition ensures that if the default theory has an extension then it is consistent.

Further, for each default $\delta \in \Pi$ of the form of Equation 1, w and each a_i are restricted to disjunctions. It can be easily seen that restricting a_i to a disjunction does not decrease the expressibility of the default theory. The same is true of the restriction on w, by virtue of the following equality;

$$\{c_1 \,\&\ldots\&\, c_r \leftarrow a_1, \ldots, a_n, M(b)\}$$

$$=$$

$$\{c_1 \leftarrow a_1, \ldots, a_n, M(b),\ \ldots,\ c_r \leftarrow a_1, \ldots, a_n, M(b)\},$$

[3] The semi-normal default theory needs some extra letters in the language, but extensions of the semi-normal theory restricted to the original language are extensions of the original theory.

where each c_i is a ground disjunction. The proof of this equality is trivial.[4]

Finally, we assume that a default theory Π consists of a possibly infinite set of ground defaults. We discuss some implications of relaxing this assumption in Section 7.

3 Proof Procedure for Normal Defaults

Much of the original work on resolution based proof procedures for default theories has been developed in Reiter [Rei80] for normal defaults.

The representation used by Reiter is not adopted here because it is not easily extendible for use in more general default theories. Further, our proof procedure has some close parallels to SLDNF (c.f. [Llo84]) as well as having parallels to the abductive refutation procedure of [EK89]. Therefore, we adopt notation that emphasizes these similarities.

Instead of defining default proofs as disjoint applications of resolution, the approach taken here is to define a default resolution procedure which "resolves" two defaults and returns a third default. Since it is expected that this procedure will be used for defaults that are more general than normal defaults, the definition of default resolution is written to include non-normal defaults as well.

Definition 15. We define *default resolution* or *DR* as follows. Let

$$\delta_1 = g_1 \vee ... \vee g_s \leftarrow a_1, ..., a_n, Mb_1, \ldots, Mb_t, \tag{4}$$

$$\delta_2 = e_1 \vee ... \vee e_q \leftarrow c_1, ..., c_p, Md_1, \ldots, Md_r, \tag{5}$$

where $s, q \geq 1$, $n, t, p, r \geq 0$. We assume, without loss of generality, that $e_1 = \neg g_1$. Then the *default resolvent* or result of applying default resolution to δ_1 and δ_2 is

$$g_2 \vee \ldots \vee g_s \vee e_2 \vee \ldots \vee e_q \leftarrow a_1, \ldots, a_n, c_1, \ldots, c_p, Mb_1, \ldots, Mb_t, Md_1, \ldots, Md_r \tag{6}$$

It can be seen that default resolution makes use of ordinary resolution on the consequents of the default rules. However, it is not class preserving. That is, if we resolve two normal defaults we do not necessarily get a normal default. Yet, default resolution does not alter the extensions of a default theory in any way.

Proposition 16. *Let Π be a default theory with defaults δ_1, $\delta_2 \in \Pi$. Suppose δ_1 and δ_2 have a default resolvent ρ. Then Π has an extension E iff $\Delta = \Pi \cup \{\rho\}$ has an extension E.*

---

[4] See also Theorem 5.14 in [MT93].

Proof: Suppose δ_1 and δ_2 has the form of Equations 4 and 5, respectively. Clearly, then ρ has the form of Equation 6.

($\Rightarrow$) Suppose Π has an extension E. We must show that the addition of ρ does not change the extension. There are two cases to consider.

Case I: Suppose ρ is activated in E, but δ_1 and δ_2 are not activated in E. Clearly, this is impossible.

Case II: Suppose ρ is not activated in E, but δ_1 and δ_2 are. Again, this is impossible.

So, ρ is activated in E whenever δ_1 and δ_2 are activated in E. But, *cons*(ρ) is in the deductive closure of E if δ_1 and δ_2 are in E. Consider the iteration on E_i. It is easy to see that E is also an extension for Δ from Definition 2.

($\Leftarrow$) Suppose Δ has an extension E. Again, ρ is activated in E whenever δ_1 and δ_2 are activated in E by the arguments above. Further, from Definition 2, E must also be an extension for Π. □

Default resolution alone is not sufficient to generate Reiter's normal default proof procedure. Reiter's proof, which consists of successive applications of default resolution on a default theory $\Pi = (\Delta, \Omega)$, employs a final check of consistency between the defaults in the proof and the formulas in Ω. In place of this we introduce the concept of meaningfulness. Meaningfulness allows us to do the consistency check as the proof is being generated.

Definition 17. We say that a ground default δ is *meaningful* with respect to a set of ground well-formed formulas W if no $j \in \neg justs(\delta)$ can be proven in W. We write *meaningful*(δ, W).

When we talk about a proof in a default theory, it is usually in terms of a query. Here we define exactly how a formula translates in default logic into a set of query defaults.

Definition 18. Let ρ be a default rule of the form $\leftarrow w_1 \vee ... \vee w_n, J$, and each w_i a conjunction of literals. Then *Query*(ρ) is defined to be the set of default rules, $\{\neg w_1 \leftarrow J, ..., \neg w_n \leftarrow J\}$.

Definition 19. Let ω be a formula in the language of a default theory $\Pi = (\Delta, \Omega)$ written in disjunctive normal form (ie. disjunctions of conjunctions of literals). A *partial inExtension derivation* of ω is a sequence of tuples

$$(\rho_1, Defaults_1, \Lambda_1), \ldots, (\rho_n, Defaults_n, \Lambda_n)$$

generated by calls to Algorithm *Partial InExtension*, where for each i, $1 \leq i \leq n$, ρ_i is a single default rule of the form,

$$c_1 \vee ... \vee c_s \leftarrow a_1, ..., a_p, Mb_1, ..., Mb_m, \tag{7}$$

Each $Defaults_i$ and each Λ_i is a set of ground defaults.

Algorithm 20 Partial InExtension.

p-ext1: If $s \neq 0$ then
1. $\rho_{i+1} = \eta$, where η is the default resolvent of some default $\nu \in (\Pi \cup Defaults_i)$ with the default rule ρ_i, such that $meaningful(\nu, Cons(\Lambda_i))$.
2. If $\nu \in \Pi$, then $\Lambda_{i+1} = \Lambda_i \cup \{\nu\}$ else $\Lambda_{i+1} = \Lambda_i$.
3. $Defaults_{i+1} = Defaults_i \cup \{\eta\}$

p-ext2: Else if $p \neq 0$, then
1. $\rho_{i+1} \in Query(\rho_i)$
2. $\Lambda_{i+1} = \Lambda_i$
3. $Defaults_{i+1} = Query(\rho_i)$

Further, $\rho_1 = \leftarrow w$, $Defaults_1 = Query(\leftarrow w)$, and Λ_1 is a Π-defining set. We call Λ_1 the *first default set.*

We call $(\rho_n, Defaults_n, \Lambda_n)$ the final tuple. The default rule ρ_n, is called the *final default rule*, and Λ_n is called the *final default set.*

A *partial inExtension refutation* of a formula w is a derivation in which ρ_n contains only justifications.

We usually begin a partial inExtension refutation with the default set $\Lambda_1 = \Omega$. In fact, unless otherwise stated it will be assumed that $\Lambda_1 = \Omega$.

Lemma 21. *Let $\Pi = (\Delta, \Omega)$ be a default theory with an extension E. Then Ω is a Π-defining set for E.*

If a partial inExtension refutation fails because there does not exist a default ν in **p-ext1**, such that $meaningful(\nu, Cons(\Lambda_i))$, we say there is *no meaningful refutation.*

Definition 22. We define a *weak partial inExtension refutation* to be the same as a partial inExtension refutation except that Λ_i does not change on any call to Algorithm *Partial inExtension.*

Theorem 23 cf. [Rei80]. *Let $\Pi = (\Delta, \Omega)$ be a normal default theory with extension E. The formula $b \in E$ iff there is a partial inExtension refutation of b in Π.*

Corollary 24. *Let $\Pi = (\Delta, \Omega)$ be a normal default theory. The formula b is not in any extension E of Π iff there are no partial inExtension refutations of b in Π.*

Proof: This is the contrapositive of Theorem 23. □

4 Proof Procedure for Simple Defaults

The partial inExtension refutations are sound and complete for simple default theories as well. Of course, the test for meaningfulness in **p-ext1** is superfluous in the case of simple defaults, because there are no justifications.

Proposition 25. *Let $\Pi = (\Delta, \Omega)$ be a simple default theory with extension E. The formula $b \in E$ iff there exists a partial inExtension refutation of b in Π.*

Proof: ($\Rightarrow$) Suppose $b \in E$. Then by Proposition 14 $norm(\Pi)$ has an extension E. Thus, there is a normal inExtension refutation $\mathcal{R}^n$, of b in $norm(\Pi)$. A parallel simple refutation, $\mathcal{R}$, can be done in Π, where $norm(\delta)$ is replaced by δ and the resolvents are changed accordingly.
($\Leftarrow$) Suppose there is a simple inExtension proof of b in Π with final default set Λ. There is a corresponding inExtension proof of b in $norm(\Pi)$, unless there is a default resolution done in **p-ext1** in Π that cannot be done in $norm(\Pi)$ because it is not meaningful. Suppose the default that is not meaningful in $norm(\Pi)$ is $b \leftarrow a_1, ..., a_p, M(Mb)$. So $\neg b$ in $th(cons(\Lambda_i))$, but b in $th(cons(\Lambda_{i+1}))$. So, $th(cons(\Lambda))$ is inconsistent. But then Π does not have an extension. This is a contradiction since Π is simple. □

Corollary 26. *Let $\Pi = (\Delta, \Omega)$ be a simple default theory with extension E. Suppose there is a partial inExtension refutation of b in Π with final default set Λ_n. If $p \in Prereqs(\Lambda_n)$, then there is a partial inExtension refutation of p in Λ_n.*

Proof: By the structure of partial inExtension refutations the Proposition above holds. □

Proposition 27. *Let $\Pi = (\Delta, \Omega)$ be a simple default theory with extension E. Suppose there is a partial inExtension refutation of b in Π with first default set Λ_1 any Π-defining default set and final default set Λ_n. Then Λ_n is a Π-defining set through E.*

Proof: Since Λ_n is simple it has an extension F. By Proposition 11, Λ_n can have only one extension. By Corollary 26, a refutation for each $p \in Prereqs(\Lambda_n)$ can be done in Π. So, by Theorem 25, each $p \in F$. However, by Proposition 10, $F = th(Cons(\Lambda'))$, where $\Lambda' \subseteq \Lambda_n$. From the arguments above, $\Lambda' = \Lambda_n$. □

5 Semi-normal defaults

Semi-normal default theories are much more complicated than either normal default theories or simple default theories.

Example 2. Let Π be the following default theory:

1. $a \leftarrow M(a \& \neg b)$
2. $b \leftarrow Mb$
   Clearly the only extension of Π is $th(\{b\})$. However, there is a partial inExtension refutation of a.
   $(\leftarrow a, \{\neg a \leftarrow\}, \{\})$
   $(\neg a \leftarrow, \{\neg a \leftarrow\}, \{\})$
   $(\leftarrow M(a \& \neg b), \{\neg a \leftarrow, \ \leftarrow M(a \& \neg b)\}, \{a \leftarrow M(a \& \neg b)\})$

Thus, partial inExtension refutations alone are not strong enough to describe when a formula is in an extension.

However, partial inExtension refutations can assist us in finding a refutation.

Proposition 28. *Let Π be a default theory with extension E. The disjunction $b \in E$ iff there is a partial inExtension refutation of b in E such that each default λ_i in the final default set Λ_n is meaningful with respect to E.*

Proof:
($\Rightarrow$) Consider Π^E. By Definition 2, we know that E is an extension for Π^E. By Theorem 25 there is a simple inExtension refutation of b in Π^E. By Corollary 26, E the extension for Π^E contains all $p \in Prereqs(\Lambda_n)$. We claim that the parallel refutation can be done in Π. The only reason it could not be done is if a refutation that was not meaningful was attempted. However, since $simple(\delta) \in \Pi^E$, where $\delta \in \Pi$, there can be no $\delta \in \Pi$, with $justs(\delta)$ in $th(Cons(\lambda_n))$.
($\Leftarrow$) Suppose each default in the final default set Λ_n is activated in E, the extension for Π. We know that $Cons(\Lambda_n) \models b$. Hence, $b \in E$. □

Corollary 29. *Let Π be a default theory with extension E. The disjunction $b \notin E$ iff for all partial inExtension refutations of b in Π, with final tuple $(\rho_n, defaults_n, \Lambda_n)$, there exists a default λ in Λ_n that is not meaningful with respect to E.*

Proof: This is the contrapositive of Proposition 28. □

5.1 The proof procedure

Definition 30. Let ω be a formula in the language of a default theory $\Pi = (\Delta, \Omega)$ written in disjunctive normal form. An *inExtension derivation* of ω is a sequence of tuples

$$(\rho_1, Defaults_1, \Lambda_1), \ldots, (\rho_n, Defaults_n, \Lambda_n)$$

as defined in Definition 19, generated by the calls to Algorithm *InExtension*.

Algorithm 31 inExtension.

ext1: Same as **p-ext1** in Definition 19.
ext2: Same as **p-ext2** in Definition 19.
ext3: Else if $m \neq 0$ then there is a notInextension refutation of $\neg b_1$ with final tuple $(\{\}, \Lambda^*)$.
1. $\rho_{i+1} = \{\leftarrow Mb_2, ..., Mb_m\}$
2. $\Lambda_{i+1} = \Lambda^*$
3. $Defaults_{i+1} = \emptyset$

An *inExtension refutation* is an inExtension derivation, where the final default rule is the empty rule denoted by □.

Definition 32. Let ω be a formula in the language of a default theory $\Pi = (\Delta, \Omega)$ written in disjunctive normal form. A *notInExtension derivation* of ω is a sequence of tuples

$$(\Phi_1, \Lambda_1) \ldots (\Phi_n, \Lambda_n)$$

generated by the calls to Algorithm *notInExtension*, such that for each i, $1 \leq i \leq n$, Φ_i is set containing ground defaults, $\{\rho_i^1, \ldots, \rho_i^t\}$ each of the form of Equation 7 and each Λ_i is a set of ground defaults.

Algorithm 33 notInExtension.

next1: Let $\Phi_i = \{\rho_i^j\} \cup \Phi_i'$. If $s > 0$, then
1. $\Phi_{i+1} = \Gamma \cup \Phi_i'$, where Γ is the set of all final defaults that are generated as a result of doing a *weak* partial inExtension refutation of ρ_i^j, with first default set Λ_i, where $\square \notin \Gamma$
2. $\Lambda_{i+1} = \Lambda_i$.

next2: Else if it is not the case that *meaningful*(ρ_i^j, Λ_i) holds, then
1. $\Phi_{i+1} = \Phi_i'$
2. $\Lambda_{i+1} = \Lambda_i$

next3: Else ρ_i^j is of the form $\leftarrow Mb_1, \ldots, Mb_m$
1. If there is an inExtension refutation $\mathcal{R}$ of $\neg b_1$ in Π, with first default set Λ_i and final tuple $(\square, defaults_n, \Lambda^*)$. Then,
   (a) $\Phi_{i+1} = \Phi_i'$
   (b) $\Lambda_{i+1} = \Lambda^*$
2. Else if $n > 1$, then
   (a) $\Phi_{i+1} = \Phi_i' \cup \{\leftarrow Mb_2, \ldots, Mb_m\}$
   (b) $\Lambda_{i+1} = \Lambda_i$

Further, $\Phi_1 = Query(\leftarrow w)$ and Λ_1 is a Π-defining set. We call Λ_1 the first default set. We call (Φ_n, Λ_n) the final tuple. Φ_n is called the *final rule set*, and Λ_n is called the *final default set.*

A *notInExtension derivation* of a formula w is a derivation in which, Φ_n is the empty set of default rules.

The following immediate consequences are useful.

Proposition 34. *In the inExtension and notInExtension refutation procedure, the default set Λ_i monotonically increases with each i.*

Proof: Obvious from the definition. $\square$

Proposition 35. *Suppose there is an InExtension refutation of w in a default theory $\Pi = (\Delta, \Omega)$ with final default set Λ. Then $E^* = th(Cons(\Lambda))$ is consistent.*

Proof: We know that $th(Cons(\Lambda_1))$ is consistent, since we assume that Ω is consistent. Suppose, $th(Cons(\Lambda_i))$ is not consistent. A default δ is only added to Λ_i

in step **ext1** and it always comes from Π. But, if δ makes $th(Cons(\Lambda_i))$ inconsistent, then δ could not have contributed to a meaningful default resolution, since we assume that the defaults are semi-normal. □

The following proposition shows that the final default set Λ of an inExtension refutation of b contains important information. This result is contingent on the fact that **next1** uses weak partial refutations, not partial refutations.

Proposition 36. *Let $\Pi = (\Delta, \Omega)$ be a default theory. Suppose there is an inExtension refutation of b in Π with final default set Λ. Then for all $j \in Justs(\Lambda)$, the following is true. For all partial refutations of $\neg j$ in Π with first default set Ω and final default ρ, there is a $k \in justs(\rho)$, such that $\neg k \in th(Cons(\Lambda))$.*

Proof: We know that δ is added to Λ_i, the current default set, only in **ext1**. Thus, for all $j \in justs(\delta)$, Mj is in a resolvent. Hence, there must be a notInExtension refutation of $\neg j$. There are two cases to consider.
Case1: Suppose there is a partial refutation of $\neg j$ in Π with final default ρ that is not meaningful with respect to Λ_i. Then, ρ will not be in the Φ_i generated by **next1**. By the monotonicity of Λ_i stated in Proposition 34, the theorem holds.
Case2: Suppose there is a partial refutation of $\neg j$ in Π with final default ρ that is meaningful with respect to Λ_i. Then, $\rho \in \Phi_i$. However, since there is an inExtension refutation of b, we must eventually get rid of every rule in Φ_i through some call to **next2** or **next3**. Clearly, if **next2** gets rid of ρ, the theorem holds, by Proposition 34. Further, if **next3** gets rid of ρ, then there is a $k \in justs(\rho)$ such that $\neg k$ is in Λ_{i+c}. Hence, by Proposition 34, the theorem holds. □

5.2 Soundness

The soundness proof is based on the assumption that every subset of the default theory has an extension. Although limiting, this class is actually larger than the class of normal default theories. This can be easily shown since the semi-normal default theory

$$\Pi = (\{p \leftarrow M(p\&\neg q), q \leftarrow M(q\&\neg p)\}, \emptyset)$$

has two extensions $\{p\}$ and $\{q\}$, and the union of these two extensions is a consistent set of formulas. Extensions of normal default theories are always pairwise inconsistent (see Theorem 4.8 in [MT93]).

Proposition 37. *Suppose there is an inExtension refutation of w in Π with final default set Λ. Then, for all $\lambda \in \Lambda$, there is a partial refutation of every $p \in prereqs(\lambda)$ in Π.*

Proof: This can be seen from the structure of the inExtension refutation procedure. □

Proposition 38. *Let $\Pi = (\Delta, \Omega)$ be a default theory. Suppose there is an inExtension refutation of w in Π with final default set Λ. Then, every $\lambda \in \Lambda$ is meaningful with respect to $E^* = th(Cons(\Lambda))$.*

Proof: The proof is by induction on the number of *inExtension* refutations that are contained in the *inExtension* refutation of w. We let Λ_i be the current default sets at step i in the proof and $E_i^* = th(Cons(\Lambda_i))$

Base: Consider the last *inExtension* refutation. We show that the last default λ added to Λ, the final default set must be meaningful with respect to E^*.

A default λ is added to Λ_i only in step **ext1**. Consider the last default added to Λ in step n. Clearly, this default is meaningful with respect to $th(Cons(\Lambda_{n-1}))$. Suppose that it is not meaningful with respect to $\Lambda_{n-1} \cup \{\lambda\}$. Thus, there is a $j \in justs(\lambda)$, such that $\neg j \in th(Cons(\Lambda_{n-1} \cup \{\lambda\}))$. But, λ is semi-normal, so there is only one justification j. Hence, j contributes to the proof of $\neg j$. Hence, by definition *meaningful*, λ is not meaningful with respect to $th(Cons(\Lambda_{n-1}))$.

Inductive: We assume that the last i λ's added to Λ are meaningful with respect to E^*. We show that the $i+1^{st}$ last λ added to Λ is also meaningful with respect to E^*.

Suppose not. Thus, there is a $j \in justs(\lambda)$, such that $\neg j$ is in E^*. However, Mj is a justification in some final default rule in a partial refutation. Thus, a *notInExtension* derivation will be done on $\neg j$. Further, we know by Proposition 36 that for all partial refutations of $\neg j$ in Π, none are meaningful with respect to E^*.

However, we know that at some point $\neg j$ must be added to E_i^*. Suppose, it was in E_k^*, $k \leq i$. Then, λ could not have been part of a meaningful refutation. Suppose, then we add $\neg j$ later. Then, by the inductive hypothesis, there is a refutation of $\neg j$ that is meaningful with respect to E^*. This is a contradiction. □

Theorem 39. *Let $\Pi = (\Delta, \Omega)$ be a default theory with the property that each subset of Π has an extension. Suppose there is an inExtension refutation of w in Π. Then, there is an extension E of Π that contains w.*

Proof: Let Λ be the final default set. First we show that Λ has the extension E^*. Look at Λ^{E^*}. By Proposition 38, each default $\delta \in \Lambda$ is meaningful with respect to $E^* = th(Cons(\Lambda))$. Thus, $\Lambda^{E^*} = Simple(\Lambda)$. But, by Proposition 37, for all $\lambda \in \Lambda$ there is a partial refutation of each $p \in prereqs(\Lambda)$ in Λ. Hence, there is also a corresponding proof of p, in $Simple(\Lambda)$. Thus, by Proposition 25, if Λ^{E^*} has an extension F, each $p \in prereqs(\Lambda)$ is in F. Thus by Proposition 10, $F = E^*$. But, Λ^{E^*} is a simple default theory then it must have an extension since E^* is consistent.

Since $w \in E^*$ by construction of inExtension refutations, we need to show that there is an extension F of Π_{E^*} that contains E^*. Look at Π_{E^*}. Clearly $\Lambda \subseteq \Pi_{E^*}$. By hypothesis, Π_{E^*} has an extension F. If $(\Pi_{E^*})^F \supseteq \Lambda^{E^*}$, then clearly $F \supseteq E^*$ because for simple defaults the operator E_i in Definition 2 is monotonically increasing with i. Suppose, $(\Pi_{E^*})^F$ does not contain one $\lambda \in \Lambda^{E^*}$. Then there is a $j \in justs(\lambda)$ such that $\neg j$ is in F. Thus, by Proposition 28, there is a partial refutation $\mathcal{R}$ of $\neg j$ in Π_{E^*} with final default rule ρ such that ρ is meaningful with respect to F. But, by Proposition 36 there is *no* partial refutation of $\neg j$ in Π that is meaningful with respect to E^*. Therefore there is no refutation of $\neg j$ in Π_{E^*}. This is a contradiction to the existence of $\mathcal{R}$ in Π_{E^*}.

Now, we show that F is also an extension for Π. Clearly, $(\Pi_{E^\bullet})^F = \Pi^F$. Thus, F is an extension for Π and $w \in F$. □

Corollary 40. *Let $\Pi = (\Delta, \Omega)$ be a default theory with the property that each subset of Π has an extension. Let Λ_1 be a Π-defining set. Suppose there is an inExtension refutation of w in Π with first default set Λ_1 and final default set Λ. Then, there is an extension E of Π that contains w, such that Λ is a Π-defining set through E.*

Proof: The proof goes the same as the proof of Theorem 39. Assume that Λ is the final default set. We add that each $p \in prereqs(\Lambda)$ has a partial refutation by both Proposition 37 and the definition of Π-defining. □

Corollary 41. *Let $\Pi = (\Delta, \Omega)$ be a default theory. Suppose there is an inExtension refutation of w in Π. Then Λ_n, the final default set, is Π-defining.*

Proof: Obvious from the proof of Theorem 39. □

5.3 Completeness

The completeness proof does not rely on the assumption that every subset of the default theory has an extension.

First we show that if there is an extension that contains a formula w, then there is always another tuple that can be generated by the inExtension refutation procedure. Then, we show that the proof procedure will eventually terminate. These two conditions are enough to guarantee completeness.

Proposition 42. *Suppose the default theory $\Pi = (\Delta, \Omega)$ has an extension E, such that $w \in E$. Then there is always a tuple that can be generated in the inExtension refutation procedure for w.*

Proof: We can build a partial inExtension refutation with final default set $(\rho, Defaults, \Lambda)$, where ρ is meaningful with respect to E and Λ is part of a Π-defining set through E, similar to the refutation built in the if part of Proposition 28. Next we can build a notInExtension refutation starting from step **next3** and the tuple $(\rho, Defaults, \Lambda)$. Further we show that each tuple (Φ_i, Λ_i) generated from the notInExtension refutation procedure has the property that each $\phi \in \Phi_i$ is not activated in E, and Λ_i is a Π-defining set through E. In addition every other tuple $(\rho_i, Defaults_i, \Lambda_i)$ generated by intermediate calls to the inExtension refutation procedure has the property that ρ is meaningful with respect to E and Λ_i is a Π-defining set through E.
Base: Clearly this is true for $(\leftarrow w, Query(\leftarrow w), \Omega)$.
Inductive:
Case1: Consider the first tuple in a notInExtension refutation, (Φ_1, Λ_1). This tuple can only be generated if **ext3** was called. By the inductive hypothesis, Λ_1 is a Π-defining default set. Further, by the inductive hypothesis and by construction each $\delta \in \Phi_1$ is not activated in E.

Case2: Suppose (Φ_i, Λ_i) is generated from a call to **next1**. Clearly, by the inductive hypothesis, Λ_i is a Π-defining default set. By the inductive hypothesis, Φ_{i-1} is not activated in E. By Proposition 28, there are no partial refutations that will result from **next1** that are meaningful with respect to E. Thus, any rule in Φ_i will not be meaningful with respect to E.
Case3: Suppose (Φ_i, Λ_i) is generated from a call to **next2**. By the inductive hypothesis, the Theorem holds.
Case4: Suppose (Φ_i, Λ_i) is generated from a call to **next3**. We know that each rule in Φ_{i-1} contains a justification j such that $\neg j \in E$, by induction. Select this Mj as the Mb_1 in **next3**. By Proposition 28, there is a partial refutation $\mathcal{R}$ of $\neg j$ in Π that is meaningful with respect to E. Hence, $\mathcal{R}$ is meaningful with respect to Λ_i. We did this partial refutation by induction. Thus, the final default set is meaningful with respect to E. Further, Φ_i satisfies the Theorem, by induction.
Case5: Suppose $(\rho_1, Defaults_1, \Lambda_1)$ is a first tuple in an inExtension refutation. By induction and the arguments in *Case4* and Proposition 28, the theorem holds.
Case6: Suppose $(\rho_i, Defaults_i, \Lambda_i)$ is a final default in a partial inExtension refutation. By the arguments in *Case4* there is a partial refutation that is meaningful with respect to E, and hence is meaningful with respect to the last Π-defining set through E, Λ_{i-c}. Further, by Proposition 27, Λ_i must be a Π-defining set through E.
Case7: Suppose $(\rho_i, Defaults_i, \Lambda_i)$ is generated ¿from **ext3**. By the inductive hypothesis for notInExtension refutations, the Theorem holds. □

For propositional refutations, it is easy to check for looping. We assume that the partial inExtension refutation procedures do these recursion checks to avoid infinite loops.

Proposition 43. *The inExtension refutation procedure must terminate.*

Proof: There are a finite number of formulas that are in justifications of defaults in a default theory $\Pi = (\Delta, \Omega)$. Except for the first tuple, the notInExtension refutation Algorithm is only called on justifications of defaults in Π. Further, we know that there are a finite number of partial inExtension refutations of each formula. We assume that we can find all of them in a finite amount of time. With a propositional default theory, this can be done with the standard checks for looping.

Suppose that notInExtension is called with first default rule set $\{\leftarrow w\}$. If there are no weak partial inExtension refutations, then the algorithm will eventually terminate. So, suppose there is a $\rho \in \Phi_i$ which is a final default in a weak partial inExtension refutation. Thus, we call inExtension on the negation of some justification j of ρ. If the inExtension refutation succeeds, any subsequent calls to the inExtension or notInExtension Algorithm will result in $\neg j \in th(Cons(\Lambda_i))$, where Λ_i, is the current default set. Thus, the particular partial refutation that Mj was in will no longer be meaningful with respect to $th(cons(\Lambda_i))$. Hence, ρ will not be in any subsequent Φ_i. Thus, on each call to inExtension (after the first call to inExtension), we will prevent one refutation from being meaningful in notInExtension, and hence Φ_i cannot contain ρ. Since there are only a finite number of possible refutations, the procedure must terminate. If the inExtension refutation procedure does not succeed, then either the algorithm fails, or it will succeed for another j in $justs(\rho)$ and the above arguments apply. □

Theorem 44. *Suppose the default theory $\Pi = (\Delta, \Omega)$ has an extension E, such that $w \in E$. Then there is an inExtension refutation of w in Π.*

Proof: Immediate from Proposition 42 and Proposition 43. □

Corollary 45. *Let Π be a default theory with extension E, such that $w \in E$. Let Λ_1 be a Π-defining default set through E. Then there is an inExtension refutation of w in Π with first default set Λ_1, that returns the final default set Λ and Λ is a Π-defining default set through E*

Proof: Immediate from the proof above. □

6 Results

In this section it is assumed that every subset of our default theory has an extension. In general this is not true. In the next section we show how this assumption may be relaxed.

Theorem 46. *Suppose that $\Pi = (\Delta, \Omega)$ is a default theory with extension E. Then $w \in E$ iff there is an inExtension refutation of w in Π where the first default set is any Π-defining default set through E.*

Proof: Immediate from Theorem 39, Theorem 44, and Corollary 40. □

Theorem 47. *Suppose that Π is a default theory. Then w is not in one extension E of Π iff there is a notInExtension refutation of w in Π where the first default set is any Π-defining default set through E.*

Proof: ($\Leftarrow$) Let Λ be the final default set. We know from Proposition 36 that for all partial refutations of w in Π, w is not meaningful with respect to Λ. But from previous arguments Λ has the extension $E^* = th(Cons(\Lambda))$, and we know that Π_{E^*} has an extension F that does not contain w and F is an extension for Π.

($\Rightarrow$) Similar to the completeness proof. □

Theorem 48. *Suppose that Π is a default theory with extension E, such that w_1 and w_2 are formula's in E. Then, there is an inExtension refutation of w_1 in Π with final default set Λ_1, and there is an inExtension refutation of w_2 in Π with first default set Λ_1 and final default set Λ.*

Proof: If $w_1 \in E$, then there is an inExtension refutation of w_1 in Π, with final default set Λ_n^1. Further, by Corollary 40, Λ_n^1 is Π-defining through E. Hence, by Theorem 46, there is an inExtension refutation of w_2 in Π with first default set Λ_n^1, that returns Λ_n^2, another Π-defining default set through E. □

The above results can be summarized in Figure 1. Notice that sometimes it is beneficial to know when a particular query fails. Particularly, if we want to solve the extension membership problem.

ρ	inExtension refutation	failed inExtension refutation
$\leftarrow a$	a is in one extension	a not in any extension
$\leftarrow \neg a$	$\neg a$ is in one extension	$\neg a$ is not in any extension
$\leftarrow Ma$	$\neg a$ is not in one extension	$\neg a$ in every extension
$\leftarrow M\neg a$	a is not in one extension	a is in every extension

Fig. 1. Results of different derivations, with first tuple $(\rho, Query(\rho), \Omega)$.

7 Relaxing Assumptions

7.1 Adding variables

Let $\Pi = (\Delta, \Omega)$ be a normal default theory with variables. The default rules δ in Π have the form:

$$c(\overline{x}) \leftarrow a_1(\overline{x}), ..., a_n(\overline{x}), M(b(\overline{x})\&c(\overline{x}))$$

Implicitly δ is quantified universally. We assume that δ is *range restricted.* In other words every variable that occurs in the default occurs in a prerequisite of δ. By definition then, everything in Ω must be ground. Further we define our algorithm to be *safe* if it only calls inExtension on ground literals. Our algorithm is safe, since the default theory is range restricted, and partial refutations are always done first. The safeness restriction is included in order to prevent *floundering* (c.f. [LMR92].) In future work we would like to consider the case where variables are allowed in defaults and queries. We believe that under natural extensions of safeness and floundering derivations of logic programs to default theories, the soundness and correctness of the proof procedure should hold.

Adding variables will also affect the termination of the algorithm. While in the propositional case it is easy to check for infinite proofs, variables makes this check much more difficult. There is a strong parallel between SLDNF and the inExtension refutation procedure. Consider the problem of finding a notInExtension refutation. It is similar to the problem of finding an SLD finite failure tree. Although, a finite failure tree may exist, SLDNF may spend an infinite amount of time determining this. This is because there is no algorithm A, which given as input a query w and a program P, can output in a finite amount of time whether or not a is in P. Similarly, the notInExtension refutation procedure may spend an infinite amount of time looking for all partial refutations.

7.2 Expanding the default class

A significant limiting assumption to the results presented above is that every subset of a default theory must have an extension for the soundness result to hold. This assumption while restrictive, is still more general than one might expect.

The class of *even default theories* has this property. Evenness is a syntactic property based on a graph of the default theory. Thus, it is quite easy to test if something is even.

Definition 49 [PS92]. A *graph* of a propositional semi-normal default theory (Δ, Ω), $G = (E, A)$ is a directed graph with defaults as nodes and whose set of arcs A are partitioned into arcs of weight 0 and arcs of weight 1.

(a) There is an arc $(\delta_1, \delta_2) \in A$ of weight 0 if there is a literal g in $cons(\delta_1)$ such that $g \in justs(\delta_2)$.
(b) There is an arc $(\delta_1, \delta_2) \in A$ of weight 1 if there is a literal g in $cons(\delta_1)$ such that $\neg g$ is in $prereqs(\delta_2)$, $justs(\delta_2)$, or $cons(\delta_2)$.
(c) There is an arc $(\delta_1, \delta_2) \in A$ of weight 0 if there is a literal g in $cons(\delta_1)$, such that $\neg g$ and e are in $\omega \in \Omega$ or $\omega = cons(\delta_3)$, where $\delta_3 \in \Delta$, and e is in $prereqs(\delta_2)$.
(d) There is an arc $(\delta_1, \delta_2) \in A$ of weight 0 if there is a literal g in $cons(\delta_1)$, such that $\neg g$ and e are in $\omega \in \Omega$ or $\omega = cons(\delta_3)$, where $\delta_3 \in \Delta$, and $\neg e$ is in $prereqs(\delta_2)$, $justs(\delta_2)$, or $cons(\delta_2)$.

An *even* propositional semi-normal default theory, is a default theory with a graph that contains only cycles of even weight.

Proposition 50 [PS92]. *Every even propositional semi-normal default theory has an extension.*

Proposition 51. *If (Δ, W) is an even default theory, then (Γ, V), where $\Gamma \subseteq \Delta$ and $V \subseteq W$, is also an even default theory.*

Proof: The graph of (Γ, V) is a subgraph of the graph of (Δ, W). A subgraph H of a graph G contains a subset of the edges, and hence cycles, in the graph G. □

Theorem 52. *The inExtension refutation procedure is sound and complete for even default theories, finite ordered default theories [Eth87] normal default theories, and propositional stratified default theories.*

Proof: Every subset of a normal default theory has an extension. Further, finite ordered default theories and stratified default theories are even. □

Because the definition of evenness is syntactic in nature, it is slightly more general than we need it to be. In particular, some odd cycles do not interfere with the extensions of default theories.

Definition 53. Let Π be a default theory with an odd cycle containing the defaults κ. Suppose that for each $\delta \in \kappa$, *meaningful*$(\delta, th(Cons(\kappa)))$. Then, we say that the cycle defined by κ is *not hazardous*. Otherwise, we say that κ is *hazardous*.

Conjecture 54. *Let Π be a default theory with no hazardous odd cycles. Then, Π has an extension.*

Proof (sketch): For every odd cycle in the graph. Choose any edge of weight 1. Change this edge to an edge of weight zero. Now the default theory must have only even cycles. Hence, by the results of [PS92], we can partition the graph into two sets such that only the edges of weight 1 run between the sets. Because the cycles are not hazardous, the defaults in one set only interfere with the activation of defaults on the other set. Hence, we should be able to follow the proof procedure in [PS92] and generate an extension for Π. □

The following definition makes use of this conjecture to insure that an in-Extension refutation of a formula b succeeds in a default theory Π only if Π contains an extension with b in it.

Definition 55. Let κ be a set of defaults. We define $dcyc(\kappa)$ to be the default,

$$@_\kappa \leftarrow p_1, ..., p_n, Mj_1, ... Mj_n,$$

where $Prereqs(\kappa) = \{p_1, ..., p_n\}$, $Justs(\kappa) = \{j_1, ..., j_n\}$, and $@_\kappa$ is a new atom not in Π.

Proposition 56. *Let Π be a default theory with one hazardous cycle containing the defaults κ. Then Π has an extension iff there is an inExtension refutation of $M@_\kappa$ in $\Gamma = \Pi \cup \{dcyc(\kappa)\}$.*

Proof: Suppose that there is an inExtension refutation of $M\neg@_\kappa$ that returns final default set δ. Let $E^* = th(Cons(\delta))$. We know that Γ_{E^*} is even. We must show that there is a default $D \in \kappa$ that is not in Γ_{E^*}. Clearly, $dcyc(\kappa)$ is not in δ or $dcyc(\kappa)$ would be satisfied, thus satisfying every default in κ, and hence resulting in E^* being non-meaningful which is a contradiction. So, if $dcyc(\kappa)$ is not in δ, then for all partial inExtension refutations of $@_\kappa$ with final default rule R, there is a $j \in Justs(R)$, such that $\neg j \in E^*$. The, the default set δ is both semi-normal and even. It thus has an extension E^*. Suppose $dcyc(\kappa)$ is in Γ_{E^*}. Then there is no partial refutation of $dcyc(\kappa)$ in Γ. So we can remove $dcyc(\kappa)$ from Γ_{E^*} and not affect its extension, if it has one. Thus, there is a $p \in prereqs(dcyc(\kappa))$ such that there is no partial refutation of p in Γ. Hence, we can remove the default $d \in \kappa$, such that $p \in prereqs(\delta)$. Now, $\Gamma' = \Gamma_{E^*} \setminus \{dcyc(\kappa), d\}$ is even and semi-normal. Hence Γ' has an extension E. Clearly, E is an extension for Γ.

Suppose Γ has an extension. Then clearly, $dcyc(\kappa)$ is not satisfied in E. Hence, we can remove $dcyc(\kappa)$ from Γ. □

The above result can be extended to default theories with many hazardous cycles.

8 Examples

The inExtension refutation procedure has been implemented in C-Prolog. We illustrate, below, several examples that were also run by this program.

Example 3. Let Π_1 be the following default theory:

$$\{q \leftarrow M(\neg p\&q), \quad q \leftarrow M(\neg q\&p)\}$$

This default theory has two extensions, $E_1 = th(\{p\})$ and $E_2 = th(\{q\})$. The following shows an inExtension refutation for q.

$(\leftarrow q, \{\neg q \leftarrow\}, \{\})$
$(\neg q \leftarrow, \{\neg q \leftarrow\}, \{\})$
$(\leftarrow M(\neg p\&q), \{\neg q \leftarrow, \ \leftarrow M(\neg p\&q)\}, \{q \leftarrow M(\neg p\&q)\})$

$(\{\leftarrow p \vee \neg q\}, \{q \leftarrow M(\neg p\&q)\})$

There does not exist a weak partial inExtension refutation of $p \vee \neg q$.

$(\{\}, \{q \leftarrow M(\neg p\&q)\})$
$(\square, \{\neg q \leftarrow, \ \leftarrow M(\neg p\&q)\}, \{q \leftarrow M(\neg p\&q)\})$

Example 4. Below we show how the algorithm performs on a default theory with 1 non-hazardous odd cycle. Let Π_2 be the following default theory.

$$\{b \leftarrow M(a\&b), \quad \neg a \vee g \leftarrow b, M(\neg a \vee f)\}$$

This default theory has one extensions, $E = th(\{b, \neg a \vee g\})$. The following shows an inExtension refutation for b.

$(\leftarrow b, \{\neg b \leftarrow\}, \{\})$
$(\neg b \leftarrow, \{\neg b \leftarrow\}, \{\})$
$(\leftarrow M(a\&b), \{\neg b \leftarrow, \ \leftarrow M(\neg a\&b)\}, \{b \leftarrow M(a\&b)\})$

$(\{\leftarrow \neg a \vee \neg b\}, \{b \leftarrow M(a\&b)\})$

There are no weak partial inExtension refutations of $\neg a \vee \neg b$.

$(\{\}, \{b \leftarrow M(a\&b)\})$
$(\square, \{\neg b \leftarrow, \ \leftarrow M(a\&b)\}, \{b \leftarrow M(a\&b)\})$

Example 5. It has not yet been discussed what the algorithm might compute when there is a hazardous odd cycle. Interestingly, the algorithm appears to give us relevant information. In Section 9, we approach this question more formally.

Let Π_3 be the following default theory with one hazardous odd cycle.

$$\{b \leftarrow M(a\&b), \quad c \leftarrow b, Mc, \quad \neg a \leftarrow c, M\neg a\}$$

This default theory has no extensions. The inExtension refutation procedure appropriately fails on the queries a, b, and c.

Observe what happens when we attempt to do an inExtension refutation for b.

$(\leftarrow b, \{\neg b \leftarrow\}, \{\})$
$(\neg b \leftarrow, \{\neg b \leftarrow\}, \{\})$

$(\leftarrow M(a\&b),\ \{\neg b \leftarrow,\ \ \leftarrow M(a\&b)\},\ \{b \leftarrow M(a\&b)\})$

$(\{\leftarrow a \vee \neg b\},\ \{b \leftarrow M(a\&b)\})$

There is one weak partial inExtension refutation of $\neg a \vee \neg b$.

$(\{\leftarrow Mc, M\neg a, M(a\&b)\},\ \{b \leftarrow M(a\&b)\})$

Applying **next3**.

There is no partial inExtension refutations of $\neg c$.

(No default has consequent $\neg c$.)

$(\{\leftarrow M\neg a, M(a\&b)\},\ \{b \leftarrow M(a\&b)\})$

There is no partial inExtension refutations of a.

(No default has consequent a.)

$(\{\leftarrow M(a\&b)\},\ \{b \leftarrow M(a\&b)q\})$

There is no partial inExtension refutations of $\neg a \vee \neg b$.

$(\leftarrow \neg a \vee \neg b,\ \{b \leftarrow,\ \ a \leftarrow\},\ \{b \leftarrow M(a\&b)\})$

(No default has consequent $\neg b$.)

$(a \leftarrow,\ \{b \leftarrow,\ \ a \leftarrow\},\ \{b \leftarrow M(a\&b)\})$

$(\leftarrow c, M\neg a,\ \{\leftarrow c, M\neg a,\ \ b \leftarrow,\ \ a \leftarrow\},\ \{b \leftarrow M(a\&b),\ \ \neg a \leftarrow c, M\neg a\})$

$(\neg c \leftarrow M\neg a,\ \{\leftarrow c, M\neg a,\ \ b \leftarrow,\ \ a \leftarrow\},\ \{b \leftarrow M(a\&b),\ \ \neg a \leftarrow c, M\neg a\})$

$(\leftarrow b, Mc, M\neg a,\ \{\leftarrow b, Mc, M\neg a,\ \ \leftarrow c, M\neg a,\ \ b \leftarrow,\ \ a \leftarrow\},$
$\{b \leftarrow M(a\&b),\ \ \neg a \leftarrow c, M\neg a,\ \ c \leftarrow b, Mc\})$

$$(\neg b \leftarrow Mc, M\neg a,\ \{\leftarrow b, Mc, M\neg a,\ \ \leftarrow c, M\neg a,\ \ b \leftarrow,\ \ a \leftarrow\},$$
$$\{b \leftarrow M(a\&b),\ \ \neg a \leftarrow c, M\neg a,\ \ c \leftarrow b, Mc\})$$

There is no meaningful default to resolve with.

Thus, notInExtension fails.
Hence, the inExtension refutation procedure fails.

9 Discussion and Conclusion

We have presented a sound and complete algorithm to compute the members of an extension for default theories in which each subset of the default theory has an extension. We have shown how this procedure can be used to solve both the entailment problem and the extension membership problem, although the latter is contingent on the proof failing, not succeeding. Further, we have shown that the algorithm returns a Π-defining set, which can be used to answer further queries in the program. In addition, we have discussed the implications of adding variables to our default theory and how to relax the assumption that every subset of the default theory has an extension.

Since the algorithm is sound and complete for *even default theories*, it might be interesting to study what implications the notion of evenness has on other nonmonotonic reasoning techniques. In particular, it seems that the abductive refutation procedure of Eshghi et.al. [EK89] might be both sound and complete for a related class of *even logic programs*, which would be constructed in a similar manner to the class of even default theories. Currently, their algorithm has been proven to be sound for the restricted case of locally stratifiable logic programs. Further, the algorithm does compute something, even if the default theory is not *even*. We propose that the algorithm is actually computing the extension classes of default theories [BS91]. Consider the following two examples.

Example 6. Consider the default theory:
$b \leftarrow M(a\&b)$
$c \leftarrow b, Mc$
$\neg a \leftarrow c, M\neg a$
It has one odd cycle and no extensions. However it has one extension class; $I_1 = (\{\neg a, b, c\}, \emptyset)$.[5] The inExtension refutation procedure will fail on the queries $\neg a$, b, and c.

Example 7. Consider the default theory:
$b \leftarrow M(\neg a \ \& \ b)$
$a \leftarrow M(\neg b \ \& \ a)$
$q \leftarrow M(\neg q \ \& \ q)$

[5] We abuse notation slightly here. Sets in the stable class actually represent deductive closure of the set. In other words the notation (A, B), actually means the two sets $th(A)$ and $th(B)$ are in the extension class.

It is not even and has no extensions. Further it has 4 extension classes; $I_1 = (\{q\}, \{a, b\})$, $I_2 = (\{a\}, \{a, q\})$, and $I_3 = (\{b, q\}, \{b\})$, and $I_4 = (\{a, b, q\}, \emptyset)$.

The inExtension refutation procedure will succeed for the queries a and b and fail for the query q. Thus, it computes the intersection of each extension class.

It would be interesting if we could prove that the inExtension refutation procedure only returns true for queries that are modeled by the intersection of all of the extension classes. We know that the extension classes are closely related to the extensions of a default theory. In particular, if a default theory has an extension E, there will always be a stable class containing the single extension E.

Proposition 57. *Let Π be a default theory such that every subset of the default theory has an extension. Then the inExtension refutation procedure computes the stable classes.*

References

[Bar94] M. Barback. *Default theories: proof procedures and the relation to nonmonotonic logics.* PhD thesis, Northwestern University, Department of Electrical Engineering and Computer Science, 1994.

[Bes89] P. Besnard. *An Introduction to Default Logic.* Springer, Berlin, Heidelberg, 1989.

[BF91] N. Bidoit and C. Froidevaux. General logical databases and programs: Default logic semantics and stratification. *Information and Computation*, 91:15–54, 1991.

[BS91] Chitta R. Baral and V.S. Subrahmanian. Stable extension class theory for logic programs and default logis. *Journal of Automated Reasoning*, pages 246–260, 1991.

[EK89] K. Eshghi and R.A. Kowalski. Abduction compared with negation by failure. In *Proceedings of the 6th ICLP*, pages 234–253, 1989.

[Eth87] David W. Etherington. Formalizing nonmonotonic reasoning systems. *Artificial Intelligence*, 31:41–85, 1987.

[Eth88] David W. Etherington. *Reasoning with Incomplete Information.* Morgan Kaufmann, 1988.

[GLPT91] M. Gelfond, V. Lifschitz, H. Przymusińska, and M. Truszczyński. Disjunctive defaults. In J. Allen, R. Fikes, and E. Sandewall, editors, *Principles of Knowledge Representation and Reasoning: Proceedings of the Second International Conference*, pages 230–237, San Mateo, California, April 22-25 1991. Morgan Kaufmann.

[Llo84] J.W. Lloyd. *Foundations of Logic Programming.* Springer-Verlag, 1984.

[LMR92] J. Lobo, J. Minker, and A. Rajasekar. *Foundations of Disjunctive Logic Programming.* The MIT Press, 1992.

[LS92] J. Lobo and V.S. Subrahmanian. Relating minimal models to prerequisite free normal defaults. *Information Processing Letters*, 44:129–133, 1992.

[MT89] W. Marek and M. Truszczynski. Stable semantics for logic programs and default theories. In *Proceedings of the NACLP*, pages 243–256, 1989.

[MT93] W. Marek and M. Truszczynski. *Non-monotonic Logic*. Springer-Verlag, 1993.

[PS92] C.H. Papadimitriou and M. Sideri. On finding extensions of default theories. In G. Goos and J. Hartmanis, editors, *International Conference on Database Theory*, pages 276–281. Springer-Verlag, 1992.

[Rei80] Raymond Reiter. A logic for default reasoning. *Artificial Intelligence*, 13:81–132, 1980.

A General Approach to Bottom-Up Computation of Disjunctive Semantics

Stefan Brass[1] and Jürgen Dix[2]

[1] Univ. of Hannover, Inst. f. Informatik,
Lange Laube 22,
D-30159 Hannover, FRG,
sb@informatik.uni-hannover.de

[2] Univ. of Koblenz, Inst. f. Informatik,
Rheinau 1,
D-56075 Koblenz, FRG
dix@informatik.uni-koblenz.de

Abstract. Our goal is to derive bottom-up query-evaluation algorithms from abstract properties of the underlying negation semantics. In this paper, we demonstrate our approach for the disjunctive stable model semantics, but the ideas are applicable to many other semantics as well. Our framework also helps to understand and compare other proposed query evaluation algorithms. It is based on the notion of conditional facts, developed by BRY and DUNG/KANCHANSUT. We start by computing a "residual program" and show that it is equivalent to the original program under very general conditions on the semantics (which are satisfied, e.g., by the well-founded, stable, stationary, and static semantics). Many queries can already be answered on the basis of the residual program. For the remaining literals, we propose to use an appropriate completion of the residual program, which syntactically characterizes the intended models. In the case of the stable model semantics, we utilize an interesting connection to CLARK's completion.

1 Introduction

In this paper, we introduce a framework for bottom-up query evaluation, and apply it to the disjunctive stable model semantics [GL91b, Prz91a]. A unique feature of our approach is that we derive the algorithms directly from abstract properties of the semantics [KLM90, Bra90, Dix92, DM94a, Dix95a, Dix95b, Dix95c]. In our case, these properties require certain elementary program transformations to be possible. Related transformational approaches have been considered in [DM93, CL95, DN95]. While in [DM93], abstract properties have been used only for speeding up query evaluation, in [CL95], the main focus of the program transformation is to make explicit possible uses of disjunctive information. The authors of [DN95, KSS91] consider only non-disjunctive programs under the well-founded semantics.

The first step of our approach is to compute the set of implied "conditional facts" [Bry89, Bry90, DK89a, DK89b, HY91]. These are rules without positive body literals, which result from delaying the evaluation of negative body literals (the delayed literals are attached as "conditions" to the derived facts). We show that this transformation preserves the semantics of the original program under very weak conditions, namely the possibility of unfolding (also called the "generalized principle of partial evaluation" GPPE [DM94b, Dix95b, SS94]) and the irrelevance of trivial tautologies (having the same atom in head and body). Of course, such a delaying of negative body literals is implicit in other query evaluation algorithms for non-stratified programs. It is nice, however, that our whole algorithm can be understood as a source level transformation. Lower level data structures are useful for speeding up certain abstract operations, but they are not essential for understanding the correctness of the algorithm.

The second step of the approach is to carry out certain reductions, namely to evaluate negative body literals if their truth value can be trivially determined. The result of this is called the *residual program*. The well-founded model (resp. a disjunctive extension of it) can be directly derived from the residual program. The computation of the residual program is also valid under many other semantics, e.g. the static [Prz95] and stationary [Prz91b] semantics. Of course, it is not necessary to have a strict separation between the first and the second step of the approach. By mixing and optimizing them, we are also able to derive the standard bottom-up query evalution algorithm for stratified non-disjunctive programs and the algorithm proposed in [KSS91] for the WFS of non-disjunctive programs. We believe that our approach can be a good framework to understand and compare other proposed (bottom-up) query evaluation algorithms.

Only the few atoms which are undefined in the WFS are considered in the third step. We propose to compute an appropriate completion of the residual program, which syntactically characterizes the intended models of the given semantics. In our case, we utilize (a disjunctive extension of) CLARK's completion [Cla78], which is equivalent to the stable model semantics for residual programs. Given such a set of formulas, standard theorem proving techniques can be used (we use hyperresolution [CL73] for model construction in an interesting way). More specialized techniques are also possible, but in the case of stable models it seems that not much can be gained. We believe that the availability of such a syntactical characterization greatly simplifies the understanding of query evaluation (compare, e.g. [BL92] and [BL93]). It certainly helps to view more specialized techniques only as possible optimizations of a simple basic approach.

Let us finally mention other proposed query evaluation algorithms for the (non-disjunctive) stable model semantics. Closest to our approach is probably [CW93]: They also compute a "residual program", but this is done top-down, and their processing of the residual program is quite different. The algorithms proposed in [BNNS93] (see also [DM93]) apply the definition or certain characterizations of the stable models quite directly, but use linear programming techniques for an efficient construction of minimal models. This is an interesting idea and could be used to replace our third step (expressing it the other way round, our computation of the residual program can be useful as a preprocessing phase for [BNNS93, DM93]). In [PAA91], a top-down algorithm for credulous query evaluation in extended stable models is presented. There, trees of ground literals are constructed which explain the truth or falsity of atoms in well-founded and stable models. As any top-down algorithm, they have to do some not easily understandable loop checking, which we get for free. On the other hand, top-down algorithms are goal-directed, which would need a "magic set" transformation in our case (this has been recently done by DEGERSTEDT/NILSSON in [DN95] for the well-founded semantics for non-disjunctive programs).

The paper is organized as follows. Section 2 contains the basic definitions, especially of the semantical properties on which the algorithm is based. In Section 3, we define the residual program, and show its equivalence to the original program. We then explain how to efficiently compute the residual program in Section 4. The usage of CLARK's completion to compute stable models is the subject of Section 5. In Section 6, we sketch how the algorithm [KSS91] for the well-founded semantics fits into our framework. We conclude with a summary and an outlook on future work. The proofs are delayed to an appendix.

2 Semantics and Program Transformations

We consider allowed disjunctive DATALOG programs over some fixed function-free finite signature Σ:

Definition 1 (Logic Program).
A program Φ is a finite set of rules of the form

$$A_1 \vee \cdots \vee A_k \leftarrow B_1 \wedge \cdots \wedge B_m \wedge \mathit{not}\ C_1 \wedge \cdots \wedge \mathit{not}\ C_n,$$

where the $A_i/B_i/C_i$ are Σ-atoms, $k \geq 1$, $m \geq 0$, $n \geq 0$, and every variable of the rule appears in one of the B_i.

We identify such a rule with the triple consisting of the following sets of atoms $\mathcal{A} := \{A_1, \ldots, A_k\}$, $\mathcal{B} := \{B_1, \ldots, B_m\}$, $\mathcal{C} := \{C_1, \ldots, C_n\}$, and write it as $\mathcal{A} \leftarrow \mathcal{B} \wedge \mathit{not}\ \mathcal{C}$.

Since not all proposed semantics are defined for the complete class of disjunctive programs, it is also possible to consider only a subset (which, however, must satisfy certain closure properties). Especially, our results remain valid when restricted to non-disjunctive or positive programs.

The following is a very general view of semantics:

Definition 2 (Semantics).
A semantics SEM is a mapping from the class of logic programs Φ over Σ into some semantic domain, e.g. sets of models or sets of consequences. The only restriction is that SEM is invariant under instantiation, i.e. $\mathrm{SEM}(\Phi) = \mathrm{SEM}(\Phi^*)$, where Φ^* denotes the full instantiation of Φ.

In this paper, we are mainly concerned with the stable model semantics of disjunctive programs [GL91b, Prz91a]:

Definition 3 (Stable Model).
A 2-valued Herbrand interpretation I is a stable model of a logic program Φ iff I is a minimal model of Φ/I, where Φ/I denotes the GELFOND/LIFSCHITZ-Transformation of Φ wrt I (instantiation of Φ and evaluation of negative body literals in I).

But our approach is not restricted to this particular semantics, it can be applied to any semantics satisfying some weak properties. Our properties all have the form that certain elementary transformations on logic programs are possible without changing the meaning of the programs. It suffices to consider instantiated (i.e. variable free) programs here, because we required that the semantics is instantiation-invariant, so it is completely determined by its values on instantiated programs.

Definition 4 (Program Transformation).
A transformation is any relation $\mapsto$ between instantiated logic programs.

Definition 5 (Equivalence Transformation).
A program transformation $\mapsto$ is a SEM-equivalence transformation if for all Φ, Φ' with $\Phi \mapsto \Phi'$: $\text{SEM}(\Phi) = \text{SEM}(\Phi')$.

A typical transformation of this kind is the elimination of tautological rules like $p \leftarrow p$, or, more general, $p \vee q \leftarrow p \wedge r \wedge \textit{not } s$. If a semantics is amendable to bottom-up evaluation, it should not depend on such tautologies, because a tautology can never yield anything new if applied from body to head.

Definition 6 (Elimination of Tautologies).
A semantics SEM allows elimination of tautologies, iff the transformation

$$\text{Delete a rule } \mathcal{A} \leftarrow \mathcal{B} \wedge \textit{not } \mathcal{C} \text{ with } \mathcal{A} \cap \mathcal{B} \neq \emptyset.$$

is a SEM-equivalence transformation.

Another, especially important transformation is partial evaluation in the sense of the "unfolding" operation. It is the "Generalized Principle of Partial Evaluation (GPPE)" of [DM94b, Dix95c, SS94]. In the case of non-disjunctive programs, the idea is simply to replace a positive body literal B by the bodies of all matching rules. This is very natural because the rules with B in their head are usually considered as the only possibilities to derive B. In the disjunctive case, we simply add the disjunctive context to the head of the resulting rule. For instance, if we apply this transformation to q in the body of $p \leftarrow q \wedge r$, and there is the rule $q \vee s \leftarrow t$, then the resulting rule is $p \vee s \leftarrow t \wedge r$.

Definition 7 (Generalized Principle of Partial Evaluation).
A semantics SEM satisfies GPPE iff the following transformation on instantiated logic programs is a SEM-equivalence transformation:

Replace a rule $\mathcal{A} \leftarrow \mathcal{B} \wedge \textit{not } \mathcal{C}$, where $\mathcal{B}$ contains an atom B, by the n rules

$$\mathcal{A} \cup (\mathcal{A}_i - \{B\}) \leftarrow (\mathcal{B} - \{B\}) \cup \mathcal{B}_i \wedge \textit{not } (\mathcal{C} \cup \mathcal{C}_i)$$

where $\mathcal{A}_i \leftarrow \mathcal{B}_i \wedge \textit{not } \mathcal{C}_i$ $(i = 1, \ldots, n)$ are all rules with $B \in \mathcal{A}_i$.

The following transformations are used in our algorithm for optimization only, so they are not as essential as the above ones. First, we can certainly evaluate negative body literals if their truth value is trivial:

Definition 8 (Reductions).
A semantics SEM allows positive/negative reduction iff the following are equivalence transformations on instantiated programs:

1. Replace a rule $\mathcal{A} \leftarrow \mathcal{B} \wedge not\ \mathcal{C}$ by $\mathcal{A} \leftarrow \mathcal{B} \wedge not\ (\mathcal{C} - \{C\})$ where C appears in no rule head.
2. Delete a rule $\mathcal{A} \leftarrow \mathcal{B} \wedge not\ \mathcal{C}$ if there is a disjunctive fact $\mathcal{A}' \leftarrow true$ with $\mathcal{A}' \subseteq \mathcal{C}$.

Second, many semantics allow to eliminate non-minimal rules, because they are logically weaker than other rules. However, this does not hold for semantics having an inclusive disjunction:

Definition 9 (Elimination of Non-Minimal Rules).
A semantics SEM allows elimination of non-minimal rules iff the following is a SEM-equivalence transformation:

Delete a rule $\mathcal{A} \leftarrow \mathcal{B} \wedge not\ \mathcal{C}$ s.t. there is another rule $\mathcal{A}' \leftarrow \mathcal{B}' \wedge not\ \mathcal{C}'$ with $\mathcal{A}' \subseteq \mathcal{A}$, $\mathcal{B}' \subseteq \mathcal{B}$, $\mathcal{C}' \subseteq \mathcal{C}$ (where at least one $\subseteq$ is proper).

Let us conclude this section with an overview of the properties of some well-known semantics (see also [BD95a] for interesting characterizations of STABLE):

Properties of Logic-Programming Semantics					
Semantics	Domain	El. Taut.	GPPE	P./N. Red.	Nonmin.
Clark's comp [Cla78]	Nondis.	—	•	•	•
GCWA [Min82]	Pos.	•	•	(trivial)	•
Positivism [BH86]	Dis.	—	•	•	•
WGCWA [RLM89][1]	Pos.	—	•	(trivial)	—
Stable [GL91b, Prz91a]	Dis.	•	•	•	•
WFS [VGRS91]	Nondis.	•	•	•	•
Strong WFS [Ros90]	Dis.	—	—	•	—
Stationary [Prz91b]	Dis.	•	•	•	•
Static [Prz95]	Dis.	•	•	•	•

3 Computing the Residual Program

In this section we explain how to compute a normal form of the given program, called the residual program, and prove that it is equivalent to the original program under very weak conditions on the semantics. Our approach is based

[1] WGCWA is equivalent to the semantics introduced by Ross/Topor in [RT88].

on the notion of "conditional facts", as developed by BRY [Bry89, Bry90] and DUNG/KANCHANSUT [DK89a, DK89b] (both for the non-disjunctive case). The idea is to delay the evaluation of negative body literals, and to attach them as conditions to the derived (disjunctive) facts. Because of the allowedness restriction on the programs, conditional facts are ground:

Definition 10 (Conditional Fact).
A conditional fact is a rule without positive body literals, i.e. it is of the form $A_1 \vee \cdots \vee A_k \leftarrow not\ C_1 \wedge \cdots \wedge not\ C_m$, where the A_i and the C_j are ground atoms ($k \geq 1$, $m \geq 0$).

The usual bottom-up fixpoint computation is also possible with conditional facts: In the non-disjunctive case, one can simply store the conditions of a fact in an additional set-valued argument. Derived facts get the union of the conditions of the facts matched with the body literals (plus the corresponding instances of the negative body literals of the rule itself). This is demonstrated in the following example:

$$p(a) \leftarrow \qquad\qquad \neg s(b) \quad \wedge \quad \neg r(b).$$
$$\uparrow \qquad\qquad\qquad \uparrow \qquad\quad \uparrow$$
$$\boxed{\quad p(X) \leftarrow q_1(X) \wedge q_2(X,Y) \wedge \neg r(Y). \quad}$$
$$\uparrow \qquad\quad \uparrow$$
$$q_1(a) \quad\ q_2(a,b) \leftarrow \neg s(b)$$

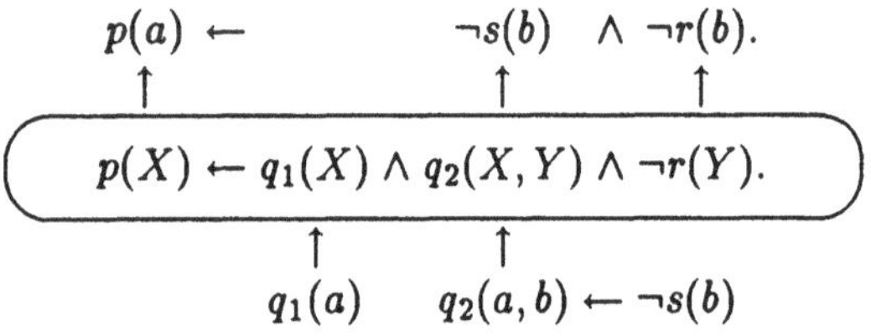

In the disjunctive case, one applies the "hyperresolution" operator, by adding to every fact also a disjunctive context [CL73, MR90, Bra95]. An implementation with database techniques has been suggested in [BL92]. Formally, the immediate consequence operator is generalized to conditional facts as follows:

Definition 11 (Immediate Consequences with Conditions).
For a set Γ of conditional facts we define:

$$T_\Phi(\Gamma) := \left\{ \left(A_0 \cup \bigcup_{i=1}^m (A_i - \{B_i\}) \right) \leftarrow \neg\left(C_0 \cup \bigcup_{i=1}^m C_i \right) \; \middle| \; \text{there are} \right.$$
$$\text{a ground instance } A_0 \leftarrow B_1 \wedge \cdots \wedge B_m \wedge \neg C_0 \text{ of a rule in } \Phi$$
$$\left. \text{and cond. facts } A_i \leftarrow \neg C_i \in \Gamma \text{ with } B_i \in A_i \ (i = 1, \ldots, m) \right\}.$$

We compute the smallest fixpoint of T_Φ as usual: We start with $\Gamma_0 := \emptyset$ and then iterate $\Gamma_i := T_\Phi(\Gamma_{i-1})$ until nothing changes. This must happen because there are only finitely many predicates and constants to build ground atoms occuring in conditional facts, and there are only finitely many subsets of all these atoms (corresponding to head and body). The transformation from the original logic program to the set of all derived conditional facts does not change the semantics of the program:

Theorem 12 ($\Phi \mapsto \mathrm{lfp}(T_\Phi)$ is a SEM-Equivalence Transformation).
Let SEM be a semantics which satisfies GPPE, and allows the elimination of tautologies. Then $SEM(\Phi) = SEM(\mathrm{lfp}(T_\Phi))$.

This is an important and non-trivial strengthening of a similar theorem from [BD95b]. Intuitively, it might seem very natural, because GPPE and T_Φ are rather similar. However, T_Φ works bottom-up, whereas GPPE works top-down. In fact, the formal proof is quite long (see the appendix). The earlier proof needed in addition the possibility to eliminate non-minimal rules, and was much simpler.

The next step of our algorithm is to reduce the derived conditional facts by evaluating the conditions where possible. For the computation of stable models, this step is not strictly necessary, but it is an important optimization. In the case of non-disjunctive programs, we simply evaluate *not* C to true if C appears in no head, and to false, if C is given as an unconditional fact. In the general case, the reduction is defined as follows:

Definition 13 (Reduction of Conditional Facts).
Let $\mathcal{P}(\Gamma)$ be the set of atoms occuring in some rule head in Γ. Then we define:

$$\begin{aligned} R(\Gamma) := \big\{\mathcal{A} \leftarrow \neg(\mathcal{C} \cap \mathcal{P}(\Gamma)) \;\big|\; & \mathcal{A} \leftarrow \neg\mathcal{C} \in \Gamma, \\ & \text{there is no } \mathcal{A}' \leftarrow \mathit{true} \in \Gamma \text{ with } \mathcal{A}' \subseteq \mathcal{C} \text{ and} \\ & \text{there is no } \mathcal{A}' \leftarrow \neg\mathcal{C}' \in \Gamma \text{ with } \mathcal{A}' \subseteq \mathcal{A},\, \mathcal{C}' \subseteq \mathcal{C} \\ & \qquad \text{(where at least one } \subseteq \text{ is proper)}\big\}. \end{aligned}$$

We again iterate this operator until nothing changes (the number of occurring literals decreases in each step). We call the result the "residual program", because it is similar to the residual program computed in [CW93]. However, our version also contains the true facts, not only conditions for the undefined facts.

Definition 14 (Residual Program).
The residual program of Φ is

$$\hat{\Phi} := R^{\omega}\big(\mathrm{lfp}(T_\Phi)\big).$$

Corollary 15 ($\Phi \mapsto \hat{\Phi}$ is a SEM-Equivalence Transformation).
Let SEM be a semantics satisfying all properties defined in Section 2. Then $SEM(\hat{\Phi}) = SEM(\Phi)$ for every logic program Φ and its residual program $\hat{\Phi}$.

So we now have a logic program equivalent to the original one under STABLE, WFS, and many other semantics. What we have gained during this computation is first that the rules have a very particular form (no positive body literals, no variables), and second that the truth value of most atoms can be trivially read from this program (because the atom is explicitly given as an unconditional fact or it does not appear in any rule head). There is usually only a very small number of proper conditional facts remaining, and this is where the various semantics differ. For instance, it follows from our results in [BD95b] that the well-founded semantics simply makes all the remaining "critical atoms" undefined.

4 Optimizations and Implementation Hints

In the last section, we gave a theoretical basis for computing the residual program. Now let us consider implementation issues in greater detail. Let us start with a trivial ("naive") implementation of the fixpoint computation:

$\Gamma_{last} := \emptyset;$
$\Gamma := \{\mathcal{A} \leftarrow not\ \mathcal{C} \mid \mathcal{A} \leftarrow not\ \mathcal{C} \in \Phi\};$
while $\Gamma \neq \Gamma_{last}$ **do**
  $\Gamma_{last} := \Gamma;$
  foreach $\mathcal{A} \leftarrow \mathcal{B} \wedge not\ \mathcal{C}$ **with** $\mathcal{B} \neq \emptyset$ **do**
    $apply(\mathcal{A} \leftarrow \mathcal{B} \wedge not\ \mathcal{C});$ /* $\Gamma := \Gamma \cup T_{\{\mathcal{A} \leftarrow \mathcal{B} \wedge not\ \mathcal{C}\}}(\Gamma_{last})$ */

We of course aim at semi-naive evaluation (see, e.g., [RSS94]). There, we have to distinguish between three sets of conditional facts:

1. The new conditional facts Γ_{new} which are generated during this iteration. We resolve with them only beginning in the next iteration (otherwise we would loose the control which resolution steps actually have been done).
2. The conditional facts Γ_{diff} generated in the last iteration. At least one body literal must be matched with them.
3. Conditional facts Γ_{old} generated before the last iteration. We guarantee that all resolution steps using only these conditional facts have already been done.

We will not consider this further here, since the standard techniques can be used.

The procedure *apply* evaluates a given rule against the current set of conditional facts. For simplicity, we show an implementation only for the case of two positive body literals. The generalization to a variable number of body literals is straightforward:

procedure $apply(\mathcal{A} \leftarrow B_1 \wedge B_2 \wedge not\ \mathcal{C})$:
  foreach $A_1 \leftarrow not\ \mathcal{C}_1 \in \Gamma_{last}$ **and** $A_1 \in \mathcal{A}_1$ **do**
    if there is θ_1 with $B_1\theta_1 = A_1$ **then**
      foreach $\mathcal{A}_2 \leftarrow not\ \mathcal{C}_2 \in \Gamma_{last}$ **and** $A_2 \in \mathcal{A}_2$ **do**
        if there is θ_2 with $B_2(\theta_1 \circ \theta_2) = A_2$ **then**
          $\theta := \theta_1 \circ \theta_2;$
          $\mathcal{A}' := \mathcal{A}_0\theta \cup (\mathcal{A}_1 - \{B_1\theta\}) \cup (\mathcal{A}_2 - \{B_2\theta\});$
          $\mathcal{C}' := \mathcal{C}_0\theta \cup \mathcal{C}_1 \cup \mathcal{C}_2;$
          $insert(\mathcal{A}' \leftarrow not\ \mathcal{C}');$
            /* $\Gamma := \Gamma \cup \{\mathcal{A}' \leftarrow not\ \mathcal{C}'\}$ */

There is a large body of knowledge on possible improvements upon this basic algorithm. Obviously, indexes are needed to speed up the search for $\mathcal{A}_i \leftarrow not\ \mathcal{C}_i$ and $A_i \in \mathcal{A}_i$ matching the body literal $B_i(\theta_1 \circ \cdots \circ \theta_{i-1})$. Note that the management of substitutions for allowed rules is very simple: The first occurrence of a variable assigns a value, later occurrences act only as a test. So if our internal representation of rules distinguishes between first and later occurrences, we do not explicitly need to undo a binding (e.g., by means of a trail).

The order of the body literals is relevant to make the best possible use of the existing indexes (and to fail a rule application as soon as possible). We should also employ "intelligent backtracking" (going back to the body literal which introduced the binding responsible for a later failed literal). Furthermore, there are of course other join techniques besides our "nested loop/index join".

The next point to consider is the procedure *insert*. Its goal is to add a newly computed conditional fact $\mathcal{A} \leftarrow \mathit{not}\, \mathcal{C}$ to the current set Γ of conditional facts. In doing so, it at least has to eliminate duplicates, otherwise even simple tautologies like $p(X) \leftarrow p(X)$ will lead to non-termination. But we can do even more. After computing the set of implied conditional facts, we will apply our reductions. So why not apply the reductions right now? Let us consider the three types of reductions in detail:

1. Elimination of non-minimal conditional facts: Suppose Γ contains a conditional fact $\mathcal{A}' \leftarrow \mathit{not}\, \mathcal{C}'$ with $\mathcal{A}' \subseteq \mathcal{A}$ and $\mathcal{C}' \subseteq \mathcal{C}$. Then of course $\mathcal{A} \leftarrow \mathit{not}\, \mathcal{C}$ will later be deleted, but also all facts derived using $\mathcal{A} \leftarrow \mathit{not}\, \mathcal{C}$ will be deleted: Let $A \in \mathcal{A}$ be matched with a body literal. If $A \in \mathcal{A}'$, we can as well use the stronger conditional fact. If $A \notin \mathcal{A}'$, the conditional fact $\mathcal{A}' \leftarrow \mathit{not}\, \mathcal{C}'$ is already stronger than the derived conditional fact. So in either case, non-minimal facts as input yield non-minimal facts as output. This allows us to delete them at once when they are generated — we do not have to wait until the reduction phase.
2. Positive reduction: This has to be delayed, because when we evaluate $\mathit{not}\, \mathcal{C}$ to true, we have to be sure that C will not later be derived.
3. Negative reduction: This can be done at once, because whenever $\mathcal{A} \leftarrow \mathit{not}\, \mathcal{C}$ is used in a resolution step, the resulting conditional fact contains also the condition $\mathit{not}\, \mathcal{C}$ (plus possibly more). So if we know already that $\mathit{not}\, \mathcal{C}$ is false, we only get superfluous conditional facts, which will later anyway be deleted. Therefore, we can delete them at once and avoid the unnecessary resolution steps.

But not only the newly computed conditional fact can be thrown away due to the reductions — we also may have to delete a member of Γ:

procedure *insert*($\mathcal{A} \leftarrow \mathit{not}\, \mathcal{C}$):
    foreach $\mathcal{A}' \leftarrow \mathit{not}\, \mathcal{C}' \in \Gamma$ **with** $\mathcal{A} \subset \mathcal{A}'$, $\mathcal{C} \subseteq \mathcal{C}'$ (or $\subseteq$, $\subset$) **do**
        $\Gamma := \Gamma - \{\mathcal{A}' \leftarrow \mathit{not}\, \mathcal{C}'\}$;
    if $\mathcal{C} = \emptyset$ **then**
        foreach $\mathcal{A}' \leftarrow \mathit{not}\, \mathcal{C}' \in \Gamma$ **with** $\mathcal{A} \subseteq \mathcal{C}'$ **then**
            $\Gamma := \Gamma - \{\mathcal{A}' \leftarrow \mathit{not}\, \mathcal{C}'\}$;
    if there is no $\mathcal{A}' \leftarrow \mathit{not}\, \mathcal{C}' \in \Gamma$ with $\mathcal{A}' \subseteq \mathcal{A}$, $\mathcal{C}' \subseteq \mathcal{C}$ **then**
        if there is no $\mathcal{A}' \leftarrow \mathit{true} \in \Gamma$ with $\mathcal{A}' \subseteq \mathcal{C}$ **then**
            $\Gamma := \Gamma \cup \{\mathcal{A} \leftarrow \mathit{not}\, \mathcal{C}\}$;

Deleting derived facts makes the immediate consequence operator nonmonotonic wrt $\subseteq$, however, it is monotonic in the lattice based on

$$\Gamma_1 \sqsubseteq \Gamma_2 \;:\Longleftrightarrow\; \text{for every } \mathcal{A}_1 \leftarrow \mathit{not}\, \mathcal{C}_1 \in \Gamma_1 \text{ there is } \mathcal{A}_2 \leftarrow \mathit{not}\, \mathcal{C}_2 \in \Gamma_2 \text{ such that } (\mathcal{A}_2 \subseteq \mathcal{A}_1 \text{ and } \mathcal{C}_2 \subseteq \mathcal{C}_1) \text{ or } (\mathcal{C}_2 = \emptyset \text{ and } \mathcal{A}_2 \subseteq \mathcal{C}_1).$$

Note also that this deletion is even compatible with semi-naive evaluation: When we delete an old conditional fact, we will insert a new "better" one for it. So there will be at least one further iteration, where we can use the new fact instead of the old one (and any rule application which uses this new fact is allowed in the next semi-naive step).

Of course, the feasibility of these reductions relies on an efficient algorithm for finding subsets/supersets. As experiments of SEIPEL [Sei94] have shown, the elimination of duplicate and subsumed disjunctive facts can take more than half of the total running time of query evaluation. The algorithm we are going to present is quite efficient; its time complexity for finding conditional facts in Γ which are affected by a newly computed fact $\mathcal{A} \leftarrow \mathit{not}\ \mathcal{C}$ is

$$O(\text{number of occurrences of literals from } \mathcal{A} \leftarrow \mathit{not}\ \mathcal{C} \text{ in } \Gamma).$$

Further improvements are subject of future research (for instance, it might be possible to generalize data structures for partial-match queries on relations).

Let us define the length of a conditional fact $\mathcal{A} \leftarrow \mathit{not}\ \mathcal{C}$ as the number of literals in it, i.e. $|\mathcal{A}| + |\mathcal{C}|$. The overlap of two disjunctive facts is the number of common literals, i.e. $|\mathcal{A}_1 \cap \mathcal{A}_2| + |\mathcal{C}_1 \cap \mathcal{C}_2|$. Now it is clear that $\mathcal{A}_1 \leftarrow \mathit{not}\ \mathcal{C}_1$ subsumes $\mathcal{A}_2 \leftarrow \mathit{not}\ \mathcal{C}_2$ (i.e. $\mathcal{A}_1 \subseteq \mathcal{A}_2$ and $\mathcal{C}_1 \subseteq \mathcal{C}_2$) iff the overlap of the two conditional facts is equal to the length of $\mathcal{A}_1 \leftarrow \mathit{not}\ \mathcal{C}_1$. The length of a conditional fact can be computed when it is constructed, we will assume that it is stored in an array *length*. Furthermore, we will use an array *overlap* to manage the overlap with the current conditional fact $\mathcal{A} \leftarrow \mathit{not}\ \mathcal{C}$. Of course, we cannot initialize it to zero every time when we want to check a new conditional fact. Therefore we use "lazy initialization": Every test is assigned a unique number *testno*, and we store in the array *lastset* the last time when the corresponding entry in *overlap* was initialized. So we refine the implementation of the procedure *insert* as follows:

```
testno := 0;
procedure insert(𝒜 ← not 𝒞):
    testno := testno + 1;
    foreach A ∈ 𝒜 do
        foreach 𝒜' ← not 𝒞' ∈ Γ with A ∈ 𝒜' do
            if inc_overlap(𝒜' ← not 𝒞', |𝒜| + |𝒞|) then
                return ; /* 𝒜 ← not 𝒞 is non-minimal */
    foreach C ∈ 𝒞 do
        foreach 𝒜' ← not 𝒞' ∈ Γ with C ∈ 𝒞' do
            if inc_overlap(𝒜' ← not 𝒞', |𝒜| + |𝒞|) then
                return ; /* 𝒜 ← not 𝒞 is non-minimal */
    .../* Negative reduction can be implemented similarly */
    Γ := Γ ∪ {𝒜 ← not 𝒞};
    length[𝒜 ← not 𝒞] := |𝒜| + |𝒞|;
    lastset[𝒜 ← not 𝒞] := 0;
```

Of course, in order to get the mentioned efficiency, our data structures must allow a direct access on the conditional facts $\mathcal{A}' \leftarrow \mathit{not}\ \mathcal{C}'$ with $A \in \mathcal{A}'$ or $C \in \mathcal{C}'$.

Now the procedure *inc_overlap* increments the overlap with a conditional fact $\mathcal{A}' \leftarrow not\ \mathcal{C}'$ and checks whether it is a subset or superset of the given conditional fact $\mathcal{A} \leftarrow not\ \mathcal{C}$:

```
procedure inc_overlap(A' ← not C', l): bool
    if lastset[A' ← not C'] = testno then
        overlap[A' ← not C'] := overlap[A' ← not C'] + 1;
    else
        overlap[A' ← not C'] := 1;
        lastset[A' ← not C'] := testno;
    if overlap[A' ← not C'] = length[A' ← not C'] then
        return true; /* A ← not C is non-minimal */
    if overlap[A' ← not C'] = l then
        delete(A' ← C');
    return false;
```

This completes our discussion of the computation of derived conditional facts.

The next step in the algorithm are the reductions. We have already eliminated non-minimal conditional facts, and done negative reduction. However, when we now evaluate negative body literals to "true", the other two reductions can become applicable again. Therefore we use the procedure *insert* for the reduced conditional facts, which automatically performs the other reductions.

So our goal now is to find efficiently occurrences of negative body literals which do not occur in any head. We already above needed data structures to locate all positive and negative occurrences of an atom. Now we suggest to introduce a counter *numpos*$[A]$ for the number of positive occurrences of A. It can easily be updated during the computation of the derived conditional facts. Furthermore, we also maintain a set *nopos* of those atoms occurring in a body, but not in a head. Then positive reduction can be implemented as follows:

```
procedure reduce:
    while nopos ≠ ∅ do
        let C ∈ nopos;
        foreach A ← not C ∈ Γ with C ∈ C do
            Γ := Γ − {A ← not C};
            insert(A ← not (C − {C}));
        nopos := nopos − {C};
```

Probably, it would slightly increase the efficiency if we immediately check the other body literals of this rule, i.e. call *insert*$(\mathcal{A} \leftarrow not\ (\mathcal{C} - nopos))$ instead. But in order not to repeat these checks later, we would have to store for every conditional fact the version number of *nopos* with which it was last reduced. The reason for this is that *nopos* is increased through the reductions performed by the call to *insert*.

The procedure *delete* called in *inc_overlap* looks as follows:

procedure *delete*($\mathcal{A}' \leftarrow not\ C'$):
  foreach $A \in \mathcal{A}'$ **do**
    $numpos[A] := numpos[A] - 1$;
    if $numpos[A] = 0$ **then**
      $nopos := nopos \cup \{A\}$;

This does not ensure that A occurs in a negative body literal when it is inserted into *nopos*, but this is not important for correctness and termination.

So we can now compute the residual program with reasonable efficiency. Especially, with the access paths discussed, we *never* have to go through the complete set Γ of conditional facts. There are two really important further optimizations, which, however, need further research in the disjunctive case.

First, it is not necessary to delay positive reduction until we have computed all derivable conditional facts. When we evaluate *not* C to *true*, we must only be sure that C will not occur in any head. In the case of Horn programs, it is known how to order the rules according to the predicate dependencies, and iterate only strongly connected components. We can do the same for conditional facts, at least if the program is non-disjunctive (for a generalization to disjunctive facts see [Bra95]). But this allows us to do positive reduction for all predicates defined in "lower" SCCs. Therefore, if the program should be stratified, we can evaluate all negative body literals immediately (and thus get the standard bottom-up query evaluation algorithm for stratified databases). Furthermore, if there are only a few parts in the program which are not stratified, we have to delay only these negative body literals.

Second, as any bottom-up approach, our technique would profit from a "magic set" transformation. However, this is only possible for semantics satisfying the "relevance" condition [Dix92, DM94c, DM94b], which the two-valued stable semantics does not. So there can be no goal-directed query evaluatation algorithm for it. However, if our method is used for computing, e.g., the WFS, then a magic set transformation would drastically increase the efficiency. In the non-disjunctive case, standard techniques may be appropriately adjusted (see [DN95, KSS91]). We only have to ensure that if we derive a conditional fact containing *not* C in its body, then we also get *magic*[C], so that rule instances possibly yielding C are not blocked. In the disjunctive case, no real magic set techniques are known, although ideas of [Dem91, Roy90, Bra95] might be used.

Finally, let us note that in the non-disjunctive case it is often possible (namely, when no predicate depends on itself positively and negatively at the same time) to introduce new predicates for conditional facts. This would allow to build an implementation on existing deductive databases.

5 Computing the Stable Semantics from the Completion

In the preceding sections, we have shown how to compute the residual program $\hat{\Phi}$. Let us repeat the two important properties of the residual program:

1. It is equivalent to the original program for a wide range of semantics (namely all semantics allowing the elementary transformations of Section 2).

2. It is much simpler than the original program, because it is ground, it contains no positive body literals, and usually only very few rules.

The truth value of most literals is already decided by the residual program, because they either are given as an unconditional fact or do not appear at all in it. We now have to treat the few difficult literals, about which conditions remained after the reductions. It is interesting to note that whatever we do with them, we get a semantics with the good properties of Section 2:

Theorem 16 [BD95b].
Let SEM be a semantics such that $SEM(\Phi) = SEM(\hat{\Phi})$ *for every logic program* Φ *and its residual program* $\hat{\Phi}$. *Then SEM allows unfolding (GPPE), elimination of tautologies and non-minimal rules, and positive and negative reduction.*

Note, however, that it is not guaranteed that any model of the residual program is also a model of the original program. So a model-theoretic semantics can only select certain models of the residual program, for instance, any subset of the supported models. It is subject of our future research to find a maximal class of three-valued models with this property.

But in this paper our main goal is to compute the stable model semantics. There we make use of a result of FAGES and BEN-ELIYAHU [AB94] that if there are no positive loops, the stable models coincide with the supported models. This is certainly the case for residual programs because they have no positive body literals at all. Furthermore, supported models correspond to CLARK's completion [Cla78, BH86]. So if we take CLARK's completion of the residual program, we get a syntactical characterization of the stable models. Of course, the previous results considered only the non-disjunctive case. However, the generalization is easy. In order to define CLARK's completion for disjunctive rules, we simply view a rule like $p \vee q \leftarrow \mathit{not}\, r$ as a shorthand for the two rules $p \leftarrow \mathit{not}\, q \wedge \mathit{not}\, r$ and $q \leftarrow \mathit{not}\, p \wedge \mathit{not}\, r$.

Definition 17 (Completion of a Residual Program).
Let $\hat{\Phi}$ be an instantiated program without positive body literals. Then we define

$$\begin{aligned}
comp^{+}(\hat{\Phi}) &:= \bigl\{A_1 \vee \cdots \vee A_m \vee C_1 \vee \cdots \vee C_n \bigm| \mathcal{A} \leftarrow \mathit{not}\, \mathcal{C} \in \hat{\Phi},\\
&\qquad\qquad \{A_1, \ldots, A_m\} = \mathcal{A},\\
&\qquad\qquad \{C_1, \ldots, C_n\} = \mathcal{C}\bigr\}.\\
comp^{-}(\hat{\Phi}) &:= \bigl\{\neg A \vee \neg C_1 \vee \cdots \vee \neg C_n \bigm| A \text{ is a ground atom},\\
&\qquad\qquad C_i \in \mathcal{C}_i \cup (\mathcal{A}_i - \{A\}),\\
&\qquad\qquad \text{where } \mathcal{A}_i \leftarrow \mathit{not}\, \mathcal{C}_i \in \hat{\Phi},\ i = 1, \ldots, n\\
&\qquad\qquad \text{are all conditional facts with } A \in \mathcal{A}_i\bigr\}.\\
comp(\hat{\Phi}) &:= comp^{+}(\hat{\Phi}) \cup comp^{-}(\hat{\Phi}).
\end{aligned}$$

For instance, consider the following residual program $\hat{\Phi}$ and the completed definitions for p and q in the standard "if and only if"-notation:

$$\begin{array}{lll}
\hat{\Phi}: & p \vee q \leftarrow \mathit{not}\, r. & \text{completion}: \quad p \leftrightarrow (\neg q \wedge \neg r) \vee (\neg s \wedge \neg t).\\
& p \leftarrow \mathit{not}\, s \wedge \mathit{not}\, t. & \qquad\qquad\qquad q \leftrightarrow (\neg p \wedge \neg r).
\end{array}$$

The direction $\leftarrow$ corresponds to the logical information in the given program, and is represented by the positive disjunctions above. The negative disjunctions are the clausal ("multiplied out") forms of the direction $\rightarrow$.

Now this completion of the residual program characterizes the stable models:

Theorem 18 (Completion Characterizes Stable Models).
A two-valued Herbrand interpretation I is a stable model of Φ iff $I \models comp(\hat{\Phi})$, where $\hat{\Phi}$ is the residual program of Φ.

So an answer θ to a query ψ is (skeptically) correct wrt the stable model semantics iff $comp(\hat{\Phi}) \vdash \psi\theta$. Any theorem prover can be used to check that (or generate answers during the proof of ψ). It is also possible to use standard model generating algorithms on $comp(\hat{\Phi})$ to construct the stable models of Φ. However, we can also make use of the very special structure of $comp(\hat{\Phi})$. In order to continue our computation bottom-up, we suggest to compute all positive consequences of $comp(\hat{\Phi})$. This is done by applying again the "hyperresolution" [CL73] technique used already in Definition 11. The negative disjunctions $\neg A_1 \vee \cdots \vee \neg A_n$ are interpreted as rules $\leftarrow A_1 \wedge \cdots \wedge A_n$. The body atoms are matched with the positive disjunctions. The result of the rule application consists of the disjunctive contexts. Note that it is possible that the empty disjunction is computed, which is interpreted as logically false. This happens if the completion is inconsistent, e.g. for the program $p \leftarrow not\ p$.

Definition 19 (Implied Positive Disjunctions).
Hyperresolution with rules from $comp^-(\hat{\Phi})$ is defined as follows:

$$H(\mathcal{D}) := \Big\{ \bigcup_{i=1}^{m} (\mathcal{A}_i - \{A_i\}) \;\Big|\; \mathcal{A}_i \in \mathcal{D},\ A_i \in \mathcal{A}_i,\ \neg A_1 \vee \cdots \vee \neg A_m \in comp^-(\hat{\Phi}) \Big\}.$$

We start with $\mathcal{D}_0 := comp^+(\hat{\Phi})$ and iterate $\mathcal{D}_i := H(\mathcal{D}_{i-1})$ until a fixpoint $\mathcal{D}_n$ is reached. Then let $comp^*(\hat{\Phi}) := \{\mathcal{A} \in \mathcal{D}_n \mid \text{for all } \mathcal{A}' \subset \mathcal{A}\text{: } \mathcal{A}' \notin \mathcal{D}_n\}$.

Let us illustrate this with an example. Consider the following residual program $\hat{\Phi}$ and its completion $comp(\hat{\Phi})$ written as facts and rules:

$\hat{\Phi}: p \vee q.$	$comp^+(\hat{\Phi})$: $p \vee q.$	$comp^-(\hat{\Phi})$: $\leftarrow p \wedge q.$
$r \leftarrow not\ p.$	$r \vee p.$	$\leftarrow q \wedge p.$
$r \leftarrow not\ q.$	$r \vee q.$	$\leftarrow r \wedge p \wedge q.$
$s \leftarrow not\ r.$	$s \vee r.$	$\leftarrow s \wedge r.$

The second and the third rule are of course superfluous. We can derive r (with the first rule applied to the second and third disjunctive fact), and after deleting non-minimal disjunctions we get $\{p \vee q,\ r\}$. This directly describes the two stable models $I_1 := \{p, r\}$ and $I_2 := \{q, r\}$. In general, we have the following:

Theorem 20 (Meaning of Implied Positive Disjunctions).
I is a stable model of Φ iff I is a minimal model of $comp^*(\hat{\Phi})$.

Obviously, a positive disjunction is skeptically implied by the stable model semantics iff it or a subdisjunction of it is contained in $comp^{+}(\hat{\Phi})$. A negative ground atom is implied iff it does not occur in $comp^{+}(\hat{\Phi})$. Arbitrary negative disjunctions require a little more computation, but still can be answered efficiently from $comp^{*}(\hat{\Phi})$:

Theorem 21 (Computation of Negative Disjunctions).
A negative disjunction $\neg A_1 \vee \cdots \vee \neg A_n$ is skeptically implied by STABLE iff there are not $\mathcal{A}_1, \ldots, \mathcal{A}_n \in comp^{*}(\hat{\Phi})$ with $A_i \in \mathcal{A}_i$ $(i = 1, \ldots, n)$, and such that neither $\bigcup_{i=1}^{n} (\mathcal{A}_i - \{A_i\})$ nor a subdisjunction of it is contained in $comp^{*}(\hat{\Phi})$.

It is interesting to note that also the dual approach is possible: If we compute all implied negative disjunctions, the maximal models of the result are the stable models of the original program.

Let us now consider the computation of the stable models themselves. In the special case that there is only a single stable model, $comp^{*}(\hat{\Phi})$ is the set of atoms true in it, so no further computation is needed. If there are multiple models, we construct them by a case analysis. Note that any atom contained in a proper disjunction of $comp^{*}(\hat{\Phi})$ can really be true or false (of course, the decision on different atoms is not independent). So we also need no further computation if we are only interested in credulous truth of ground literals. In the general case, we choose a truth value for a ground atom, and then compute the implied positive disjunctions which follow from this new information. We repeat this process until no proper disjunctions remain:

> **procedure** *model_generation*$\big(comp^{+}(\hat{\Phi}),\ comp^{-}(\hat{\Phi})\big)$:
>   **compute** $comp^{*}(\hat{\Phi})$;
>   **if** $comp^{*}(\hat{\Phi})$ contains no proper disjunction **then**
>   **print** $comp^{*}(\hat{\Phi})$;
>   **else**
>   **let** A be contained in a proper disjunction;
>   *model_generation*$\big(comp^{+}(\hat{\Phi}) \cup \{A\},\ comp^{-}(\hat{\Phi})\big)$;
>   *model_generation*$\big(comp^{+}(\hat{\Phi}),\ comp^{-}(\hat{\Phi}) \cup \{\neg A\}\big)$;

Note that by the completeness of hyperresolution, we can be sure that if we choose A to be true or false, there is really a stable model in which A has this truth value. So our algorithm never runs into "dead ends". This is an important difference to the algorithm used in [CW93] for propagating guessed truth values of atoms. For instance, the following residual program has only a single stable model (namely $\{p, \neg q, r\}$), but it is reduced in the sense of [CW93], so their algorithm has to guess a truth value of some atom:

$$p \leftarrow not\ p.$$
$$p \leftarrow not\ q.$$
$$q \leftarrow not\ r.$$
$$r \leftarrow not\ q.$$

Of course, this example is quite pathological, and their reduction algorithm works well in the more usual simpler cases. However, it is also not clear how to generalize it to the disjunctive case.

Let us conclude this section by giving an implementation of the computation of $comp^*(\hat{\Phi})$. When we have $\hat{\Phi}$, it is a simple restructuring task to construct $comp^+(\hat{\Phi})$ and $comp^-(\hat{\Phi})$. The interesting point is the hyperresolution. Of course, in principle it would be possible to re-use the implementation of Section 4, but since we now have only ground literals (and no rule heads or negative body literals), a more specialized implementation can be faster.

It is interesting that hyperresolution can also be done by "pushing the facts through the rules", whereas in Section 4 the rules had the control. By using this idea, we immediately get a semi-naive behaviour (doing no derivation twice). The approach is also natural because we now often have more rules than facts. In the following algorithm, we use the set Q to "queue" the disjunctions we still have to treat. The set $\mathcal{D}$ is the result, i.e. at the end it will be $comp^*(\hat{\Phi})$:

$\mathcal{D} := \emptyset$;
$Q := comp^+(\hat{\Phi})$;
while $Q \neq \emptyset$ **do**
  let $\mathcal{A} \in Q$;
  $Q := Q - \{\mathcal{A}\}$;
  $ins\_dis(Q, \mathcal{A})$;   /* $\mathcal{D} := \mathcal{D} \cup \{\mathcal{A}\}$ */
  $conseq(\mathcal{A})$;
print $\mathcal{D}$;

Besides inserting a disjunctive fact into a set, the procedure *ins_dis* also eliminates non-minimal disjunctions from $\mathcal{D} \cup Q$ (as shown for *insert* in Section 4). The procedure *conseq* computes the immediate consequences using the disjunctive fact $\mathcal{A}$ and possibly other facts in $\mathcal{D}$:

procedure $conseq(\mathcal{A})$:
  foreach $A \in \mathcal{A}$ **do**
    foreach $\leftarrow \mathcal{B} \in comp^-(\hat{\Phi})$ **with** $A \in \mathcal{B}$ **do**
      $resolve(\mathcal{B} - \{A\},\ \mathcal{A} - \{A\})$;

The procedure *resolve* matches the remaining body literals with disjunctive facts from $\mathcal{D}$:

procedure $resolve(\mathcal{B}, \mathcal{A})$:
  if $\mathcal{B} = \emptyset$ **then**
    $ins\_dis(Q, \mathcal{A})$;   /* $Q := Q \cup \{\mathcal{A}\}$ */
  else
    let $A \in \mathcal{B}$;
    foreach $\mathcal{A}' \in \mathcal{D}$ **with** $A \in \mathcal{A}'$ **do**
      $resolve(\mathcal{B} - \{A\},\ \mathcal{A} \cup (\mathcal{A}' - \{A\}))$;

6 Comparison With Other Bottom-Up Algorithms

We claimed that our approach can also be used as a framework for understanding and comparing other query evaluation algorithms. Let us consider for example the algorithm proposed in [KSS91] for computing the WFS of non-disjunctive programs. The well-founded semantics follows from the residual program by making all difficult atoms undefined:

Theorem 22 (Computation of WFS) [BD95b].
The well-founded model of a non-disjunctive program Φ can be derived from its residual program $\hat{\Phi}$ as follows:

1. *If $A \leftarrow true \in \hat{\Phi}$, then A is true in the well-founded model.*
2. *If A does not occur in $\hat{\Phi}$, then A is false in the well-founded model.*
3. *All other ground atoms are undefined in the well-founded model.*

The algorithm of [KSS91] is based on VAN GELDER's alternating fixpoint method. In order to understand it in our framework, the main difference is that they store not the complete conditional facts, but only their head literals and one further bit indicating whether there is a non-trivial body or not. This is done by introducing two versions of every IDB-predicate: The predicate p contains the facts currently known to be true (the conditional facts with body "*true*"), while the predicate p' contains the facts currently not known to be false (the heads of all conditional facts). It is of course a loss of information to code the rule bodies in a single bit, but this can be compensated by recomputing them in each step of the reduction phase.

Let us consider as an example the following rule (similar to the classical "winning state" example, but the "move" relation is computed by a join):

$$p(X) \leftarrow q(X,Y) \wedge r(Y,Z) \wedge \neg p(Z).$$

We assume that q and r are EDB-relations. In our approach, we start by computing the conditional facts as follows:

$$p\_if\_not\_p(X,Z) \leftarrow q(X,Y) \wedge r(Y,Z).$$

In order to simplify the comparision, we have introduced a new predicate to store the conditional facts. Obviously, $p\_if\_not\_p(X,Z)$ represents $p(X) \leftarrow \neg p(Z)$.

An optimization applied in [KSS91] is to precompute the surely true facts and to combine the first derivation of conditional facts already with the first reduction, but in this example p is simply initialized to the empty relation (since there are no purely positive rules about p). Then the first step of [KSS91] is

$$p'(X) \leftarrow q(X,Y) \wedge r(Y,Z) \wedge \neg p(Z).$$

Since $\neg p(Z)$ is always true, this exactly corresponds to our first step, only the bodies of the derived conditional facts are forgotten.

Now in our approach, we apply iteratively the reduction operator R. On the one hand, this produces facts which are known to be true:

$$p(X) \leftarrow p\_if\_not\_p(X, Z) \wedge \neg p\_if\_not\_p(Z, \_).$$

The same facts are computed in the next step of the [KSS91]-approach:

$$p(X) \leftarrow q(X, Y) \wedge r(Y, Z) \wedge \neg p'(Z).$$

On the other hand, we reduce the pending conditional facts by the following deletion:

$$p\_if\_not\_p(X, Z) -= \ p\_if\_not\_p(X, Z) \wedge p(Z).$$

Again, the same is done in [KSS91]:

$$p'(X) \leftarrow q(X, Y) \wedge r(Y, Z) \wedge \neg p(Z).$$

Both approaches iterate these two steps until a fixpoint is reached.

To summarize, the difference between both approaches is that we explicitly represent the conditional facts, whereas [KSS91] recompute them in each step. It is also interesting to note that our final set of conditional facts still contains enough information to compute the stable models, whereas this information is lost by reducing them only to their heads.

7 Conclusions

We proposed a general framework for computing semantics of disjunctive logic programs. Especially important for our approach is the residual program which can be computed by delaying negative body literals unless their truth value is trivial. We have shown that it is equivalent to the original program for a wide range of semantics. We also gave a detailed explanation how to compute the residual program bottom-up (including many interesting optimizations).

We illustrated our method in the case of the disjunctive stable semantics, where we used a disjunctive extension of CLARK's completion to characterize the stable models syntactically. Furthermore, we also considered the non-disjunctive well-founded semantics, and compared our approach to the algorithm of [KSS91].

A first prototype implementation of our approach can be obtained from "ftp://ftp.informatik.uni-hannover.de/software/index.html". We plan to further develop this program and investigate additional optimizations.

Furthermore, we will of course look at other semantics, especially we are working on PRZYMUSINSKI's stationary and static semantics. It is also interesting what happens when we use a three-valued completion instead of the two-valued CLARK's completion (we will in general not get the three-valued stable models, since these can violate GPPE in the disjunctive case).

Acknowledgement

The comments of HENDRIK DECKER, UDO LIPECK, and TEODOR PRZYMUSINSKI have been very helpful. We would like to thank also DIRK HILLBRECHT and MICHAEL SALZENBERG for implementing our approach.

References

[AB94] Krzysztof R. Apt and Roland N. Bol. Logic programming and negation: A survey. *The Journal of Logic Programming*, 19/20:9–71, 1994.

[BD95a] Stefan Brass and Jürgen Dix. Caracterizations of the Stable Semantics by Partial Evaluation. In A. Nerode, W. Marek, and M. Truszczyński, editors, *Logic Programming and Non-Monotonic Reasoning, Proceedings of the Third International Conference.* Springer LNCS, to appear, June 1995.

[BD95b] Stefan Brass and Jürgen Dix. Disjunctive Semantics based upon Partial and Bottom-Up Evaluation. In Leon Sterling, editor, *Proceedings of the 12th Int. Conf. on Logic Programming, Tokyo.* MIT, June 1995.

[BH86] Nicole Bidoit and Richard Hull. Positivism vs. minimalism in deductive databases. In *Proc. of the 5th ACM Symp. on Principles of Database Systems (PODS'86)*, pages 123–132, 1986.

[BL92] Stefan Brass and Udo W. Lipeck. Generalized bottom-up query evaluation. In Alain Pirotte, Claude Delobel, and Georg Gottlob, editors, *Advances in Database Technology — EDBT'92, 3rd Int. Conf.*, number 580 in LNCS, pages 88–103. Springer-Verlag, 1992.

[BL93] Stefan Brass and Udo W. Lipeck. Bottom-up query evaluation with partially ordered defaults. In *Proceedings of the 3rd International Conference on Deductive and Object-Oriented Databases (DOOD'93)*, pages 253–266, LNCS 769. Springer, 1993.

[BNNS93] Colin Bell, Anil Nerode, Raymond Ng, and V. S. Subrahmanian. Implementing stable semantics by linear programming. In Luís Moniz Pereira and Anil Nerode, editors, *Logic Programming and Non-monotonic Reasoning, Proc. of the Second Int. Workshop (LPNMR'93)*, pages 23–42. MIT Press, 1993.

[Bra90] Stefan Brass. Beginnings of a theory of general database completions. In Serge Abiteboul and Paris C. Kanellakis, editors, *Third International Conference on Database Theory (ICDT'90)*, number 470 in LNCS, pages 349–363. Springer-Verlag, 1990.

[Bra95] Stefan Brass. Bottom-up query evaluation in disjunctive deductive databases. Research report, Institut für Informatik, Universität Hannover, 1995.

[Bry89] François Bry. Logic programming as constructivism: A formalization and its application to databases. In *Proc. of the Eighth ACM SIGACT-SIGMOD-SIGART Symposium on Principles of Database Systems (PODS'89)*, pages 34–50, 1989.

[Bry90] François Bry. Negation in logic programming: A formalization in constructive logic. In Dimitris Karagiannis, editor, *Information Systems and Artificial Intelligence: Integration Aspects*, pages 30–46. Springer, 1990.

[CL73] Chin-Liang Chang and Richard C.-T. Lee. *Symbolic Logic and Mechanical Theorem Proving.* Academic Press, New York, 1973.

[CL95] Stefania Costantini and Gaetano Lanzarone. Static Semantics as Program Transformation and Well-founded Computation. this Volume, pages 156–180, 1995.

[Cla78] K. L. Clark. Negation as Failure. In H. Gallaire and J. Minker, editors, *Logic and Data-Bases*, pages 293–322. Plenum, New York, 78.

[CW93] Weidong Chen and David S. Warren. Computation of stable models and its integration with logical query processing. Technical report, SUNY at Stony Brook, 1993.

[Dem91] Robert Demolombe. An efficient strategy for non-horn deductive databases. *Theoretical Computer Science*, 78:245–259, 1991.

[Dix92] Jürgen Dix. A framework for representing and characterizing semantics of logic programs. In B. Nebel, C. Rich, and W. Swartout, editors, *Principles of Knowledge Representation and Reasoning: Proc. of the Third Int. Conf. (KR'92)*, pages 591–602. Morgan Kaufmann, 1992.

[Dix95a] Jürgen Dix. A Classification-Theory of Semantics of Normal Logic Programs: I. Strong Properties. *Fundamenta Informaticae*, XXII:227–255, 1995.

[Dix95b] Jürgen Dix. A Classification-Theory of Semantics of Normal Logic Programs: II. Weak Properties. *Fundamenta Informaticae*, XXII:257–288, 1995.

[Dix95c] Jürgen Dix. Semantics of Logic Programs: Their Intuitions and Formal Properties. An Overview. In Andre Fuhrmann and Hans Rott, editors, *Logic, Action and Information. Proceedings of the Konstanz Colloquium in Logic and Information (LogIn '92)*, pages 227–313. DeGruyter, 1995.

[DK89a] Phan Minh Dung and Kanchana Kanchansut. A fixpoint approach to declarative semantics of logic programs. In *Proc. NACLP'89*, pages 604–625, 1989.

[DK89b] Phan Minh Dung and Kanchana Kanchansut. A natural semantics of logic programs with negation. In *Proc. of the Ninth Conf. on Foundations of Software Technology and Theoretical Computer Science*, pages 70–80, 1989.

[DM93] Jürgen Dix and Martin Müller. Implementing Semantics for Disjunctive Logic Programs Using Fringes and Abstract Properties. In Luis Moniz Pereira and Anil Nerode, editors, *Logic Programming and Non-Monotonic Reasoning, Proceedings of the Second International Workshop*, pages 43–59. Lisbon, MIT Press, July 1993.

[DM94a] Jürgen Dix and Martin Müller. An Axiomatic Framework for Representing and Characterizing Semantics of Disjunctive Logic Programs. In Pascal Van Hentenryck, editor, *Proceedings of the 11th Int. Conf. on Logic Programming, S. Margherita Ligure*, pages 303–322. MIT, June 1994.

[DM94b] Jürgen Dix and Martin Müller. Partial Evaluation and Relevance for Approximations of the Stable Semantics. In Z.W. Ras and M. Zemankova, editors, *Proceedings of the 8th Int. Symp. on Methodologies for Intelligent Systems, Charlotte, NC, 1994*, pages 511–520. Springer, Lecture Notes in Artificial Intelligence 869, 1994.

[DM94c] Jürgen Dix and Martin Müller. The Stable Semantics and its Variants: A Comparison of Recent Approaches. In L. Dreschler-Fischer and B. Nebel, editors, *Proceedings of the 18th German Annual Conference on Artificial Intelligence (KI '94), Saarbrücken, Germany*, pages 82–93. Springer, Lecture Notes in Artificial Intelligence 861, 1994.

[DN95] Lars Degerstedt and Ulf Nilsson. Magic Computation of Well-founded Semantics. This volume, pages 127–155, 1995.

[GL91b] Michael Gelfond and Vladimir Lifschitz. Classical Negation in Logic Programs and Disjunctive Databases. *New Generation Computing*, 9:365–387, 1991. (Extended abstract appeared in: Logic Programs with Classical Negation. *Proceedings of the 7-th International Logic Programming Conference, Jerusalem*, pages 579-597, 1990. MIT Press.).

[HY91] Yong Hu and Li Yan Yuan. Extended well-founded model semantics for general logic programs. In Koichi Furukawa, editor, *Proc. of the 8th Int. Conf. on Logic Programming (ICLP'91)*, pages 412–425. MIT Press, 1991.

[KLM90] Sarit Kraus, Daniel Lehmann, and Menachem Magidor. Nonmonotonic reasoning, preferential models and cumulative logics. *Artificial Intelligence*, 44:167–207, 1990.

[KSS91] David B. Kemp, Peter J. Stuckey, and Divesh Srivastava. Magic sets and bottom-up evaluation of well-founded models. In *Proc. of the 1991 Int. Symposium on Logic Programming*, pages 337–351. MIT Press, 1991.

[Min82] Jack Minker. On indefinite databases and the closed world assumption. In *Proceedings of the 6th Conference on Automated Deduction, New York*, pages 292–308. Springer, 1982.

[MR90] Jack Minker and Arcot Rajasekar. A fixpoint semantics for disjunctive logic programs. *The Journal of Logic Programming*, 9:45–74, 1990.

[PAA91] Luís Moniz Pereira, Joaquim N. Aparício, and José J. Alferes. Derivation procedures for extended stable models. In *Proc. of the 12th Int. Joint Conf. on Artificial Intelligence (IJCAI'91)*, pages 863–868, 1991.

[Prz91a] Teodor Przymusinski. Stable Semantics for Disjunctive Programs. *New Generation Computing Journal*, 9:401–424, 1991. (Extended abstract appeared in: Extended stable semantics for normal and disjunctive logic programs. *Proceedings of the 7-th International Logic Programming Conference, Jerusalem*, pages 459–477, 1990. MIT Press.).

[Prz91b] Teodor C. Przymusinski. Semantics of disjunctive logic programs and deductive databases. In Claude Delobel, Michael Kifer, and Yoshifumi Masunaga, editors, *Deductive and Object-Oriented Databases, 2nd Int. Conf. (DOOD'91)*, number 566 in LNCS, pages 85–107. Springer-Verlag, 1991.

[Prz95] Teodor Przymusinski. Static semantics for normal and disjunctive logic programs. *Annals of Mathematics and Artificial Intelligence*, 1995. To appear.

[RLM89] Arcot Rajasekar, Jorge Lobo, and Jack Minker. Weak Generalized Closed World Assumption. *Journal of Automated Reasoning*, 5:293–307, 1989.

[Ros90] Kenneth A. Ross. The well founded semantics for disjunctive logic programs. In Won Kim, Jean-Marie Nicolas, and Shojiro Nishio, editors, *Deductive and Object-Oriented Databases, Proc. of the First International Conference (DOOD'89)*, pages 385–402. North-Holland, 1990.

[Roy90] Véronique Royer. Backward chaining evaluation in stratified disjunctive theories. In *Proc. of the Ninth ACM SIGACT-SIGMOD-SIGART Symposium on Principles of Database Systems (PODS'90)*, pages 183–195, 1990.

[RSS94] Raghu Ramakrishnan, Divesh Srivastava, and S. Sudarshan. Rule ordering in bottom-up fixpoint evaluation of logic programs. *IEEE Transactions on Knowledge and Data Engineering*, 6(4):501–517, 1994.

[RT88] Kenneth A. Ross and Rodney W. Topor. Inferring negative information from disjunctive databases. *Journal of Automated Reasoning*, 4:397–424, 1988.

[Sei94] Dietmar Seipel. An efficient computation of the extended generalized closed world assumption by support-for-negation sets. In *Proc. Int. Conf. on Logic Programming and Automated Reasoning (LPAR'94)*, number 822 in LNAI, pages 245–259. Springer, 1994.

[SS94] Chiaki Sakama and Hirohisa Seki. Partial Deduction of Disjunctive Logic Programs: A Declarative Approach. In *Fourth International Workshop on Logic Program Synthesis and Transformation (LOPSTR'94)*. Lecture Notes in Computer Science, Springer-Verlag, July 1994.

[VGRS91] Allen Van Gelder, Kenneth A. Ross, and John S. Schlipf. The well-founded semantics for general logic programs. *Journal of the Association for Computing Machinary (JACM)*, 38:620–650, 1991.

A Proofs

A.1 Proof of Theorem 12

Our goal is to show that it is possible to reach $\mathrm{lfp}(T_\Phi)$ from Φ by a series of GPPE- and "Elimination of Tautology"-steps. In this process, we have to be very careful with non-minimal conditional facts, since we allow semantics for which they are relevant. The problem is illustrated by the following examples:

Example 1. We once hoped that if Φ' results from Φ by an application of GPPE, then $\mathrm{lfp}(T_\Phi) = \mathrm{lfp}(T_{\Phi'})$. This, however, does not hold. Let Φ be:

$$p \vee q \leftarrow r.$$
$$r \leftarrow q.$$
$$q \vee r.$$

For this program, we get $\mathrm{lfp}(T_\Phi) = \{q \vee r, p \vee q, r, p \vee r\}$. Now if we apply GPPE to r in the first rule, we replace this rule by

$$p \vee q \leftarrow q.$$
$$p \vee q.$$

Note that $p \vee q \leftarrow q$ is a tautology, and in fact, it is the source of the problem, because with it it is possible to derive $p \vee q \vee r$ which is not in $\mathrm{lfp}(T_\Phi)$.

Example 2. In the above example, it would have been possible to simply eliminate the tautology before further applications of GPPE to avoid the derivation of the critical conditional fact. But this is not always correct, because if the program Φ itself contains a tautology, e.g.

$$p \vee q \leftarrow q.$$
$$q \vee r.$$

then we of course have to apply the tautology to get the conditional fact $p \vee q \vee r$ contained in $\mathrm{lfp}(T_\Phi)$.

Example 3. In fact, tautologies can also occur as intermediate results because GPPE in contrast to hyperresolution evaluates only one body literal at a time. Consider for example the following program:

$$p \leftarrow q \wedge r.$$
$$q \vee r.$$
$$r \vee s.$$

If we evaluate the first body literal by GPPE, we get $p \vee r \leftarrow r$. Then another application of GPPE yields $p \vee r \vee s$, the result of hyperresolution.

Lemma 23. *Let Φ be an instantiated logic program containing the two rules*

$$\mathcal{A} \leftarrow B_0 \wedge B_1 \wedge \cdots \wedge B_m \wedge not\, \mathcal{C}.$$
$$B_0 \vee \mathcal{A}' \leftarrow B_1' \wedge \cdots \wedge B_n' \wedge not\, \mathcal{C}'.$$

Let Φ' contain in addition the result of an unfolding step, i.e.

$$\Phi' := \Phi \cup \{(\mathcal{A} \cup \mathcal{A}') \leftarrow B_1 \wedge \cdots \wedge B_m \wedge B_1' \wedge \cdots \wedge B_n' \wedge not\, (\mathcal{C} \cup \mathcal{C}')\}.$$

If the added rule is not a tautology, then $\mathrm{lfp}(T_{\Phi'}) \subseteq \mathrm{lfp}(T_\Phi)$.

Proof. To simplify the notation, we consider only the case without $\mathcal{C}, \mathcal{C}'$. This is no real restriction, since negative body literals can be moved into the heads if they are distinguished by making their predicate symbols disjoint from the positive head- and body-literals.

Now let the new rule be applied to disjunctive facts $\mathcal{A}_i$, $i = 1, \ldots, m$, and $\mathcal{A}_j'$, $j = 1, \ldots, n$. Then the resulting disjunctive fact is

$$\mathcal{A} \cup \mathcal{A}' \cup \bigcup_{i=1}^{m} (\mathcal{A}_i - \{B_i\}) \cup \bigcup_{j=1}^{n} (\mathcal{A}_j' - \{B_j'\}). \qquad (*)$$

Now we have to distinguish several cases to show that this conditional fact is also derivable in Φ. Each case fills a hole in the preceding case.

1. The natural idea to derive this disjunctive fact would be to first apply the rule $B_0 \vee \mathcal{A}' \leftarrow B_1' \wedge \cdots \wedge B_n'$ and get

   $$\{B_0\} \cup \mathcal{A}' \cup \bigcup_{j=1}^{n} (\mathcal{A}_j' - \{B_j'\}).$$

   We then enter this for B_0 into $\mathcal{A} \leftarrow B_0 \wedge B_1 \wedge \cdots \wedge B_m$. This results in

   $$\mathcal{A} \cup (\mathcal{A}' - \{B_0\}) \cup \bigcup_{j=1}^{n} (\mathcal{A}_j' - \{B_j', B_0\}) \cup \bigcup_{i=1}^{m} (\mathcal{A}_i - \{B_i\}).$$

   Of course, $\mathcal{A}'$ does not contain B_0, so this set-difference is effectless and $(\mathcal{A}' - \{B_0\})$ can be simplified to $\mathcal{A}'$. However, we have to assume that the $\mathcal{A}_j'$, $j = 1, \ldots, n$, do not contain B_0 (or that $B_j' = B_0$) in order to really get $(*)$. This hole is treated in case 2.

2. Now we assume that $B_0 \in \mathcal{A}'_j$ and $B_0 \neq B'_j$ for at least one $1 \leq j \leq n$. Without loss of generality, we can choose $j = 1$ to simplify the notation. Then we first apply the rule $\mathcal{A} \leftarrow B_0 \wedge B_1 \wedge \cdots \wedge B_m$ and enter $\mathcal{A}'_1$ for the body literal B_0. This results in

$$\mathcal{A} \cup (\mathcal{A}'_1 - \{B_0\}) \cup \bigcup_{i=1}^{m} (\mathcal{A}_i - \{B_i\}).$$

Since $B_0 \neq B'_1$, the generated disjunctive fact contains B'_1. Therefore, we can insert it into $B_0 \vee \mathcal{A}' \leftarrow B'_1 \wedge \cdots \wedge B'_n$. This gives

$$\{B_0\} \cup \mathcal{A}' \cup (\mathcal{A} - \{B'_1\}) \cup (\mathcal{A}'_1 - \{B_0, B'_1\})$$
$$\cup \bigcup_{i=1}^{m} (\mathcal{A}_i - \{B_i, B'_1\}) \cup \bigcup_{j=2}^{n} (\mathcal{A}'_j - \{B'_j\}).$$

Now let us check that this is equivalent to $(*)$. First, $\{B_0\} \cup (\mathcal{A}'_1 - \{B_0, B'_1\})$ can be simplified to $\mathcal{A}'_1 - \{B'_1\}$, since $B_0 \in \mathcal{A}'_1$ and $B_0 \neq B'_1$. Second, $\mathcal{A}$ cannot contain B'_1, since otherwise the combined rule would be a tautology. However, we have to assume now that $B'_1 \notin \mathcal{A}_i$ or $B'_1 = B_i$ for $i = 1, \ldots, m$ (otherwise see case 3). Then the above expression is equivalent to $(*)$.

3. The current situation is as follows: $B_0 \in \mathcal{A}'_j$ and $B_0 \neq B'_j$ for at least one $1 \leq j \leq n$, furthermore $B'_j \in \mathcal{A}_i$ and $B'_j \neq B_i$ for at least one $1 \leq i \leq m$. Again, without loss of generality, we can choose $j = 1$ and $i = 1$. Then we first enter $\mathcal{A}_1$ for B'_1 in the rule $B_0 \vee \mathcal{A}' \leftarrow B'_1 \wedge \cdots \wedge B'_m$. This results in

$$\{B_0\} \cup \mathcal{A}' \cup (\mathcal{A}_1 - \{B'_1\}) \cup \bigcup_{j=2}^{n} (\mathcal{A}'_j - \{B'_j\}).$$

Since $B'_1 \neq B_1$, the generated disjunctive fact contains B_1. Therefore, we can insert it for B_1 in the rule $\mathcal{A} \leftarrow B_0 \wedge B_1 \wedge \cdots \wedge B_m$, and insert $\mathcal{A}'_1$ for B_0. The result is

$$\mathcal{A} \cup (\mathcal{A}'_1 - \{B_0\}) \cup (\{B_0\} - \{B_1\}) \cup (\mathcal{A}' - \{B_1\}) \cup (\mathcal{A}_1 - \{B'_1, B_1\})$$
$$\cup \bigcup_{j=2}^{n} (\mathcal{A}'_j - \{B'_j, B_1\}) \cup \bigcup_{i=2}^{m} (\mathcal{A}_i - \{B_i\}).$$

Now let us check that this is indeed equivalent to $(*)$. First, we allow no duplicate body literals, so $B_0 \neq B_1$, therefore the term $\{B_0\} - \{B_1\}$ entails that B_0 is contained in the result, and we already know that it is also contained in $(*)$. Second, we have $\mathcal{A}'_1 - \{B_0\}$ instead of $\mathcal{A}'_1 - \{B'_1\}$. But the result already contains B_0, so the set-difference has no effect on the total result, and $(*)$ also contains B'_1 (because $B'_1 \in \mathcal{A}_1$ and $B'_1 \neq B_1$), so it is correct that the result contains B'_1 (since $B'_1 \neq B_0$). Third, $\mathcal{A}'$ cannot contain B_1, since otherwise the combined rule would be a tautology. Fourth, we eliminate B'_1 from $\mathcal{A}_1$, but it is still contained in the result as explained above. Finally, we have to assume that $B_1 \notin \mathcal{A}'_j$ (or else $B_1 = B'_j$) for $j = 2, \ldots, n$ (see case 4).

4. Now, the remaining little hole can be described as follows: As in case 3, we have $B_0 \in \mathcal{A}'_1$, $B_0 \neq B'_1$ and $B'_1 \in \mathcal{A}_1$, $B'_1 \neq B_1$. Now in addition, there is a $2 \leq j \leq n$, with $B_1 \in \mathcal{A}'_j$ and $B_1 \neq B'_j$. To simplify the notation, we choose $j = 2$. In this case, we first apply the rule $\mathcal{A} \leftarrow B_0 \wedge B_1 \wedge \cdots \wedge B_m$ and insert $\mathcal{A}'_1$ for B_0 and $\mathcal{A}'_2$ for B_1. This results in

$$\mathcal{A} \cup (\mathcal{A}'_1 - \{B_0\}) \cup (\mathcal{A}'_2 - \{B_1\}) \cup \bigcup_{i=2}^{m} (\mathcal{A}_i - \{B_i\}).$$

Now we apply the rule $B_0 \vee \mathcal{A}' \leftarrow B'_1 \wedge \cdots \wedge B'_n$ and insert $\mathcal{A}_1$ for B'_1 and the above constructed disjunctive fact for B'_2 (Since $B'_2 \neq B_1$, the constructed disjunctive fact really contains B'_2.). The result is

$$\begin{aligned}\{B_0\} \cup \mathcal{A}' \cup (\mathcal{A}_1 - \{B'_1\}) \cup (\mathcal{A} - \{B'_2\}) \\ \cup (\mathcal{A}'_1 - \{B_0, B'_2\}) \cup (\mathcal{A}'_2 - \{B_1, B'_2\}) \\ \cup \bigcup_{i=2}^{m} (\mathcal{A}_i - \{B_i, B'_2\}) \cup \bigcup_{j=3}^{n} (\mathcal{A}'_j - \{B'_j\}).\end{aligned}$$

Now the result contains
   - B_0,
   - B_1, since $B_1 \in \mathcal{A}_1$ and $B'_1 \neq B_1$,
   - B'_1 since $B'_1 \in \mathcal{A}'_1$, $B_0 \neq B'_1$ and $B'_2 \neq B'_1$ (we allow no duplicate body literals).

   So set-differences with these atoms have no effect. Next, $\mathcal{A} - \{B'_2\} = \mathcal{A}$, since $B'_2 \in \mathcal{A}$ would make the combined rule a tautology. By applying these simplifications, we get:

$$\begin{aligned}\{B_0\} \cup \mathcal{A}' \cup \mathcal{A}_1 \cup \mathcal{A} \cup (\mathcal{A}'_1 - \{B'_2\}) \cup (\mathcal{A}'_2 - \{B'_2\}) \\ \cup \bigcup_{i=2}^{m} (\mathcal{A}_i - \{B_i, B'_2\}) \cup \bigcup_{j=3}^{n} (\mathcal{A}'_j - \{B'_j\}).\end{aligned}$$

   Note that also (*) contains
   - B_0 (since $B_0 \in \mathcal{A}'_1$ and $B_0 \neq B'_1$),
   - B_1 (since $B_1 \in \mathcal{A}'_2$ and $B_1 \neq B'_2$), and
   - B'_1 (since $B'_1 \in \mathcal{A}_1$ and $B'_1 \neq B_1$).

   Therefore, in order to get from the above expression to (*), we only need the following assumptions: $B'_2 \notin \mathcal{A}'_1$ and $B'_2 \notin \mathcal{A}_i$ (or $B'_2 = B_i$) for $i = 2, \ldots, m$ (otherwise see case 5).
5. The current situation is as follows: The resulting disjunctive fact (*) contains
   - B_0 (because $B_0 \in \mathcal{A}'_1$, $B_0 \neq B'_1$),
   - B'_1 (because $B'_1 \in \mathcal{A}_1$, $B'_1 \neq B_1$),
   - B_1 (because $B_1 \in \mathcal{A}'_2$, $B_1 \neq B'_2$), and
   - B'_2 (because either $B'_2 \in \mathcal{A}'_1$, $B'_2 \neq B'_1$ or $B'_2 \in \mathcal{A}_i$, $2 \leq i \leq m$, $B'_2 \neq B_i$).

If we apply the rules as in case 1 (i.e. in the most natural way), our only risk is to loose B_0. Let the result be $\hat{\mathcal{A}}_1$. Next, we apply the rules as in case 3. This time, we may loose B_1. Let the result be $\hat{\mathcal{A}}_2$. Since $B_0 \neq B_1'$, $\hat{\mathcal{A}}_1$ contains B_1', and since $B_1 \neq B_2'$, $\hat{\mathcal{A}}_2$ contains B_2'. Therefore, we can insert $\hat{\mathcal{A}}_1$ and $\hat{\mathcal{A}}_2$ for B_1' and B_2' into $B_0 \vee \mathcal{A}' \leftarrow B_1' \wedge B_2' \wedge \cdots \wedge B_n'$. The result surely contains B_0, and also B_1 (from $\hat{\mathcal{A}}_1 - \{B_1'\}$), as well as B_1' (from $\hat{\mathcal{A}}_2 - \{B_2'\}$), and B_2' (from $\hat{\mathcal{A}}_1 - \{B_1'\}$ or directly if $B_2' = B_0$). The rest of (*) was already contained in the intermediate result and simply carries through. □

Lemma 24. *Let Φ be an instantiated logic program containing a rule*

$$\mathcal{A} \leftarrow B_0 \wedge B_1 \wedge \cdots \wedge B_m \wedge not\ \mathcal{C}$$

and a conditional fact $B_0 \vee \mathcal{A}' \leftarrow not\ \mathcal{C}'$. Let

$$\Phi' := \Phi \cup \big\{(\mathcal{A} \cup \mathcal{A}') \leftarrow B_1 \wedge \cdots \wedge B_m \wedge not\ (\mathcal{C} \cup \mathcal{C}')\big\}.$$

Then $\mathrm{lfp}(T_{\Phi'}) \subseteq \mathrm{lfp}(T_\Phi)$.

Proof. This is trivial: If something is derivable using the new rule, then we can also use the old rule with the conditional fact. □

Theorem 12 ($\Phi \mapsto \mathrm{lfp}(T_\Phi)$ is a SEM-Equivalence Transformation). *Let SEM be a semantics which satisfies GPPE, and allows the elimination of tautologies. Then $SEM(\Phi) = SEM\big(\mathrm{lfp}(T_\Phi)\big)$.*

Proof. We have to construct $\mathrm{lfp}(T_\Phi)$ from Φ by using only semantics preserving steps. This works as follows:

1. First, we completely instantiate the given program Φ. By our definition of a semantics, we have $\mathrm{SEM}(\Phi) = \mathrm{SEM}(\Phi^*)$. Note also that Φ^* is finite because of our restriction on Σ.
2. Next, we add the tautological rule $A \leftarrow A$ for every ground atom A. Since tautologies are irrelevat for SEM it is not only possible to delete them, but also to add them without changing the semantics of the given program. Because of these tautologies, applications of GPPE never delete the original rule, they only add the partially evaluated rules to the program.
3. We now apply GPPE until nothing changes. However, directly after every appliction of GPPE, we delete every newly generated tautology, which did not result from applying a conditional fact. Therefore, the added rules do not increase the set of derivable conditional facts by Lemma 23 and Lemma 24. This means especially that all generated conditional facts are contained in $\mathrm{lfp}(T_\Phi)$. On the other hand, every conditional fact in $\mathrm{lfp}(T_\Phi)$ is generated: For instance, consider the rule $\mathcal{A} \leftarrow B_1 \wedge \cdots \wedge B_n \wedge not\ \mathcal{C}$ applied to conditional facts $\mathcal{A}_i \leftarrow not\ \mathcal{C}_i$. The result contained in $\mathrm{lfp}(T_\Phi)$ is

$$\mathcal{A} \cup \bigcup_{i=1}^{n} (\mathcal{A}_i - \{B_i\}) \leftarrow not\ \big(\mathcal{C} \cup \bigcup_{i=1}^{n} \mathcal{C}_i\big).$$

By applying GPPE to the first body literal, we get

$$\mathcal{A} \cup (\mathcal{A}_1 - \{B_1\}) \leftarrow B_2 \wedge \cdots \wedge B_n \wedge not\ (\mathcal{C} \cup \mathcal{C}_1).$$

Next, we apply GPPE to B_2 in this rule, and especially insert $\mathcal{A}_2 \leftarrow not\ \mathcal{C}_2$. And so on.

4. Finally, we delete all rules which still have positive body literals by applying GPPE. In order to do this, we first delete all tautologies (we also delete immediately any tautology which is later generated). Since there are no tautologies, an application of GPPE to some positive body literal generates only rules without this body literal. And once this body literal has vanished from all rules in the program, it can never be created by an application of GPPE. Therefore, all occurring positive body literals can be eliminated one after the other. Note also that no rules are created which are not already contained in the program due to phase 2. Therefore, the set of conditional facts does not increase, and after all other rules are eliminated, $\text{lfp}(T_\Phi)$ remains. □

A.2 Proof of Theorems 18, 20, 21

In order to prove that CLARK's completion of the residual program characterizes the stable models, we use the supported models as an intermediate step. Note that we cannot formally use the result of FAGES and BEN-ELIYAHU because we consider disjunctive logic programs. First we have to generalize the notion of a supported model:

Definition 25 (Supported Model).
A two-valued Herbrand-interpretation I is a supported model of a logic program Φ iff for every ground atom A with $I \models A$ there is a ground instance $\mathcal{A} \leftarrow \mathcal{B} \wedge not\ \mathcal{C}$ of a rule in Φ such that $I \models \mathcal{B} \wedge not\ \mathcal{C}$ and $I \not\models \mathcal{A} - \{A\}$.

Lemma 26.

1. *If Φ has no positive body literals, then a supported model of Φ is also stable.*
2. *For any Φ, a stable model of Φ is also supported.*

Proof. 1. Let I be a supported model of Φ. Clearly, I is also a supported model of Φ/I. But Φ/I is a set of disjunctive facts of the form $\mathcal{A} \leftarrow \mathit{true}$. Now the supportedness-condition means that every true atom occurs in a disjunction where all other atoms are false. So no smaller model than I can still be a model of Φ/I.

2. Let I be a stable model of Φ, i.e. a minimal model of Φ/I. Let A be an atom true in I and $I' := I - \{A\}$. So I' is smaller than I and must violate a rule $\mathcal{A} \leftarrow \mathcal{B}$ in Φ/I. This means especially $I' \models \mathcal{B}$, and therefore $I \models \mathcal{B}$. Furthermore, I satisfies also the negative body literals (because the rule is contained in Φ/I). Finally we have $I' \not\models \mathcal{A}$, i.e. $I \not\models \mathcal{A} - \{A\}$, so A is contained in $\mathcal{A}$, and this rule supports it. □

Lemma 27.
Let $\hat{\Phi}$ be an instantiated program without positive body literals. I is a supported model of $\hat{\Phi}$ iff $I \models comp(\hat{\Phi})$.

Proof. 1. Let I be a supported model of $\hat{\Phi}$, but suppose that it does not satisfy one of the constructed negative disjunctions, e.g. $\neg A \vee \neg C_1 \vee \cdots \vee \neg C_n$. So $I \models A$, but A is not supported, since $I \models C_i$ makes the rule $\mathcal{A}_i \leftarrow not\ \mathcal{C}_i$ not applicable as a support for A: Either one of the negative body literals is false, or another head literal is true.

2. Let $I \models comp(\hat{\Phi})$, but suppose that I were not a supported model of $\hat{\Phi}$. Since $I \models comp^+(\hat{\Phi})$, I obviously is a model of $\hat{\Phi}$. So it is only possible that the support for some ground atom A is missing in I. Let $\mathcal{A}_i \leftarrow not\ \mathcal{C}_i$ $(i = 1, \ldots, n)$ be all rules with $A \in \mathcal{A}_i$. Since none of these supports A, in every rule either a negative body literal must be false in I, or another head literal besides A must be true. So choose the corresponding atoms as C_i. Then I does not satisfy $\neg A \vee \neg C_1 \vee \cdots \vee \neg C_n$, which is a contradiction. □

Theorem 18 (Completion Characterizes Stable Models).
A two-valued Herbrand interpretation I is a stable model of Φ iff $I \models comp(\hat{\Phi})$, where $\hat{\Phi}$ is the residual program of Φ.

Proof. This is now an immediate consequence of Theorem 12 and Lemmas 26 and 27. □

Lemma 28.
Let $\hat{\Phi}$ be an instantiated program without positive body literals. An interpretation I is a model of $comp(\hat{\Phi})$ iff it is a minimal model of $comp^*(\hat{\Phi})$.

Proof. 1. Let I be a minimal model of $comp^*(\hat{\Phi})$, and let $I_1, \ldots, I_m$ be all models of $comp(\hat{\Phi})$. We have to show that I is among the I_i. Suppose it were not. Since I is a minimal model of $comp^*(\hat{\Phi})$, and the I_i are also models of $comp^*(\hat{\Phi})$ (since $comp(\hat{\Phi}) \vdash comp^*(\hat{\Phi})$), there must be ground atoms A_i with $I_i \models A_i$ and $I \not\models A_i$ (if for some I_i there were no such atom, we would have $I_i \preceq I$, and together with $I_i \neq I$ this would imply $I_i \prec I$). Now consider the disjunction $A_1 \vee \cdots \vee A_m$. It (or a subdisjunction of it) is contained in $comp^*(\hat{\Phi})$, because all the models of $comp(\hat{\Phi})$ satisfy it, i.e. $comp(\hat{\Phi}) \vdash A_1 \vee \cdots \vee A_m$. However, I does not satisfy it, which is a contradiction.

2. Now let I be a model of $comp(\hat{\Phi})$. Since $comp(\hat{\Phi}) \vdash comp^*(\hat{\Phi})$, I is also a model of $comp^*(\hat{\Phi})$. Now suppose that there were a smaller model I_1 of $comp^*(\hat{\Phi})$, and let I_0 be a minimal model of $comp^*(\hat{\Phi})$ with $I_0 \preceq I_1$, i.e. $I_0 \prec I$. By the already proven other direction, we get $I_0 \models comp(\hat{\Phi})$. Let A be a ground atom with $I \models A$ and $I_0 \not\models A$. By Lemma 27, I is a supported model of $\hat{\Phi}$, so let $\mathcal{A} \leftarrow not\ \mathcal{C}$ be the supporting rule for A. Since $I \models not\ \mathcal{C}$, and $I_0 \prec I$, it follows that $I_0 \models not\ \mathcal{C}$. In the same way, $I \not\models \mathcal{A} - \{A\}$ implies $I_0 \not\models \mathcal{A} - \{A\}$. Finally, we know $I_0 \not\models A$. But this means $I_0 \not\models \mathcal{A} \leftarrow not\ \mathcal{C}$, which is a contradiction. □

Theorem 20 (Meaning of Implied Positive Disjunctions).
I is a stable model of Φ iff I is a minimal model of comp$^*(\hat{\Phi})$.

Proof. This follows immediately from Theorem 18 and Lemma 28. □

Theorem 21 (Computation of Negative Disjunctions).
A negative disjunction $\neg A_1 \vee \cdots \vee \neg A_n$ is skeptically implied by STABLE iff there are not $\mathcal{A}_1, \ldots, \mathcal{A}_n \in comp^*(\hat{\Phi})$ with $A_i \in \mathcal{A}_i$ $(i = 1, \ldots, n)$, and such that neither $\bigcup_{i=1}^{n}(\mathcal{A}_i - \{A_i\})$ nor a subdisjunction of it is contained in comp$^*(\hat{\Phi})$.

Proof. 1. Let $\neg A_1 \vee \cdots \vee \neg A_n$ be skeptically implied by STABLE, i.e. true in every minimal model of *comp*$^*(\hat{\Phi})$. Let $\mathcal{A}_1, \ldots, \mathcal{A}_n \in comp^*(\hat{\Phi})$ with $A_i \in \mathcal{A}_i$ $(i = 1, \ldots, n)$. Since one of the A_i is false in every minimal model of *comp*$^*(\hat{\Phi})$, the corresponding rest disjunction $\mathcal{A}_i - \{A_i\}$ must be true in that minimal model, so $\bigcup_{i=1}^{n}(\mathcal{A}_i - \{A_i\})$ is true in every minimal model of *comp*$^*(\hat{\Phi})$, and since it is a positive disjunction, it is also true in every model. By the transitivity of $\vdash$, all positive disjunctions which follow from *comp*$^*(\hat{\Phi})$, are already represented by a subdisjunction in *comp*$^*(\hat{\Phi})$.

2. Now let $\neg A_1 \vee \cdots \vee \neg A_n$ be not skeptically implied by STABLE, so there is a stable model I of $\hat{\Phi}$ with $I \models A_i$ $(i = 1, \ldots, n)$. By Lemma 28, I is a minimal model of *comp*$^*(\hat{\Phi})$, therefore $I_i := I - \{A_i\}$ cannot be a model of it, i.e. there must be a disjunction $\mathcal{A}_i$ with $I_i \not\models \mathcal{A}_i$. Since I satisfies it, $A_i \in \mathcal{A}_i$ follows. However, $\bigcup_{i=1}^{n}(\mathcal{A}_i - \{A_i\})$ is false in I, so neither it nor a subdisjunction of it can be contained in *comp*$^*(\hat{\Phi})$. □

Static Semantics as Program Transformation and Well-Founded Computation *

Stefania Costantini,[1] and Gaetano A. Lanzarone[1]

Università degli Studi di Milano, Dip. di Scienze dell'Informazione
via Comelico 39/41, I-20135 Milano, Italy
costanti@imiucca.csi.unimi.it lanzarone@hermes.mc.dsi.unimi.it

Abstract. In this paper, we propose a new constructive characterization of those semantics for disjunctive logic programs which are extensions of the well-founded semantics for normal programs. Based on considerations about how disjunctive information is treated by a given semantics, we divide the computation of that semantics into two phases. The first one is a program transformation phase, which applies axiom schemata expressing how derivations involving disjunctions are made in the given semantic framework. The second one is a constructive phase, based on a variation of the well-founded model construction for normal programs. We apply this two-phases procedural semantics to the computation of the static semantics of disjunctive logic programs as a case-study, showing how it works and what its results are in several examples. A main perspective of this proposal is a procedural semantics for disjunctive programs consisting of an inefficient preprocessing phase (implementing the program transformation procedure), to be however performed only once, and of an efficient runtime computation, obtained as a variation of any effective procedural semantics for the well-founded model.

1 Introduction

Disjunctive logic programs are significantly more expressive than normal programs; thus, all the semantics proposed for them are of very high complexity (for an overview of recently proposed semantics, their properties and their complexity, see [Bar91], [Dix91], [Dix92], [Got92], [JL92]). This means that it is not easy to conceive reasonable proof procedures for this kind of program.

In this paper, we propose an approach to computing a class of semantics of disjunctive logic programs. The approach divides the construction of a given semantics into parts, to be computed separately.

In our opinion, the following components underly any semantics for disjunctive programs with negation: (i) the specification of how to use explicit disjunctive information in derivation; (ii) the specification of how to relate explicit and

* We thank the anonymous referees for their careful readings of the manuscript and many useful comments.

implicit disjunctive information; (iii) the specification of how to relate disjunction and negation. By varying the choices for (i)-(iii), different (though related) semantics can be obtained.

Our proposal concerns those semantics which are extensions/modifications of the well-founded model semantics (like for instance [CB92], [Prz94]). We define a program transformation procedure, which includes the formalization of points (i)-(ii). To the resulting program, it is then possible to apply a variation of any procedure for the well-founded model construction for normal programs (see [Sch92] for a survey). The variation is defined by modifying the base step of the procedure so as to include the choice for point (iii), i.e. for relating negation and disjunction.

We illustrate our proposal with respect to the Static Semantics for disjunctive programs [Prz94], which appears to be a natural generalization of the well-founded model semantics. We believe, although this is still only a conjecture, that the approach could be easily adapted to other similar existing semantics.

A main perspective of this proposal is a procedural semantics for disjunctive programs consisting of an inefficient preprocessing phase (implementing the program transformation procedure), to be however performed only once, and of an efficient runtime computation, obtained as a variation of any effective procedural semantics for the well-founded model.

Trying to cope with the complexity of declarative and procedural semantics of disjunctive logic programs has been a motivating point of this research. In the present paper, however, the complexity issue is not specifically addressed. In fact, the main aim has been that of investigating the abstract properties of these semantics, independently of computational issues. We defer to future work a precise analysis of the complexity of the steps involved by the proposed approach.

After some preliminary definitions (Section 2) and a summary of the static semantics (Section 3) with some observations (Section 4), we introduce the program transformation procedure (Section 5) and the modified well-founded computation (Section 6). In Section 7 we discuss some examples, and in Section 8 we propose some final remarks.

2 Preliminary Definitions

A *disjunctive logic program* P is a set of clauses of the form:

$$A_1 \vee \ldots \vee A_l \leftarrow B_1 \wedge \ldots \wedge B_m \wedge not\ C_1 \wedge \ldots \wedge not\ C_n \quad (1)$$

where $l \geq 1$, $m, n \geq 0$ and A_i, B_i and C_i's are atomic formulae. We will call the A_i's and B_i's *atoms*, or *positive literals*, and the *not* C_i's *negative literals*. If, for every clause, $l = 1$, then the program is called *normal*. If, in addition, $n = 0$, then the program is called *definite*.

As it is customary in the literature (see [HP90]), we assume that the program has already been instantiated, i.e. all its (possibly infinitely many) clauses are propositional. By *not* we mean a non-monotonic, commonsense negation whose informal meaning is: *notC holds whenever C is believed to be false, i.e. whenever ¬C is believed to be true*, where ¬ is classical negation of first-order predicate logic.

For the semantics of definite logic programs and the semantics of normal logic programs we will follow [Llo87] and [HP90], respectively. By "interpretations" and "models" we mean Herbrand interpretations and Herbrand models. B_P is, as usual, the Herbrand base of P. In the following, we will consider the *well-founded model semantics* of normal programs. The well-founded model of P (for short WFM_P , or simply WFM) is unique, and is in general 3-valued. Following [Prz89], [HP90] we indicate WFM_P with $< T(P); F(P) >$, or with $< T; F >$ if there is no ambiguity about P. T is the set of atoms which are true w.r.t. the WFM, F the set of atoms which are false. All atoms belonging to $B_P - (T \cup F)$ have truth value undefined.

Various equivalent definitions of the well-founded model can be found in the literature, for instance [AVG90], [Gel93] [Prz89], [HP90], [SC94]. In the examples, we will use the constructive definition introduced in [Gel93] and [SC94], that we rephrase below.

Here and in the rest of the paper, literals *not* A are considered to be new atoms. We conventionally assume that, for every atom A in the language of P, B_P contains both A and *not* A. The following definitions introduce the computation of the WFM by means of the computation of all the literals which are true with respect to the WFM. The connection to the standard formulation in terms of the sets T and F is then stated in Theorem 4.

Definition 1 Enhanced Immediate Consequence Operator.
Let $J \subseteq B_P$ be the set of literals currently known to be true. I.e., J is the current approximation of the WFM. The VanEmden-Kowalski's operator T [Llo87] is modified into T_J, as follows. In particular, in the base step, the negation *not* A of every atom A not belonging to J is assumed. The subsequent steps simply apply the clauses of the program, given the set of literals already computed.

$$\begin{aligned} T_J \uparrow 0 &= \{not\, A \in B_P : A \notin J\} \\ T_J \uparrow n+1 &= \{A \in B_P : \\ &\quad A \leftarrow B_1, \ldots, B_k \text{ is a clause in } P, \{B_1, \ldots, B_k\} \subseteq B_P\} \end{aligned}$$

Let $S(J) = T_J \uparrow \omega$.

Let us now assume to iteratively apply the function S, starting from $J = \emptyset$, and then taking J to be the result obtained at the previous iteration. We may notice that $S(\emptyset) = T_\emptyset \uparrow \omega$ will contain an overestimated set of consequences, since *not* A will be assumed for every $A \in B_P$. Vice versa, at the second iteration, $S(S(\emptyset)) = T_{S(\emptyset)} \uparrow \omega$ will contain an underestimated set of consequences, since the negation of atoms in $S(\emptyset)$ cannot be assumed. Similarly, the subsequent iteration steps will develop into an *iterated fixpoint computation* [Gel93]. At each second step, an underestimated set of consequences, of growing size with respect to the previous one, is obtained. I. e., at every second step a better approximation of the *WFM* is computed. To capture this behaviour, a function Σ corresponding to a double application of S is defined below.

Definition 2 Alternating Fixpoint Computation. Let $\Sigma = S^2$ correspond to a double application of S, i.e.

$$\begin{aligned} \Sigma \uparrow 0 &= \emptyset \\ \Sigma \uparrow n+1 &= \Sigma(\Sigma \uparrow n) = S(S(\Sigma \uparrow n)) \end{aligned}$$

The following theorems state that Σ computes as least fixed point a set *WFC* of literals, which exactly correspond to the set of literals which are true with respect to the *WFM*.

Theorem 3 Well-founded Model Construction.
Σ is monotonically increasing, and therefore for some ordinal δ:

$$\Sigma \uparrow \delta = \Sigma \uparrow \delta + 1 = WFC$$

Theorem 4.
Let A be an atom. Let $T = \{A \in WFC\}$ and $F = \{A : not\ A \in WFC\}$.
We have $WFM_P =< T; F >$.

Example 1.
Given the normal program:

$$\begin{aligned} a &\leftarrow not\ b \\ b &\leftarrow not\ a \\ e &\leftarrow f \\ f &\leftarrow not\ g \\ g &\leftarrow h \end{aligned}$$

the computation of the well-founded model by means of the above procedure is the following.

$$\begin{aligned} &\Sigma \uparrow \mathbf{0} &&= \emptyset \\ &S(\emptyset) &&= \{not\ a, not\ b, not\ e, not\ f, not\ g, not\ h \\ & &&\quad a, b, e, f\} \\ &\Sigma \uparrow \mathbf{1} &&= S(S(\emptyset)) = \{not\ g, not\ h \\ & &&\quad e, f\} \\ &S(\Sigma \uparrow 1) &&= \{not\ a, not\ b, not\ g, not\ h \\ & &&\quad a, b, e, f\} \\ &\Sigma \uparrow \mathbf{2} &&= S(S(\Sigma \uparrow 1)) = \Sigma \uparrow 1 \end{aligned}$$

Therefore, the fixpoint of the sequence is $WFC = \Sigma \uparrow 1 = \{not\ g, not\ h, e, f\}$, and thus $T = \{e, f\}$ and $F = \{g, h\}$.

For the sake of simplicity, by abuse of notation, conjunctions and disjunctions will be treated as *sets*, so as not to be concerned about the order of the literals composing them. Conjunctions of positive (respectively, negative) literals will be denoted by names starting with $\mathcal{C}$ (respectively, $\overline{\mathcal{C}}$). Conjunctions of possibly intermixed positive and negative literals will be denoted by names starting with $\hat{\mathcal{C}}$. Disjunctions of positive (respectively, negative) literals will be denoted by names starting with $\mathcal{D}$ (respectively, $\overline{\mathcal{D}}$). Disjunctions of possibly intermixed positive and negative literals will be denoted by names starting with $\hat{\mathcal{D}}$. By $\sim$ we will mean the operation of negating all the literals composing a conjunction or disjunction: e.g., if $\mathcal{D}A = A \vee B$, we have $\overline{\mathcal{D}}A = \sim\mathcal{D}A = notA \vee notB$. We will call $\sim \mathcal{D}D$ the *negation* of $\mathcal{D}D$. Literals can be seen as particular cases of conjunctions and disjunctions (singleton sets). Again by abuse of notation, we will apply to conjunctions and disjunctions the usual set operators $\in$, $\cup$, $-$ (set difference). Set operators will be used also for comparing disjunctions and conjunctions. For instance, given disjunction $\mathcal{D}A$ and conjunction $\mathcal{C}B$ we will write $\mathcal{C}B \not\subseteq \mathcal{D}A$ to mean that the atoms composing $\mathcal{C}B$ are not a subset of the atoms composing $\mathcal{D}A$.

In this notation, a disjunctive clause of the form 1 is written as:

$$\mathcal{D}A \leftarrow \mathcal{C}B, \overline{\mathcal{C}}C$$

3 A Summary of the Static Semantics

In this section we report the main definitions and results about the static semantics, as introduced in [Prz94]. The static semantics can be seen as an extension of the well-founded model semantics to disjunctive logic programs. In fact, it derives a minimal, in some sense, set of conclusions that can be inferred from a disjunctive program. This is obtained by translating the (instantiated version of) the program into a first-order *Autoepistemic Logic of Knowledge and Beliefs*. The language of these kinds of theories is a propositional language $\mathcal{L}_{\mathcal{B}}$, with standard connectives ($\vee$, and, $\wedge$, or, $\supset$, material implication, $\neg$, negation), the propositional letter $\bot$ (denoting *false*) and a modal operator $\mathcal{B}$, called the *belief* operator. The atomic formulae of the form $\mathcal{B}F$, where F is an arbitrary formula of $\mathcal{L}_{\mathcal{B}}$, are called *belief atoms.* $\mathcal{B}F$ intuitively means "F is believed" The formulae of $\mathcal{L}_{\mathcal{B}}$ in which $\mathcal{B}$ does not occur are called *objective* and the set of such formulae is denoted by $\mathcal{L}$.

Definition 5 Belief Theory.
An *autoepistemic theory of beliefs*, or just a *belief theory*, is an arbitrary theory in the language $\mathcal{L}_{\mathcal{B}}$.

Definition 6 Affirmative Belief Theory.
An *affirmative belief theory*, is a theory in the language $\mathcal{L}_{\mathcal{B}}$ consisting of a (possibly infinite) set of clauses of the form:

$$B_1 \wedge \ldots \wedge B_m \wedge \mathcal{B}G_1 \wedge \ldots \wedge \mathcal{B}G_k \wedge \neg\mathcal{B}F_1 \wedge \ldots \wedge \neg\mathcal{B}F_n \supset A_1 \vee \ldots \vee A_l \quad (2)$$

where $l > 0$, $k, m, n \geq 0$, A_i's and B_i's are objective atoms and F_i's and G_i's are arbitrary formulae.

A disjunctive logic program P is translated into a special case of affirmative belief theory, where every clause of the form 1 is considered to be translated into the corresponding axiom:

$$B_1 \wedge \ldots \wedge B_m \wedge \mathcal{B}\neg C_1 \wedge \ldots \wedge \mathcal{B}\neg C_n \supset A_1 \vee \ldots \vee A_l \quad (3)$$

where the A_i's, B_i's, and C_i's are objective atoms.

A *model* of a belief theory is a consistent set of literals. All models are assumed to be *total*, i.e., given atom A, either A or $\neg A$ belongs to M. An atom A is *true* in a model M (resp. *false*) if A (resp. $\neg A$) belongs to M. A model M is smaller than a model N, if it contains less positive literals (atoms).

Definition 7 Minimal Model of a Belief Theory.
A *minimal model* of a belief theory T is a model M of T such that there is no smaller model N of T which coincides with M on belief atoms.

$T \models_{min} F$ means that F is true in all minimal models of T, i.e. F is *minimally entailed* by T.

In a theory T, the following axioms are given, describing obvious properties of belief atoms.

(D) Consistency Axiom:

$$\neg\mathcal{B}\bot$$

(K) Normality Axiom: For any formulae F and G

$$\mathcal{B}(F \supset G) \supset (\mathcal{B}F \supset \mathcal{B}G)$$

(N) Necessitation Rule: For any formula F

$$\frac{F}{\mathcal{B}F}$$

Axiom (N) implies that beliefs are distributive with respect to conjunctions, namely, for any formaulae F and G,

$$\mathcal{B}(F \wedge G) \equiv (\mathcal{B}F \wedge \mathcal{B}G)$$

Instead, it is not assumed that the belief operator is distributive with respect to disjunctions. A variation of the semantics can, however, be easily defined by assuming the

(J) Disjunctive belief axiom

$$\mathcal{B}(F \vee G) \equiv \mathcal{B}F \vee \mathcal{B}G$$

Definition 8 Formulae Derivable from a Belief Theory.
A formula F is derivable from a belief theory if it belongs to the smallest set, $Cn_*(T)$, of formulae of the language $\mathcal{L}_\mathcal{B}$ which contains the theory T and all (the substitution instances of) the axioms (K), (D), and is closed under the necessitation rule (N). This is denoted by $T \vdash_* F$. Consequently,

$$Cn_*(T) = \{F : T \vdash_* F\}$$

A belief theory T is called *consistent* if $Cn_*(T)$ is consistent. Thus, T is consistent if $T \not\vdash_* \perp$.

Notice that, by the consistency axiom (D),

$$\forall F \text{ such that } \mathcal{B}F \in T,\ T \models \neg\mathcal{B}\neg F$$

The *Belief Closure Operator* defined below is based on the idea of building extensions of a belief theory T based on another belief theory S, obtained by augmenting T with precisely those belief atoms $\mathcal{B}F$ which satisfy the condition that F is true in all minimal models of S.

Definition 9 Belief Closure Operator.
For any belief theory T define the *belief closure* operator Ψ_T by the formula:

$$\Psi_T(S) = Cn_*(T \cup \{\mathcal{B}F : S \models_{min} F\})$$

where S is an arbitrary belief theory and F ranges over all formulae of $\mathcal{L}_\mathcal{B}$

Theorem 10 Monotonicity of the Belief Closure Operator.
Suppose that the theories V' and V'' are extensions of a belief theory T obtained by adding some belief atoms $\mathcal{B}F$ to T, and let $T' = Cn_*(V')$ and $T'' = Cn_*(T'')$.

$$\textit{If } T \subseteq T' \textit{ then } \Psi_T(T') \subseteq \Psi_T(T'')$$

A *Static Expansion* of a belief theory T is a fixed point of the operator Ψ_T.

Definition 11 Static Expansions.
A theory $\hat{T}$ is a static expansion of the belief theory T iff $\hat{T} = \Psi_T(\hat{T})$.

Static expansions $\hat{T}$ of a belief theory T are first-order extensions of T, and thus provide the meaning of T consisting of the sentences logically derivable from $\hat{T}$. Since Ψ_T is monotonic, it has a least fixed point, as stated below.

Theorem 12 Least Static Expansion.
Every belief theory T has the least *static expansion $\overline{T}$, namely the least fixed point of the operator Ψ_T.*

Definition 13 Static Completion.
The *least* static expansion $\overline{T}$ of a belief theory T is called the *static completion* of T.

Theorem 14 Consistency of Static Completions.
The static completion $\overline{T}$ of any affirmative belief theory T is always consistent.

As a special case, the static completion of a belief theory which is the translation of a disjunctive logic program P is consistent.

Definition 15 Static Semantics.
The static semantics of a belief theory T is the set of all formulae which belong to the static completion $\overline{T}$ of T.

In agreement with Minker's *Generalized Closed Word Assumption GCWA*) [Min82] and with McCarthy's *Circumscription* [McC80], a formula F is believed to be true in the static semantics if and only if it is minimally entailed by $\overline{T}$. Thus, $\mathcal{B}F$ means that F is believed to be true, i.e. that F is true in all minimal models of $\overline{T}$. By definition, *not* F means $\mathcal{B}\neg F$, i.e. F is believed to be false, i.e. F is false in all the minimal models of $\overline{T}$, i.e. $\neg F$ is believed to be true.

For normal programs, the well-founded, static and stationary [Prz91] semantics coincide. For positive disjunctive programs, the static semantics coincides with the minimal model semantics.

In the rest of the paper, let $\overline{P}$ be the static completion of the affirmative belief theory corresponding to a disjunctive logic program P.

Remark.
Notice that, in the context of an affirmative belief theory which is the translation of a disjunctive logic program P, we are interested in a subset of $\overline{P}$, consisting of the belief atoms $\mathcal{B}D$ or $\mathcal{B} \sim D$, where D is either a literal or a disjunction, containing at least one atom/disjunction which appears as the conclusion of a clause in P. We will call this subset the *interesting subset* of $\overline{P}$.

4 Observations on the Static Semantics

In this section we propose some observations about the static semantics, useful for what follows. Conventionally, we extend the notation for disjunctions and conjunctions introduced in Section 2 to conjunctions/disjunctions of formulae of $\mathcal{L}_{\mathcal{B}}$.

An affirmative belief theory is, as defined in the previous section, composed of a set of axioms represented as implications. Some of the axioms may have empty conditions, and will be called *facts*. In the following, given any extension $\hat{P}$ of the belief theory corresponding to a disjunctive program P, we will call *interesting subset* of $\hat{P}$ the set of axioms whose conclusion is a disjunction (as a particular case, an atom) containing at least one atom/disjunction which appears as the conclusion of a clause in P.

Since any logical theory implies all the tautologies, this is also the case for belief theories, and for their static expansions. From the necessitation rule (N), it is thus possible to derive belief atoms corresponding to all the instances of all the tautologies of propositional logic over the language $\mathcal{L}_{\mathcal{B}}$, like for instance

$\mathcal{B}(F \vee \neg F)$ for any formula F of $\mathcal{L}_\mathcal{B}$. From the consistency axiom (D), formulae corresponding to the negation of all the tautologies are symmetrically obtained, like for instance $\neg\mathcal{B}((F \wedge \neg F))$. Axiom (K) is a distributive axiom which allows modus ponens to be applied to belief formulae. In an affirmative belief theory, several disjunctions can be derived, not only those explicitly present in the conditions of some of the axioms.

Example 2.
From theory:

$$A \vee B$$
$$A \supset C$$

where A, B and C are objective atoms, given tautology

$$((A \supset C) \supset ((A \vee B) \supset (C \vee B)))$$

by axiom (N) it is possible to derive

$$\mathcal{B}(A \vee B)$$
$$\mathcal{B}(A \supset C)$$
$$\mathcal{B}((A \supset C) \supset ((A \vee B) \supset (C \vee B)))$$

From the last formula, by axiom (K), applied twice, we obtain

$$\mathcal{B}(A \supset C) \supset (\mathcal{B}(A \vee B) \supset \mathcal{B}(C \vee B))$$

Now, by modus ponens it follows

$$\mathcal{B}(A \vee B) \supset \mathcal{B}(C \vee B)$$

and then

$$\mathcal{B}(C \vee B)$$

The following is a trivial consequence of the definitions reported in the previous section.

Proposition 16.
Let $Z \subseteq \overline{P}$ be a set of belief atoms. $\Psi_P(P \cup Z) \subseteq \overline{P}$.

Proof. Since $Z \subseteq \overline{P}$, clearly $(P \cup Z) \subseteq (P \cup \overline{P})$. By the monotonicity of Ψ_P, $\Psi_P(P \cup Z) \subseteq \Psi_P(P \cup \overline{P})$. Since $P \subseteq \overline{P}$, and $\overline{P}$ is a fixed point of Ψ_P, it follows $\Psi_P(P \cup Z) \subseteq \overline{P})$. □

In order to compute the static completion of disjunctive logic programs, it is important to characterize the formulae F such that $T \models_{min} F$, given an affirmative belief theory T. The definitions imply that one has to assign arbitrary truth values to belief atoms which are not in T, then minimize the objective atoms, and select those which have the same truth value in all the minimal models. Some observations are in order about what this means.

Lemma 17.
Let A be an objective atom. Let $\hat{\mathcal{D}}D$ be a disjunction such that $T \models_{min} \hat{\mathcal{D}}D$, and $A \in \hat{\mathcal{D}}D$ (or, respectively, $\neg A \in \hat{\mathcal{D}}D$). Assume $\nexists \hat{\mathcal{D}}H$, $\hat{\mathcal{D}}H \subseteq \hat{\mathcal{D}}D$, such that $A \in \hat{\mathcal{D}}H$ (or, respectively, $\neg A \in \hat{\mathcal{D}}H$). Then, $T \not\models_{min} \neg A$

Proof. By hypothesis, $\hat{\mathcal{D}}D$ is not redundant with respect to A (respectively, $\neg A$). Since it cannot be decided which of the literals composing $\hat{\mathcal{D}}D$ are true, any of them can be assumed in a minimal model. Thus, there will be minimal models where A is true, and others where it is false. Therefore, $\neg A$ can't be minimally entailed. □

Example 3.
From theory T

$$A \vee B \vee C$$

one cannot decide which literal is true. Thus, every minimal model will entail $A \vee B \vee C$, but there will be three models, entailing A, B and C respectively. Thus, $T \not\models_{min} A$, $T \not\models_{min} B$, and $T \not\models_{min} C$.
Given instead T',

$$A \vee B \vee C$$

$$B \vee C$$

since the first disjunction is redundant with respect to the second one, every minimal model will entail $\neg A$, and thus $T' \models_{min} \neg A$.

Lemma 18.
If for every axiom in T of the form $\hat{C}G \supset F$, $\exists \mathcal{B}L \in \hat{C}G \; : \; T \not\models \mathcal{B}L$ then $T \not\models_{min} F$ and $T \not\models_{min} \neg F$

Proof. If we consider such an axiom, by varying the truth value of $\mathcal{B}L$, F becomes alternatively true or false. Thus, neither F nor its negation may belong to all minimal models. □

Theorem 19.
For any formula F and any affirmative belief theory T, $T \models_{min} F$ iff one of the following cases holds:

(i) *F is an atom or a disjunction, and there exists an axiom $\hat{C}G \supset F$ in T where $T \models \hat{C}G$*
(ii) *$F = \neg A$, where A is an objective atom to which Lemma 17 does not apply, and for every axiom $\hat{C}G \supset A$ in T there exists an objective formula $R \in \hat{C}G$ such that $T \not\models R$.*
(iii) *$F = \neg A$ where A is an objective atom to which Lemma 17 does not apply, and there is no axiom $CG \supset A$ in T.*
(iv) *$F = \neg A$ where A is an objective atom, (i) does not apply to A, and $T \models_{min} \mathcal{D}D$, $T \models_{min} \mathcal{D}H$, $H \subseteq D$, $A \in D$, $A \notin H$.*
(v) *F is a negative disjunction $\overline{\mathcal{D}}D$, $T \models_{min} \mathcal{D}D$ and $\exists L \in \mathcal{D}D$, $T \not\models_{min} L$.*
(vi) *F is a logical consequence of formulae which fit in cases (i)-(v).*

Proof. Case (i) is fairly obvious. In cases (ii)-(iv), if Lemma 17 does not apply we can conclude that every minimal model will entail $\neg A$, since it does not entail A, and it is total. Case (v) holds because

$$\neg(A \wedge B) \equiv (\neg A \vee \neg B)$$

is a tautology of first-order propositional logic. Case (vi) is also obvious. All the formulae not considered in cases (i)-(vi) are not minimally entailed since they are not necessary for satisfying axioms in T, and are not logical consequences of those which are necessary. □

In [Prz94], the static completion is shown to be the least fixed point of a monotonic minimal model operator, based on the belief closure operator Ψ_T, so that it can be iteratively constructed starting from P. In the following sections, we propose an analogous characterization, given by splitting the construction into two parts: a preliminary part of simplification of the program w.r.t. disjunction, and then a constructive part based on a variant of the well-founded model computation.

5 Program Transformation

The objective of the program transformation procedure described in this section is that of identifying and making explicit all potential deductions which can be performed, according to a given semantics, by means of the disjunctive knowledge represented in the program. The result is a new program P' (containing P as a proper subprogram) where disjunction may occur also in the conditions of the axioms. Thus, the definition of the procedure formalizes the rules for using disjunction in the inference process.

For the static semantics, that we are considering as a case-study, a disjunction of literals is transposed, by necessitation (axiom (N)), into a single belief atom, which is then used in derivations according to the usual first-order-logic rules. In the static semantics, in fact, it is not assumed that the belief operator is distributive with respect to disjunctions. It is however possible, as we will see, to optionally introduce the disjunctive belief axiom.

Following [Prz94], and as summarized in the previous section, we consider every clause in a disjunctive logic program P to be translated into a corresponding axiom of an affirmative belief theory, of the form 2. Therefore, we are able to use all features of first-order predicate logic (including moving literals from one side of the implication to the other, and introducing disjunctions in the conditions). Since we will not explicitly use this notation, please recall that *notA* means $\mathcal{B}\neg A$. All disjunctions in the conditions of clauses will be enclosed in brackets, to indicate that they correspond to a single belief atom. Axioms in P and P' will be also called, by abuse of notation, *clauses*.

As shown in Example 2, in the context of theories which are the translation of disjunctive logic programs, a way for deriving new disjunctions is that of using tautologies of propositional logic. Useful tautologies concerning disjunction can be represented by means of the following axiom schemata. Let Q, R, S, W be objective atoms, D be a disjunction of objective atoms, and C any conjunction.

$$((C \wedge W \supset Q) \supset (C \wedge (W \vee S)) \supset (Q \vee S)) \tag{4}$$

$$((C \supset D) \supset (C \wedge W \supset (D \vee S)) \tag{5}$$

The purpose of axiom 4 is that of introducing disjunctions in the conditions of clauses, so as to derive new disjunctions from those which are conclusions of some other clause in P. Axiom 5, insted, has the aim of eliminating redundant clauses.

Proposition 20.
Axiom schema 4 represents all possible derivations of disjunction from other disjunctions.

Proof. This is easy to see, since this axiom potentially introduces in the conditions and conclusion of clauses all possible disjunctions over the language of the program. □

In order to generate only the interesting clauses (in the sense specified in Section 4), we also introduce the following restricted form of axiom schema 4.

$$((C \wedge W \supset Q) \wedge (C \wedge R \supset S) \supset (C \wedge (W \vee R)) \supset (Q \vee S)) \tag{6}$$

Axiom 6 joins two clauses, thus obtaining a new one with disjunctive conditions and conclusion.

The program transformation procedure performs a controlled application of the above schemata to the given program, so as to generate interesting axioms only. To do this, the application takes as basis disjunctions $\mathcal{D}D$ appearing as the conclusion of a clause in P, and their negation $\sim\mathcal{D}D$. With this limitation, only the significant subset of the static completion is computed in the constructive step. Other limitations are introduced to avoid the generation of redundant clauses.

The program transformation procedure for the static semantics consists in repeatedly applying the steps defined below in the given order, each step being repeated until no further transformation is possible. Each transformation will be first illustrated by means of examples, and then defined formally.

Initial Step

The aim of this step is that of relating disjunctions expressed explicitly with disjunctions expressed implicitly, by applying axiom schema 6.

Example 4.
Given clauses:

$$a \leftarrow b, g$$
$$a \leftarrow c, h$$
$$b \vee c \leftarrow e, f$$

add axiom:

$$a \leftarrow (b \vee c), g, h$$

Example 5.
Similarly to the previous example, given clauses:

$$a \vee b$$
$$c \leftarrow a,\ e$$
$$d \leftarrow b,\ not\, f$$

add axiom:

$$c \vee d \leftarrow (a \vee b), e, not\, f$$

Formally, this transformation step is defined as follows.

Definition 21.
Given clauses:

$$\mathcal{D}D_1 \leftarrow \mathcal{C}B_1, \overline{\mathcal{C}}C_1$$
$$\ldots$$
$$\mathcal{D}D_n \leftarrow \mathcal{C}B_n, \overline{\mathcal{C}}C_n$$
$$\mathcal{D}T \leftarrow \mathcal{C}H, \overline{\mathcal{C}}K$$

if $\forall \mathcal{C}B_i \;\; i = 1, \ldots, n \;\; \exists A_i \in \mathcal{C}B_i$ such that $A_i \in \mathcal{D}T$, then:
let $\mathcal{C}B'_i = \bigcup_{i=1}^{n} (\mathcal{C}B_i - A_i)$;
let $\overline{\mathcal{C}}C'_i = \bigcup_{i=1}^{n} \overline{\mathcal{C}}C_i$;
let $\mathcal{D}D' = \bigcup_{i=1}^{n} \mathcal{D}D_i$;
let $\mathcal{D}A = A_1 \vee \ldots \vee A_n$;
add axiom:

$$\mathcal{D}D' \leftarrow \mathcal{D}A, \mathcal{C}B', \overline{\mathcal{C}}C'$$

As a special case, we may have $\mathcal{D}D_1 = \ldots = \mathcal{D}D_n$.

An analogous transformation involving negative literals allows us to optionally introduce the disjunctive belief axiom.

Example 6.
Given clauses:

$$a \leftarrow not\, b$$
$$a \leftarrow not\, c$$
$$b \vee c \leftarrow e, f$$

the axiom:

$$a \leftarrow (not\, b \vee not\, c)$$

is an application of the disjunctive belief axiom. In fact, in terms of belief theories, the axiom schema which has been applied in this case is:

$$((\mathcal{B}\neg b \supset a) \wedge (\mathcal{B}\neg c \supset a)) \supset (\mathcal{B}(\neg b \vee \neg c) \supset a)$$

which is equivalent to

$$((\mathcal{B}\neg b \vee \mathcal{B}\neg c) \supset a)) \supset (\mathcal{B}(\neg b \vee \neg c) \supset a) \; .$$

Notice that, in performing derivations from the program P, the disjunctive belief axiom makes sense only if applied to negative atoms, which are the only belief atoms in the program. An example of application is shown in Section 6.

Formally, we have the following

Definition 22.
Given the same clauses as in previous definition,
if $\forall \overline{\mathcal{C}}C_i \;\; i = 1, \ldots, n \;\; \exists\, notA_i \in \overline{\mathcal{C}}C_i$ such that
$notA_i \in \sim\mathcal{D}T$, then:
let $\overline{\mathcal{C}}C_i' = \overline{\mathcal{C}}C_i - notA_i$;
let $\mathcal{C}P = \bigcup_{i=1}^{n} \mathcal{C}B_i$ and $\overline{\mathcal{C}}Q = \bigcup_{i=1}^{n} \overline{\mathcal{C}}C_i'$;
let $\mathcal{D}D' = \bigcup_{i=1}^{n} \mathcal{D}D_i$;
let $\overline{\mathcal{D}}D = notA_1 \vee \ldots \vee notA_n$;
add axiom:

$$\mathcal{D}D' \leftarrow \overline{\mathcal{D}}D, \mathcal{C}P, \overline{\mathcal{C}}Q$$

Intermediate Step

This step carefully applies axiom schema 4, so as to exploit disjunctions which appear as the conclusion of some clause in P.

Example 7.
Consider the following clauses.

$$t \leftarrow a, f$$
$$a \vee b \leftarrow p, not\; q$$

add axiom:

$$t \vee b \leftarrow (a \vee b), f$$

The formal definition of this transformation is the following.

Definition 23.
Given clauses:

$$\mathcal{D}A \leftarrow \mathcal{C}B, \overline{\mathcal{C}}C$$
$$\mathcal{D}D \leftarrow \mathcal{C}P, \overline{\mathcal{C}}Q$$

if $\mathcal{D}A \not\subseteq \mathcal{D}D$ and $\exists\, A \in \mathcal{C}B$ such that $A \in \mathcal{D}D$, then:
let $\mathcal{C}B' = \mathcal{C}B - \{A\}$;
let $\mathcal{D}D' = \mathcal{D}D - \{A\}$;
let $\mathcal{D}A' = \mathcal{D}A \cup \mathcal{D}D'$;
add axiom:

$$\mathcal{D}A' \leftarrow \mathcal{D}D, \mathcal{C}B', \overline{\mathcal{C}}Q$$

The limitation $\mathcal{D}A \not\subseteq \mathcal{D}D$ is aimed at avoiding redundancies, as exemplified below.

Example 8.
Given clauses:
$a \vee b \vee c$
$c \vee b \leftarrow c$
it is useless to generate the axiom:
$a \vee b \vee c \leftarrow (a \vee b \vee c)$

Example 9.
Consider the following clauses.

$$g \leftarrow k, not\ c$$
$$c \vee d \leftarrow m, not\ n$$

The situation is similar to previous example, but the condition *not c* in the first clause corresponds to the negation of atom c, that appears in the disjunction $c \vee d$, which is the conclusion of the second clause. In this case, add axiom:

$$g \vee not\ d \leftarrow k, (not\ c \vee not\ d)$$

Formally, we have

Definition 24.
Given the same clauses as in previous definition,
if $\mathcal{D}A \not\subseteq \mathcal{D}D$ and $\exists\, notA \in \overline{\mathcal{C}}C$ such that $notA \in {\sim}\mathcal{D}D$, then:
let $\overline{\mathcal{C}}C' = \overline{\mathcal{C}}C - \{notA\}$;
let $\overline{\mathcal{D}}D = {\sim}\mathcal{D}D$;
let $\overline{\mathcal{D}}D' = \overline{\mathcal{D}}D - \{notA\}$; let $\hat{\mathcal{D}}E = \mathcal{D}A \vee \overline{\mathcal{D}}D'$
add axiom:

$$\hat{\mathcal{D}}E \leftarrow \overline{\mathcal{D}}D, \mathcal{C}B, \overline{\mathcal{C}}C'$$

Again, the limitation $\mathcal{D}A \not\subseteq \mathcal{D}D$ is aimed at avoiding redundancies, such as the following.

Example 10.
Given clauses:
$a \vee b \vee c$
$a \vee b \leftarrow not\ c$
it is useless to generate the axiom:
$a \vee b \vee not\ a \vee not\ b \leftarrow (not\ a \vee not\ b \vee not\ c)$

Final Step

The aim is to eliminate redundant axioms, i.e. those axioms whose head and body are included in that of another (according to axiom schema 5).

Example 11.
Consider the following axioms.

$$a \vee b \leftarrow f, g$$
$$a \vee b \vee c \leftarrow f, g, h$$

The second axiom can be removed, since its conclusion is a trivial consequence of the conclusion of the first one.

Formally, we have

Definition 25.
Let $C1$ be the axiom

$$\mathcal{D}A \leftarrow \mathcal{C}B, \overline{\mathcal{C}}C$$

and $C2$ be the axiom

$$\mathcal{D}F \leftarrow \mathcal{C}G, \overline{\mathcal{C}}H$$

If $\mathcal{D}A \subseteq \mathcal{D}F$ and $\mathcal{C}B \subseteq \mathcal{C}G$ and $\overline{\mathcal{C}}C \subseteq \overline{\mathcal{C}}H$, then remove $C2$.

In the rest of this paper, when considering one of the following: the disjunctive logic program P; the new program P' obtained by applying the transformation procedure defined above; the consequences of P'; the results of the constructive phase; we will say that they *correspond* to an affermative belief theory (or more generally to a set of formulae of $\mathcal{L}_{\mathcal{B}}$) in the sense that: every atom *not* A must be read as $\mathcal{B}\neg A$ and every disjunction $A \vee B$ in the conditions of axioms must be read read as $\mathcal{B}(A \vee B)$. By abuse of notation, we indicate with the same names P and P' also the corresponding belief theories. By "model" we mean a model of a belief theory, as defined in Section 3.

Proposition 26.
P' corresponds to an affirmative belief theory.

Proof. From the definition of the program transformation steps, it is easy to see that the resulting axioms are still of the form 2. □

Theorem 27.
M is a model of P iff M is a model of P'.

Proof. The axioms added to P by the program transformation procedure are logical consequences of P, and therefore adding them explicitly does not change the models of the theory. □

Theorem 28.
$Cn_*(P) = Cn_*(P')$

Proof. The consequences obtained from the axioms of P' added by the program transformation procedure can be derived directly ¿from P, given the tautologies of propositional logic. Therefore, the overall set of consequences is the same. □

Corollary 29.
The static completion of P is the same as the static completion of P'.

Proof. By the definition of belief closure operator, since the set of minimal models and the consequences Cn_* are the same for P and P', the fixed points of the belief closure operators Ψ_P and and $\Psi_{P'}$ must also be the same. □

The previous results imply that we can indifferently consider the minimal models and the static completion of P and P'. In particular, we are entitled to compute the static completion of P by means of the transformed program P'.

6 Iterated Fixpoint Computation

The static semantics can be computed by applying to the program P', resulting from the above-defined transformation procedure, a variation of the construction summarized in Section 2. In particular, it is only necessary to modify the base step, while the rest of the procedure remains the same.

Preliminarly, we assume that the Herbrand base of P' contains (as new atoms): all negative literals appearing in P'; all disjunctions appearing in P'; and the negation of each disjunction appearing in P'. This extended Herbrand base will be denoted by B_P^C. In this way, the program P' can be treated, basically, as a definite Horn-clause program.

Notice that any set $Z \subseteq B_P^C$ corresponds to an affirmative belief theory composed of facts. Again by the abuse of notation, this affirmative belief theory will be called Z.

Proposition 30. *Given a set $Z \subseteq B_P^C$, the logical consequences of $P' \cup Z$ correspond to the interesting subset of $Cn_*(P \cup Z)$.*

Proof. The program transformation procedure has added to P' new axioms which simulate the application of axioms (K) and (N), taking (D) into account. All the belief formulae in P' and Z are represented as atoms of B_P^C. The axioms are formulated so as to derive interesting disjunctions. Thus, this corresponds to applying Cn_* to $P \cup Z$. □

Proposition 31. *Given a set $Z \subseteq B_P^C$, $Cn_*(P \cup Z)$ is equivalent to the least Herbrand model of $P \cup Z$.*

Proof. This holds because, in the extended Herbrand base, $P \cup Z$ (or, equivalently, $P' \cup Z$) is a definite program. □

For the static semantics, in order to compute what is true in *all* minimal models of a belief theory corresponding to the translation of a disjunctive logic program, it is necessary to consider the requirements stated in Theorem 19. Since the steps of the iterated fixpoint procedure start from a current set of beliefs, which is an approximation of the final one, some of the requirements can be taken into account also in the base step.

Definition 32 Modified Base Step.
Let $A, notA, \mathcal{D}D, \overline{\mathcal{D}}D \in B_P^C$. Let $J \subseteq B_P^C$.

$$
\begin{aligned}
T_J \uparrow 0 \;=\; & \\
& \textbf{(1)}\ \{\ notA : A \notin J \\
& \quad \text{and } \forall \mathcal{D}D \text{ such that } A \in \mathcal{D}D\ \ \mathcal{D}D \notin J \\
& \quad \text{and } \forall \overline{\mathcal{D}}D \text{ such that } notA \in \overline{\mathcal{D}}D\ \ \overline{\mathcal{D}}D \notin J\} \quad \bigcup \\
& \textbf{(2)}\ \{\ notA : A \notin J \\
& \quad \text{and } \forall \mathcal{D}D \text{ such that } A \in \mathcal{D}D \\
& \quad \mathcal{D}D' = \mathcal{D}D - \{A\} \in J\} \quad \bigcup \\
& \textbf{(3)}\ \{\ \overline{\mathcal{D}}D = {\sim}\mathcal{D}D \text{ such that} \\
& \quad \exists A \in \mathcal{D}D, A \notin J\}
\end{aligned}
$$

Lemma 33.
Let $J \subseteq B_P^C$, and let J be consistent. Let F be a negative literal or a negative disjunction. $T_J \uparrow 0$ corresponds to the set $\{\mathcal{B}F\ :\ J \models_{min} F\}$.

Proof. J corresponds to an affirmative belief theory composed of facts. Points (1)-(3) of Definition 32 exactly correspond to points (iii)-(v) of Theorem 32, which are those applicable to this kind of theory. □

We will still call Σ the function resulting from Definitions 1 and 2 by substituting, in Definition 1, the original base step with the modified base step.

Theorem 34.
Σ is monotonically increasing, and therefore for some ordinal δ:

$$\Sigma \uparrow \delta = \Sigma \uparrow \delta + 1 = WFD$$

The proof is like those in [Gel93] and [SC94], since the modified base step does not actually affect this point.

In the following, given $Z \subseteq B_P^C$, the comparison between $\Sigma(Z)$ and $\Psi_P(P \cup Z)$ (which is equal, by the results given in previous section, to $\Psi_{P'}(P' \cup Z)$) is meant with respect to the interesting subset of $\Psi_P(P \cup Z)$.

Theorem 35.
Let $Z \subseteq B_P^C$, $Z \subseteq \overline{P}$. $P \cup \Sigma(Z) = \Psi_P(P \cup Z)$.

Proof. By the definition of Σ,

$$\Sigma(Z) = S(S(Z)) = T_Z \uparrow \omega$$

By Proposition 31 and Lemma 33,

$$S(Z) = Cn_*(P \cup \{\mathcal{B}F \ : \ Z \models_{min} F\}$$

where F is either a negative literal or a negative disjunction. Notice, however, that these belief atoms (beliefs about negative formulae) are the only interesting ones in this context: in fact, they are the only belief atoms explicitly present in the clauses of *P'*.

$S(Z)$ is an overestimated, possibly inconsistent set of consequences. In fact, it will contain both A and $not\ A$ any time that $Z \models_{min} not\ A$, but A is instead a consequence of $P \cup \{not\ A\}$. When computing $S(S(Z))$, however, these inconsistent conclusions will be excluded, since point (1) of the modified base step will exclude $not\ A$. Then, the modified base step will compute the negative formulae F that are minimally entailed by the consistent subset of S(Z).

Since $Z \subseteq \overline{P}$, this corresponds to finding the formulae F that are minimally entailed by $P \cup Z$. Thus, by applying again the definition of Σ and Proposition 31, we have

$$P \cup S(S(Z)) = P \cup \Sigma(Z) = Cn_*(P \cup \{\mathcal{B}F \ : \ P \cup Z \models_{min} F\}$$

which is exactly $\Psi_P(P \cup Z)$. □

Corollary 36.
$\Sigma(Z) \subseteq \overline{P}$.

Proof. The result follows from the above Theorem, and from Proposition 16. □

Lemma 37.
$P \cup (\Sigma \uparrow n+1) = P \cup (\Sigma(\Sigma \uparrow n)) = \Psi_P(P \cup (\Sigma \uparrow n))$.

Proof. Since $\Sigma \uparrow 0 = \emptyset$, and clearly $\emptyset \subseteq \overline{P}$, by Theorem 35 $P \cup (\Sigma \uparrow 1) = \Psi_P(P \cup (\Sigma \uparrow 0))$. The thesis easily follows by induction, assuming that $\Sigma \uparrow n \subseteq \overline{P}$, and applying Theorem 35. □

Corollary 38.
The sequence $\Psi_P(P \cup \Sigma \uparrow n)$ is monotonically increasing, and thus has a least fixed point.

Proof. It is an immediate consequence of Theorem 34 and Theorem 35. □

Corollary 39.
The fixed point of the sequence $\Psi_P(P \cup \Sigma \uparrow n)$ is the least fixed point of the operator Ψ_P.

Proof. This follows from Corollary 36, since the fixed point of the sequence $\Psi_P(P \cup \Sigma \uparrow n)$ is reached in correspondence of the least fixed point $\Sigma \uparrow \delta$ of the sequence $\Sigma \uparrow n$. In fact, by Theorem 35, $P \cup \Sigma \uparrow \delta = \Psi_P(P \cup \Sigma \uparrow \delta)$ □

Therefore, we have proved the correspondence between the (set of consequences of) *WFD* and the static completion. In the next section we show this correspondence with respect to some examples.

7 Examples

In this Section we give some examples of the proposed approach. First, we consider two of the sample programs discussed in [Prz94] so as to show that the proposed constructive approach gives the same results. Then, we propose more complex new examples, in order to better illustrate the program transformation procedure.

Example 1. ([Prz94, Example 5.2] Let *wp1* stand for *Write_Paper_1*, *wp2* stand for *Write_Paper_2*, *gc* stand for *Get_Crazy*, *gf* stand for *Get_Fired*, and let the given program *P* be the following.

$$wp1 \vee wp2$$
$$gc \leftarrow wp1,\ wp2$$
$$gf \leftarrow not\ wp1,\ not\ wp2$$

The program transformation procedure does not modify the program. The computation of the static completion by the proposed extended well-founded computation is the following.

$$\begin{aligned}
\Sigma \uparrow \mathbf{0} \quad &= \emptyset \\
S(\emptyset) \quad &= \{not\ wp1 \vee not\ wp2, not\ wp1, not\ wp2, not\ gc, not\ gf, \\
&\quad wp1 \vee wp2, gf\} \\
\Sigma \uparrow \mathbf{1} \quad &= S(S(\emptyset)) = \{not\ wp1 \vee not\ wp2, not\ gc, \\
&\quad wp1 \vee wp2\} \\
S(\Sigma \uparrow 1) &= \{not\ wp1 \vee not\ wp2, not\ gc, not\ gf, \\
&\quad wp1 \vee wp2\} \\
\Sigma \uparrow \mathbf{2} \quad &= S(S(\Sigma \uparrow 1)) = S(\Sigma \uparrow 1)
\end{aligned}$$

Therefore, the fixpoint of the sequence is
$WFD = \Sigma \uparrow 2 = \{not\ wp1 \vee not\ wp2, not\ gc, not\ gf, wp1 \vee wp2\}$. In fact, given the belief theory T corresponding to P, the static completion is
$\overline{T} = Con*\ (T \cup \{\mathcal{B}(\neg wp1 \vee \neg wp2), \mathcal{B}\neg gc, \mathcal{B}\neg gf, \mathcal{B}(wp1 \vee wp2)\})$.

Example 2. ([Prz94, Example 5.4] Let *w* stand for *Work*, *t* stand for *Tired*, *s* stand for *Sleep*, *p* stand for *Paid*, *u* stand for *Unhappy*, and let the given program *P* be the following.

$$\begin{aligned}
&w \vee t \vee s \\
&\qquad w \leftarrow not\ t \\
&\qquad s \leftarrow not\ w \\
&\qquad t \leftarrow not\ s \\
&\qquad u \leftarrow w,\ not\ p \\
&\qquad p
\end{aligned}$$

The program transformation procedure does not modify the program. The computation of the static completion is the following.

$$\begin{aligned}
\Sigma \uparrow \mathbf{0} \quad &= \emptyset \\
S(\emptyset) \quad &= \{not\ w \vee not\ t \vee not\ s, not\ w, not\ t, not\ s, not\ u, not\ p, \\
&\quad w \vee t \vee s, w, t, s, u, p\} \\
\Sigma \uparrow \mathbf{1} \quad &= S(S(\emptyset)) = \{not\ w \vee not\ t \vee not\ s, \\
&\quad w \vee t \vee s, p\} \\
S(\Sigma \uparrow 1) &= \{not\ w \vee not\ t \vee not\ s, not\ u \\
&\quad w \vee t \vee s, p\} \\
\Sigma \uparrow \mathbf{2} \quad &= S(S(\Sigma \uparrow 1)) = S(\Sigma \uparrow 1)
\end{aligned}$$

Therefore, the fixpoint of the sequence is $WFD = \Sigma \uparrow 1 = \{not\ w \vee not\ t \vee not\ s, not\ u, p, w \vee t \vee s\}$. In fact, given the belief theory T corresponding to P, the static completion is $\overline{T} = Con*\ (T \cup \{\mathcal{B}(\neg w \vee \neg t \vee \neg s), \mathcal{B}\neg u, \mathcal{B}p, \mathcal{B}(w \vee t \vee s)\})$.

It is easy to see that the correspondence between *WFD* and Static Completion also holds for [Prz94, Example 5.3].

Example 3. Let us reconsider the predicates in Example 1, together with: *gs* standing for *Get_Salary*, *gr* standing for *Get_Rich*, *gf* standing for *Get_Famous*, *gh* standing for *Get_Happy*, *ga* standing for *Get_Angry*. Let the given program P be the following.

$$\begin{aligned}
&wp1 \vee wp2 \\
&\qquad gr \leftarrow wp1 \\
&\qquad gf \leftarrow wp2 \\
&\qquad gc \leftarrow gr,\ gf \\
&\qquad gh \leftarrow gr \\
&\qquad gh \leftarrow gf \\
&\qquad gs \leftarrow wp1 \\
&\qquad gs \leftarrow wp2 \\
&\qquad ga \leftarrow not\ wp1 \\
&\qquad ga \leftarrow not\ wp2
\end{aligned}$$

The initial step of the program transformation procedure adds the axioms:

$$gs \leftarrow (wp1 \lor wp2)$$
$$gh \leftarrow (gr \lor gf)$$

The intermediate and final steps add the axioms:

$$gr \lor wp2 \leftarrow (wp1 \lor wp2)$$
$$gf \lor wp1 \leftarrow (wp1 \lor wp2)$$
$$ga \lor not\ wp1 \leftarrow (not\ wp1 \lor not\ wp2)$$
$$ga \lor not\ wp2 \leftarrow (not\ wp1 \lor not\ wp2)$$

The computation of the static completion by the proposed procedure is the following.

$$\begin{array}{ll}
\Sigma \uparrow \mathbf{0} & = \emptyset \\
S(\emptyset) & = \{not\ wp1 \lor not\ wp2, not\ gr \lor not\ gf, \\
& \quad not\ wp1, not\ wp2, not\ gr, not\ gf, \\
& \quad not\ gh, not\ gc, not\ gs, not\ ga, \\
& \quad gr \lor wp2, gf \lor wp1, \\
& \quad ga \lor not\ wp1, ga \lor not\ wp2, \\
& \quad wp1 \lor wp2, gr \lor gf, \\
& \quad gh, gs, ga\} \\
\Sigma \uparrow \mathbf{1} & = S(S(\emptyset)) = \{not\ wp1 \lor not\ wp2, not\ gr \lor not\ gf, not\ gc, \\
& \quad wp1 \lor wp2, gr \lor gf, \\
& \quad gr \lor wp2, gf \lor wp1, \\
& \quad ga \lor not\ wp1, ga \lor not\ wp2, \\
& \quad gh, gs\} \\
S(\Sigma \uparrow 1) & = \{not\ wp1 \lor not\ wp2, not\ gr \lor not\ gf, not\ gc, \\
& \quad wp1 \lor wp2, gr \lor gf, \\
& \quad gr \lor wp2, gf \lor wp1, \\
& \quad ga \lor not\ wp1, ga \lor not\ wp2, \\
& \quad gh, gs\} \\
\Sigma \uparrow \mathbf{2} & = S(S(\Sigma \uparrow 1)) = S(\Sigma \uparrow 1)
\end{array}$$

Therefore, the fixpoint of the sequence is
$WFD = \Sigma \uparrow 2$.

By applying the negative part of the initial step, it is possible to implement the *disjunctive belief axiom*

$$\mathcal{B}(F \lor G) \equiv \mathcal{B}F \lor \mathcal{B}G$$

In this case, in fact, we would add axiom

$$ga \leftarrow not\ wp1 \lor not\ wp2$$

which would lead to adding conclusion ga to WFD.

Example 4. Let *gq* stand *Good_Quality*, *rf* stand for *Refunded*, *st* stand for *Satisfied*, *ba* stand for *Buy_Again*, and let the given program P be the following.

$$gq \vee rf$$
$$st \leftarrow gq$$
$$ba \leftarrow st$$
$$ba \leftarrow rf$$

The program transformation procedure (initial and intermediate steps) adds the axioms:

$$ba \leftarrow st \vee rf$$
$$st \vee rf \leftarrow (gq \vee rf)$$

The first new axiom is obtained by joining the third and fourth clauses, thus making explicit the disjunctive information that they express. The second new axiom is obtained by a derivation involving the first two clauses. It is easy to verify that:
$WFD = \{not\ gq \vee not\ rf, not\ st \vee not\ rf, gq \vee rf, st \vee rf, ba\}$

Thus, it is clear that any shop which satisfies the condition $st \vee rf$, represented in the first clause of the program, is a good shop, where a customer will buy again.

8 Concluding Remarks

The idea of applying program transformation techniques for characterizing/computing the semantics of normal and disjunctive programs is not new in itself. It has been used, for instance, in [Cos95] for characterizing the stable model semantics [MG88] for normal programs, and in [MM93] for computing the well-founded and stationary semantics for normal and disjunctive programs.

In this paper, however, a main aim has been that of abstracting from computational issues and trying to analyze and characterize the general features of any semantics of disjunctive programs. An analysis and a classification of semantics for disjunctive programs have been proposed in [Dix92] [JD94]. We are indebted to these papers, and the spirit of the present paper is very much the same.

The perspective of this proposal is twofold. On the one hand, as already mentioned, the proposed approach might constitute the formal foundation of efficient procedural semantics for disjunctive logic programs. On the other hand, it is aimed to be a step towards the definition of a general framework for comparing different related semantics, and for possibly specifying parametrized definitions of semantics, to be adapted to the application domain at hand. What can be parametrized is the following. First, the choice of the axiom schemata on which the program transformation procedure is based. This influences the treatment of disjunctive information: in fact, the set of conclusions potentially derivable by the axioms given in Section 5 can be restricted, or changed, according to some kind of reasoning principle. Second, the modified base step, which basically defines the relationship between disjunction and negation. Also in this case, some other reasoning principles could be adopted, instead of minimal entailment.

The proposal in the present form could be potentially extended to versions of the stable model semantics for disjunctive programs, by suitably adapting those procedures which compute the stable models on the basis of the well-founded model, such as [Cos95], [VS92].

References

[AVG90] J.S. Schlipf A. Van Gelder, K.A. Ross. The well-founded semantics for general logic programs. *Journal of the ACM*, 38(3), 1990. abstract in: Proc. of the Seventh ACM SIGACT-SIGMOD Symposium on Principles of Database Systems, 1988.

[Bar91] C. Baral. *Issues in knowledge representation: semantics and knowledge combination.* PhD thesis, Department of Computer Science, 1991.

[CB92] J. Minker C. Baral, J. Lobo. Generalized disjunctive well-founded semantics for logic programs. *Annals of Mathematics and Artificial Intelligence*, 5, 1992.

[Cos95] S. Costantini. Contributions to the stable model semantics of logic programs with negation. *Theoretical Computer Science*, forthcoming, 1995. abstract in: A. Nerode (ed.), Logic Programming and Non-Monotonic Reasoning, Proc. of the Second International Workshop, The MIT Press, 1993.

[Dix91] J. Dix. Classifying semantics of logic programs. In V. S. Subrahmanian A. Nerode, W. Marek, editor, *Proc. of the First International Workshop on Logic Programming and Non-Monotonic Reasoning.* The MIT Press, 1991. Washington D. C., July 1991.

[Dix92] J. Dix. Classifying semantics of disjunctive logic programs. In K. Apt, editor, *Logic Programming, Proc. of the 1992 Joint Conference and Symposium.* The MIT Press, 1992. Washington D. C., November 1991.

[Gel93] A. Van Gelder. The alternating fixpoint of logic programs with negation. *Journal of Computer and System Sciences*, 47(1), 1993. abstract in: Proc. of the Eight ACM SIGACT-SIGMOD-SIGART Symposium on Principles of Database Systems, 1989.

[Got92] G. Gottlob. The complexity of propositional default reasoning under the stationary semantics. Technical Report CD-TR-92/42, Institut fur Information-Systeme, Technische University, A-1040 Wien, Austria, 1992.

[HP90] T. C. Przymusinski H. Przymusinska. Semantic issues in deductive databases and logic programs. In R.B. Banerji, editor, *Formal Techniques in Artificial Intelligence.* North Holland, Amsterdam, 1990.

[JD94] M. Müller J. Dix. An axiomatic framework for representing and characterizing semantics of disjunctive logic programs. In P. Van Hentenryck, editor, *Logic Programming, Proc. of the 11th International Conference.* The MIT Press, 1994. Santa Margherita Ligure, June 1994.

[JL92] A. Rajasekar J. Lobo, J. Minker. *Foundations of Disjunctive Logic Programming.* The MIT Press, 1992.

[Llo87] J. W. Lloyd. *Foundations of Logic Programming.* Springer-Verlag, Berlin, second, extended edition, 1987.

[McC80] J. McCarthy. Circumscription - a form of non-monotonic reasoning. *Artificial Intelligence*, 13, 1980.

[MG88] V. Lifschitz M. Gelfond. The stable model semantics for logic programming. In R.A. Kowalski K. Bowen, editor, *Logic Programming, Proceedings of the Fifth Symposium.* The MIT Press, 1988.

[Min82] J. Minker. On indefinite data bases and the closed world assumption. In *Proc. of the 6th Conference on Automated Deduction*, New-York, 1982. Springer-Verlag.

[MM93] J. Dix M. Müller. Implementing semantics of disjunctive logic programs using fringes and abstract properties. In A. Nerode, editor, *Logic Programming and Non-Monotonic Reasoning, Proc. of the Second International Workshop.* The MIT Press, 1993.

[Prz89] T. C. Przymusinski. Every logic program has a natural stratification and an iterated fixpoint model. In *Proc. of the Eight ACM SIGACT-SIGMOD-SIGART Symposium on Principles of Database Systems.* ACM Press, 1989. Philadelphia, Pennsylvania.

[Prz91] T. C. Przymusinski. Semantics of disjunctive logic programs and deductive databases. In Y. Masunega C. Delobel, M. Kifer, editor, *DOOD'91, Proc. of the 2nd International Conference on Deductive and Object-Oriented Databases*, Berlin, 1991. Springer-Verlag. Munich, Germany.

[Prz94] T. C. Przymusinski. Static semantics for normal and disjunctive logic programs. *the Annals of Mathematics and Artificial Intelligence*, ??, 1994. Special Issue on Disjunctive Programs.

[SC94] G.A. Lanzarone S. Costantini. Metalevel negation and non-monotonic reasoning. *Methods of Logic in Computer Science: An International Journal*, 1(1), 1994. abstract in: Proc. of the Workshop on Non-Monotonic Reasoning and Logic Programming, Austin, TX, November 1-2, 1990.

[Sch92] J.S. Schlipf. *A survey of complexity and undecidability results in logic programming.* In *Proc. of the Workshop on Structural Complexity and Recursion-Theoretic Methods in Logic Programming*, November 1992. held in conjunction to JICSLP'92, Washington, D. C.

[VS92] C.Vago V.S. Subrahmanian, D. Nau. Wfs + branch and bound = stable models. Technical Report CS-TR-2935 UMIACS-TR-92_82, University of Maryland, July 1992. submitted to IEEE Transactions on Knowledge and Data Engineering.

Magic Computation for Well-founded Semantics

Lars Degerstedt[1] and Ulf Nilsson[1]

Department of Computer and Information Science
Linköping University
S-581 83 Linköping, SWEDEN
{larde,ulfni}@ida.liu.se

Abstract. We propose a new realization of goal-directed query evaluation of (non-floundering) normal logic programs for the well-founded semantics. To this end we introduce a new magic templates transformation and give a new fixed point characterization of the well-founded semantics, lifting an existing definition from the ground to the non-ground case. The new fixed point characterization enables us to show a step-by-step correspondence between the naive bottom-up evaluation of the transformed program and a class of top-down search strategies defined in terms of the search forest framework of Bol and Degerstedt. This correspondence implies that the magic transformation is sound and complete. Hence, it provides an upper bound on the search space that must be considered in order to preserve completeness of the bottom-up approach.

1 Introduction

Bol and Degerstedt [BD93a] have proposed a concept of *search forest* to characterize a reasonably sized search space for goal-directed query evaluation of normal programs using *well-founded semantics* (van Gelder et. al. [VRS91]) as the underlying declarative semantics. The framework is based on tabulated resolution, but unlike for instance Tamaki and Sato's OLDT-resolution [TS86], it possesses the additional property that it strictly separates the *search space* (that is, the search forest) from the *search strategy*. For positive programs a general concept of search strategy has been proposed (Bol and Degerstedt [BD93b]) in which some basic search strategies are formulated: depth-first, breadth-first and so-called magic-search. The latter being proven step-wise equivalent to bottom-up evaluation using magic templates (Ramakrishnan [Ram88]). However, for normal programs the search strategy problem has not been thoroughly addressed.

In this paper we propose a new *magic transformation* for normal logic programs and modify the fixed point definition of well-founded semantics of Bonnier et.al [BNN91] to work on a non-ground representation of interpretations. We then show that the resulting bottom-up computation of the transformed program corresponds, step-by-step, to a *class* of search strategies, called *magic strategies*, for non-floundering queries. As a consequence, the well-founded model of the transformed program is shown to be sound and complete wrt a given program and query. Unlike Kemp, Stuckey and Srivastava [KSS91], [KSS92] and

Morishita [Mor93] our goal is not to describe a specific *algorithm* for computing answers to queries. Our aim is rather (1) to define an *upper bound* on the *search space* needed to compute answers bottom-up using magic templates and (2) to relate the magic approach to the search forest of Bol and Degerstedt [BD93a]. The problem of actually computing answers to queries efficiently is a subsequent problem, not addressed in this paper. However, the approach is *constructive* in nature and a naive prototype implementation exists.

The rest of this paper is organized accordingly: in Section 2 we give basic notation and terminology used throughout the paper. In Section 3 we recapture a somewhat simplified version of the search forest for normal programs: informally in Section 3.1 and formally in Sections 3.2–3.3. The new fixed point operators and magic transformation follow in Section 4. Again we start with an informal description of the method in Section 4.1 before giving the formal definitions in Sections 4.2–4.3. In Section 5 we define the class of *magic* search strategies for the search forest and in Section 6 we finally show how the class of magic search strategies correspond, step-by-step, to a naive bottom-up computation of magic programs (in Section 6.1) and prove soundness and completeness of the magic transformation (in Section 6.2).

2 Preliminaries

We presuppose familiarity with standard terminology and notation from logic programming (cf. Lloyd [Llo87] or Apt [Apt90]) and only briefly review concepts that may be ambiguous. In particular we assume that the reader is familiar with the well-founded semantics of van Gelder et. al. [VRS91]. (See also Apt and Bol [AB94] for a comprehensive survey of negation in logic programming.)

By A we denote the set of all atomic formulas. If $\alpha \in A$ then $ground(\alpha)$ denotes the set of all ground instances of α (given a fixed Herbrand universe). By $ground(\{\alpha_1, \alpha_2, \ldots\})$ we denote the set $ground(\alpha_1) \cup ground(\alpha_2) \cup \ldots$.

An *interpretation* $\Im$ is a set of ground literals such that if $\alpha \in \Im$ then $\sim\alpha \notin \Im$. We say that $\Im$ is total if it is always the case that either $\alpha \in \Im$ or $\sim\alpha \in \Im$. Otherwise $\Im$ is said to be partial. A ground atom α is said to be true (respectively false) if $\alpha \in \Im$ (respectively $\sim\alpha \in \Im$). Otherwise α is said to be undefined. For computational reasons we prefer to encode interpretations by so-called *interpretation frames*:

Definition 1 (Interpretation frames).
An *interpretation frame* (T, U) is a pair of sets of (possibly non-ground) atoms where $T \subseteq U$.

An interpretation frame (T, U) encodes the least (set-wise) interpretation $\Im$ such that:

- $\alpha \in \Im$ if $\alpha \in ground(T)$;
- $\sim\alpha \in \Im$ if $\alpha \notin ground(U)$.

Thus, T represents true atoms and U the complement of false atoms (consequently $ground(U) \setminus ground(T)$ is the set of all undefined atoms). In particular, the interpretation $\emptyset$ may be represented by the interpretation frame $(\emptyset, A)$. Similarly $(\emptyset, \emptyset)$ encodes the interpretation $\{\sim\alpha \mid \alpha \in ground(A)\}$.

We finally survey a couple of inference rules used in Section 3 for defining the search forest and in Section 4.3 to define the well-founded semantics.

Definition 2 (ℓ-instantiation).
Let P be a program and ℓ a literal of the form α or $\sim\alpha$. Let $\beta \leftarrow \ell_1, \ldots, \ell_n$ be a variant of a clause $C \in P$, standardized apart from α. If θ is a most general unifier of β and α, then we call the clause $(\beta \leftarrow \ell_1, \ldots, \ell_n)\theta$ an *ℓ-instantiation of C*. By $P|\ell$ we denote a set that contains one ℓ-instantiation of C for each clause $C \in P$ that has ℓ-instantiations.[1]

Notice that $P|\ell$ is unique up to renaming of variables. In order to distinguish these derived clauses from program clauses, we refer to them as *resultants* (a concept from partial deduction as defined by Lloyd and Shepherdson [LS91]).

In addition to ordinary resultants, that rely on the ordinary (three-valued) implication $\leftarrow$, we also need resultants that make use of a non-standard connective, denoted by $\leftarrow_u$. The intended interpretation of $\alpha \leftarrow_u \beta$ is that *α is not false as long as β is not false*. Thus, if β is true then $\alpha \leftarrow \beta$ implies that α is true whereas $\alpha \leftarrow_u \beta$ implies that α is true *or* undefined. (An alternative notation is Nilsson's [Nil93] and Przymusinski and Warren's [PW92] $\alpha \leftarrow \mathbf{u}, \beta$.)

Definition 3 (Resultant).
Let α be an atom and L a sequence of literals. A *resultant* is a formula $\alpha \leftarrow L$; a *u-resultant* is a formula $\alpha \leftarrow_u L$.

The body literals of a resultant are called *subgoals*. Moreover, by the (*original*) *query* we understand a given atomic formula, subsequently denoted by q.

Definition 4 (Answer).
A resultant of the form $\alpha \leftarrow$ is called an *answer* and a u-resultant of the form $\alpha \leftarrow_u$ is called a *u-answer*.

By analogy to the discussion above an answer describes a true fact and a u-answer a non-false fact (that is, something that is either true or undefined).

By a *computation rule* R we mean a rule which selects one literal in the body of every (u-)resultant. A (u-)resultant G and a (u-)answer can be used to produce a new (u-)resultant by *atom-resolution* of the subgoal of G, if the subgoal is positive:

Definition 5 (Atom resolvent).
Let G be a resultant $\alpha \leftarrow \ell_1, \ldots, \ell_n$ and R a computation rule. Assume that $R(G) = \ell_i$ is a positive literal, G' is an answer $\beta \leftarrow$, and σ a renaming of

[1] Note that the definition differs slightly from the original one ([BD93a])

variables in G' such that $var(G) \cap var(G'\sigma) = \emptyset$. If θ is a most general unifier of ℓ_i and $\beta\sigma$, then $(\alpha \leftarrow \ell_1, \ldots, \ell_{i-1}, \ell_{i+1}, \ldots, \ell_n)\theta$ is called an *atom resolvent of G using G′* (via R).

If at least one of G and G' is a u-resultant the same definition applies, but the resolvent is *always* a u-resultant in such cases.

3 The Search Forest

Bol and Degerstedt [BD93a] have provided two alternative definitions of the search forest — the first is an over-estimation of the second, but in the case of "loops through negation" they coincide. As will be shown, naive bottom-up computation with magic templates corresponds step-by-step to certain ways of traversing the first forest; providing us with the relation between these upper bounds of the magic and search forest approach. This section recaptures the search forest framework: first informally — in operational terms — and then formally using a declarative style.

3.1 Outline of the Method

Tabulated resolution, as understood here, is goal-directed and lemma-driven. As in Prolog computation, *goal-directedness* essentially means: (1) selection and instantiation of relevant clauses and (2) resolution of body literals using computed answers or, in the case of negative literals, lack of computed answers. By *lemma-driven* computation we understand computation viewed as derivation of a set of atomic consequences, or lemmas. Thus, just as in ordinary bottom-up computation the tabulation-based approach is a kind of saturation process (in contrast to "linear" algorithms such as SLD-resolution).

Intuitively, the search forest captures this saturation process by construction of a forest of "search trees" by means of *extension steps*. In a tree, each node is meant to model a state of computation corresponding to a program point in a particular clause, for a particular call. To reflect this, the nodes are labelled with (u-)resultants. In operational terms, we have one extension step corresponding to a *procedure call* ℓ; namely we start up new trees with roots labelled by resultants from the set $P|\ell$, if they are not already in the forest (ℓ is either the original query or a subgoal selected at some node in the forest). The step is called *extension by clause*. In addition, we have some extension steps corresponding to various kinds of *procedure return*. These steps all add a new child to a calling node, where the next subgoal of the resultant will be considered. The final forest obtained at the (possibly transfinite) limit of this construction, the *search forest*, is thus a description of the *search space* for tabulation-based methods, for which we (separately) may discuss different *search strategies*.

The extension steps for procedure return differ depending on whether a calling subgoal is a positive or negative literal. In the positive case, there is a step using an ordinary answer based on atom resolution, *extension by answer*, and a similar step for u-answers, called *extension by u-answer*. Similarly, for negative

$1: w(b){\leftarrow}m(b,\,Y),\,{\sim}w(Y)$	$8: w(a){\leftarrow}m(a,\,Y),\,{\sim}w(Y)$	$2: m(b,a){\leftarrow}$
$4: w(b){\leftarrow}{\sim}w(a)$　$5: w(b){\leftarrow}{\sim}w(c)$	$13: w(a){\leftarrow}{\sim}w(b)$	$3: m(b,c){\leftarrow}$
$6: w(b){\leftarrow}u$　$7: w(b){\leftarrow}u$	$15: w(a){\leftarrow}u$	$10: m(a,b){\leftarrow}$
$9: w(c){\leftarrow}m(c,\,Y),\,{\sim}w(Y)$	$16: w(d){\leftarrow}m(d,\,Y),\,{\sim}w(Y)$	$11: m(c,d){\leftarrow}$
$12: w(c){\leftarrow}{\sim}w(d)$		
$14: w(c){\leftarrow}u$		

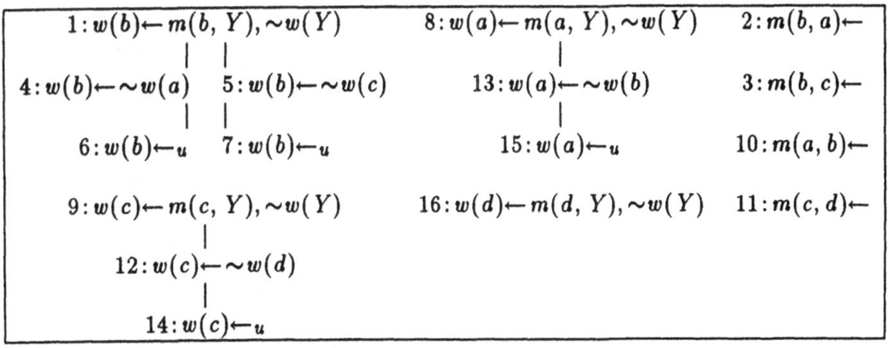

Fig. 1. Forest F^1 closed under positive extensions

literals we have two steps. The first, *extension by negation as failure*, corresponds to successful proof of the negative literal, i.e. exhaustion of possible successes for the positive counterpart. Finally there is a step returning value undefined. This step will be used as a first "approximate" answer of a negative call, which is needed in particular if there are loops through negation. (Notice, the resemblance with how the well-founded model is defined). We will use the step, called *extension by u-assumption* blindly; namely as soon as a negative literal is selected. (Thus, giving us some "unnecessary" u-resultants in the forest as u-assumptions are not always needed.)

Consider the following program P_1 (van Gelder et. al. [VRS91]):[2]

$win(X){\leftarrow}move(X,Y),{\sim}win(Y).$
$move(a,b){\leftarrow}.$　$move(b,a){\leftarrow}.$　$move(b,c){\leftarrow}.$　$move(c,d){\leftarrow}.$

Figure 1 depicts the forest for the query $win(b)$, when repeatedly applying all possible *positive extensions* — that is, all extension steps but extension by negation as failure. In the example we assume that the leftmost computation rule is used. Let us call this forest F^1. The numbers in the figure are not formally part of the forest. However, they suggest one possible way of constructing the forest. The nodes $1,2,3,8,9,10,11,16$ are obtained through extension by clause. Nodes $4,5,12,13$ through extension by answer. Nodes $6,7,14,15$ through extension by u-assumption. (This particular example does not make use of extension by u-answer.)

For definition of extension by negation as failure we need the notion of a proven false (or failed) atom in a forest such as F^1, closed under the positive extensions. A first attempt is to say that an atom β is failed in F iff there is no (u)-answer $\beta{\leftarrow}_{(u)}$ in F. However, this is not quite correct as the u-assumption, although sound at the moment of application, may turn out to be unsound. Take

---

[2] Notice that the program P_1 will be used frequently in subsequent examples.

for instance, the program $\{p \leftarrow \quad q \leftarrow \sim p\}$. In the forest for the query q there will be a node $q \leftarrow_u$, as a result of extension by u-assumption. Clearly, $q \leftarrow_u$ is unsound w.r.t. the semantics of the program, as our intended reading of $q \leftarrow_u$ is that q is not false. Any branch relying on such an "unsound" u-assumption may be viewed as a derivation needed at a preliminary stage of computation. We do not remove "unsound" branches from the forest, but instead just mark them as "no-good" and neglect them in the future. This is a natural solution as the search forest is meant to capture the search space of computation, and not the state. Formally we identify these "unsound" branches by means of an *unsound set* Ω_F which contains all nodes occurring in any such branch in the forest F.

In other words, we define Ω_F in such a way that Ω_F contains any node from F with an ancestor node added either by an extension by u-assumption, which has turned out to be unsound, or by extension by u-answer using a u-answer from Ω_F. Hence, in a declarative spirit, Ω_F provides a concise description of exactly *when* a node can be considered to be "unsound".

Thus more precisely, an atom β is said to be failed in F iff all (u)-answers of the form $\beta\theta \leftarrow_{(u)}$ in F are contained in Ω_F (assuming that F is closed under positive extensions). For F^1 the unsound set Ω_{F^1} is empty. Accordingly, any atom α for which there are no (u)-answers $\alpha\theta$ in F^1, is failed in F^1. In particular, the atoms $move(d, Y)$ (which is selected at node 16) and $win(d)$ (which is in the selected subgoal at node 12) are failed in F^1.

Extension by negation as failure is called a *negative extension* as it relies on a closure property — it can only be applied if, for a negative literal $\sim\beta$, the positive counterpart β *cannot* be proven. Hence, the forest is constructed iteratively by, in each step, closing the forest under positive extensions and negative extensions w.r.t. the forest in the previous step. Thus, a forest F^2 may be obtained by positive extension steps and by negative extension w.r.t. F^1 as shown in Figure 2. Note that F^2 extends F^1 due to its construction. In Figure 2 the horizontal line marks where the forest F^1 ends. Node 17 is added through extension by negation as failure (as $win(d)$ is failed in F^1). For F^2, the unsound set Ω_{F^2} contains node 7 (as $win(c) \leftarrow$ is an answer in F^2). However, no new negative extension is possible; hence F^2 is the final search forest. The computed result for the $win(b)$ is interpreted as undefined, as there are no answer for $win(b)$ in the search forest but a u-answer which is not in Ω_F.

Notice, that the depth of each tree in the search forest is no greater than the number of body literals at the root of the tree. It follows that the forest is finite for function-free programs (as the Herbrand base is finite). However, in the general case branching may be infinite and there may be infinitely many trees.

3.2 Positive and Negative Extensions

In this section we formally define the extension steps used in the search forest. First some auxiliary definitions: we define a *forest* to be any set of trees whose nodes are labelled with (u-)resultants.[3] By a *tree for β* in a forest, we refer to

[3] Formally we must separate between a node and its label. However, for readability nodes are usually identified with their labels.

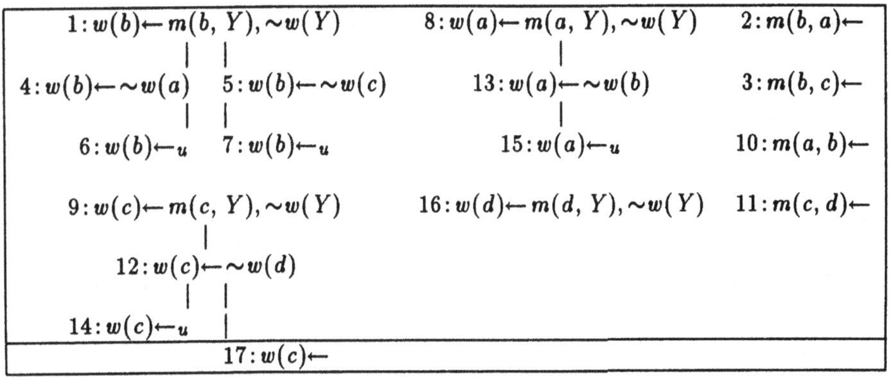

Fig. 2. Forest F^2 closed under positive extensions and closed under negative extensions w.r.t. F^1.

a tree whose root is a β-instantiation of a program clause (which program is involved shall always be clear from the context). We say that the forest F_1 is a *subforest* of F_2, notation $F_1 \sqsubseteq F_2$, if we can obtain F_1 (modulo the renaming of variables within resultants) by removing zero or more nodes (and all their descendants) from F_2.

Throughout the remains of Section 3 we assume a fixed program P, a leftmost computation rule R and an atomic query q. Our discussion is only concerned with *non-floundering* queries under the leftmost computation rule — that is, any q for which no non-ground negative literal is a subgoal (using R) in the search forest for q. As a consequence our exposition can exclude the notion of "extension by floundering" used by Bol and Degerstedt [BD93a]. Moreover, we consider resultants equal up to renaming of variables. The following auxiliary notion will be useful.

Definition 6 (Selected literal).
A literal ℓ is called *selected* in F if either $\ell = q$ or $\ell = R(G)$ for some node G in F. Moreover, ℓ must be ground if ℓ is a negative literal.

We have the following *positive extensions*.

Definition 7 (Positive Extensions).
Let F be a forest. F is closed under

- *extension by clause*, if
  if ℓ is selected in F and $G \in P|\ell$, then F contains a tree with a root labelled by G;
- *extension by answer*, if
  if G is a node in F with $R(G) = \beta$, and there is an answer $\beta\theta\leftarrow$ in a tree

for an instance[4] of β in F, then G has a child labelled by an atom resolvent of G and $\beta\theta\leftarrow$;
- *extension by u-answer*, if
  if G is a node in F with $R(G) = \beta$, and there is a u-answer $\beta\theta\leftarrow_u$ in a tree for an instance[4] of β in F, then G has a child labelled by an atom resolvent of G and $\beta\theta\leftarrow_u$;
- *extension by u-assumption*, if
  if G is a node in F and $R(G) = \sim\beta$ is ground, then G has a child labelled by the u-resultant that is obtained by removing $R(G)$ from G (thus this child contains the connective $\leftarrow_u$).

As mentioned above, the use of u-assumption in the final extension may produce resultants which are unsound if the negative literal turns out to be false. This comes from the fact that the u-assumption is not sound w.r.t. the truth-ordering ($\mathbf{f} < \mathbf{u} < \mathbf{t}$).

Definition 8 (Computed and Potential Answers).
Let F be a forest and β an atom.

- We say that $\beta\theta$ is a *computed answer* for β in F, if a tree for β in F contains a leaf (*computed answer node*) $\beta\theta\leftarrow$.
- We say that $\beta\theta$ is a *potential answer* for β in F, if a tree for β in F contains a leaf (*potential answer node*) $\beta\theta\leftarrow_{(u)}$ (i.e. $\beta\theta\leftarrow$ or $\beta\theta\leftarrow_u$).

Example 1. Figure 1 contains four computed answer nodes (2, 3, 10 and 11) and four additional potential answer nodes (6, 7, 14 and 15).

We next define what it means for an atom to be *failed* and *successful* in a forest. To this end we first introduce the notion of the *unsound set*, thereby identifying the part of the forest which contains the unsound u-answers.

Definition 9 (Unsound set).
The *unsound set* Ω_F of F is the least set of nodes of F that satisfies for every node G of F:

- If $R(G) = \sim\beta$, β is ground, and β is a computed answer for β in F, then the child of G (obtained by extension by u-assumption) is contained in Ω_F.
- If $R(G) = \beta$, G' is a potential answer for β in F, G has a child obtained by extension by u-answer using G' and all variants of G' that are potential answers for β in F are contained in Ω_F, then the child is contained in Ω_F.
- If the parent of G is contained in Ω_F, then G is contained in Ω_F.

Definition 10 (Successful and failed atoms).
Let β be an atom and let F be a forest. (This definition will always be used in a context where F is closed under the positive extensions and β or $\sim\beta$ is selected in F.)

[4] Actually, it is enough to consider only the trees for β. However, as discussed by Bol and Degerstedt [BD93b] it is important to consider *all* instances of β in order to get a one-to-one correspondence between the search forest and the "magic" approach.

- β is *successful* in F if there is a computed answer for β in F.
- β is *failed* in F if all potential answer nodes for β in F are contained in Ω_F.

Example 2. The atom $move(b, Y)$ is successful in F^1 (cf. Figure 1) since it has a computed answer (for instance, $move(b, c)$). On the other hand, the atoms $move(d, Y)$ and $win(d)$ are failed in F^1. The unsound set Ω_{F^1} is empty.

We have the following *negative extension.*

Definition 11 (Negative extensions).
Let F and F' be forests, such that F extends F'. F is closed w.r.t. F' under

- *extension by negation as failure*, if
  if G is a node in F, $R(G) = \sim\beta$ is ground, and β is failed in F', then G has a child in F labelled by the goal obtained by removing $R(G)$ from G.

3.3 Definition of the Search Forest

We define the *search forest* as the limit of a (possibly transfinite) sequence of partial forests $F^1, F^2, \ldots$ closed under positive and negative extensions. We take care that the sequence is *cumulative*, i.e. each forest F^i extends its predecessors F^j, $j < i$, and that an atom that is successful (failed) in one forest, remains successful (failed) in the rest of the sequence.

Definition 12 (Search forest).
Let P be a program and q an atomic query:

- The forest $F_P^1(q)$ is the $\sqsubseteq$-smallest forest that is closed under the positive extensions.
- The forest $F_P^{i+1}(q)$ is the $\sqsubseteq$-smallest forest that is closed under the positive extensions and closed under the negative extensions w.r.t. $F_P^i(q)$.
- Let i be a limit ordinal, and let $S = \{F_P^j(q) \mid j < i\}$. The forest $F_P^i(q)$ is the least upper bound of S w.r.t. $\sqsubseteq$.
- The *search forest* $F_P(q)$ of P and q (via the leftmost computation rule) is the forest $F_P^i(q)$ of the smallest rank i such that $F_P^i(q) = F_P^{i+1}(q)$.

Notice that the set of literals selected in F^i ($i \geq 1$) is constant — all new nodes in F^j ($j > 1$) are mere copies of nodes in F^1 but for the implication arrow $\leftarrow / \leftarrow_u$. This is a consequence of the blind use of extension by u-assumption.

Example 3. Figure 1 depicts the forest $F_{P_1}^1(win(b))$ (the $\sqsubseteq$-smallest forest closed by positive extensions). Figure 2 depicts the forest $F_{P_1}^2(win(b))$ (the smallest forest closed by positive extensions and negative extension w.r.t. the forest $F_{P_1}^1(win(b))$). No further extensions are possible. Thus, Figure 2 depicts the search forest of P_1 and $win(b)$ using the leftmost computation rule. Note that $\Omega_{F^2} = \{7\}$. That is, node 7 is now an unsound conclusion. (Of course, in our example it makes no difference since node 6 is still sound.)

It follows immediately from Bol and Degerstedt's discussion [BD93a] that for any non-floundering query q, our somewhat simplified definition of $F_P(q)$ is both sound and complete (as formulated in [BD93a]).

Hence, for a (non-floundering) query q and a grounding substitution θ, the results in $F_P(q)$ are extracted in the following way:

- $q\theta$ is true in WFM(P) if $q\theta$ is an instance of a computed answer for q;
- $q\theta$ is false in WFM(P) if all potential answers more general than $q\theta$ are contained in Ω_F;
- $q\theta$ is undefined in WFM(P), otherwise.

4 A Bottom-up Approach

In this section we propose a new way of using bottom-up evaluation for normal programs by means of a magic transformation. If executed naively the transformation captures and encodes the intuition behind a goal-directed top-down computation with a leftmost positivistic computation rule (that is, a computation rule which "prefers" leftmost positive literal over negative literals). In the following sections we will show that the well-founded model of the transformed program provides valuable information about relevant parts of the well-founded model of the original program when given a query — namely those parts that are needed to answer the query in a goal-directed manner.

4.1 Outline of the method

The well-founded model of a program is naturally described as a least fixed point. Hence, we may use any such characterization as a basis for bottom-up evaluation of the well-founded semantics. For database applications bottom-up evaluation is often used as basis for computation. The *set-at-a-time* execution is well-suited for cases where *all* answers are desired. The method is also *lemma-driven* which means that it supports the idea of a "cache", for keeping already computed results, in the database system.

In Section 4.3 we consider one particular fixed point characterization of the well-founded model proposed by Bonnier et. al. [BNN91] for ground programs. In their approach the model is obtained as the least fixed point of an operator Ψ_P which in turn is defined as the least fixed point of a second operator $\Phi_{P,I}$. We generalize these operators to work directly on non-ground clauses and literals (although still restricted to the ground case for negative literals) using interpretation frames. By these adjustments we make the operators amenable to actual implementation.

If executed naively the approach amounts to a process $I^0, I^1, \ldots$ where Ψ_P is iteratively used to construct better and better approximations of the well-founded model, starting from an interpretation frame where everything is undefined. In each iteration, I^i, additional information is obtained using the operator Φ_{P,I^i} — yielding all consequences of the program given that the truth-value of negative literals is kept fixed w.r.t. I^i. For the program $P_1 \cup \{\ move(d,e)\leftarrow\ \}$ the iterations look as follows (for notational reasons we have omitted the true atoms from the U-part of the interpretation frames) :

$$
\begin{aligned}
I^0 &= (\emptyset, A)\\
I^1 &= (\{m(a,b), m(b,a), m(b,c), m(c,d), m(d,e)\}, \{w(a), w(b), w(c), w(d)\})\\
I^2 &= (\{w(d), m(a,b), m(b,a), m(b,c), m(c,d), m(d,e)\}, \{w(a), w(b), w(c)\})\\
I^3 &= (\{w(d), m(a,b), m(b,a), m(b,c), m(c,d), m(d,e)\}, \{w(a), w(b)\})\\
I^4 &= (\{w(b), w(d), m(a,b), m(b,a), m(b,c), m(c,d), m(d,e)\}, \{w(a), w(b)\})\\
I^5 &= (\{w(b), w(d), m(a,b), m(b,a), m(b,c), m(c,d), m(d,e)\}, \{w(b)\})\\
I^6 &= (\{w(b), w(d), m(a,b), m(b,a), m(b,c), m(c,d), m(d,e)\}, \emptyset)\\
I^7 &= I^6
\end{aligned}
$$

Notice, that $win(c)$ is identified as false for the first time in iteration I^3. However, as the falsity depends only on $\sim win(d)$ being false, i.e. $win(d)$ being true, this could actually have been detected already in iteration I^2. In fact, this observation reveals a subtle difference between detection of falsity in our bottom-up method and detection of failure in the construction of the search forest.

Straightforward bottom-up evaluation is not goal-directed. To deal with this problem it is common to *transform* the program in such a way that computation concerns only those parts of the model(s) of the original program that are needed to answer the query. (And some auxiliary atoms that encode the introduced filtering mechanism.)

In the next section we define a new transformation method for normal programs that resembles the so-called magic-transformation for positive programs. First, we insert "filter" atoms in all clause bodies in order to impose control over the firing of clauses during the bottom-up computation: in the program P_1 the transformed clauses looks as follows (the notation $call(\beta)$, for any β of the form $p(\bar{x})$, abbreviates an atom $call\_p(\bar{x})$ with a new predicate symbol $call\_p$):

$$
\begin{aligned}
&win(X)\leftarrow call(win(X)), move(X,Y), \sim win(Y).\\
&move(a,b)\leftarrow call(move(a,b)).\\
&\quad\ldots\\
&move(c,d)\leftarrow call(move(c,d)).
\end{aligned}
$$

Notice that the new "filter atoms" do not only control *when* a clause is fired but can also contribute by instantiating the clause. In fact, atom resolution of a clause w.r.t. its "filter atom" is used for the same purpose here as "extension by clause" in the search forest. Namely, to select and instantiate clauses for all "procedure calls" derived from the original query. Hence, the predicates given by $call(\beta)$, for any clause head β in the original program, should be defined in such a way that they encode these "procedure calls".

The *call*-predicates should be two-valued. Therefore we define them solely in terms of positive clauses, as an over-approximation of the part of the program that is needed in order to answer the query. We do this by encoding a top-down computation rule which picks literals from left-to-right as if negative literals never failed. Thus, in the case of program P_1 we get the following clauses:

$call(win(Y)) \leftarrow call(win(X)), move^{+}(X, Y).$
$call(move(X, Y)) \leftarrow call(win(X)).$

$win^{+}(X)) \leftarrow call(win(X)), move^{+}(X, Y).$
$move^{+}(a, b) \leftarrow call(move(a, b)).$
...
$move^{+}(c, d) \leftarrow call(move(c, d)).$

The filter atom $call(win(Y))$ says that $win(Y)$ is called (that is, needed) if $call(win(X))$ is needed and $move^{+}(X, Y)$ succeeds; that is, $move(X, Y)$ is *potentially true*. The subprogram defining the predicates win^{+} and $move^{+}$ is simply a copy of the subprogram for *win* and *move* with all negative literals removed.

Since the β^{+}-construction does not take negative literals into account, the derivation of *call*-atoms over-estimates the needed "procedure calls" in the same way as the blind use of extension by u-assumption leads to unnecessary selections in the forest.

Finally, to use the transformed program to answer a particular query, such as $win(b)$, we just add a fact:

$call(win(b)) \leftarrow .$

Bottom-up computation of the well-founded model of the transformed program yields a query answering procedure for the original program where the computed result for $win(b)$, i.e. that $win(b)$ is undefined, is extracted from the computed model of the transformed program.

4.2 Magic Transformation

The extended magic transformation that will now be formally defined relies on an extended alphabet of predicate symbols. To this end we assume the existence of two distinct predicate symbols, denoted by p^{+}/n and $call\_p/n$, for each predicate symbol p/n. Given an atomic formula α of the form $p(t_1, \ldots, t_n)$ we sometimes write $call(\alpha)$ (respectively α^{+}) to denote the atoms $call\_p(t_1, \ldots, t_n)$ (respectively $p^{+}(t_1, \ldots, t_n)$).

Definition 13 (Magic transformation).
Let P be a normal program. Then $magic(P)$ is the smallest set of clauses such that if $\alpha_0 \leftarrow L \in P$ then:

1. $\alpha_0 \leftarrow call(\alpha_0), L \in magic(P)$;
2. if $\alpha_1, \ldots, \alpha_n$ are the positive literals in L, then $\alpha_0^{+} \leftarrow call(\alpha_0), \alpha_1^{+}, \ldots, \alpha_n^{+} \in magic(P)$;
3. if $\ell = \beta$ or $\ell = \sim\beta$ is a literal in L and $\alpha_1, \ldots, \alpha_k$ are all positive literals to the left of ℓ in L, then $call(\beta) \leftarrow call(\alpha_0), \alpha_1^{+}, \ldots, \alpha_k^{+} \in magic(P)$.

Given an atomic query q, we define $magic(P, q)$ to be the program $magic(P) \cup \{call(q) \leftarrow\}$. The transformed program is intended to be such that if $q\theta$ is ground then $q\theta$ has the same truth-value in WFM(P) as in WFM($magic(P, q)$). (This will be formally verified in Section 6.2 for the class of programs considered in this paper.)

Note that (2) and (3) together form a positive program. That is, neither $call(\beta)$ nor β^+ may be undefined in the well-founded model of $magic(P, q)$ for any query q.

4.3 Bottom-up Interpreter

In the following we present the fixed point characterization of the well founded semantics which originates from the description of Bonnier et. al. [BNN91]. First let:

- L (with or without adornments) denote a sequence of literals;
- $I^+ = (T^+, U^+)$ and $I^- = (T^-, U^-)$ be interpretation frames;

We need the following transition relation based on resolution on resultants:[5]

- $(\alpha_0 \leftarrow L_1) \overset{I^+I^-}{\Longrightarrow} (\alpha_0 \leftarrow L_2)\theta$ if there is a $\beta \in T^+$ and $(\alpha_0 \leftarrow L_2)\theta$ is an atom resolvent[6] of $(\alpha_0 \leftarrow L_1)$ using $\beta \leftarrow$;
- $(\alpha_0 \leftarrow_{(u)} L_1) \overset{I^+I^-}{\Longrightarrow} (\alpha_0 \leftarrow_u L_2)\theta$ if there is a $\beta \in U^+$ and $(\alpha_0 \leftarrow_u L_2)\theta$ is an atom resolvent[6] of $(\alpha_0 \leftarrow_{(u)} L_1)$ using $\beta \leftarrow$;
- $(\alpha_0 \leftarrow_{(u)} L_1, \sim\alpha, L_2) \overset{I^+I^-}{\Longrightarrow} (\alpha_0 \leftarrow_{(u)} L_1, L_2)$ if α is ground and $\sim\alpha$ is true in I^-;
- $(\alpha_0 \leftarrow_{(u)} L_1, \sim\alpha, L_2) \overset{I^+I^-}{\Longrightarrow} (\alpha_0 \leftarrow_u L_1, L_2)$ if α is ground and α is undefined in I^-;
- $(\alpha_0 \leftarrow_{(u)} L) \overset{I^+I^-}{\Longrightarrow} (\alpha_0 \leftarrow_{(u)} L)\theta$ if L consists of non-ground negative literals only and $L\theta$ is ground.

The last case is a (usually impractical) way of avoiding *floundering*. It is a case which is needed for Proposition 14 to hold for arbitrary programs, but it is a case which will not be needed when considering programs $magic(P, q)$ where q is not floundering in the search forest $F_P(q)$.[7]

We may now define the following fixed point operator on interpretation frames:

$$\Phi_{P,I^-}(I^+) = (T_P(I^-, I^+), U_P(I^-, I^+))$$

where:

---

[5] To avoid doubling some rules we sometimes write $\leftarrow_{(u)}$. Our intention is that there is one transition for the connective $\leftarrow$ and one for $\leftarrow_u$.

[6] In contrast to extension by (u-)answer we do not presuppose a fixed computation rule, but may select any positive literal.

[7] This follows from the proof of Proposition 17.

$$T_P(I^-,I^+) = \{\alpha\theta \mid \exists(\alpha\leftarrow L) \in P \text{ such that } (\alpha\leftarrow L) \overset{I^+I^-}{\Longrightarrow} \ldots \overset{I^+I^-}{\Longrightarrow} (\alpha\theta\leftarrow)\}$$
$$U_P(I^-,I^+) = \{\alpha\theta \mid \exists(\alpha\leftarrow L) \in P \text{ s. t. } (\alpha\leftarrow L) \overset{I^+I^-}{\Longrightarrow} \ldots \overset{I^+I^-}{\Longrightarrow} (\alpha\theta \leftarrow_{(u)})\}$$

Given an ordering where $(T_1, U_1) \leq (T_2, U_2)$ iff $T_1 \subseteq T_2$ and $U_1 \subseteq U_2$ (modulo renaming of variables), it follows that Φ_{P,I^-} is continuous. Thus, Φ_{P,I^-} has a $\leq$-least fixed point which can be obtained as the limit of the iteration $\Phi_{P,I^-} \uparrow k$ defined thus:

$$\begin{aligned} \Phi_{P,I^-} \uparrow 0 &= (\emptyset, \emptyset) \\ \Phi_{P,I^-} \uparrow (k+1) &= \Phi_{P,I^-}(\Phi_{P,I^-} \uparrow k) \end{aligned}$$

We may also define an "outer" fixed point operator:

$$\Psi_P(I^-) = \text{LFP}_{\leq}(\Phi_{P,I^-}) = \lim_{k\rightarrow\infty} \Phi_{P,I^-} \uparrow k$$

Formally Ψ_P is a mapping on interpretation frames, but if interpretation frames are viewed as codings of regular interpretations it follows that Ψ_P is monotonic on the standard information ordering ($\subseteq$). By a simple generalization of Przymusinski's result [Prz90] to the non-ground case it can be shown that:

Proposition 14. *$\text{LFP}_{\subseteq}(\Psi_P)$ encodes the well-founded model $\text{WFM}(P)$ of P.*

Define the ascending ordinal powers of Ψ_P thus:

$$\begin{aligned} \Psi_P \uparrow 0 &= (\emptyset, A) \\ \Psi_P \uparrow i+1 &= \Psi_P(\Psi_P \uparrow i) \\ \Psi_P \uparrow i &= \bigcup\{\Psi_P \uparrow j \mid j \leq i\} \quad \text{(for limit ordinals } i) \end{aligned}$$

The well-founded model of P, $\text{WFM}(P)$, is encoded by the least upper bound of the (possibly transfinite) sequence:

$$I_0^0, I_1^0, \ldots, I_0^1, I_1^1, \ldots, I_0^2, I_1^2, \ldots$$

where:

$$\begin{aligned} I_k^i &= \Phi_{P,I^i} \uparrow k \text{ for any integer } k. \\ I^i &= \Psi_P \uparrow i \quad \text{for any ordinal } i; \end{aligned}$$

5 Magic search

Bol and Degerstedt [BD93b] describe search strategies for forests in terms of sequences of forests. A search sequence for a positive search forest F is a sequence of forests $\{F\}_i = F_1, F_2, \ldots$, such that $F_i \sqsubseteq F$, and F_{i+1} extends F_i with one new node: we say that we *visit a node in F_i for extension*. We briefly outline how this framework carries over to naive search for normal programs: to deal with extension by negation as failure we have to generalize the notion of search sequence to transfinite sequences. Hence, by a (*naive*) *search sequence* $\{F\}_i^j$ we mean a sequence $F_0^0, F_1^0, \ldots, F_0^1, F_1^1, \ldots, F_0^2, F_1^2 \ldots$ such that:

1. $F_0^i = \emptyset$ for any ordinal i.
2. F_{k+1}^i extends F_k^i by visiting at most one node in F_k^i for one positive or one negative extension[8].

The limits in the search sequence are defined thus:

$$F^0 = \emptyset$$
$$F^{i+1} = \bigsqcup_{j<\omega} F_j^i$$
$$F^i = \bigsqcup_{j<i} F^j \qquad \text{for limit ordinals } i$$

By a *partial description* $\{F\}_k^i$ of a search sequence S we mean a subsequence of S which preserves the limits of S, where $F_0^i = \emptyset$ and where F_{k+1}^i is obtained from F_k^i by adding finitely many nodes to F_k^i. We say that S *satisfies* $\{F\}_k^i$.

Within this framework we may now describe a class of "magic" search sequences corresponding to how the bottom-up interpreter introduced above behave on magic programs. This class extends the notion of "magic" sequences for positive programs, as defined by Bol and Degerstedt [BD93b].

Definition 15. A search sequence S is *magic* iff S satisfies a partial description $\{F\}_k^i$ such that for any ordinal i and integer k:

1. Let Γ_{k+1}^i be the (intermediate) forest obtained from F_k^i by visiting each node in F_k^i for every possible extension by clause and repeatedly visiting each node for extension by u-assumption.
2. F_{k+1}^i is obtained from Γ_{k+1}^i by repeatedly visiting each node in Γ_{k+1}^i for extension by (u-)answer using (u-)answers from F_k^i, and repeatedly visit each node in Γ_{k+1}^i for extension by negation as failure using failed atoms from:
   (a) F^1 when $i = 1$.
   (b) F^j, $i = j + 1$, when i is a successor ordinal $i > 1$.
   (c) F^j, for some $j < i$ when i is a limit ordinal.

Notice, that while $2(a)$ may use failed atoms from its predecessor limit this is not possible in $2(b) - (c)$. The reason for the difference is due to the asymmetry between how the bottom-up operator deals with falsity due to false positive literals only and falsity due to false negative literals. This introduces a subtlety in the correspondence between the two methods defined in the next section — in the construction of the search forest, atoms "fail faster" than in the naive magic approach. The reason being that, in the forest, if we have a selected negative subgoal $\sim\alpha$ in a tree for β and an answer $\alpha\leftarrow$ then we may immediately use this

[8] To be more precise we have to guarantee extension by negation as failure only refers to forests where the part in focus is closed under the positive extensions. We omit this discussion here, but just note that any search sequence that we consider in the following fulfills this requirement if we assume that there are no failed atoms in the empty forest.

fact in the process of failing β. However, in the bottom-up case the interpretation of negative literals is kept fixed in each iteration and the falsity of β therefore shows up in the next iteration.

Example 4. All magic search sequences for the program P_1 with the query $win(b)$ satisfy the partial description:

$$
\begin{aligned}
&F_0^0 = \emptyset \\
&F_1^0 = \{1\} \\
&F_2^0 = \{1,2,3\} \\
&F_3^0 = \{1,2,3,4,5,6,7\} \\
&F_4^0 = \{1,2,3,4,5,6,7,8,9\} \\
&F_5^0 = \{1,2,3,4,5,6,7,8,9,10,11\} \\
&F_6^0 = \{1,2,3,4,5,6,7,8,9,10,11,12,13,14,15\} \\
&F_7^0 = \{1,2,3,4,5,6,7,8,9,10,11,12,13,14,15,16\} \\
&F_8^0 = \{1,2,3,4,5,6,7,8,9,10,11,12,13,14,15,16\} = F^1 \\
&\quad\vdots \\
&F_0^1 = \emptyset \\
&\quad\vdots \\
&F_5^1 = \{1,2,3,4,5,6,7,8,9,10,11\} \\
&F_6^1 = \{1,2,3,4,5,6,7,8,9,10,11,12,13,14,15,17\} \\
&F_7^1 = \{1,2,3,4,5,6,7,8,9,10,11,12,13,14,15,17,16\} \\
&F_8^1 = \{1,2,3,4,5,6,7,8,9,10,11,12,13,14,15,17,16\} = F^2 = F^3 = \ldots \\
&\quad\vdots
\end{aligned}
$$

6 Bottom-up $\simeq$ Top-down

The step-by-step correspondence for positive programs between magic templates and the search forest presented by Bol and Degerstedt [BD93b], was done by coupling derived call patterns and atoms of magic programs with derived subgoal selections and computed answers in the search forest. In this section we extend the correspondence to normal programs. To do this we first define how atoms in interpretation frames *correspond* to nodes in forests. Second, we show that the correspondence holds at each step of computation, thereby proving the step-by-step equivalence between the two methods.

In the following definition of the correspondence we separate between the true and the undefined atoms, as their role will be somewhat different. The following auxiliary notation will be used to reason about an interpretation frame (T, U):

$$
\begin{aligned}
&\text{TRUE}((T, U)) &= T \\
&\text{UNDEF}((T, U)) &= U \setminus T
\end{aligned}
$$

Definition 16 (Correspondence).
Let I be an interpretation frame and F a forest. We say that I and F *t-correspond* iff for each α:

(a) $call(\alpha) \in \text{TRUE}(I)$ iff α or $\sim\alpha$ is selected in F;
(b) $\alpha^+ \in \text{TRUE}(I)$ iff α is a potential answer in F;
(c) $\alpha \in \text{TRUE}(I)$ iff α is a computed answer in F.

We say that I and F *u-correspond* iff for each α:

(d) $\alpha \in \text{UNDEF}(I)$ iff α is not a computed answer in F and there is a potential answer node $\alpha \leftarrow_u$ in F which is not in Ω_F.

Due to the two-valued interpretation of the new auxiliary atoms, the four points completely covers all possible interpretation frames for magic programs.

6.1 Step-by-step Correspondence

As already pointed out (Section 5) there is an asymmetry in the correspondence between the two methods that shows up as follows: while both methods treat true atoms similarly, it turns out that atoms become false one level later (in the outermost iteration) in the bottom-up computation compared with the forest. Thus there are two cases for each fixed point operator in the correspondence proposition. For notational convenience, let:

$$I^i = \Psi_{magic(P,q)} \uparrow i$$
$$I^i_k = \Phi_{magic(P,q),I^i} \uparrow k$$

for a fixed program P and query q.

Proposition 17 (Step-wise equivalence).
Let P be a program and q a non-floundering query w.r.t. P. Each magic search sequence S for P and q satisfies a partial description $\{F\}^i_k$ such that for any ordinal i and integer k:

1. *I^i_{k+1} and F^i_k t-correspond;*
2. *I^i_{k+1} and F^j_k u-correspond, for any $j < i$;*
3. *if $i > 0$ then I^i and F^i t-correspond;*
4. *if $i > 1$ then I^i and F^j u-correspond, for any $j < i$;*

Before proving the proposition we first prove the following lemma using some auxiliary notation: let $Q(i,k)$ stand for the points 1 and 2 in Proposition 17. Similarly let $P(i)$ stand for points 3 and 4.

Lemma 18. *For any integer k and ordinal i: $P(j)$ for all $j \leq i$ implies $Q(i,k)$.*

Proof. Let i be any ordinal. First assume that $P(j)$ is true for $j \leq i$. The proof is by induction on k. The base case, $k = 0$, is trivial so let $k > 0$ and assume that $Q(i, k_0)$ is true for any $k_0 < k$. There are four cases to consider:

(a) $call(\beta\theta) \in \text{TRUE}(I^i_{k+1})$
 $\Leftrightarrow$ there exists a clause $call(\beta) \leftarrow call(\alpha_0), \alpha_1^+, \ldots, \alpha_m^+ \in magic(P)$ and there are atoms $call(\beta_0), \beta_1^+, \ldots, \beta_m^+ \in \text{TRUE}(I^i_k)$ such that:

$$\text{MGU}(\{\beta_j = \alpha_j\}_{0 \leq j \leq m}) = \theta;$$

$\Leftrightarrow$ there exists a clause $\alpha_0 \leftarrow L_1, (\sim)\beta, L_2 \in P$ such that $\alpha_1, \ldots, \alpha_m$ are all positive literals in L_1 and (by induction) β_0 or $\sim\beta_0$ is selected in F^i_{k-1}. Hence, $(\alpha_0 \leftarrow L_1, (\sim)\beta, L_2)\sigma$ (where $\sigma = \text{MGU}(\beta_0 = \alpha_0)$) is a node in Γ^i_k (as defined in Definition 15). By induction we also have that $\beta_1, \ldots, \beta_m$ are potential answers in F^i_{k-1};

$\Leftrightarrow$ there exists a node $(\alpha_0 \leftarrow_{(u)} (\sim)\beta, L_2)\theta$ in F^i_k (obtained through extension by (u)-answer and u-assumption[9]);

$\Leftrightarrow$ $\beta\theta$ or $\sim\beta\theta$ is selected in F^i_k.

(b) $\beta^+\theta \in \text{TRUE}(I^i_{k+1})$

$\Leftrightarrow$ /* *The proof is more or less identical to* (a) */

$\Leftrightarrow$ $\beta\theta$ is a potential answer in F^i_k.

(c) A non-magic atom $\beta\theta \in \text{TRUE}(I^i_{k+1})$

$\Leftrightarrow$ there exists a clause $\beta \leftarrow call(\beta), L_1, \sim L_2 \in magic(P)$. Moreover, there exists an atom $call(\beta') \in \text{TRUE}(I^i_k)$, a sequence L'_1 of atoms in $\text{TRUE}(I^i_k)$ such that $\theta = \text{MGU}(\{\beta' = \beta, L_1 = L'_1\})$ and $L_2\theta$ are false in I^i;

$\Leftrightarrow$ there exists a clause $\beta \leftarrow L_1, \sim L_2 \in P$ and, by induction, β' or $\sim\beta'$ is selected in F^i_{k-1} (in which case Γ^i_k contains a node $(\beta \leftarrow L_1, \sim L_2)\sigma$ where $\sigma = \text{MGU}(\beta = \beta')$). Moreover, L'_1 are computed answers in F^i_{k-1} and $L_2\theta$ are failed in $F^j, F^{j+1}, \ldots$ for some $j < i$ (due to $P(i)$ and the cumulativity of the sequence $F^0, F^1, \ldots$);

$\Leftrightarrow$ there exists a node $\beta\theta \leftarrow$ in F^i_k (obtained by means of extension by answer and negation as failure);

$\Leftrightarrow$ $\beta\theta$ is a computed answer in F^i_k.

Thus I^i_{k+1} and F^i_k t-correspond.

(d) A non-magic atom $\beta\theta \in \text{UNDEF}(I^i_{k+1})$ iff

$\Leftrightarrow$ *i.* there exists $\beta \leftarrow call(\beta), L_1, \sim L_2 \in magic(P)$. There also exists $call(\beta') \in \text{TRUE}(I^i_k)$ and $L'_1 \in \text{TRUE}(I^i_k) \cup \text{UNDEF}(I^i_k)$ such that $\theta = \text{MGU}(\{\beta' = \beta, L_1 = L'_1\})$. Finally, none of $L_2\theta$ are true in I^i;

ii. $\beta\theta \notin \text{TRUE}(I^i_{k+1})$.

$\Leftrightarrow$ *i.* there exists $\beta \leftarrow L_1, \sim L_2 \in P$. Moreover, β' or $\neg\beta'$ is selected in F^j_k (for all $j \leq i$) and L'_1 are potential answers in F^j_k which are not in Ω_F. Finally, none of $L_2\theta$ are computed answers in I^j;

ii. $\beta\theta$ is not a computed answer in F^j_k for all $j < i$ (by (a) and cumulativity);

$\Leftrightarrow$ $\beta\theta \leftarrow_u$ is a potential answer in F^j_k which is not in Ω_F (for all $j < i$) and $\beta\theta$ is not a computed answer in F^j_k.

Hence, I^i_{k+1} and F^j_k u-correspond for any $j < i$. □

[9] For this to be possible we require that the initial query is non-floundering.

i	Potentially true facts		Forest nodes
	$\text{TRUE}(I_i^0)$	$\text{UNDEF}(I_i^0)$	
0			
1	$call(w(b))$		
2	$call(m(b, A))$		1
3	$m(b, a), m(b, c), m^+(b, a), m^+(b, c)$		2, 3
4	$w^+(b), call(w(a)), call(w(c))$	$w(b)$	4, 5, 6, 7
5	$call(m(a, A)), call(m(c, B))$		8, 9
6	$m(a, b), m(c, d), m^+(a, b), m^+(c, d)$		10, 11
7	$w^+(a), w^+(c), call(w(d))$	$w(a), w(c)$	12, 13, 14, 15
8	$call(m(d, B))$		16

Fig. 3. Iteration of $\Phi_{P,I^0} \uparrow i$ (i.e. I_i^0)

Proof (of Proposition 17).
Points 3 and 4: the proofs are done by induction on i. First let $i > 0$ be an ordinal and assume that $P(j)$ holds for any $j < i$. Then by Lemma 18 we get that $Q(j, k)$ holds for any k in which case point 3 follows no matter if i is a successor or limit ordinal. Next let $i > 1$. Then the following points are equivalent:

$\beta \in \text{UNDEF}(I^i)$

$\Leftrightarrow$ $\beta \in \text{UNDEF}(I)$, for all I in $I^j_{\ell_j}, I^j_{\ell_j+1}, \ldots$ for all $j < i$ (by monotonicity of $\Phi_{magic(P,q),I^j}$)

$\Leftrightarrow$ $\beta \leftarrow_u$ is a sound potential answer, but not a computed answer, in F for F in $F^{j'}_{\ell_{j'}-1}, F^{j'}_{\ell_{j'}}, \ldots$ for all $j' < j < i$ (due to $Q(j, k)$)

$\Leftrightarrow$ $\beta \leftarrow_u$ is a potential answer in F^j which is not in Ω_F, and β is not a computed answer in F^j $(j < i)$.

Thus point 4 holds. Points 1 and 2 follow from 3 and 4 — for all i, $P(i)$ — and Lemma 18 □

Remark: We have restricted our discussion to programs with "non-floundering queries" to avoid selection of non-ground negative literals in the search forest. We conjecture that the magic approach avoids resolving non-ground negative literals (i.e. avoids using the last transition in Section 4.3) for exactly the same class of programs/queries. However, this has not been formally verified.

Example 5. Let P be $magic(P_1, win(b))$ where P_1 is the program in Section 3.1. Figure 3 depicts the computation of $I^1 = \text{LFP}_{\preceq}(\Phi_{P,I^0})$ where I^0 is the interpretation frame that represents the interpretation $\emptyset$ (that is, everything is undefined). The computation is actually cumulative — that is, everything that is true (potentially true) in an iteration remains true (potentially true) in subsequent iterations. However, for typographical reasons we prefer to depict only

i	POTENTIALLY TRUE FACTS		FOREST
	TRUE(I_i^1)	UNDEF(I_i^1)	NODES
⋮	⋮	⋮	⋮
7	$w(c), w^+(a), w^+(c), call(w(d))$	$w(a)$	12, 13, 14, 15, 17
8	$call(m(d, B))$		16

Fig. 4. Iteration of $\Phi_{P,I^1} \uparrow i$ (i.e. I_i^1)

increments. To the very right is shown how iterations correspond to extensions in Figure 1. Also, note the correspondence with the partial description in Example 4.

Figure 4 depicts the fixed point computation of Φ_{P,I^1}. The only difference compared with the first iteration is that $win(d)$ which was assumed to be undefined in I^0 is known to be false in I^1. We are thus able to infer that $win(c)$ is true in I^2.

6.2 Soundness and Completeness of the Magic Transformation

Proposition 17 implies that $\text{LFP}_{\subseteq}(\Psi_{magic(P,q)})$ and $F_P(q)$ t-correspond and u-correspond. As a consequence both the soundness and completeness results of Degerstedt [Deg93] can be applied to $\text{LFP}_{\subseteq}(\Psi_{magic(P,q)})$ (which according to Proposition 14 encodes $\text{WFM}(magic(P, q))$).

Corollary 19 (Soundness of $\Psi_{magic(P,q)}$).
Let P and q be a program and a query. Let $(T, U) = \text{LFP}_{\subseteq}(\Psi_{magic(P,q)})$.

1. *If $q\theta \in T$, then all ground instances of $q\theta$ are true in $\text{WFM}(P)$.*
2. *If there exists no θ such that $q\theta \in U$, then all ground instances of q are false in $\text{WFM}(P)$.*

Corollary 20 (Completeness of $\Psi_{magic(P,q)}$).
Let P and q be a program and a query. Let $(T, U) = \text{LFP}_{\subseteq}(\Psi_{magic(P,q)})$.

1. *If a ground instance $q\gamma$ of q is true in $\text{WFM}(P)$, then there exists $q\theta \in T$, such that $q\theta$ is more general than $q\gamma$.*
2. *If all ground instances of q are false in $\text{WFM}(P)$, then there exists no θ such that $q\theta \in U$.*
3. *Let P' be the augmented version of P.[10] If for some substitution σ, all ground instances of $q\sigma$ are true in $\text{WFM}(P')$, then for some $q\theta$ more general than $q\sigma$, $q\theta \in T$*

[10] I.e., $P' = P \cup \{p'(f'(c'))\}$, such that none of the symbols p', f', or c' appear in P or q. This construction is needed to handle the *universal query problem*. See e.g. Ross [Ros92] for details.

Notice, that the soundness and completeness theorems are not restricted to non-floundering queries — according to Proposition 17 our step-wise equivalence holds for ground programs as a special case. Thus, since the well-founded model for a program is equal to its ground instantiation, the theorems hold also for the non-ground case.

Remark: Note that $\text{LFP}_{\subseteq}(\Psi_{magic(P,q)})$ encodes the well-founded model of the program $magic(P, q)$. Thus, both soundness and completeness are properties of the well-founded model rather than properties of the particular fixed point characterization.

7 Discussion

In this paper we have proposed a new magic transformation for normal programs based on the transformation of Nilsson [Nil93]. Moreover, we have generalized the characterization of the well-founded semantics of Bonnier et. al. [BNN91] from the ground to the non-ground case. If the original program is datalog then the transformed program is as well. Hence, we introduce goal-directedness without losing termination. We have shown how the class of, so-called, magic search strategies for the search forest using the leftmost computation rule correspond, step-by-step, to naive bottom-up evaluation of magic programs for non-floundering queries. As a consequence, we have shown (1) a correspondence between the well-founded model of the magic program and the search forest and (2) soundness and completeness of our magic method.

Although constructive in nature, the framework described in this paper is not primarily intended for direct implementation. It defines a search space and a class of search strategies that guarantee soundness and completeness, but exactly how to traverse the search space *efficiently* is a separate issue. However, some obvious refinements come to mind:

- There are many regularities in clauses of $magic(P, q)$. One can easily extend the transformation to include, for instance, supplementary predicates to avoid recomputations of e.g. α^+-atoms; Moreover, using differential techniques (such as semi-naive evaluation) much overhead can be eliminated;
- The asymmetry between how the bottom-up operator and the search forest deals with falsity (respectively failure) indicates a possible optimization of the bottom-up approach;
- In some cases it is not necessary to traverse the complete search space. As already pointed out, we consider the search space to be an upper limit. For instance, each time a negative literal is first encountered we have blindly assumed that the literal is undefined. If there are loops through negation this is necessary, but if the program, for instance, is (locally) stratified it is not. In such cases the magic approach can be modified so that we deal with one strata at a time, using information from lower strata when negative literals are encountered. Such a "layered" bottom-up evaluation is made possible

since clauses defining *call*(α) and α^+ do not rely on negation; A similar optimization was introduced within the search forest framework of Bol and Degerstedt [BD93a].

The blind use of u-assumptions employed above can be seen as an effective realization of SLS-resolution using a positivistic computation rule (cf. Ross [Ros92] or Przymusinski [Prz89]) as observed by Bol and Degerstedt [BD93a]. Our computation of the magic program can thus be seen as an effective bottom-up counterpart of SLS-resolution.

The correspondence to the search forest also indirectly relates our approach to a top-down framework called *SLG-resolution*, proposed by Chen and Warren [CW93a]. SLG-resolution is similar to the search forest in many respects. One difference is that the purpose of the search forest is to provide an upper bound on the common search space that must be searched by any complete interpreter. In SLG-resolution the idea is rather to give a non-deterministic framework based on a set of inference rules (much in the same way as in e.g. OLDT-resolution [TS86]).

Moreover, the methods differ in that SLG-resolution uses the notion of delayed negative literals. Such literals are explicitly kept and carried around in resultants (extended for this purpose). This is to permit the method to be used also for computation of the stable model semantics. The search forest, on the other hand, is intended only to handle well-founded semantics and therefore made it possible to use the notion of u-assumption and abortion of "unsound" branches instead.

If negative literals are always delayed in SLG-resolution it seems to correspond to complete search in the search forest when u-assumptions are made blindly.

Kemp, Stuckey and Srivastava [KSS92] have a similar approach to ours but intertwine the magic transformation and the fixed point computation whereas our approach separates the two. In addition their approach seems to presuppose a particular fixed point characterization. The transformation described here is independent of any such characterization. As a consequence, our transformation appears suitable for more complex semantics such as stable model semantics [CW93b] and semantics for disjunctive programs (cf. Brass and Dix [BD94]) for the purpose of constructing a residual program in a goal-oriented way.

The magic transformation and fixed point computation described in Section 4 have been implemented in SICStus Prolog as a first step towards efficient implementation of the well-founded semantics.

References

[AB94] Krzysztof Apt and Roland Bol. Logic Programming and Negation: A Survey. *J. of Logic Programming*, 19/20:9–71, 1994.

[Apt90] Krzysztof Apt. Introduction to Logic Programming. In J. van Leeuwen, editor, *Handbook of Theoretical Computer Science: Formal Models and Semantics*, volume B, chapter 10, pages 493–574. Elsevier, 1990.

[BD93a] R. Bol and L. Degerstedt. Tabulated Resolution for Well Founded Semantics. In *Proc. of the International Logic Programming Symposium,* Vancouver, pages 199–219. The MIT Press, 1993.

[BD93b] R. Bol and L. Degerstedt. The Underlying Search for Magic Templates and Tabulation. In *Proc. of International Conf. on Logic Programming,* Budapest, pages 793–811. The MIT Press, 1993.

[BD94] S. Brass and J. Dix. A General Approach to Bottom-up Computation of Disjunctive Semantics. pages 127–155, this volume

[BNN91] S. Bonnier, U. Nilsson, and T. Näslund. A Simple Fixed Point Characterization of Three-valued Stable Model Semantics. *Information Processing Letters*, 40(2):73–78, 1991.

[CW93a] W. Chen and D. S. Warren. Query Evaluation under the Well-founded Semantics. In *Proc. of SIGACT-SIGMOD-SIGART Symposium on Principles of Database Systems*, pages 168–179, Washington DC, 1993.

[CW93b] W. Chen and D.S. Warren. Computation of Stable Models and its Integration with Logical Query Processing. Technical report, Comp. Sci. Dept, SUNY ant Stony Brook, 1993.

[Deg93] L. Degerstedt. *Tabulated Resolution for Well-Founded Semantics.* Licentiate thesis no 402, Dept. of Computer and Information Science, Linköping University, 1993.

[KSS91] D. Kemp, P. Stuckey, and D. Srivastava. Magic Sets and Bottom-up Evaluation of Well-founded Models. In *Proc. of 1991 International Logic Programming Symposium,* San Diego, pages 337–351. The MIT Press, 1991.

[KSS92] D. Kemp, P. Stuckey, and D. Srivastava. Query Restricted Bottom-up Evaluation of Normal Logic Programs. In K. Apt, editor, *Proc. of Joint International Conf. and Symp. on Logic Programming,* Washington, pages 288–302. The MIT Press, 1992.

[Llo87] John W. Lloyd. *Foundations of Logic Programming.* Springer-Verlag, second edition, 1987.

[LS91] J. Lloyd and J. Shepherdson. Partial Evaluation in Logic Programming. *J. of Logic Programming,* 11(3-4):217–242, 1991.

[Mor93] S. Morishita. An Alternating Fixpoint Tailored to Magic Programs. In *Proc. of SIGACT-SIGMOD-SIGART Symposium on Principles of Database Systems*, pages 123–134, Washington DC, 1993.

[Nil93] U. Nilsson. Goal-directed Bottom-up Evaluation of Normal Logic Programs. In *Proc. of the International Logic Programming Symposium*, Vancouver, 1993. The MIT Press. (Abstract).

[Prz89] T. Przymusinski. Every Logic Program has a Natural Stratification and an Iterated Fixed Point Model. In *Proc. of the 8th Symposium on Principles of Database Systems*, pages 11–21, 1989.

[Prz90] T. Przymusinski. The Well-founded Semantics Coincides with the Three-valued Stable Semantics. *Fundamenta Informaticae*, 13(4):445–464, 1990.

[PW92] T. Przymusinski and D. S. Warren. Well Founded Semantics: Theory and Implementation. Draft, 1992.

[Ram88] R. Ramakrishnan. Magic Templates: A Spellbinding Approach to Logic Programming. In *Proc. of Fifth International Conf/Symposium on Logic Programming,* Seattle, pages 140–159. The MIT Press, 1988.

[Ros92] K. Ross. A Procedural Semantics for Well-founded Negation in Logic Programs. *J. of Logic Programming,* 13(1):1–22, 1992.

[TS86] H. Tamaki and T. Sato. OLD Resolution with Tabulation. In E Shapiro, editor, *Proc. of Third International Conf. on Logic Programming,* London, Lecture Notes in Computer Science 225, pages 84–98. Springer-Verlag, 1986.

[VRS91] A. Van Gelder, K. Ross, and J. Schlipf. The Well-Founded Semantics for General Logic Programs. *J. of the ACM*, 38(3):620–650, 1991.

Computing Stable and Partial Stable Models of Extended Disjunctive Logic Programs*

Carolina Ruiz and Jack Minker

Department of Computer Science and
Institute for Advanced Computer Studies
University of Maryland. College Park, MD 20742 U. S. A.
{cruizc, minker}@cs.umd.edu

Abstract. In [Prz91], Przymusinski introduced the partial (or 3-valued) stable model semantics which extends the (2-valued) stable model semantics defined originally by Gelfond and Lifschitz [GL88]. In this paper we describe a procedure to compute the collection of all partial stable models of an extended disjunctive logic program. This procedure consists in transforming an extended disjunctive logic program into a constrained disjunctive program free of negation-by-default whose set of 2-valued minimal models corresponds to the set of partial stable models of the original program.

Keywords: Extended disjunctive logic programs, Negation, Stable models, Partial stable models, Three valued semantics, Well-supportedness.

1 Introduction

The partial (or 3-valued) stable model semantics defined by Przymusinski in [Prz91] is a three-valued semantics for the class of extended disjunctive logic programs (*edlps*). This class of programs consists of disjunctive logic programs that may contain two kinds of negations: negation-by-default and explicit negation. The definition of this semantics extends the (2-valued) stable model semantics given by Gelfond and Lifschitz ([GL88]) to the 3-valued disjunctive case.

The original definitions of both the 2-valued and the 3-valued stable model semantics are not constructive. They give criteria to check whether or not a given model of the program is (partial) stable. Some procedures to compute the 2-valued stable model semantics of disjunctive logic programs have been described ([BNNS93, FLMS93, IKH92]).

The purpose of this paper is to provide a procedure that constructs the collection of 3-valued stable models of any *edlp*. To prove that our procedure is correct, we introduce a new characterization of the partial stable model semantics in terms of well-supported 3-valued models of *edlps*. The notion of well-supported 2-valued models was introduced by Fages ([Fag91]) for the class of definite normal

* Support for this paper was provided by the Air Force Office of Scientific Research under grant number 91-0350, and the National Science Foundation under grant numbers IRI-8916059 and IRI 9300691.

programs. Here we extend that notion to *edlps* and to the 3-valued case. As stated by Fages, well-supported models are supported models with loop-free finite justifications. We show that the notions of partial stability and 3-valued well-supportedness are equivalent. This result generalizes Fages work to the 3-valued disjunctive framework. To prove this characterization, we introduce a fixpoint operator that computes the minimal (with respect to the *truth ordering*) 3-valued models of an *edlp* free of negation-by-default.

It is worth noticing that even for the propositional case, the problem of constructing the collection of partial stable models of an *edlp* is not tractable. [1] This is a consequence of the fact that skeptical reasoning in this semantics (i.e. determining if a literal is *true* in every partial stable model of the program) is Π_2^P-complete (see [EG93]).

Our construction of the collection of partial stable models of a given *edlp* P is as follows: first P is translated into a new constrained *edlp*, called P^{3S}, free of negation-by-default whose syntax captures the well-supported semantics of P, in the sense that P^{3S} contains clauses stating explicitly when there is support for an atom to be *true*, *false* or *unknown*. Furthermore, constraints appearing in the clauses are used to guarantee that those supports are loop-free. Subsequently, the minimal 2-valued models of P^{3S} are computed. These models, when translated to the language of P, are precisely the well-supported (and hence the partial stable) models of P.

This paper is organized as follows: Section 2 presents background on the partial stable model semantics needed in the following sections. Section 3 provides both a characterization of partial stable models as well-supported 3-valued models and a fixpoint operator that computes the minimal (with respect to the *truth ordering*) 3-valued models of *edlps* free of negation-by-default. Section 4 is concerned with the computation of the 3-valued stable models of an *edlp*. We introduce a transformation, called the *3S-transformation*, that, given an *edlp* P, computes a constrained *edlp* P^{3S}. We prove that there is a one-to-one correspondence between the minimal 2-valued models of P^{3S} and the 3-valued well-supported models (and consequently the 3-valued stable models) of the original program. An algorithm to compute the minimal 2-valued models of P^{3S} is given in section 4.2. In section 5 we draw some conclusions.

2 Background

Classical logic assumes that the truth value of every sentence is either *true* or *false*. 3-valued semantics allow the additional possibility that the truth value of a statement is *unknown*. In this section we make precise what an *edlp* is and define the notions of 3-valued interpretation and 3-valued model of an *edlp*. We describe alternative orderings on the three truth values and study the orderings among 3-valued interpretations that they induce. Finally, the set of 3-valued stable models of an *edlp* is defined.

[1] Assuming that P $\neq$ NP.

Definition 1 (Extended disjunctive logic programs).
Let $\mathcal{L}$ denote a first order language.

1. An **extended disjunctive clause** is a clause of the form:

$$l_0 \vee \ldots \vee l_k \leftarrow l_{k+1}, \ldots, l_m, \textit{not } l_{m+1}, \ldots, \textit{not } l_n$$

   where $0 \leq k \leq m \leq n$ and the l's are literals (i.e. atoms and explicitly negated atoms) in the language $\mathcal{L}$ and *not* is the negation-by-default operator.
2. An **extended disjunctive logic program** (*edlp*) is a set of extended disjunctive clauses.

In what follows we sometimes abbreviate an extended disjunctive clause of the form $l_0 \vee \ldots \vee l_k \leftarrow l_{k+1}, \ldots, l_m, \textit{not } l_{m+1}, \ldots, \textit{not } l_n$ as $H \leftarrow B$ where $H = l_0 \vee \ldots \vee l_k$ and $B = l_{k+1}, \ldots, l_m, \textit{not } l_{m+1}, \ldots, \textit{not } l_n$.

Since an *edlp* is equivalent to the set of all its ground instances, we consider here only propositional *edlps*, and so the language $\mathcal{L}$ is just a set of propositional symbols. We require that $\mathcal{L}$ contain special propositions **t**, **f** and **u**, that are intended to denote *true, false* and *unknown*, respectively.

Minker and Ruiz ([MR93, MR94]) give techniques to obtain the semantics of an *edlp* in term of the semantics of a corresponding *edlp* free of explicit negation. Therefore, without loss of generality we consider in the sequel only programs free of explicit negation. With this in mind, we say that an *edlp* is *positive* when it is free of negation-by-default.

Definition 2 (Ordering among truth values).
Consider the following orderings among truth values:

1. *Truth Ordering* ($<_t$) *on truth values:*

$$\textit{false} <_t \textit{unknown} <_t \textit{true}.$$

2. *Knowledge Ordering* ($<_k$) *on truth values:*

$$\textit{unknown} <_k \textit{false} \text{ and } \textit{unknown} <_k \textit{true}.$$

Graphically,

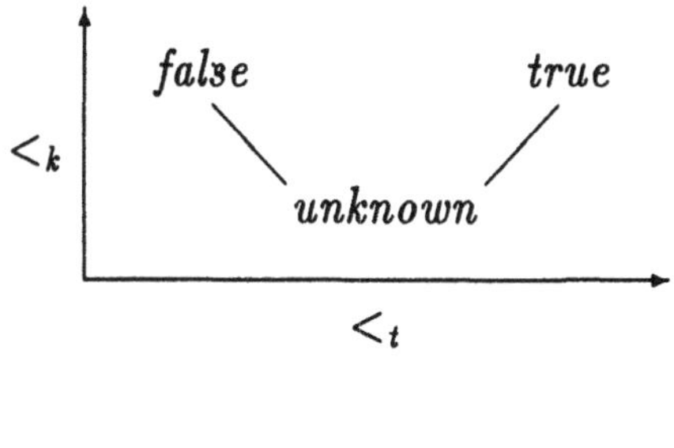

Given a propositional language $\mathcal{L}$, a 3-valued interpretation is a 3-valued truth assignment to the propositions in $\mathcal{L}$. It is commonly represented as a partial function (hence the name of *partial* interpretation) $I : \mathcal{L} \rightarrow \{true, false\}$ in which the truth value of a proposition that does not belong to the domain of I is taken to be *unknown*. A concise way of writing such a partial function is as a pair $\langle I^+; I^- \rangle$ where I^+ and I^- consist of the propositions in $\mathcal{L}$ that are mapped to *true* and to *false* respectively. (All the remaining propositions are mapped to *unknown*.)

Definition 3 (3-valued interpretations).
Let P be an *edlp* written in a propositional language $\mathcal{L}$.

1. A 3-valued interpretation I of P is a pair $\langle I^+; I^- \rangle$ where I^+ and I^- are disjoint subsets of $\mathcal{L}$ and such that $\mathbf{t} \in I^+$, $\mathbf{f} \in I^-$ and $\mathbf{u} \notin I^+ \cup I^-$.
2. A proposition $a \in \mathcal{L}$ is *true* in I if $a \in I^+$; a is *false* in I if $a \in I^-$; and a is *unknown* in I otherwise. The truth values of more complex sentences with respect to I are computed using the Kleene truth tables (in which we have abbreviated *true*, *false* and *unknown* as t, f and u respectively):

$\wedge$	t	u	f
t	t	u	f
u	u	u	f
f	f	f	f

$\vee$	t	u	f
t	t	t	t
u	t	u	u
f	t	u	f

a	t	u	f
not a	f	u	t

3. The truth value of a sentence φ with respect to an interpretation I is denoted by $\mathcal{V}_I(\varphi)$.
4. $I^{\mathbf{u}}$ denotes $\mathcal{L} - (I^+ \cup I^-)$, i.e., the set of propositions that are *unknown* in I.

Based on the orderings on truth values given before, the 3-valued interpretations can be ordered in the following ways.

Definition 4 (Orderings among 3-valued interpretations).
Let P be an *edlp*. Given two 3-valued interpretations $I = \langle I^+; I^- \rangle$ and $J = \langle J^+; J^- \rangle$, the following are two possible ways of ordering I and J:

1. *Truth Ordering* ($\preceq_t$) *on 3-valued interpretations*:

$$I \preceq_t J \text{ iff } \mathcal{V}_I(a) \leq_t \mathcal{V}_J(a) \text{ for all } a \in \mathcal{L}.$$

2. *Knowledge Ordering* ($\preceq_k$) *on 3-valued interpretations*:

$$I \preceq_k J \text{ iff } \mathcal{V}_I(a) \leq_k \mathcal{V}_J(a) \text{ for all } a \in \mathcal{L}.$$

Equivalent definitions of these orderings that appear frequently in the literature (see e.g [Prz91]) are $I \preceq_t J$ iff $I^+ \subseteq J^+$ and $I^- \supseteq J^-$; and $I \preceq_k J$ iff $I^+ \subseteq J^+$ and $I^- \subseteq J^-$.

As usual, a model of an *edlp* is an interpretation that satisfies all the clauses of the program.

Definition 5 (3-valued (minimal) models).
Let P be an *edlp*.

1. A 3-valued interpretation M is a 3-valued model of P if for every clause $H \leftarrow B$ in P , $\mathcal{V}_M(H) \geq_t \mathcal{V}_M(B)$.
2. M is said to be a $\prec_t$*-minimal* (respectively $\prec_k$*-minimal*) 3-valued model of P if there is no 3-valued model N of P such that $N \neq M$ and $N \prec_t M$ (respectively $N \prec_k M$).

A semantics of an *edlp* is captured by a subcollection of its set of models. In particular, the 3-valued stable model semantics of an *edlp* is given by the set of its 3-valued stable models as defined below.

Definition 6 (3-valued (or Partial) Stable Model [Prz91]).
Let P be an *edlp* and let M be any 3-valued model of P.

1. The *Gelfond–Lifschitz* transformation P^M of P with respect to M is the *edlp* free of negation-by-default obtained by replacing in every clause of P all negated-by-default premises $l = not\ c$ which are *true* (respectively *unknown*; respectively *false*) in M by the proposition **t** (respectively **u**; respectively **f**).
2. M is a *3-valued (or partial) stable model* of P if M is a $\prec_t$-minimal model of P^M.

Given an *edlp* P, Przymusinski proved the following relationships among the collections of partial stable models *3-STABLE(P)*, stable models *2-STABLE(P)* and the well-founded model *WFS(P)* of P.

Proposition 7 ([Prz91]).
Let P be an edlp *and let M be a 3-valued model of P.*

1. *If $M \in$ 3-STABLE(P) then M is a $\prec_t$-minimal 3-valued model of P.*
2. *If $M \in$ 2-STABLE(P) then $M \in$ 3-STABLE(P).*
3. *If P is a normal logic program and $M =$ WFS(P) then $M \in$ 3-STABLE(P). In addition, M is $\prec_k$-minimal among the partial stable models of P, i.e. for all $N \in$ 3-STABLE(P), $M \preceq_k N$.*

Notice that the notion of partial stability is defined using the truth ordering $\prec_t$, and henceforth we consider only this ordering.

3 Characterization of Partial Stable Models of *edlps*

In this section we prove a new characterization of the partial stable model semantics in terms of well-supported 3-valued models of *edlps*. As stated in the introduction, the notion of well-supported 2-valued models was introduce by Fages ([Fag91]) for the class of normal logic programs. In section 3.2 we summarize the relevant definitions in [Fag91] and extend that notion to *edlps* and to the 3-valued case. We show that the notions of partial stability and 3-valued well-supportedness are equivalent. The proof of this characterization is based in the existence of a fixpoint operator that computes the $\prec_t$-minimal 3-valued models of a positive *edlp*. We introduce such an operator in section 3.1.

3.1 Computing Minimal Partial Models of Positive *edlps*

We define a fixpoint operator $\tilde{T}_P$ which computes the 3-valued $\prec_t$-minimal models of an *edlp* free of negation-by-default P. It is worth noticing that the Fitting immediate consequence operator ([Fit85]) for the 3-valued case computes the $\prec_k$-minimal models of P and so a different operator is needed to compute with respect to the truth ordering $\prec_t$.

Definition 8 ($\langle Dom, \prec_t \rangle$).

1. A set of interpretations $\mathcal{I}$ is called *canonical* if all interpretations in $\mathcal{I}$ are $\prec_t$-incomparable, i.e. if for all distinct $I, J \in \mathcal{I}, I \not\prec_t J$ and $J \not\prec_t I$.
2. Consider the partially ordered set $\langle Dom, \prec_t \rangle$ defined by:
   - *Dom* is the collection of all sets of canonical interpretations in the language $\mathcal{L}$.
   - the order $\prec_t$ on interpretations is extended to *Dom* as follows: Given two canonical sets of interpretations $\mathcal{I}, \mathcal{J} \in Dom$,
     $\mathcal{I} \preceq_t \mathcal{J}$ iff for all $J \in \mathcal{J}$ there exists $I \in \mathcal{I}$ such that $I \preceq_t J$.

Given a set of interpretations $\mathcal{I}$ we define $min(\mathcal{I})$ as the subset of $\mathcal{I}$ containing just the $\prec_t$-minimal 3-valued interpretations in $\mathcal{I}$. Notice that $min(\mathcal{I})$ is a canonical set of interpretations.

It is straightforward to check that $\langle Dom, \prec_t \rangle$ is a lower semi-lattice whose bottom element is $\bot = \langle \{\mathbf{t}\}; \mathcal{L} - \{\mathbf{t}, \mathbf{u}\} \rangle$, whose top element is $\top = \langle \mathcal{L} - \{\mathbf{f}, \mathbf{u}\}; \{\mathbf{f}\} \rangle$ and where the greatest lower bound (glb) of a collection X of canonical sets of interpretations is given by: glb(X)= $min(\cup X)$.

Definition 9 (T_P **operator**).
Let P be an *edlp* free of negation-by-default and $C = a_1 \vee \ldots \vee a_k \leftarrow b_1, \ldots, b_m$ be a clause in P. Let B denote the body of C, i.e. $B = b_1, \ldots, b_m$. Given an interpretation I of P, we define the *operator* T_P on I and C as the following set of interpretations:

$$T_P(I, C) = \begin{cases} min[\{\langle I^+ \cup \{a_i\}; I^- - \{a_i\}\rangle : 1 \leq i \leq k\}], & \text{if } \mathcal{V}_I(B) = \mathit{true} \\ min[\{\langle I^+; I^- - \{a_i\}\rangle : 1 \leq i \leq k\}], & \text{if } \mathcal{V}_I(B) = \mathit{unknown} \\ \{I\}, & \text{if } \mathcal{V}_I(B) = \mathit{false} \end{cases}$$

Lemma 10.
Let C an arbitrary but fixed clause. Then, $T_P(\_, C)$ is monotonic on its first argument. In other words, given interpretations I and J, if $I \preceq_t J$ then $T_P(I, C) \preceq_t T_P(J, C)$.

Proof. Let C be of the form $a_1 \vee \ldots \vee a_k \leftarrow B$. Note first that for any interpretation I, $\{I\} \preceq_t T_P(I, C)$. Let I and J be interpretations such that $I \preceq_t J$. We need to show that $T_P(I, C) \preceq_t T_P(J, C)$, that is, that for every $J' \in T_P(J, C)$ there is an $I' \in T_P(I, C)$ such that $I' \preceq_t J'$.

Case 1: $\mathcal{V}_I(B) = \mathit{true}$. This implies that $\mathcal{V}_J(B) = \mathit{true}$ and hence, if $J' \in T_P(J, C)$, J' is of the form $\langle J^+ \cup \{a_i\}; J^- - \{a_i\}\rangle$ for some $i \in \{1, \ldots, k\}$. Since $I \preceq_t J$ then $I' = \langle I^+ \cup \{a_i\}; I^- - \{a_i\}\rangle \preceq_t J'$.

Case 2: $\mathcal{V}_I(B) = \mathit{unknown}$. This implies that $\mathcal{V}_J(B)$ is either *true* or *unknown*. Let $J' \in T_P(J, C)$. If $\mathcal{V}_J(B)$ is *true* then $J' = \langle J^+ \cup \{a_i\}; J^- - \{a_i\}\rangle$ and if $\mathcal{V}_J(B)$ is *unknown* then $J' = \langle J^+; J^- - \{a_i\}\rangle$, for some $i \in \{1, \ldots, k\}$. In both cases, $I' = \langle I^+; I^- - \{a_i\}\rangle \preceq_t J'$.

Case 3: $\mathcal{V}_I(B) = \mathit{false}$. This implies that $I' = I \preceq_t J \preceq_t J'$ for all $J' \in T_P(J, C)$.

In any of these three cases, either $I' \in T_P(I, C)$ or there is some $I'' \in T_P(I, C)$ such that $I'' \preceq_t I' \preceq_t J'$. □

Definition 11 ($\tilde{T}_P$ operator).
Let P be an *edlp* free of negation-by-default and let $\{C_1, \ldots, C_n\}$, for some $n \geq 0$, be the set of clauses in P. The *operator* $\tilde{T}_P$ *on* $\langle Dom, \prec_t\rangle$ is defined as follows: Given a canonical set of interpretations $\mathcal{I}_0$, consider the sequence of canonical sets of interpretations $\langle \mathcal{I}_0, \ldots \mathcal{I}_n\rangle$, defined inductively by:

$$\mathcal{I}_{i+1} = min[\bigcup_{I \in \mathcal{I}_i} T_P(I, C_{i+1})],$$

then $\tilde{T}_P(\mathcal{I}_0) = \mathcal{I}_n$.

Proposition 12.
$\tilde{T}_P$ is monotonic on $\langle Dom, \prec_t\rangle$.

Proof. Given $\mathcal{I}, \mathcal{J} \in Dom$, it is enough to show that $\mathcal{I} \preceq_t \mathcal{J}$ implies that $min[\bigcup_{I \in \mathcal{I}} T_P(I, C)] \preceq_t min[\bigcup_{J \in \mathcal{J}} T_P(J, C)]$ for every clause C in P. Assume $\mathcal{I} \preceq_t \mathcal{J}$ and let $J' \in min[\bigcup_{J \in \mathcal{J}} T_P(J, C)]$. Then $J' \in T_P(J, C)$ for some $J \in \mathcal{J}$. By hypothesis, there is some $I \in \mathcal{I}$ such that $I \preceq_t J$. By Lemma 10, $T_P(I, C) \preceq_t T_P(J, C)$ and therefore there is some $I' \in T_P(I, C)$ such that $I' \preceq_t J'$. Since $I' \in \bigcup_{I \in \mathcal{I}} T_P(I, C)$ then there is some $I'' \in min[\bigcup_{I \in \mathcal{I}} T_P(I, C)]$ for which $I'' \preceq_t I' \preceq_t J'$. □

Lemma 13.
Let P be an edlp, M be a 3-valued model of P and $\mathcal{I}$ be a canonical set of interpretations. Then, for every clause $C \in P$, if $\mathcal{I} \preceq_t \{M\}$ then $min[\bigcup_{I \in \mathcal{I}} T_P(I, C)] \preceq_t \{M\}$.

Proof. Let $C = a_1 \vee \ldots \vee a_k \leftarrow B$. Assume that $\mathcal{I} \preceq_t \{M\}$ and let $I \in \mathcal{I}$ such that $I \preceq_t M$.

Case 1 If $\mathcal{V}_I(B) = \mathit{true}$ then $\mathcal{V}_M(B) = \mathit{true}$ and therefore there is some $a_i \in M^+$ since M models C. Hence, $I' = \langle I^+ \cup \{a_i\}; I^- - \{a_i\}\rangle \preceq_t M$.

Case 2 If $\mathcal{V}_I(B) = \mathit{unknown}$ then $\mathcal{V}_M(B)$ is either *true* or *unknown*. Hence, there is some a_i for which $\mathcal{V}_M(a_i) \geq_t \mathit{unknown}$ and so $I' = \langle I^+; I^- - \{a_i\}\rangle \preceq_t M$.

Case 3 If $\mathcal{V}_I(B) = \mathit{false}$ then $I' = I \preceq_t M$.

In any of these three cases $I' \in \bigcup_{I \in \mathcal{I}} T_P(I, C)$. Therefore, there is some $I'' \in \mathit{min}[\bigcup_{I \in \mathcal{I}} T_P(I, C)]$ such that $I'' \preceq_t I' \preceq_t M$. □

Since the operator $\tilde{T}_P$ is monotonic on the lower semi-lattice $\langle \mathit{Dom}, \prec_t \rangle$, then it has a least fixed point on the semi-lattice. Furthermore this least fixed point is given by $\tilde{T}_P {\uparrow}^{\infty}(\bot)$. The following result shows that this least fixed point consists of the set of $\prec_t$-minimal 3-valued models of P.

Theorem 14.
$\tilde{T}_P {\uparrow}^{\infty}(\bot)$ is the canonical set of $\prec_t$-minimal 3-valued models of P.

Proof. By construction, every $I \in \tilde{T}_P {\uparrow}^{\infty}(\bot)$ satisfies all the clauses in P and therefore I is a 3-valued model of P. Now, let M be a 3-valued model of P. Since $\bot \preceq_t M$, a simple induction together with Lemma 13 shows that $\tilde{T}_P {\uparrow}^{\infty}(\bot) \preceq M$. Hence, there exists a 3-valued model $M_0 \in \tilde{T}_P {\uparrow}^{\infty}(\bot)$ such that $M_0 \preceq M$. This implies that if M is a $\prec_t$-minimal 3-valued model of P then $M \in \tilde{T}_P {\uparrow}^{\infty}(\bot)$. In other words, $\tilde{T}_P {\uparrow}^{\infty}(\bot)$ contains all the $\prec_t$-minimal 3-valued models of P. Since $\tilde{T}_P {\uparrow}^{\infty}(\bot)$ is a canonical set of interpretations, $\tilde{T}_P {\uparrow}^{\infty}(\bot)$ cannot contain any other model of P. Hence $\tilde{T}_P {\uparrow}^{\infty}(\bot)$ contains precisely the $\prec_t$-minimal 3-valued models of P. □

Example 1.
Consider the following positive *edlp* P.

$$
\begin{aligned}
P = \{\ & C_1 : a \vee b \leftarrow c \\
& C_2 : \quad d \leftarrow \\
& C_3 : \quad c \leftarrow d, \mathbf{u}\ \}
\end{aligned}
$$

$\tilde{T}_P(\bot)$:

$T_P(\bot, C_1) = \{I_1 = \bot\} = \mathcal{I}_1$
$T_P(I_1, C_2) = \{I_2 = \langle\{\mathbf{t}, d\}; \{\mathbf{f}, a, b, c\}\rangle\} = \mathcal{I}_2$
$T_P(I_2, C_3) = \{I_3 = \langle\{\mathbf{t}, d\}; \{\mathbf{f}, a, b\}\rangle\} = \mathcal{I}_3$
So, $\tilde{T}_P(\bot) = \mathcal{I}_3$.

$\tilde{T}_P {\uparrow}^2 (\bot)$:

$T_P(I_3, C_1) = \{I_4 = \langle\{\mathbf{t}, d\}; \{\mathbf{f}, a\}\rangle, I_5 = \langle\{\mathbf{t}, d\}; \{\mathbf{f}, b\}\rangle\} = \mathcal{I}_4$
$T_P(I_4, C_2) = \{I_4\}$ $\quad T_P(I_5, C_2) = \{I_5\}$
$T_P(I_4, C_3) = \{I_4\}$ $\quad T_P(I_5, C_3) = \{I_5\}$
So, $\tilde{T}_P {\uparrow}^2 (\bot) = \mathcal{I}_4$.

$\tilde{T}_P {\uparrow}^3 (\bot) = \tilde{T}_P {\uparrow}^2 (\bot) = \mathcal{I}_4$.

Hence P has two $\prec_t$-minimal 3-valued models, namely I_4 and I_5.

As shown in Theorem 14, $\tilde{T}_P {\uparrow}^{\infty}(\bot)$ is the set of $\prec_t$-minimal 3-valued models of P. Therefore the least fixed point of $\tilde{T}_P$ is independent of the ordering of the clauses in the program.

Finally, we point out that for a positive *edlp* P in which the proposition $\mathbf{u}$ does not appear, $\tilde{T}_P\uparrow^\infty(\bot)$ consists of the set of minimal (2-valued) models of P, and so, for this case the least fixed point of $\tilde{T}_P$ coincides with the least fixed point of the Minker/Rajasekar fixpoint operator ([MR90]).

3.2 Well-Supported 3-valued Models

We start this section by briefly surveying the definition of 2-valued well-supported models given by Fages [Fag91] and his characterization of the 2-valued stable model semantics. Then we introduce our extended definition and characterization for the disjunctive 3-valued case.

Definition 15 (Well-supported 2-valued interpretations [Fag91]).
A Herbrand interpretation I is a *well-supported* 2-valued interpretation of a normal logic program P iff there exists a strict well-founded partial ordering $<$ on I such that for any $a \in I$ there is a ground instance of a clause

$$C = a \leftarrow \underbrace{b_1, \ldots, b_m, not\ c_1, \ldots, not\ c_n}_{B}$$

in P satisfying the following conditions:

1. $a > b_i$ for all $i \in \{1, \ldots, m\}$ and
2. $\mathcal{V}_I(B) = true$.

Theorem 16 ([Fag91]).
Let P be a normal logic program and let M be a Herbrand interpretation of P. Then, M is a stable model of P iff M is a well-supported model of P.

Condition 2 guarantees that C is a support for a to be *true*. Condition 1 guarantees that this support is loop-free, that is, the justifications for the b's to be *true* do not depend on the fact that a is *true*. We extend those conditions to disjunctive clauses.

Definition 17 (Well-supported 3-valued interpretations).
A Herbrand 3-valued interpretation I is a *well-supported 3-valued interpretation* of an *edlp* P iff there exists a strict well-founded partial ordering $<$ on $I^+ \cup I^{\mathbf{u}}$ such that for any $a \in I^+ \cup I^{\mathbf{u}}$ there is a ground instance of a clause

$$C = a \vee \underbrace{a_1 \vee \ldots \vee a_k}_{H} \leftarrow \underbrace{b_1, \ldots, b_m, not\ c_1, \ldots, not\ c_n}_{B}$$

in P satisfying the following conditions:

1. $a > b_i$ for all $i \in \{1, \ldots, m\}$ and
2. **Case 1:** If $a \in I^+$, then $\mathcal{V}_I(B) = true$ and $\mathcal{V}_I(H) <_t true$, or
   Case 2: If $a \in I^{\mathbf{u}}$, then $\mathcal{V}_I(B) = unknown$ and $\mathcal{V}_I(H) = false$.
   (These two cases can be summarized as: $\mathcal{V}_I(H) <_t \mathcal{V}_I(B) = \mathcal{V}_I(a)$.)

The 3-valued well-supported models of an *edlp* P are exactly the 3-valued stable models of the program as the following theorem shows. The proof of this result is based on the fact that a 3-valued stable model M of P is a $\prec_t$-minimal 3-valued model of P^M and therefore it can be constructed using the fixpoint operator $\tilde{T}_{P^M}$ defined in section 3.1 whose iterations provide a well-founded order on $M^+ \cup M^{\mathbf{u}}$.

Theorem 18.
Let P be an edlp and let M be a 3-valued interpretation of P. Then, M is a 3-valued stable model of P iff M is a well-supported 3-valued model of P.

Proof. "$\Rightarrow$" Let $C_0, \ldots, C_{n-1}$ list all the clauses in P. If M is a 3-valued stable model of P then M is a $\prec_t$-minimal 3-valued model of P^M. Then M can be rebuilt using the fixpoint operator $\tilde{T}_{P^M}$. Let α be the smallest ordinal for which $\tilde{T}_{P^M} \uparrow^{\alpha} (\bot)$ is the least fixed point of $\tilde{T}_{P^M}$. Let

$$\langle \bot = M_0, \underbrace{M_1, \ldots, M_n}_{\tilde{T}_{P^M}\uparrow^1(\bot)}, \underbrace{M_{n+1}, \ldots, M_{2n}}_{\tilde{T}_{P^M}\uparrow^2(\bot)}, \ldots, \underbrace{M_{(\alpha-1)n+1}, \ldots, M_{\alpha n}}_{\tilde{T}_{P^M}\uparrow^\alpha(\bot)} = M \rangle$$

be a trace of the construction of M, i.e. a sequence of interpretations that converges to M and such that for all i, $M_i \preceq_t M$ and $M_{i+1} \in T_P(M_i, C_{i \bmod n})$, where mod$n$ denotes the modulo n function. Such a trace exists due to Lemma 13. Given an element $a \in M^+ \cup M^{\mathbf{u}}$, we say that the *rank* of a, denoted by rank(a), with respect to the trace is i if i is the smallest integer for which $\mathcal{V}_{M_i}(a) = \mathcal{V}_M(a)$ (notice that the rank of every element in $M^+ \cup M^{\mathbf{u}}$ is always greater than 0). Let $<$ be the strict well-founded partial ordering on $M^+ \cup M^{\mathbf{u}}$ given by

$$a < b \text{ iff } \begin{cases} a, b \in M^+ \text{ and rank}(a) < \text{rank}(b) \text{ or} \\ a, b \in M^{\mathbf{u}} \text{ and rank}(a) < \text{rank}(b) \text{ or} \\ a \in M^+ \text{ and } b \in M^{\mathbf{u}}. \end{cases}$$

This order is a well-supported order on M. To see this, let $a \in M^+ \cup M^{\mathbf{u}}$ and suppose that a is of rank $i+1$. By definition of $\tilde{T}_{P^M}$, there is a clause

$$C = a \vee \underbrace{a_1 \vee \ldots \vee a_k}_{H} \leftarrow \underbrace{b_1, \ldots, b_m, \textit{not } c_1, \ldots, \textit{not } c_n}_{B}$$

in P and consequently there is a clause

$$C^M = a \vee \underbrace{a_1 \vee \ldots \vee a_k}_{H} \leftarrow \underbrace{b_1, \ldots, b_m, \mathcal{V}_M(\textit{not } c_1), \ldots, \mathcal{V}_M(\textit{not } c_n)}_{B^M}$$

in P^M such that:

Case 1: If $a \in M^+_{i+1}$, then $\mathcal{V}_{M_i}(B^M) = \textit{true}$, and so $\mathcal{V}_M(B) = \textit{true}$, which implies that $a > b_i$ for all $i \in \{1, \ldots, m\}$. Furthermore C can be selected in such a way that $\mathcal{V}_{M_i}(H) <_t \textit{true}$, since otherwise $\langle M^+ - \{a\}; M^- \rangle$ would be a model of P^M contradicting the $\prec_t$-minimality of M.

Case 2: If $a \in M^{\mathbf{u}}_{i+1}$, then $\mathcal{V}_{M_i}(B^M) = \mathit{unknown}$ which implies that $a > b_i$ for all $i \in \{1, \ldots, m\}$. Furthermore C can be selected in such a way that $\mathcal{V}_{M_i}(H) = \mathit{false}$, because otherwise $\langle M^+; M^- \cup \{a\}\rangle$ would be a model of P^M contradicting the $\prec_t$-minimality of M.

Hence, M is a well-supported 3-valued model of P.

"$\Leftarrow$" Let M be a well-supported model of P. Since M is a model of P then M is a model of P^M. We need to show that M is a $\prec_t$-minimal model of P^M. Assume that M is not a $\prec_t$-minimal model of P^M. Let N be a $\prec_t$-minimal model of P^M such that $N \prec_t M$. Let a be a smallest element (with respect to the well-founded order $<$) for which $\mathcal{V}_N(a) \prec_t \mathcal{V}_M(a)$.

Since M is well-supported, there is a clause

$C = a \vee \underbrace{a_1 \vee \ldots \vee a_k}_{H} \leftarrow \underbrace{b_1, \ldots, b_m, \mathit{not}\ c_1, \ldots, \mathit{not}\ c_n}_{B}$ in P such that:

1. $a > b_i$ for all $i \in \{1, \ldots, m\}$ and
2. **Case 1:** If $a \in M^+$, then $\mathcal{V}_M(B) = \mathit{true}$ and $\mathcal{V}_M(H) <_t \mathit{true}$. Since $a > b_i$ for all $i \in \{1, \ldots, m\}$, then the truth-values of the b's are the same under M and under N so $\mathcal{V}_N(B^M) = \mathcal{V}_M(B) = \mathit{true}$ and since $N \prec_t M$ then $\mathcal{V}_N(H) \leq_t \mathcal{V}_M(H) <_t \mathit{true}$ and so if $\mathcal{V}_N(a) <_t \mathcal{V}_M(a)$, N would not be a model of P^M contradicting the choice of N.

   Case 2: If $a \in M^{\mathbf{u}}$, then $\mathcal{V}_M(B) = \mathit{unknown}$ and $\mathcal{V}_M(H) = \mathit{false}$. Since $a > b_i$ for all $i \in \{1, \ldots, m\}$, then $\mathcal{V}_N(B^M) = \mathcal{V}_M(B) = \mathit{unknown}$ and since $N \prec_t M$ then $\mathcal{V}_N(H) = \mathit{false}$. Therefore, if $\mathcal{V}_N(a) <_t \mathit{unknown}$ then N is not a model of P^M which is a contradiction.

Hence, M is a $\prec_t$-minimal model of P^M. □

4 Computing Partial Stable Models of *edlps*

This section is concerned with the computation of the 3-valued stable models of an *edlp*. We introduce a transformation, called the *3S–transformation*, that, given an *edlp* P, computes a new *edlp* P^{3S} free of negation-by-default whose set of minimal 2-valued models corresponds to the 3-valued stable models of the original program. An algorithm to compute the minimal 2-valued models of an *edlp* free of negation-by-default is given in section 4.2.

4.1 The 3S–transformation

Given an *edlp* P, the 3S–transformation performs case analysis to construct all potential justifications or supports for a proposition to be *true*, *false* or *unknown*. Those justifications are written as constrained clauses and collected to form a positive *edlp* called P^{3S}. The constraints ensure that the justifications are loop-free.

P^{3S} is written in a richer language $\hat{\mathcal{L}}$ which is obtained by adding to $\mathcal{L}$ new propositional symbols ua and na for each propositional symbol $a \in \mathcal{L}$. Intuitively, a will be understood as a is *true*, ua as a is *unknown* and na as a is *false*.

Definition 19 (Extended language $\hat{\mathcal{L}}$).
Let $\mathcal{L}$ be a propositional language. $\mathcal{L}$ is extended to the propositional language $\hat{\mathcal{L}} = \{a, ua, na | a \in \mathcal{L}\}$.

We introduce operators $\mathcal{T}, \mathcal{F}$ and $\mathcal{U}$ which, applied to a sentence in the language $\mathcal{L}$, produce sets of all possible justifications in the expanded language $\hat{\mathcal{L}}$ under which the given sentence is *true*, *false* or *unknown* respectively. In other words, a sentence φ is *true* (resp. *false*, resp. *unknown*) if and only if at least one of the supporting sentences in $\mathcal{T}(\varphi)$ (resp. $\mathcal{F}(\varphi)$, resp. $\mathcal{U}(\varphi)$) holds.

In what follows we inductively define these operators.

Definition 20 (Operators $\mathcal{T}, \mathcal{F}$ and $\mathcal{U}$ on normal literals).
Let $a \in \mathcal{L}$. The *operators* $\mathcal{T}, \mathcal{F}$ *and* $\mathcal{U}$ are defined on a and on *not* a as follows:

$$\begin{array}{ll} \mathcal{T}(a) = \{a\} & \mathcal{T}(not\ a) = \{na\} \\ \mathcal{U}(a) = \{ua\} & \mathcal{U}(not\ a) = \{ua\} \\ \mathcal{F}(a) = \{na\} & \mathcal{F}(not\ a) = \{a\} \end{array}$$

A disjunction of propositions $H = a_1 \vee \ldots \vee a_k$, is *true* when at least one of the propositions $a_1, \ldots, a_k$ is *true*; *false* when all these propositions are *false* and *unknown* when at least one of these propositions is *unknown* and the remaining ones are either *unknown* or *false*. We codify all possibilities under which H is unknown by using k-tuples of 0's and 1's that contain at least one 1. Such a tuple $\langle \lambda_1, \ldots, \lambda_k \rangle$ can be seen as stating that a_i is *false* if $\lambda_i = 0$ and *unknown* if $\lambda_i = 1$. If at least one λ_j is 1, then H is *unknown*. We express this formally in the language $\hat{\mathcal{L}}$ in the following definition.

Definition 21 (Operators $\mathcal{T}, \mathcal{F}$ and $\mathcal{U}$ on disjunctions).
Let $H = a_1 \vee \ldots \vee a_k$, $k \geq 0$, be an arbitrary disjunction of propositions. The *operators* $\mathcal{T}, \mathcal{F}$ *and* $\mathcal{U}$ are defined on H as follows:

$\mathcal{T}(H) = \{a_1 \mid \ldots \mid a_k\}$ [2]
$\mathcal{F}(H) = \{na_1 \wedge \ldots \wedge na_k\}$
$\mathcal{U}(H) = \{(\mathcal{F}/\mathcal{U})^{\lambda_1}(a_1) \wedge \ldots \wedge (\mathcal{F}/\mathcal{U})^{\lambda_k}(a_k) : \langle \lambda_1, \ldots, \lambda_k \rangle \in \mathcal{B}^k\}$

where:

- $\mathcal{B}^k = \{\langle \lambda_1, \ldots, \lambda_k \rangle : \lambda_1, \ldots, \lambda_k \in \{0,1\} \text{ and } \exists j \in \{1, \ldots, k\}, \lambda_j = 1\}$.
- $(\mathcal{F}/\mathcal{U})^{\lambda}(a) = \begin{cases} \mathcal{F}(a), & \text{If } \lambda = 0 \\ \mathcal{U}(a), & \text{If } \lambda = 1 \end{cases}$

Notice that when H is an empty disjunction (i.e. when $k = 0$) the previous definition makes $\mathcal{T}(H) = \mathcal{U}(H) = \{\} \equiv \{\mathbf{f}\}$ and $\mathcal{F}(H) = \{\mathbf{t}\}$.

We follow a similar process to define the truth value of a conjunction of normal literals $B = b_1, \ldots, b_m, not\ c_1, \ldots, not\ c_n$. B is *true* if all b's are *true* and all c's are *false*. It is *false* if at least one of the b's is *false* or one of the

[2] We use the symbol "|" to separate elements in a set.

c's is *true*. And it is *unknown* if the truth values of the b's and (*not* c)'s are greater than or equal to *unknown* (i.e. *unknown* or *true*) and at least one of them is *unknown*. Again, we codify all possibilities under which B is *unknown* by using $(m+n)$-tuples of 0's and 1's that contain at least one 1. Such a tuple $\langle \lambda_1, \ldots, \lambda_{m+n} \rangle$ can be seen as stating that the b's and the (*not* c)'s are *true* if the corresponding entries in the tuple equal 0 or are *unknown* if they are equal to 1. Since at least one entry is 1, then B is *unknown*. The following definition formalizes this in the language $\hat{\mathcal{L}}$.

Definition 22 (Operators $\mathcal{T}, \mathcal{F}$ and $\mathcal{U}$ on conjunctions).
Let $B = b_1, \ldots, b_m, \textit{not } c_1, \ldots, \textit{not } c_n$, where $m, n \geq 0$. The *operators* $\mathcal{T}, \mathcal{F}$ *and* $\mathcal{U}$ are defined on B as follows:

$$\mathcal{T}(B) = \{b_1 \wedge \ldots \wedge b_m \wedge nc_1 \wedge \ldots \wedge nc_n\}$$
$$\mathcal{F}(B) = \{nb_1 \mid \ldots \mid nb_m \mid c_1 \mid \ldots \mid c_n\}$$
$$\begin{aligned}\mathcal{U}(B) = \{\ &(\mathcal{T}/\mathcal{U})^{\lambda_1}(b_1) \wedge \ldots \wedge (\mathcal{T}/\mathcal{U})^{\lambda_m}(b_m) \wedge \\ &(\mathcal{T}/\mathcal{U})^{\lambda_{m+1}}(\textit{not } c_1) \wedge \ldots \wedge (\mathcal{T}/\mathcal{U})^{\lambda_{m+n}}(\textit{not } c_n) : \\ &\langle \lambda_1, \ldots, \lambda_{m+n} \rangle \in \mathcal{B}^{m+n}\}\end{aligned}$$

where:

$$(\mathcal{T}/\mathcal{U})^{\lambda}(\varphi) = \begin{cases} \mathcal{T}(\varphi), & \text{If } \lambda = 0 \\ \mathcal{U}(\varphi), & \text{If } \lambda = 1 \end{cases}$$

When B is an empty conjunction (i.e. when $m, n = 0$), $\mathcal{T}(B) = \{\mathbf{t}\}$ and $\mathcal{F}(B) = \mathcal{U}(B) = \{\} \equiv \{\mathbf{f}\}$, according to the previous definition.

We concentrate now on determining when a clause is a support for a proposition with respect to a model M of the clause. Assume that there is a well-founded partial order $<$ on $M^+ \cup M^{\mathbf{u}}$. Let a be an arbitrary but fixed proposition and let $C = a \vee H \leftarrow B$, where $B = b_1, \ldots, b_m, \textit{not } c_1, \ldots, \textit{not } c_n$. C is a *support* for a with respect to M if one of the following cases holds.

1. If $\mathcal{V}_M(a)$ is *true* then $\mathcal{V}_M(H) <_t \mathcal{V}_M(B) = \textit{true}$ and $a > b_i$ for all $i \in \{1, \ldots, m\}$.
2. If $\mathcal{V}_M(a)$ is *unknown* then $\mathcal{V}_M(H) <_t \mathcal{V}_M(B) = \textit{unknown}$ and $a > b_i$ for all $i \in \{1, \ldots, m\}$.
3. If $\mathcal{V}_M(a)$ is *false* then $\mathcal{V}_M(H) \geq_t \mathcal{V}_M(B)$ (this happens when $\mathcal{V}_M(H)$ is *true*, when $\mathcal{V}_M(B)$ is *false* or when both values are *unknown*).

These three cases are explicitly coded in the operators $\tilde{\mathcal{T}}_a, \tilde{\mathcal{U}}_a$ and $\tilde{\mathcal{F}}_a$ in the following definition. A set of constraints $\{a > b_i : 1 \leq i \leq m\}$ with respect to a clause $C = a \vee H \leftarrow b_1, \ldots, b_m, \textit{not } c_1, \ldots, \textit{not } c_n$ can be understood as requiring that if the clause C is used to support that a is either *true* or *unknown*, then the proofs that the b's are *true* or *unknown* should not rely on the proof for a. Then we say that a set of constraints is satisfied when $<$ is a partial order (i.e. $a > b$ and $b > a$ are not required simultaneously). Since the definition of well-supportedness calls only for the existence of a partial order in the set of *true* and *unknown* propositions of a model, we do not have to add constraints to clauses supporting a to be *false*.

Definition 23 (Operators $\tilde{\mathcal{T}}_a, \tilde{\mathcal{F}}_a$, and $\tilde{\mathcal{U}}_a$).
Let $a \in \mathcal{L}$ and let $C = a \vee H \leftarrow \underbrace{b_1, \ldots, b_m, not\ c_1, \ldots, not\ c_n}_{B}$ be a clause in P.

- Let $\mathcal{C}_a(B)$ be the following set of constraints:

$$\mathcal{C}_a(B) = \{a > b_i : 1 \leq i \leq m\}.$$

- The *operators* $\tilde{\mathcal{T}}_a, \tilde{\mathcal{F}}_a$, *and* $\tilde{\mathcal{U}}_a$ on the clause C are defined as follows:

$\tilde{\mathcal{T}}_a(H, B) = \mathcal{T}(B), [\mathcal{F}(H) \mid \mathcal{U}(H)]$ under constraints $\mathcal{C}_a(B)$.
$\tilde{\mathcal{F}}_a(H, B) = \mathcal{F}(B) \mid \mathcal{T}(H) \mid (\mathcal{U}(B), \mathcal{U}(H))$ under no constraints.
$\tilde{\mathcal{U}}_a(H, B) = (\mathcal{U}(B), \mathcal{F}(H))$ under constraints $\mathcal{C}_a(B)$.

The operators "," and "|" between sets stand for the usual operators "×" (Cartesian product) and "∪" (union) respectively. (We use here "," and "|" to preserve the flavor of logic programming syntax.)

Example 2.
Let $C = a \leftarrow b, not\ c$. Then, all possible supports for the three possible truth values of a are listed below:
$\tilde{\mathcal{T}}_a((), (b, not\ c)) = \{b \wedge nc\}$ under $\mathcal{C}_a(B) = \{a > b\}$,
$\tilde{\mathcal{F}}_a((), (b, not\ c)) = \{nb \mid c\}$ under no constraints,
$\tilde{\mathcal{U}}_a((), (b, not\ c)) = \{(ub \wedge nc) \mid (b \wedge uc) \mid (ub \wedge uc)\}$ under $\mathcal{C}_a(B)$,
which state that the only justification for a to be *true* is that b be *true* and c be *false* simultaneously. There are two supports for a to be *false*, namely b is *false* or c is *true*. All the remaining possibilities support a to be *unknown*.

We apply now case analysis to construct all possible justifications of a proposition a with respect to a program P. Consider the set of all clauses defining a in P (i.e. the set of clauses containing a in their heads). With respect to a well-supported 3-valued model of P, a is *true* when at least one of these clauses supports a to be *true*, a is *false* if all clauses in its definition support a to be *false*, and a is *unknown* when none of these clauses supports a to be *true* but at least one of them supports a to be *unknown*. Since one of these cases must hold, the clause $a \vee ua \vee na$ must be satisfied in the well-supported model.

It is worth noticing that if a proposition a is not defined in P (it does not appear in the head of any clause in P) then there is no support for it to be *true* or *unknown* and therefore it is taken to be *false*.

Definition 24 (3S–transformation).
Let P be an *edlp*.

1. Let $a \in \mathcal{L}$. Let the definition of a in P consist of the following set of clauses:

$$a \vee H_1 \leftarrow B_1$$
$$\vdots$$
$$a \vee H_r \leftarrow B_r$$

where $r \geq 0$. The *3S-transformation of the definition of* a, denoted by a^{3S}, is given by the following set of clauses:

If $r = 0$:

$$na \leftarrow$$

If $r > 0$:

$$a \leftarrow \{\tilde{\mathcal{T}}_a(H_1, B_1) \mid \ldots \mid \tilde{\mathcal{T}}_a(H_r, B_r)\}$$

$$ua \leftarrow \{(\tilde{\mathcal{F}}_a/\tilde{\mathcal{U}}_a)^{\lambda_1}(H_1, B_1), \ldots, (\tilde{\mathcal{F}}_a/\tilde{\mathcal{U}}_a)^{\lambda_r}(H_r, B_r) : \langle\lambda_1, \ldots, \lambda_r\rangle \in \mathcal{B}^r\}$$

$$na \leftarrow \tilde{\mathcal{F}}_a(H_1, B_1), \ldots, \tilde{\mathcal{F}}_a(H_r, B_r)$$

$$a \vee ua \vee na \leftarrow$$

(here, $\varphi \leftarrow \{\psi_1 \mid \ldots \mid \psi_n\}$ is a shorthand for the set of clauses $\left\{\begin{array}{c} \varphi \leftarrow \psi_1 \\ \vdots \\ \varphi \leftarrow \psi_n \end{array}\right\}$)

where:

$$(\tilde{\mathcal{F}}_a/\tilde{\mathcal{U}}_a)^{\lambda}(H, B) = \begin{cases} \tilde{\mathcal{F}}_a(H, B), & \text{If } \lambda = 0 \\ \tilde{\mathcal{U}}_a(H, B), & \text{If } \lambda = 1 \end{cases}$$

2. The *3S-transformation* P^{3S} *of* P is obtained by applying the 3S-transformation to each proposition in the language of P.

The number of clauses in P^{3S} is, in general, exponential on the number of clauses in P since all possible supports for each truth value of a proposition in $\mathcal{L}$ are considered.

As noted before, the 3S-transformation requires that each proposition a assumes a truth value. However, it may be the case that, say, a and ua are both *true* in P^{3S}. Since this is clearly undesirable, we impose a set of denial rules on the models of P^{3S} to eliminate such possibilities.

Definition 25 (Denial rules IC_P).
Let P be a disjunctive logic program and let IC_P denote the following set of denial rules:

$$IC_P = \{\Leftarrow a, ua; \Leftarrow a, na; \Leftarrow ua, na : a \in \mathcal{L} - \{\mathbf{t}, \mathbf{u}, \mathbf{f}\}\}.$$

An interpretation I of P^{3S} is any subset of $\hat{\mathcal{L}}$ satisfying the denial rules IC_P. I^+, I^- and $I^{\mathbf{u}}$ denote respectively the positive, the negative and the uncertain parts of I, i.e., $I^+ = \{a \in \mathcal{L} : a \in I\}$, $I^- = \{a \in \mathcal{L} : na \in I\}$ and $I^{\mathbf{u}} = \{a \in \mathcal{L} : ua \in I\}$. I^3 denote the 3-valued interpretation $\langle I^+; I^-\rangle$.

Associated with each $a \in I^+ \cup I^{\mathbf{u}}$ there is a collection $\mathcal{C}_a^I$ that contains all the sets of constraints that appear in clauses supporting a (or ua) with respect to I (for an illustration see Example 4 below), i.e.

$$\mathcal{C}_a^I = \{C_a(B) : \text{there is a clause } a \leftarrow B \text{ (or } ua \leftarrow B\text{) under constraints } C_a(B) \text{ in } P^{3S} \text{ such that } \mathcal{V}_I(B) = \mathit{true}\}.$$

Let $\mathcal{C}^I = \{\mathcal{C}^I_a : a \in I^+ \cup I^{\mathbf{u}}\}$. We say that I *satisfies the constraints in* $\mathcal{C}^I$ if and only if for every $a \in I^+ \cup I^{\mathbf{u}}$ there is some $C_a(B_a) \in \mathcal{C}^I_a$ such that $[\bigcup_{(a \in I^+ \cup I^{\mathbf{u}})} C_a(B_a)]$ defines a partial order in $I^+ \cup I^{\mathbf{u}}$.

We make precise now the notion of (minimal) 2-valued models of P^{3S}.

Definition 26 (2-valued models of P^{3S}).

1. A *2-valued model of* P^{3S} is a subset M of $\hat{\mathcal{L}}$ satisfying all clauses in the program and the constraints in $\mathcal{C}^M$.
2. Let M and N be 2-valued models of P^{3S}. We say that $M \leq N$ iff $M^+ \subseteq N^+$ and $N^- \subseteq M^-$.

A 3-valued interpretation J of P can be transformed into a 2-valued interpretation J^2 of P^{3S} by defining $J^2 = J^+ \cup \{ua : a \in J^{\mathbf{u}}\} \cup \{na : a \in J^-\}$.

The set of minimal 2-valued models of P^{3S} (denoted by $\mathcal{M}^{IC_P}_{P^{3S}}$) is closely related to the set of 3-valued stable models of P, as the following examples show.

Example 3.
Let $P = \{b \vee c; a \leftarrow not\ b; a \leftarrow not\ c\}$.

$$
\begin{array}{llll}
P^{3S} = \{ & b \leftarrow (uc \mid nc) & & C_b = \emptyset \\
& nb \leftarrow c & & \\
& c \leftarrow (ub \mid nb) & & C_c = \emptyset \\
& nc \leftarrow b & & \\
& a \leftarrow nb \mid nc & & C_a = \emptyset \\
& na \leftarrow b, c & & \\
& ua \leftarrow (ub, c) \mid (b, uc) \mid (ub, uc) & & C_a = \emptyset \\
a \vee ua \vee na \leftarrow & & & \\
b \vee ub \vee nb \leftarrow & & & \\
c \vee uc \vee nc \leftarrow & & & \}
\end{array}
$$

$IC_P = \{\Leftarrow x, ux; \Leftarrow x, nx; \Leftarrow ux, nx : x \in \{a, b, c\}\}$

The minimal 2-valued models of P^{3S} are

$$\mathcal{M}^{IC_P}_{P^{3S}} = \{M_1 = \{a, b, nc\}, M_2 = \{a, nb, c\}\}.$$

Here, $\mathcal{C}^{M_1} = \{\mathcal{C}^{M_1}_a = \{\emptyset\}, \mathcal{C}^{M_1}_b = \{\emptyset\}\}$ and $\mathcal{C}^{M_2} = \{\mathcal{C}^{M_2}_a = \{\emptyset\}, \mathcal{C}^{M_2}_c = \{\emptyset\}\}$. Clearly, M_1 and M_2 respectively satisfy the constraints in $\mathcal{C}^{M_1}$ and $\mathcal{C}^{M_2}$ since an empty set of constraints defines a partial order on any set. M_1 and M_2 correspond to the partial stable models of P: *3-STABLE*$(P) = \{\langle\{a, b\}; \{c\}\rangle, \langle\{a, c\}; \{b\}\rangle\}$.

Example 4.
Let $P = \{a \leftarrow b; b \leftarrow a; c \leftarrow not\ a\}$.

$$
\begin{array}{llll}
P^{3S} = \{ & a \leftarrow b & C_a = \{a > b\} & \\
& ua \leftarrow ub & C_a = \{a > b\} & \\
& na \leftarrow nb & & \\
& b \leftarrow a & C_b = \{b > a\} & \\
& ub \leftarrow ua & C_b = \{b > a\} & \\
& nb \leftarrow na & & \\
& c \leftarrow na & C_c = \emptyset & \\
& uc \leftarrow ua & C_c = \emptyset & \\
& nc \leftarrow a & & \\
& a \vee ua \vee na \leftarrow & & \\
& b \vee ub \vee nb \leftarrow & & \\
& c \vee uc \vee nc \leftarrow & & \}
\end{array}
$$

$$IC_P = \{\Leftarrow x, ux; \Leftarrow x, nx; \Leftarrow ux, nx : x \in \{a, b, c\}\}$$

There are three minimal models of P^{3S}:
$M_1 = \{a, b, nc\}$ with $\mathcal{C}^{M_1} = \{C_a = \{a > b\}, C_b = \{b > a\}\}$,
$M_2 = \{ua, ub, uc\}$ with $\mathcal{C}^{M_2} = \{C_a = \{a > b\}, C_b = \{b > a\}, C_c = \{\emptyset\}\}$ and
$M_3 = \{na, nb, c\}$ with $\mathcal{C}^{M_3} = \{C_c = \{\emptyset\}\}$.
Notice, however that the sets of constraints on M_1 and on M_2 are unsatisfiable since $\{a > b, b > a\}$ is not a partial order. Therefore, $\mathcal{M}^{IC_P}_{P^{3S}} = \{\{na, nb, c\}\}$ which corresponds to the unique 3-valued stable (and hence well-founded) model of P, namely $\{\langle\{c\}; \{a, b\}\rangle\}$.

Indeed, there is a one-to-one correspondence between the minimal models of the constrained logic program P^{3S} and the 3-valued well-supported (and hence partial stable) models P as the following theorem shows.

Theorem 27.
Let P be an edlp *and let M be a 3-valued interpretation of P. Then M is a 3-valued well-supported model of P iff $M^2 \in \mathcal{M}^{IC_P}_{P^{3S}}$.*

Proof. "$\Leftarrow$" Assume $M^2 \in \mathcal{M}^{IC_P}_{P^{3S}}$. Let $a \in \mathcal{L}$.

Case 1: If $a \in M^2$, then there is some clause

$$C = a \vee \underbrace{a_1 \vee \ldots \vee a_k}_{H} \leftarrow \underbrace{b_1, \ldots, b_m, not\ c_1, \ldots, not\ c_n}_{B}$$

in P for which $\tilde{\mathcal{T}}_a(H, B) = true$, i.e. $\mathcal{V}_M(B) = true$, $\mathcal{V}_M(H) <_t true$ and M^2 satisfies the constraints $\{a > b_i : 1 \leq i \leq m\}$. If there were no such a clause, then for every clause $a \vee H \leftarrow B \in P$ either $\tilde{\mathcal{F}}_a(H, B)$ or $\tilde{\mathcal{U}}_a(H, B)$ would be $true$. Hence, either ua or na would belong to M^2 contradicting the assumption that M^2 satisfies IC_P.

Case 2: If $ua \in M^2$, then there exists some $\langle\lambda_1, \ldots, \lambda_r\rangle \in \mathcal{B}^r$, where r is the number of clauses in the definition of a in P, for which the conjunction $(\tilde{\mathcal{F}}_a/\tilde{\mathcal{U}}_a)^{\lambda_1}(H_1, B_1), \ldots, (\tilde{\mathcal{F}}_a/\tilde{\mathcal{U}}_a)^{\lambda_r}(H_r, B_r)$ is $true$ in M^2 (otherwise either a or na would belong to M^2). Hence, there is some $\lambda_j = 1$ and so there is a clause

$$C = a \vee \underbrace{a_1 \vee \ldots \vee a_k}_{H} \leftarrow \underbrace{b_1, \ldots, b_m, not\ c_1, \ldots, not\ c_n}_{B}$$

in P for which $\tilde{\mathcal{U}}_a(H, B)$ is *true* in M^2, which means that $\mathcal{V}_M(B) =$ *unknown*, $\mathcal{V}_M(H) =$ *false* and M^2 satisfies the constraints $\{a > b_i : 1 \leq i \leq m\}$.

Therefore M is a well-supported model of P.

"$\Rightarrow$" Assume that M is a well-supported model of P. First, we show that M^2 is a model of P^{3S}. Since M is a 3-valued model, M^2 satisfies all the clauses of the form $a \vee ua \vee na$ and also satisfies the denial rules IC_P. Let $a \in \mathcal{L}$ and let the definition of a in P consist of the following set of clauses:

$$(C_1)\ a \vee H_1 \leftarrow B_1$$

$$\vdots$$

$$(C_r)\ a \vee H_r \leftarrow B_r$$

where $r \geq 0$. The 3S–transformation of the definition of a is given by the following set of clauses:

If $r = 0$:

$$na \leftarrow$$

If $r > 0$:

(t_a1) $\quad a \leftarrow \tilde{\mathcal{T}}_a(H_1, B_1)$

$\vdots$

(t_ar) $\quad a \leftarrow \tilde{\mathcal{T}}_a(H_r, B_r)$

(u_a) $\quad ua \leftarrow \{(\tilde{\mathcal{F}}_a/\tilde{\mathcal{U}}_a)^{\lambda_1}(H_1, B_1), \ldots, (\tilde{\mathcal{F}}_a/\tilde{\mathcal{U}}_a)^{\lambda_r}(H_r, B_r) : \langle \lambda_1, \ldots, \lambda_r \rangle \in \mathcal{B}^r\}$

(f_a) $\quad na \leftarrow \tilde{\mathcal{F}}_a(H_1, B_1), \ldots, \tilde{\mathcal{F}}_a(H_r, B_r)$

$(3v_a)$ $a \vee ua \vee na \leftarrow$

Notice that if $r = 0$, there is no support for a to be *true* or *unknown* so a must be *false* in M and then M^2 is a model of $na \leftarrow$. To prove the statement when $r > 0$, we consider three cases corresponding to the three possible truth values of a with respect to M. It is clear that in each of these cases the clause $(3v_a)$ is satisfied by M.

Case 1: a is *true* in M.

Clearly, M^2 models $(t_a1), \ldots, (t_ar)$. Since M is a well-supported model of P there is some j, $1 \leq j \leq r$ for which the clause

$$C_j = a \vee \underbrace{a_1 \vee \ldots \vee a_k}_{H_j} \leftarrow \underbrace{b_1, \ldots, b_m, not\ c_1, \ldots, not\ c_n}_{B_j}$$

in P satisfies the following conditions:

1. $a > b_i$ for all $i \in \{1, \ldots, m\}$.
2. $\mathcal{V}_M(B_j) = true$ and $\mathcal{V}_M(H_j) <_t true$.

Therefore $\mathcal{V}_M(\tilde{\mathcal{T}}_a(H_j, B_j)) = true$ and consequently $\mathcal{V}_M(\tilde{\mathcal{F}}_a(H_j, B_j)) = \mathcal{V}_M(\tilde{\mathcal{U}}_a(H_j, B_j)) = false$ and so M^2 models (f_a) and (u_a).

Case 2: a is *unknown* in M.

Clearly, M^2 models (u_a). Notice that there is no clause in the definition of a in P for which $\mathcal{V}_M(B_i) = true$ and $\mathcal{V}_M(H_i) < true$. Otherwise a would have to be *true* in M in order for M to be a model of P. Hence, for every $i \in \{1, \ldots, r\}$, either $\mathcal{V}_M(\tilde{\mathcal{U}}_a(H_i, B_i)) = true$ or $\mathcal{V}_M(\tilde{\mathcal{F}}_a(H_i, B_i)) = true$ and so, M^2 models $(t_a 1), \ldots, (t_a r)$.

Since a is *unknown* in M and M is a well-supported model of P there is a clause

$$C_j = a \vee \underbrace{a_1 \vee \ldots \vee a_k}_{H_j} \leftarrow \underbrace{b_1, \ldots, b_m, not\ c_1, \ldots, not\ c_n}_{B_j}$$

in P satisfying the following conditions:

1. $a > b_i$ for all $i \in \{1, \ldots, m\}$.
2. $\mathcal{V}_M(B_j) = unknown$ and $\mathcal{V}_M(H_j) = false$.

and therefore $\mathcal{V}_M(\tilde{\mathcal{U}}_a(H_j, B_j)) = true$ which implies that $\mathcal{V}_M(\tilde{\mathcal{F}}_a(H_j, B_j)) = false$ and so M^2 models (f_a).

Case 3: a is *false* in M.

Clearly, M^2 models (f_a). Since a is *false* in M and M is a model of P, $\mathcal{V}_M(B_j) \leq_t \mathcal{V}_M(H_j)$ for all $j, 1 \leq j \leq r$. This implies that M^2 models $(t_a 1), \ldots, (t_a r)$ and also that $\mathcal{V}_M(\tilde{\mathcal{U}}_a(H_j, B_j)) = false$ for all j and so M^2 models (u_a).

Hence, M^2 is a model of P^{3S}. It remains to be shown that M^2 is a *minimal* model of P^{3S}. Suppose, by way of contradiction, that there is some $N \in \mathcal{M}^{IC_P}_{P^{3S}}$ such that N is smaller than M^2. It is straightforward to check that N^3 is a 3-valued model of P and that $N^3 \prec_t M$. This yields a contradiction since M is a $\prec_t$-minimal 3-valued model of P due to Proposition 7 together with the assumption that M is a well-supported (and hence, partial stable) model of P. □

Corollary 28.
Let P be an edlp and let M be a 3-valued interpretation of P. Then M is a 3-valued stable model of P iff $M^2 \in \mathcal{M}^{IC_P}_{P^{3S}}$.

Proof. This follows immediately from Theorems 18 and 27 □

4.2 Computing Minimal 2-valued Models of P^{3S}

In this section we give an algorithm to construct the minimal models of P^{3S} and show how to check which of those models satisfy the constraints in the program.

We start by noticing that P^{3S} contains two types of clauses: Horn clauses and disjunctive facts. Let P_H^{3S} and P_D^{3S} denote the subsets of P^{3S} containing respectively the Horn clauses and the disjunctive facts in P.

An approach to compute the minimal 2-valued models of P^{3S} is the following: we start with the empty interpretation and apply an immediate consequence operator to P_H^{3S} until a fixpoint I is reached. If I satisfies all the clauses in P_D^{3S} we are done. Otherwise, we select one clause $a \vee ua \vee na \in P_D^{3S}$ that is not satisfied by I and split I into three interpretations: $I \cup \{a\}$, $I \cup \{ua\}$, and $I \cup \{na\}$. For each such interpretation we apply again the immediate consequence operator with respect to P_H^{3S} to find a revised fixed point, which is tested to determine if it models P_D^{3S}. If it does, we are done and if not, we repeat the process until all interpretations obtained satisfy every disjunction in P_D^{3S}. If at any point during this process an interpretation inconsistent with the set of denial rules IC_P is reached, then that interpretation is thrown away. At the end of the process, we check which of the resulting interpretations satisfy their own set of constraints.

Figure 1 provides an algorithm to compute $\mathcal{M}_{P^{3S}}^{IC_P}$, where $T_{P_H^{3S}}$ is any immediate consequence operator defined for Horn programs.

1. $\mathcal{M}' := \{\emptyset\}$
2. **repeat**
3. $\quad \mathcal{M} := \mathcal{M}'$
4. $\quad \mathcal{M}' := \emptyset$
5. $\quad$ **for each** $I \in \mathcal{M}$ **do**
6. $\quad\quad I := T_{P_H^{3S}} \uparrow^{\infty} (I)$
7. $\quad\quad$ **if** I satisfies IC_P **then**
8. $\quad\quad\quad$ **if** there is some $C = a \vee ua \vee na \in P_D^{3S}$ s.t. $I \not\models C$ **then**
9. $\quad\quad\quad\quad \mathcal{M}' := \mathcal{M}' \cup \{I \cup \{a\}, I \cup \{ua\}, I \cup \{na\}\}$
10. $\quad\quad\quad$ **else** $\mathcal{M}' := \mathcal{M}' \cup \{I\}$
11. **until** $\mathcal{M} = \mathcal{M}'$
12. $\mathcal{M} := min(\mathcal{M})$
13. $\mathcal{M}_{P^{3S}}^{IC_P} := \{M \in \mathcal{M} : M$ satisfies the constraints in $C^M\}$

Fig. 1. Algorithm to compute $\mathcal{M}_{P^{3S}}^{IC_P}$

We detail now instruction 6 to show how the set of constraints C^I associated with an interpretation I can be computed simultaneously to the iterations of the fixpoint operator.

6.1. **repeat**
6.2. $\quad I_0 := I$
6.3. $\quad I' := \emptyset$
6.4. $\quad$ **for each** clause $x \leftarrow B$ under constraints $C_x(B)$ in P_H^{3S}
$\quad$ such that $\mathcal{V}_I(B) = \mathit{true}$ **do**
6.5. $\qquad I' := I' \cup \{x\}$
6.6. $\qquad$ **if** x is of the form a or ua for some $a \in \mathcal{L}$ **then**
6.7. $\qquad\quad C_a^I := C_a^I \cup \{C_x(B)\}$
6.8. $\quad I := I'$
6.9. **until** $I = I_0$

We point out that instruction 13 can be implemented in terms of a search in a particular graph. It is easy to see that a set of constraints $\mathcal{C}$ of the form $a > b$ defines a partial order on $\hat{\mathcal{L}}$ if and only if the directed graph $G = \langle V = \hat{\mathcal{L}}, E = \{(a,b) : a > b \in \mathcal{C}\}\rangle$ is acyclic. Checking if this graph is acyclic can be done in time $O(|\hat{\mathcal{L}}| + |\mathcal{C}|)$ (see e.g. [AHU83]).

We illustrate how the algorithm works for different *edlps*.

Example 5.
Let $P = \{a \leftarrow not\ b; b \leftarrow not\ a\}$.

$$P^{3S} = \{ \quad \begin{array}{rlll} & a \leftarrow nb & C_a = \emptyset & \\ & ua \leftarrow ub & C_a = \emptyset & \\ & na \leftarrow b & & P_H^{3S} \\ & b \leftarrow na & C_b = \emptyset & \\ & ub \leftarrow ua & C_b = \emptyset & \\ & nb \leftarrow a & & \\ \hline a \vee ua \vee na \leftarrow & & & \\ b \vee ub \vee nb \leftarrow & & & P_D^{3S}\} \end{array}$$

$$IC_P = \{\Leftarrow x, ux; \Leftarrow x, nx; \Leftarrow ux, nx : x \in \{a, b\}\}$$

We start with the empty interpretation $I = \{\}$. Since the Horn part of P^{3S} has no facts, the empty set is the fixed point obtained for I. We then select $a \vee ua \vee na$ from P_D^{3S}, which is not satisfied by I and form three interpretations, as shown by the first level of the tree of Figure 2. We find the fixpoint for $I_1 = \{a\}$ with respect to P_H^{3S} to obtain nb (on the second level of the tree). The interpretation $I_1' = \{a, nb\}$ now satisfies all the clauses in P^{3S}. The same is done for $I_2 = \{ua\}$ and for $I_3 = \{na\}$ to obtain ub and b respectively. $I_2' = \{ua, ub\}$ and $I_3' = \{na, b\}$ satisfy all clauses in P^{3S}. Notice that the three interpretations satisfy the denial rules IC_P and they are $\prec_t$-incomparable so each of them is $\prec_t$-minimal. Finally, each of them satisfies the associated set of constraints: $\mathcal{C}^{I_1'} = \{C_a^{I_1'} = \{\emptyset\}\}$, $\mathcal{C}^{I_2'} = \{C_a^{I_2'} = \{\emptyset\}, C_b^{I_2'} = \{\emptyset\}\}$ and $\mathcal{C}^{I_3'} = \{C_a^{I_3'} = \{\emptyset\}\}$. Therefore, $\mathcal{M}_{P^{3S}}^{IC_P} = \{\{a, nb\}, \{ua, ub\}, \{na, b\}\}$.

The corresponding 3-valued stable models of the program P are $\{\langle\{a\};\{b\}\rangle, \langle\emptyset;\emptyset\rangle, \langle\{b\};\{a\}\rangle\}$. I'_2 corresponds to the well-founded model $\langle\emptyset;\emptyset\rangle$ of P.

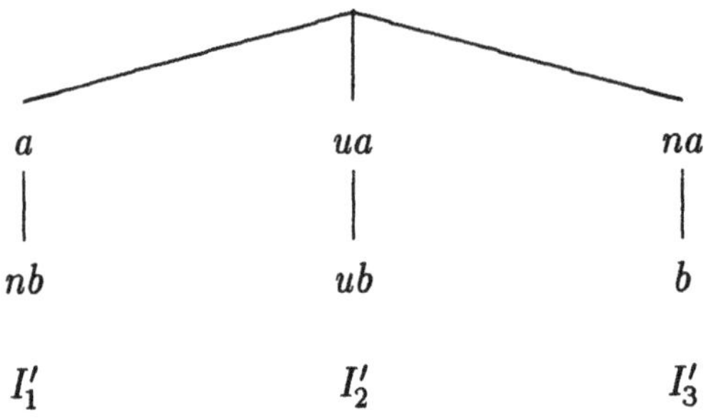

Fig. 2. Minimal 2-valued models of P^{3S} in Example 5.

Example 6.
Let $P = \{a \leftarrow c; a \leftarrow b; b \leftarrow a; c \leftarrow\}$.

$$
P^{3S} = \{ \quad
\begin{array}{rll}
a & \leftarrow c & C_a = \{a > c\} \\
a & \leftarrow b & C_a = \{a > b\} \\
ua & \leftarrow uc, nb & C_a = \{a > c\} \\
ua & \leftarrow nc, ub & C_a = \{a > b\} \\
ua & \leftarrow uc, ub & C_a = \{a > b, a > c\} \\
na & \leftarrow nc, nb & \\
b & \leftarrow a & C_b = \{b > a\} \\
ub & \leftarrow ua & C_b = \{b > a\} \\
nb & \leftarrow na & \\
c & \leftarrow & C_c = \emptyset \\
a \vee ua \vee na & \leftarrow & \\
b \vee ub \vee nb & \leftarrow & \\
c \vee uc \vee nc & \leftarrow & \quad \}
\end{array}
$$

$$IC_P = \{\Leftarrow x, ux; \Leftarrow x, nx; \Leftarrow ux, nx : x \in \{a, b, c\}\}$$

The immediate consequence operator applied to P_H^{3S} produces the only model of P^{3S}, namely $M = \{a, b, c\}$. The set of constraints associated with M is $\mathcal{C}^M = \{\mathcal{C}_a^M = \{\{a > c\} | \{a > b\}\}, \mathcal{C}_b^M = \{\{b > a\}\}, \mathcal{C}_a^M = \{\emptyset\}\}$. M satisfies this set of constraints since $\{a > c, b > a\}$ is a partial order on $\{a, b, c\}$. Hence, $\mathcal{M}_{P^{3S}}^{IC_P} = \{\{a, b, c\}\}$ and *3-STABLE*$(P) = \langle\{a, b, c\}; \emptyset\rangle$.

The algorithm in Figure 1 constructs every minimal model of P^{3S} and hence, in the worst case, runs in exponential time on the size of P^{3S}.

A global improvement to the process of computing the partial stable models of P is to partition P into several connected components using the notion of semi-stratification described in [FLMS93] and to apply the 3S–transformation and the algorithm in Figure 1 just to each component of the program.

A local speed–up in the algorithm can be achieved by selecting in instruction 8, a clause from P_D^{3S} that maximizes the number of clauses in P_H^{3S} that are usable in the next application of the fixpoint operator $T_{P_H^{3S}}$.

We end this section by showing how the algorithm works with a program that does not have any partial stable models.

Example 7.
Let $P = \{w \vee s \vee t;\, w \leftarrow not\ t;\, s \leftarrow not\ w;\, t \leftarrow not\ s\}$.

$$
\begin{array}{lrll}
P^{3S} = \{ & w & \leftarrow (us|ns), (ut|nt) & C_w = \emptyset \\
 & w & \leftarrow nt & C_w = \emptyset \\
 & uw & \leftarrow (s|t), ut & C_w = \emptyset \\
 & nw & \leftarrow (s|t), t & \\
 & s & \leftarrow (uw|nw), (ut|nt) & C_s = \emptyset \\
 & s & \leftarrow nw & C_s = \emptyset \\
 & us & \leftarrow (w|t), uw & C_s = \emptyset \\
 & ns & \leftarrow (w|t), w & \\
 & t & \leftarrow (uw|nw), (us|ns) & C_t = \emptyset \\
 & t & \leftarrow ns & C_t = \emptyset \\
 & ut & \leftarrow (w|s), us & C_t = \emptyset \\
 & nt & \leftarrow (w|s), s & \\
 & w \vee uw \vee nw & \leftarrow & \\
 & s \vee us \vee ns & \leftarrow & \\
 & t \vee ut \vee nt & \leftarrow & \}
\end{array}
$$

$$IC_P = \{\Leftarrow x, ux; \Leftarrow x, nx; \Leftarrow ux, nx : x \in \{w, s, t\}\}$$

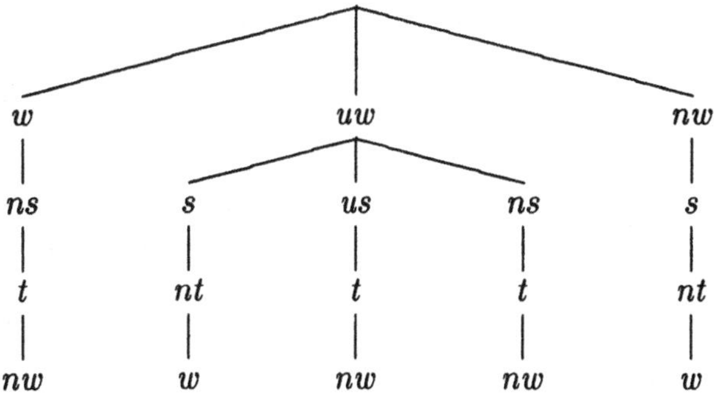

Fig. 3. Computation of the minimal 2-valued models of P^{3S} in Example 7.

Figure 3 shows that every interpretation obtained during the computation of the minimal 2-valued models of P^{3S} is inconsistent with respect to the denial rules IC_P. Then $\mathcal{M}^{IC_P}_{P^{3S}} = \{\}$ and consequently *3-STABLE*$(P) = \{\}$.

5 Conclusions

We have provided an effective procedure that computes the partial stable models of an *edlp*. We have shown that there is a one-to-one correspondence between the partial stable models of an *edlp* and the minimal models of a constrained *edlp* free of negation-by-default (or equivalently, the well-supported models of an *edlp* free of negation-by-default). Strictly speaking, this implies that the use of negation-by-default under the interpretation of the partial stable model semantic does not increase the expressive power of constrained positive programs. The same observation is applicable to the (total) stable model and the well-founded semantics since these semantics are easily derived from the set of partial stable models of the program.

Nevertheless, the presence of the negation-by-default operator is undoubtly useful in the sense that it allows us to write concise programs independent of the number of truth values being considered.

The procedure presented here to compute the 3-valued stable models of an *edlp* is based on case analysis. An implementation of that procedure has been completed and we expect to experiment with it. We believe that the approach can be adapted to compute the 2-valued as well as the 4-valued stable models [Fit93] of the program. We plan to investigate these topics.

References

[AHU83] A. Aho, J. Hopcroft, and J. Ullman. *Data Structures and Algorithms*. Addison-Wesley, 1983.

[BNNS93] C. Bell, A. Nerode, R. Ng, and V.S. Subrahmanian. Implementing stable model semantics by linear programming. In *Proceedings of the 1993 International Workshop on Logic Programming and Non-monotonic Reasoning*, June 1993.

[EG93] T. Eiter and G. Gottlob. Complexity aspects of various semantics for disjunctive databases. In *Proceedings of the Twelfth ACM SIGART-SIGMOD-SIGART Symposium on Principles of Database Systems (PODS-93)*, pages 158–167. ACM Press, May 1993.

[Fag91] F. Fages. A new fixpoint semantics for general logic programs compared with the well-founded and the stable model semantics. *New Generation Computing*, 9:425–443, 1991.

[Fit85] M. Fitting. A Kripke-Kleene semantics of logic programs. *Journal of Logic Programming*, 2(4):295–312, December 1985.

[Fit93] M. Fitting. The family of stable models. *Journal of Logic Programming*, 17(2, 3 & 4):197–226, 1993.

[FLMS93] J.A. Fernández, J. Lobo, J. Minker, and V.S. Subrahmanian. Disjunctive lp + integrity constrains = stable model semantics. *Annals of Mathematics and Artificial Intelligence*, 8(3-4):449–474, 1993.

[GL88] M. Gelfond and V. Lifschitz. The stable model semantics for logic programming. In R. Kowalski and K. Bowen, editors, *Proceedings of the Fifth International Conference and Symposium on Logic Programming*, pages 1070–1080, Seattle, WA, USA, Aug. 1988. The MIT Press.

[IKH92] K. Inoue, M. Koshimura, and R. Hasegawa. Embedding negation as failure into a model generation theorem prover. In D. Kapur, editor, *Proceedings of the Eleventh International Conference on Automated Deduction*, pages 400–415, Saratoga Springs NY, USA, June 1992. Springer-Verlag.

[MR90] J. Minker and A. Rajasekar. A fixpoint semantics for disjunctive logic programs. *Journal of Logic Programming*, 9(1):45–74, July 1990.

[MR93] J. Minker and C. Ruiz. On extended disjunctive logic programs. In J. Komorowski and Z.W. Raś, editors, *Proceedings of the Seventh International Symposium on Methodologies for Intelligent Systems*, pages 1–18. Lecture Notes in AI. Springer-Verlag, June 1993. (Invited Paper).

[MR94] J. Minker and C. Ruiz. Semantics for disjunctive logic programs with explicit and default negation. *Fundamenta Informaticae*, 20(3/4):145–192, 1994. Anniversary Issue edited by H. Rasiowa.

[Prz91] T. C. Przymusinski. Stable semantics for disjunctive programs. *New Generation Computing*, 9:401–424, 1991.

Springer-Verlag and the Environment

We at Springer-Verlag firmly believe that an international science publisher has a special obligation to the environment, and our corporate policies consistently reflect this conviction.

We also expect our business partners – paper mills, printers, packaging manufacturers, etc. – to commit themselves to using environmentally friendly materials and production processes.

The paper in this book is made from low- or no-chlorine pulp and is acid free, in conformance with international standards for paper permanency.

Lecture Notes in Artificial Intelligence (LNAI)

Vol. 728: P. Torasso (Ed.), Advances in Artificial Intelligence. Proceedings, 1993. XI, 336 pages. 1993.

Vol. 743: S. Doshita, K. Furukawa, K. P. Jantke, T. Nishida (Eds.), Algorithmic Learning Theory. Proceedings, 1992. X, 260 pages. 1993.

Vol. 744: K. P. Jantke, T. Yokomori, S. Kobayashi, E. Tomita (Eds.), Algorithmic Learning Theory. Proceedings, 1993. XI, 423 pages. 1993.

Vol. 745: V. Roberto (Ed.), Intelligent Perceptual Systems. VIII, 378 pages. 1993.

Vol. 746: A. S. Tanguiane, Artificial Perception and Music Recognition. XV, 210 pages. 1993.

Vol. 754: H. D. Pfeiffer, T. E. Nagle (Eds.), Conceptual Structures: Theory and Implementation. Proceedings, 1992. IX, 327 pages. 1993.

Vol. 764: G. Wagner, Vivid Logic. XII, 148 pages. 1994.

Vol. 766: P. R. Van Loocke, The Dynamics of Concepts. XI, 340 pages. 1994.

Vol. 770: P. Haddawy, Representing Plans Under Uncertainty. X, 129 pages. 1994.

Vol. 784: F. Bergadano, L. De Raedt (Eds.), Machine Learning: ECML-94. Proceedings, 1994. XI, 439 pages. 1994.

Vol. 795: W. A. Hunt, Jr., FM8501: A Verified Microprocessor. XIII, 333 pages. 1994.

Vol. 798: R. Dyckhoff (Ed.), Extensions of Logic Programming. Proceedings, 1993. VIII, 360 pages. 1994.

Vol. 799: M. P. Singh, Multiagent Systems: Intentions, Know-How, and Communications. XXIII, 168 pages. 1994.

Vol. 804: D. Hernández, Qualitative Representation of Spatial Knowledge. IX, 202 pages. 1994.

Vol. 808: M. Masuch, L. Pólos (Eds.), Knowledge Representation and Reasoning Under Uncertainty. VII, 237 pages. 1994.

Vol. 810: G. Lakemeyer, B. Nebel (Eds.), Foundations of Knowledge Representation and Reasoning. VIII, 355 pages. 1994.

Vol. 814: A. Bundy (Ed.), Automated Deduction — CADE-12. Proceedings, 1994. XVI, 848 pages. 1994.

Vol. 822: F. Pfenning (Ed.), Logic Programming and Automated Reasoning. Proceedings, 1994. X, 345 pages. 1994.

Vol. 827: D. M. Gabbay, H. J. Ohlbach (Eds.), Temporal Logic. Proceedings, 1994. XI, 546 pages. 1994.

Vol. 830: C. Castelfranchi, E. Werner (Eds.), Artificial Social Systems. Proceedings, 1992. XVIII, 337 pages. 1994.

Vol. 833: D. Driankov, P. W. Eklund, A. Ralescu (Eds.), Fuzzy Logic and Fuzzy Control. Proceedings, 1991. XII, 157 pages. 1994.

Vol. 835: W. M. Tepfenhart, J. P. Dick, J. F. Sowa (Eds.), Conceptual Structures: Current Practices. Proceedings, 1994. VIII, 331 pages. 1994.

Vol. 837: S. Wess, K.-D. Althoff, M. M. Richter (Eds.), Topics in Case-Based Reasoning. Proceedings, 1993. IX, 471 pages. 1994.

Vol. 838: C. MacNish, D. Pearce, L. M. Pereira (Eds.), Logics in Artificial Intelligence. Proceedings, 1994. IX, 413 pages. 1994.

Vol. 847: A. Ralescu (Ed.) Fuzzy Logic in Artificial Intelligence. Proceedings, 1993. VII, 128 pages. 1994.

Vol: 861: B. Nebel, L. Dreschler-Fischer (Eds.), KI-94: Advances in Artificial Intelligence. Proceedings, 1994. IX, 401 pages. 1994.

Vol. 862: R. C. Carrasco, J. Oncina (Eds.), Grammatical Inference and Applications. Proceedings, 1994. VIII, 290 pages. 1994.

Vol 867: L. Steels, G. Schreiber, W. Van de Velde (Eds.), A Future for Knowledge Acquisition. Proceedings, 1994. XII, 414 pages. 1994.

Vol. 869: Z. W. Raś, M. Zemankova (Eds.), Methodologies for Intelligent Systems. Proceedings, 1994. X, 613 pages. 1994.

Vol. 872: S Arikawa, K. P. Jantke (Eds.), Algorithmic Learning Theory. Proceedings, 1994. XIV, 575 pages. 1994.

Vol. 878: T. Ishida, Parallel, Distributed and Multiagent Production Systems. XVII, 166 pages. 1994.

Vol. 886: M. M. Veloso, Planning and Learning by Analogical Reasoning. XIII, 181 pages. 1994.

Vol. 890: M. J. Wooldridge, N. R. Jennings (Eds.), Intelligent Agents. Proceedings, 1994. VIII, 407 pages. 1995.

Vol. 897: M. Fisher, R. Owens (Eds.), Executable Modal and Temporal Logics. Proceedings, 1993. VII, 180 pages. 1995.

Vol. 898: P. Steffens (Ed.), Machine Translation and the Lexicon. Proceedings, 1993. X, 251 pages. 1995.

Vol. 904: P. Vitányi (Ed.), Computational Learning Theory. EuroCOLT'95. Proceedings, 1995. XVII, 415 pages. 1995.

Vol. 912: N. Lavrač, S. Wrobel (Eds.), Machine Learning: ECML – 95. Proceedings, 1995. XI, 370 pages. 1995.

Vol. 918: P. Baumgartner, R. Hähnle, J. Posegga (Eds.), Theorem Proving with Analytic Tableaux and Related Methods. Proceedings, 1995. X, 352 pages. 1995.

Vol. 927: J. Dix, L. Moniz Pereira, T.C. Przymusinski (Eds.), Non-Monotonic Extensions of Logic Programming. Proceedings, 1994. IX, 229 pages. 1995.

Lecture Notes in Computer Science

Vol. 891: C. Lewerentz, T. Lindner (Eds.), Formal Development of Reactive Systems. XI, 394 pages. 1995.

Vol. 892: K. Pingali, U. Banerjee, D. Gelernter, A. Nicolau, D. Padua (Eds.), Languages and Compilers for Parallel Computing. Proceedings, 1994. XI, 496 pages. 1995.

Vol. 893: G. Gottlob, M. Y. Vardi (Eds.), Database Theory – ICDT '95. Proceedings, 1995. XI, 454 pages. 1995.

Vol. 894: R. Tamassia, I. G. Tollis (Eds.), Graph Drawing. Proceedings, 1994. X, 471 pages. 1995.

Vol. 895: R. L. Ibrahim (Ed.), Software Engineering Education. Proceedings, 1995. XII, 449 pages. 1995.

Vol.896: R. N. Taylor, J. Coutaz (Eds.), Software Engineering and Human-Computer Interaction. Proceedings, 1994. X, 281 pages. 1995.

Vol. 897: M. Fisher, R. Owens (Eds.), Executable Modal and Temporal Logics. Proceedings, 1993. VII, 180 pages. 1995. (Subseries LNAI).

Vol. 898: P. Steffens (Ed.), Machine Translation and the Lexicon. Proceedings, 1993. X, 251 pages. 1995. (Subseries LNAI).

Vol. 899: W. Banzhaf, F. H. Eeckman (Eds.), Evolution and Biocomputation. VII, 277 pages. 1995.

Vol. 900: E. W. Mayr, C. Puech (Eds.), STACS 95. Proceedings, 1995. XIII, 654 pages. 1995.

Vol. 901: R. Kumar, T. Kropf (Eds.), Theorem Provers in Circuit Design. Proceedings, 1994. VIII, 303 pages. 1995.

Vol. 902: M. Dezani-Ciancaglini, G. Plotkin (Eds.), Typed Lambda Calculi and Applications. Proceedings, 1995. VIII, 443 pages. 1995.

Vol. 903: E. W. Mayr, G. Schmidt, G. Tinhofer (Eds.), Graph-Theoretic Concepts in Computer Science. Proceedings, 1994. IX, 414 pages. 1995.

Vol. 904: P. Vitányi (Ed.), Computational Learning Theory. EuroCOLT'95. Proceedings, 1995. XVII, 415 pages. 1995. (Subseries LNAI).

Vol. 905: N. Ayache (Ed.), Computer Vision, Virtual Reality and Robotics in Medicine. Proceedings, 1995. XIV, 567 pages. 1995.

Vol. 906: E. Astesiano, G. Reggio, A. Tarlecki (Eds.), Recent Trends in Data Type Specification. Proceedings, 1995. VIII, 523 pages. 1995.

Vol. 907: T. Ito, A. Yonezawa (Eds.), Theory and Practice of Parallel Programming. Proceedings, 1995. VIII, 485 pages. 1995.

Vol. 908: J. R. Rao Extensions of the UNITY Methodology: Compositionality, Fairness and Probability in Parallelism. XI, 178 pages. 1995.

Vol. 909: H. Comon, J.-P. Jouannaud (Eds.), Term Rewriting. Proceedings, 1993. VIII, 221 pages. 1995.

Vol. 910: A. Podelski (Ed.), Constraint Programming: Basics and Trends. Proceedings, 1995. XI, 315 pages. 1995.

Vol. 911: R. Baeza-Yates, E. Goles, P. V. Poblete (Eds.), LATIN '95: Theoretical Informatics. Proceedings, 1995. IX, 525 pages. 1995.

Vol. 912: N. Lavrač, S. Wrobel (Eds.), Machine Learning: ECML – 95. Proceedings, 1995. XI, 370 pages. 1995. (Subseries LNAI).

Vol. 913: W. Schäfer (Ed.), Software Process Technology. Proceedings, 1995. IX, 261 pages. 1995.

Vol. 914: J. Hsiang (Ed.), Rewriting Techniques and Applications. Proceedings, 1995. XII, 473 pages. 1995.

Vol. 915: P. D. Mosses, M. Nielsen, M. I. Schwartzbach (Eds.), TAPSOFT '95: Theory and Practice of Software Development. Proceedings, 1995. XV, 810 pages. 1995.

Vol. 916: N. R. Adam, B. K. Bhargava, Y. Yesha (Eds.), Digital Libraries. Proceedings, 1994. XIII, 321 pages. 1995.

Vol. 917: J. Pieprzyk, R. Safavi-Naini (Eds.), Advances in Cryptology - ASIACRYPT '94. Proceedings, 1994. XII,

Vol. 918: P. Baumgartner, R. Hähnle, J. Posegga (Eds.), Theorem Proving with Analytic Tableaux and Related Methods. Proceedings, 1995. X, 352 pages. 1995. (Subseries LNAI).

Vol. 919: B. Hertzberger, G. Serazzi (Eds.), High-Performance Computing and Networking. Proceedings, 1995. XXIV, 957 pages. 1995.

Vol. 920: E. Balas, J. Clausen (Eds.), Integer Programming and Combinatorial Optimization. Proceedings, 1995. IX, 436 pages. 1995.

Vol. 921: L. C. Guillou, J.-J. Quisquater (Eds.), Advances in Cryptology – EUROCRYPT '95. Proceedings, 1995. XIV, 417 pages. 1995.

Vol. 923: M. Meyer (Ed.), Constraint Processing. IV, 289 pages. 1995.

Vol. 924: P. Ciancarini, O. Nierstrasz, A. Yonezawa (Eds.), Object-Based Models and Languages for Concurrent Systems. Proceedings, 1994. VII, 193 pages. 1995.

Vol. 925: J. Jeuring, E. Meijer (Eds.), Advanced Functional Programming. Proceedings, 1995. VII, 331 pages. 1995.

Vol. 926: P. Nesi (Ed.), Objective Software Quality. Proceedings, 1995. VIII, 249 pages. 1995.

Vol. 927: J. Dix, L. Moniz Pereira, T. C. Przymusinski (Eds.), Non-Monotonic Extensions of Logic Programming. Proceedings, 1994. IX, 229 pages. 1995. (Subseries LNAI).